PRACTICAL RESEARCH WITH CHILDREN

Practical Research with Children is designed to help the reader understand techniques for research with children, based on real world experience. The book describes a wide range of research methods, focusing equally on quantitative and qualitative approaches, and considers how different methods can be integrated. It highlights the benefits and challenges of each method and gives emphasis to best practice, with expert guidance on how to avoid potential pitfalls in order to obtain valuable insights into how children develop.

The volume includes fifteen chapters arranged over three sections: quantitative, qualitative and mixed methods. Each chapter explores a particular method, or combination of methods, and discusses both theoretical and practical issues, using a diversity of domains, including different ages, cultures, populations and settings. Uniquely, the book includes newer methods, such as eye-tracking and digital technologies, alongside well-established behavioural methods which are used for research with children.

With contributions from internationally renowned researchers and practitioners from a range of disciplines, the book will be indispensable reading for a wide audience, including students in psychology, education and nursing undertaking research projects with children, and also anyone looking to understand the research behind current theories in child development.

Jess Prior is a Senior Lecturer in the Department of Psychology at Kingston University, UK.

Jo Van Herwegen is an Associate Professor in the Department of Psychology at Kingston University, UK.

RESEARCH METHODS IN DEVELOPMENTAL PSYCHOLOGY
A Handbook Series

Research Methods in Developmental Psychology is a series of edited books focusing upon research challenges for conducting research in developmental psychology. Ideally suited to both students coming to this area for the first time and more experienced researchers each volume provides an invaluable overview of research in this growing field, and how it can inform both education and interventions. Volumes include research challenges in neurodevelopmental disorders, child development and gerontology.

Published titles:

Neurodevelopmental Disorders: Research Challenges and Solutions
Edited by Jo Van Herwegen and Deborah Riby

Practical Research with Children
Edited by Jess Prior and Jo Van Herwegen

PRACTICAL RESEARCH WITH CHILDREN

*Edited by Jess Prior and
Jo Van Herwegen*

Routledge
Taylor & Francis Group

LONDON AND NEW YORK

First published 2016
by Routledge
2 Park Square, Milton Park, Abingdon, Oxon OX14 4RN

and by Routledge
711 Third Avenue, New York, NY 10017

Routledge is an imprint of the Taylor & Francis Group, an informa business

© 2016 Jess Prior and Jo Van Herwegen

British Library Cataloguing in Publication Data
A catalogue record for this book is available from the British Library

Library of Congress Cataloging in Publication Data
A catalog record for this book has been requested

ISBN: 978-1-138-93788-8 (hbk)
ISBN: 978-1-138-93789-5 (pbk)
ISBN: 978-1-315-67606-7 (ebk)

Typeset in Bembo and Stone Sans
by Florence Production Ltd, Stoodleigh, Devon, UK

CONTENTS

FIGURES

CONTRIBUTORS

Caspar Addyman
Research Fellow
Centre for Brain and Cognitive
    Development
Birkbeck, University of London
United Kingdom

Daniel Ansari
Professor
Department of Psychology
University of Western Ontario
Canada

Ana Aznar
Research Fellow
School of Psychology
University of Surrey
United Kingdom

Charlotte Brownlow
Senior Lecturer
School of Psychology and Counselling
University of Southern Queensland
Australia

Dagmara Dimitriou
Senior Lecturer
Lifespan Learning And Sleep
    Laboratory
UCL Institute of Education
United Kingdom

Robert Dudley
Medical Director for School Based
    Health Services
Community Health Centre of New
    Britain
Associate Clinical Professor
University of Connecticut School of
    Medicine
United States of America

Eva Gulløv
Associate Professor
Department of Education
Aarhus University, Denmark
Professor
Department of Education
University of Agder, Norway

Isabel T. Gutiérrez
Psychology Instructor
Raritan Valley Community College
New Jersey
United States of America

Jayme Hannay
Consultant, Program Development
 and Evaluation
Longmeadow, MA
United States of America

Matthew J. Jiang
Graduate Student
Department of Psychology
University of Wisconsin-Madison
United States of America

Natalia Kucirkova
Senior Lecturer
Faculty of Education
Manchester Metropolitan University
United Kingdom

Paula Kellogg Leibovitz
Registered Dietitian and Freelance
 project consultant
Southington, CT
United States of America

Frances Le Cornu Knight
Research Assistant
Lifespan Learning And Sleep
 Laboratory
UCL Institute of Education
United Kingdom

Patrick Leman
Professor
Institute of Psychiatry, Psychology and
 Neuroscience
King's College, London
United Kingdom

Lisbeth Ljosdal Skreland
Assistant Professor
Department of Education
University of Agder
Norway

Luke Mason
Research Fellow
Centre for Brain and Cognitive
 Development
Birkbeck, University of London
United Kingdom

Anna A. Matejko
PhD student
Department of Psychology
University of Western Ontario
Canada

David Messer
Professor
Centre for Research in Education and
 Educational Technology
The Open University
United Kingdom

Stephanie Milan
Associate Professor
Department of Psychology
University of Connecticut
United States of America

Lindsay O'Dell
Director of Postgraduate Studies
Faculty of Health and Social Care
The Open University
United Kingdom

Larry Owens
Professor
School of Education
Flinders University
Adelaide
Australia

Jess Prior
Senior Lecturer
School of Psychology, Criminology
    and Sociology
Kingston University
United Kingdom

Harry Purser
Assistant Professor
School of Psychology
University of Nottingham
United Kingdom

Valerie L. Rodino
Community Wellness Director
YWCA of New Britain
United States of America

Karl S. Rosengren
Professor
Department of Psychology
University of Wisconsin-Madison
United States of America

Douglas E. Sperry
Assistant Professor of Psychology
Department of Social and Behavioral
    Sciences
Saint Mary-of-the-Woods College
United States of America

Linda L. Sperry
Professor
Department of Communication
    Disorders and Counseling, School,
    and Educational Psychology
Bayh College of Education
Indiana State University
United States of America

Harriet Tenenbaum
Reader
School of Psychology
University of Surrey
United Kingdom

Cheryl To
Teaching Fellow
School of Psychology
University of Surrey
United Kingdom

Jo Van Herwegen
Associate Professor
School of Psychology, Criminology
    and Sociology
Kingston University
United Kingdom

Stephan E. Vogel
Assistant Professor
Educational Neuroscience
Institute of Psychology
University of Graz
Austria

Sam V. Wass
Lecturer
University of East London
London
United Kingdom

Karen Winter
Lecturer
School of Sociology, Social Policy
    and Social Work
Queen's University Belfast
United Kingdom

ABOUT THE EDITORS

Dr Jess Prior

Jess Prior is a Senior Lecturer in the department of Psychology at Kingston University, London. After being awarded a Quintin Hogg Research Scholarship, she completed her PhD at the University of Westminster, exploring young children's abilities to describe and recall faces. After her PhD, Jess worked as a Lecturer in Psychology at the University of North London (now London Metropolitan University), before being appointed as a Senior Lecturer in Psychology at Kingston University in September 2003. Her research focuses on appearance and visible differences in childhood and adolescence. She is interested in how children, adolescents and emerging adults *live with* visible differences, and various psychosocial issues including coping, resiliency and identity. More recently, she has become interested in the social representations of disabled and Paralympic athletes by disabled children and their families. She employs a number of qualitative research methods, including focus groups, semi-structured interviews and dyadic interviews with young children and parents in order to understand children's social worlds and experiences.

Dr Jo Van Herwegen

Jo Van Herwegen is an Associate Professor in the Department of Psychology at Kingston University. She is co-ordinator of the Child Development and Learning Difficulties Unit and course director for the MSc Child Psychology. After working as a researcher at the Institute of Child Health (UCL) and at the Institute of Education, Jo completed her PhD in 2010 at King's College London in which she investigated metaphor and metonymy comprehension in Williams syndrome. After a short post-doc position at Middlesex University, Jo was appointed as a lecturer at Kingston University in September 2010. Her research focuses mainly on language and number development in both typical and atypical populations, such as Williams syndrome, Autism Spectrum Disorders, Down syndrome and Specific Language Impairment. Linking the aforementioned areas of research activity, she explores individual differences, as well as what cognitive abilities and strategies relate to successful performance in typical populations and how these differ in atypical populations, in order to aid the development of economically valid training programmes. Jo studies cognitive abilities from infancy onwards in order to obtain a better understanding of how they develop over time and how performances across different cognitive areas relate to each other. In her research she employs a range of methods and experimental designs, including spontaneous language samples, preferential looking, experimental tasks and eye-tracking. Lately her research has focused also on the design and validity of new intervention programmes for preschool children. She has obtained funding from British Academy and Nuffield Foundation to support her research.

PREFACE

Developmental psychology is an eclectic field that incorporates a broad range of areas that include social development, cognitive development, neurological development, child psychopathology, ecological psychology, cultural psychology and educational psychology. Within these areas developmental researchers explore a wide variety of topics including emotional development, development of the self, personality development, psycho-physiological processes, number development, language development, concept development and many more. Although current research within developmental psychology focuses on the entire lifespan, there are particular issues that need consideration when planning or conducting research with children. Research with children is different from research with adult participants in that children are not always able to explain their thoughts or feelings in the same way that an adult can. Therefore, methods that have been designed for use with adult populations have been adapted, and some specific methods have been designed over the years in order to research child development. To give one example, in neuropsychology templates had to be specially created in order to interpret neuroimaging data from children (see discussion Chapter 3).

Research with children is not only challenging because young children or infants cannot easily explain their thoughts or feelings. There are also numerous practical issues to consider when working with children. Many qualitative and quantitative researchers have found that when they try to pilot a well-designed, well-constructed, well-planned study or experiment, they encounter unexpected challenges. The child may have a shorter attention span than anticipated, or differ from other children of the same age, they may find it hard to stay still in a brain imaging scanner or eye-trackers, they might not want to participate at all, even after they have initially agreed, they may tell you confidential information or ask challenging questions, they may not seem to have the language abilities to understand your interview questions or be able to follow the instructions of your experimental task. They might find some other aspects of the task more interesting than the task that you want them to focus on, or want to spend their time playing rather than following a set task or activity. On some occasions they perform much better than you might have expected and perform at ceiling (see discussion Chapter 4) or make a task seem rather easy. All of these (and many other) challenges will have to be considered and addressed by the researcher before he or she can start any data collection with children.

The current book is a practical textbook where researchers using quantitative, qualitative or a mixture of different research methods with children reflect on their decisions to use a particular method or combination of methods, the advantages and disadvantages of their chosen method, and its suitability for their chosen research question. The authors of each chapter discuss the kinds of data that they have collected through their chosen method(s), some of which has not been previously published. They are also able to offer suggestions and ideas for collecting high quality data that will be useful for researchers who are considering using a similar method. This book is therefore emphatically not a traditional research methods textbook. It gives all sorts of advice and tips that are usually missing from research methods textbooks, concerning things 'I wish I had known'.

At the end of each chapter practical tips for good practice have been provided, which are practical in their scope and content. Importantly, we hope that the advice, explanations and illustrations included in all of the chapters serve to bring the different methods alive to the reader, and allow them to reflect on how to develop their own ideas for future studies.

The chapters in this volume reflect a wide range of disciplines from across the social sciences including Psychology, Neuroscience, Clinical Psychology, Education, Medicine and Sociology. Some of the included chapters have been written by established researchers who are very well known experts in their discipline, as well as by early career researchers from around the world. The range of topics and methods, as well as the practical solutions included within the chapters will be of interest to students who are starting out to develop their own research agendas and questions, including final year undergraduate students, master students and PhD students who are at the start of their career.

Although the book discusses different research techniques used with children, we assume that readers will have basic knowledge of research methods and concepts (i.e., sampling issues, validity, reliability, quality of coding) and are familiar with different types of experimental designs (quasi, experimental, etc.) or qualitative methods (semi-structured interviews, case studies, observations, ethnography). It may well be that novice researchers will therefore need to read more broadly around their chosen method or area to supplement their reading, or to understand the theoretical underpinnings of some of the ideas presented in the chapters within this book.

Quantitative versus qualitative

There has been a longstanding debate about whether psychology, including developmental psychology, is a science that should borrow some of the scientific, quantitative methods traditionally employed by physical sciences or use more qualitative methodologies that allow for the emotions, the subjectivity, beliefs and values of an individual to be included within the research. Nowadays, there is a strong consensus that one should avoid a strong dichotomy between quantitative and qualitative research methods. The current textbook is unique in that it focuses equally on both quantitative and qualitative methods and explores how different methods can be integrated in order to obtain valuable insights into how children develop.

Both qualitative and quantitative researchers at times face some similar challenges in their research with children. For example, all researchers will need to consider formulating a research question, the design of their study, and how to code or classify their data corpus, alongside issues of quality, validity and reliability of the data. The current book will provide the reader with some very detailed and explicit illustrations of ways of coding and recording data using quantitative as well as qualitative methods, above and beyond that which could be reasonably expected in a standard research methods textbook.

Moreover, as developmental psychologists are mainly interested in how certain groups of children develop, both qualitative and quantitative researchers need to pay careful attention to the age of the child when choosing research tools and conducting their studies. In this book we have included research examples from researchers working with infants (for example Chapter 1 and 2); preschool children (Chapters 9 and 10); older teenagers (Chapters 8 and 12); alongside some chapters that consider the notion of age in research with children in more general terms (see for example Chapters 5 and 7). In addition, the book includes examples from a wide range of populations, including typically and atypically developing children (see Chapters 1, 3, 4 and 13) as well as from different cultures and ethnicities (see Chapters 10, 11 and 12).

Finally, both qualitative and quantitative researchers have to consider the setting for their research: how the setting will impact on the children and their behaviours as well as the impact of the setting on the measures used in the research. For example, one could choose to work with children in a naturalistic or semi-naturalistic setting (see Chapters 6, 7, 8 and 9) in contrast to a clinical or laboratory setting (Chapters 1, 2, 3 and 4). It can be argued that clinical or laboratory settings allow more control so that specific factors can be manipulated, while naturalistic settings provide data that is more ecologically valid. Therefore, some researchers combine data from different settings in order to try to maximise the benefits of these different settings in their data collection (Chapters 11 and 14).

The field of developmental psychology is a rapid developing one and this is also reflected in the development and use of novel methods and techniques, both qualitative and quantitative ones, for researching development in children. For example, the use of digital technologies (see Chapter 14) as well as eye-tracking (see Chapter 2) allow for a wide range of research questions to be asked, including not only how children use new technologies but also how these technologies can aid the researcher to answer certain research questions. Therefore, the book includes a discussion of well-established research methods and techniques in research with children as well as some novel ones.

The book is not exhaustive: due to the volume of different existing techniques, perspectives and methods concerning research with children, it was not possible for all methods or subject areas of research with children to be included within the book. We have, however, aimed to incorporate a range of methods that 1) include a wide range of ages of children, 2) pay attention to the setting of the research with children, 3) focus on established as well as innovative methods, 4) provide a balance of qualitative, quantitative and mixed methods chapters that consider theoretically based but practical applied research questions.

Structure of the book

The book contains three parts. The first part discusses quantitative methods and techniques while the second part focuses on qualitative approaches. The final part of the book discusses examples of mixed approaches, as in many cases the division between quantitative and qualitative approaches does not always allow for the best answer to a certain research question. However, in our own experience some students do not always understand where their chosen method falls within the division (and what advantages or disadvantages relate to this division). We hope that clearly labelling the different sections of the book will improve this understanding.

There are a number of issues of research with children that are common for a number of methodologies (for example inter-rater reliability, reliability of the data, establishing rapport between the child and adult researcher, making a task accessible for the child, researching the child as a member of his/her society). We will direct the reader to chapters that discuss similar issues or use cross-references where we feel this is beneficial.

Finally, working with children involves some specific ethical issues such as the fact that children might not be able to understand what they are consenting to. The final chapter of the book discusses a number of ethical issues that will be important to any researcher working with children, regardless of the research methodology they choose to employ.

Part 1 discusses quantitative research methods. **Chapter 1** focuses on development in infancy and discusses a range of methods, including preferential looking paradigms and eye-tracking as well as practical issues and solutions when working with non-verbal infants. Leading on directly from Chapter 1, **Chapter 2** continues with a more detailed discussion of eye-tracking as a technique for studying child development. It discusses a wide range of uses, including how eye movements can provide insight into individual differences and higher-level aspects of cognitive functions as well as how eye-tracking can be used to deliver intervention programmes. **Chapter 3** focuses on brain development and provides an overview of how to design child-friendly functional and structural MRI experiments, discusses common caveats associated with neuroimaging, how they affect data interpretation, and provides practical guidelines for conducting MRI research with children. Using examples from both typically as well as atypically developing children, **Chapter 4** discusses practical issues related to behavioural experimental and standardised psychological tasks that are used with children, including issues with regards to the administration and scoring of tasks. The final chapter in this section, **Chapter 5,** focuses on conversational data from children and explains how to elicit conversations from semi-naturalistic and naturalistic settings and provides a step-by-step guide, including a discussion of inter-rater reliability, and analysing conversation data quantitatively.

Part 2 focuses on qualitative approaches. The first chapter, **Chapter 6**, explores the practical and theoretical issues to be considered when using semi-structured interviews with young children. Using practical examples from research with children with *visible differences*, the chapter explains some key considerations for the researcher, including the advantages and limitations of this method, designing an interview schedule and conducting the interview. It considers innovative uses of activities in interviews, such as drawings and dyadic interviews. **Chapter 7** focuses on ethnographic studies with children and discusses methodological aspects and considerations concerning the need to reflect on preconceptions, ways of observing and interviewing children, and dilemmas that the adult ethnographer must consider. The theme of participatory research continues in **Chapter 8**, which focuses on Community based participatory research (CBPR) and the advantages of using a mixed methods approach combining focus groups with Photovoice in CBPR projects with teens. Finally, **Chapter 9** explores the importance of novel and transformational methodologies, including the use of reality boxes and picture construction in research with very young children, and how applications of these can be used with very young children in 'out-of-home' care to explore sensitive issues.

The final part of the book considers mixed methods approaches to research with children. **Chapter 10** starts the debate on mixed methods and discusses the advantages and difficulties of answering a certain research question using different methods. The authors contextualise the use of multiple methods using their own research that examined children's scale errors-behaviours where children attempt to perform an action on an object that is too small to accommodate the action – and children's understanding of death. **Chapter 11** considers the mixed approach of using the quantitative analysis of ethnographic data collected to examine the emergence of narrative-like talk in children from low-income families. **Chapter 12** focuses on a very specific mixed methods approach, namely Q sort, in which qualitative data is analysed using quantitative methods. It uses three studies related to teenage girls' constructions of popularity as illustrations of the methodology's usefulness in research with young people. **Chapter 13** discusses a specific topic in research with children, namely the importance of sleep, and what different methods and tools can be used by the paediatric sleep researcher. **Chapter 14** concentrates on the way that new technologies are providing a range of research tools to gather data and information about children. This chapter considers the methods that are used to answer important questions about young people's use of technology and raises questions, particularly for psychologists, about their role in investigating technology and educational processes as well as future directions. The final chapter in this section, **Chapter 15**, relates to all types of research methods and discusses the ethical implications of research with children.

Although each of these techniques and methods provides insight into the development and behaviour of children, they all have particular advantages and disadvantages. By reading these chapters as a whole collection, the reader will be in a better position to make informed choices about which method to use, and appreciate both the advantages and some of the disadvantages of a particular method, as well as how the technique might impact on their theoretical understandings of a phenomenon. Of course the reader is to make up his/her own mind about the strengths and weaknesses of certain methodologies and in deciding which methodology to use, or perhaps which combination of methods to use, they will need to be mindful of the aims and research questions of their proposed study. We hope that early career researchers and students will find this edited volume a useful collection of manuscripts for their own research throughout their research career, and that it will be a valuable resource to turn to when designing new studies in child development.

ACKNOWLEDGEMENTS FROM THE EDITORS

This book could not have been realized without the support of a number of people. First of all, we are indebted to the authors who have contributed to the book. We would like to thank all of them for their wonderful contributions and continued support, for keeping to the deadlines, and for sharing their expertise and examples of practical issues when working with children.

Our gratitude also extends to the reviewers who have provided us, as well as the authors, with valuable comments and suggestions. We would like to thank our colleagues in the Department of Psychology at Kingston for their encouragement and support, and in particular Professor Evanthia Lyons for her insights. Our thanks also extend to our publishers Taylor and Francis, especially Dr Michael Fenton and Lucy Kennedy, along with other staff for their help with the manuscript.

Finally, Jess would like to thank her family, Justin, Tara, Maisie and Maggie. Jo thanks Rob and William for their continued support.

ACKNOWLEDGEMENTS FROM THE AUTHORS

Chapter 1

The authors would like to thank Leslie Tucker, Denis Mareschal, Emily Jones and Irati Saez de Urabain for comments on an earlier draft of the chapter.

Chapter 2

This chapter was supported by a British Academy Postdoctoral Fellowship to SW. The author would like to thank Emily Jones for the use of the photograph in Figure 2.3.

Chapter 6

The author wishes to thank Justin Clegg and Amy Prior for their comments on earlier drafts of this chapter. The author also thanks Wiley Publishers for permission to reproduce the drawing in Figure 6.1. Any third party material is expressly excluded from this permission. If any of the material you wish to use appears within our work with credit to another source, authorization from that source must be obtained. This permission does not include the right to grant others permission to photocopy or otherwise reproduce this material except for accessible versions made by non-profit organizations serving the blind, visually impaired and other persons with print disabilities (VIPs).

Chapter 8

We are especially indebted to the teens and parents who participated as co-researchers in Photovoice workshops and focus groups. Special thanks are owed to Rosemarie Burgos, Melanie Benitez, Monica Little, Veronica Simon-Tirado, Kassandra Negron, Yetsaida Velez, Vilma Padilla, Keisha Torres, Vilmary Torres and Angel Torres.

Chapter 9

Dr Winter wishes to thank her participants for allowing her to use images of their artwork.

Chapter 12

The author thanks Professor Steven Brown, Kent State University who critically read and commented on an earlier version of this manuscript.

PART 1

Quantitative methods in research with children

1

RESEARCHING COGNITIVE DEVELOPMENT IN INFANCY

Caspar Addyman and Luke Mason

1.1 Introduction

Infancy is the time of greatest change and fastest learning. The brain is still growing and at its most malleable. This is when the foundations of cognition are laid down. Starting from scratch, infants must learn to walk, talk, classify all the objects in their world and learn how to manipulate them. They must learn how to regulate their emotions and interact with other people. Infancy should therefore be of interest to researchers across all areas of psychology. But infants cannot answer questionnaires or press buttons. Their attention span is even worse than undergraduates'. Infants are hard participants to find, to recruit and to schedule. They can be expensive and time consuming to test and only give small amounts of intrinsically noisy data. Research with infants presents considerable challenges and requires substantial ingenuity.

The challenges are both practical and conceptual. How do we run experiments with infants and how do we interpret the results? There are four interrelated challenges that are unique to research with infants. These are the conceptual limitations imposed by infant perception and cognition as well as the practical limitations imposed by infant attention and by infant responding. All four factors may affect an experiment to a greater or lesser degree. Methods in infancy research have been developed largely in response to these constraints. For the youngest ages perceptual limitations are the major consideration and may even be a topic of research in their own right. What is the resolution of infant vision? How well can they localise sounds in space? When do they develop the ability to smoothly track moving objects? Most important from a theoretical point of view are the limitations imposed by infant cognition. Very often these are precisely the questions we are trying to answer. How limited is infant memory? How limited is infant vocabulary, object concepts or category knowledge? How early do abilities arise? How similar or different are they to their adult equivalents? It is crucial to remember that these factors are interrelated. An infant's very limited working memory could affect their performance in any number of tasks. Object knowledge precedes word learning and so on.

The limitations imposed by infant attention and response options are more practical in nature. The biggest challenge is that infants do not know they are in an experiment. Experiments must therefore be built around infants' natural behaviours or non-behavioural measures. Behavioural measures are usually visual, namely what infants choose to look at and for how long, but can also involve physical responses like touching or pointing. Non-behavioural measures include physiological markers such as heart rate variation or electrical potentials on the scalp related to underlying brain activity. Responses must be evoked by relatively naturalistic settings that engage infants with simple tasks in a single session of several minutes to half an hour. Whatever the task, infants will get bored very quickly. Indeed, as we discuss below, many classic behavioural paradigms such as habituation exploit this. But infants are not just habituating to the stimuli on the screen, they become bored of the screen itself and of being in the quiet, darkened room where you run the study. Infants' limited attention makes every experiment a race against time.

The investigation of cognitive development in infancy has also been shaped by the technologies that are available. This chapter therefore takes a historical approach to the field, starting with a survey of classical behavioural methods that capitalise on infants' tendency to get bored very quickly and to seek out novelty and play games. We go on to describe the revolution brought about by the introduction of eye-trackers and the benefits and difficulties of using electroencephalography (EEG) with infants. We finish by discussing some recent innovations such as Near Infrared Spectroscopy (NIRS).

However, before discussing the experimental methods themselves we take a step back and consider the broader context of research with infants. There are many practical considerations unique to testing with infants and very young children. The first section of this chapter addresses those issues. We consider the designing of a lab space suitable for infant testing, recruiting and getting infants to the lab, making the visit safe and enjoyable for parents and infants.

1.2 Practical considerations

It may be tempting to focus on the methodological and technological requirements of conducting infant research, but the reality is that a variety of other factors begin exerting an influence on infants' behaviour before they even arrive at the lab.

1.2.1 The physical and social environment

Ensure that the facilities in your lab are appropriate for parents and babies. There should be space to park buggies, toys to play with before the experiment begins (and the ability to disinfect these afterwards), and facilities for baby changing and breastfeeding. In spaces where experimental sessions are filmed, ensure that the cameras can be switched off during feeding.

Infants' sleep patterns are markedly different from those of children and adults, and vary across age and between individuals. When booking babies for an experiment, it is vital to take naps into account. Parents know their child's schedule and duration of naps, so gather this information and plan around it. Be aware that an unfamiliar environment, unfamiliar people and the energy-sapping nature of experimental tasks will all work to increase nap duration and decrease the time between naps. A 6-month-old infant who has recently napped has a maximum of 1.5 hours of useful attention available to us as researchers before they need to take a break and, in most cases, to sleep. The clock starts ticking from the moment they walk through the door.

Parents are your greatest allies in gathering good data from their child. Even very young infants are constantly monitoring their parents' mood and a comfortable and relaxed parent will transmit this state to their child. It is essential to take time to explain clearly to parents what will happen, and why the research their child is taking part in is important. Parents may worry whether their child 'has passed the test' or met the requirements of the experiment. Emphasise that researchers are interested in how children naturally respond so there is never a 'right answer'. Equally, they should not feel pressured to continue if their baby is unhappy. Babies are people too with the same rights as adults and all experiments need to comply with the Helsinki convention and local ethics committees (see Chapter 15 for a detailed discussion of ethical issues when working with children and infants). But it is parents who give their consent and judge that their babies are happy. Unhappy babies give bad data. Remember too, that parental recommendations are a fantastic way of recruiting future participants.

Interacting with the infants themselves requires sensitivity on the part of the researcher and benefits greatly from experience. Just like adults, infants vary in temperament and sociability. Some will approach you immediately to play, others will become very upset if you approach them within 10 minutes of their arrival. Infants and toddlers generally view new people with mistrust until they prove themselves to be friendly, fun and non-threatening; rapport built with parents will usually rub off on infants. Limit the number of people that the infant meets to the bare minimum necessary for running the experiment. Making yourself physically less threatening, by coming down to the level of the child, using infant directed speech, and allowing the infant to come to you are all helpful in warming them up to your presence. An experienced infant researcher once remarked that when interacting with babies you must 'leave your dignity at the door'!

1.2.2 Maximising attention and compliance

Infants' attentional capacity is extremely limited and their mood is easily disrupted. Ensure that you set up everything you can in advance of the infant arriving, so that when they move into the lab proper to begin an experiment there is the minimum possible delay. Any technology must be tested and confirmed working before the baby even enters the building – do not let them sit there while a computer boots and cables are plugged in.

It is tempting to play videos to infants before a screen-based task begins, but this is usually a bad idea (although very short videos *between* tasks do help keep infants engaged). Young infants will habituate to screens and rooms reducing the time they will attend to your experimental stimuli. Older infants and toddlers will enjoy watching their favourite cartoon while an EEG net is applied, but woe betide the researcher who switches off a 2-year-old's *Peppa Pig* video and attempts to replace it with boring experimental stimuli! Instead, blow bubbles for younger infants, and use quiet, unstimulating toys with toddlers.

Over the course of the session, infants will rarely remain stationary, often leaning backward, hunching forward, or tilting their upper torso to one side or another (a particular problem for eye-tracking methods; Hessels, Cornelissen, Kemner, & Hooge, 2014). Seating the infant in a high chair or car seat will reduce the range of possible motion compared with having her sat on the parent's lap, but lap-based babies can be more easily repositioned by their parents during an experiment, and are less likely to fuss out. A middle ground that some researchers adopt is to have the parent wear a front-facing baby carrier, maximising the ability of the parent to intervene while holding the infant in a relatively constrained position in which they feel comfortable and safe.

1.2.3 Design and pacing of stimulus presentation

It is often desirable to use the same underlying paradigm with infants as with adults, in order to acquire comparable data across development. Simply taking an experiment that works with adults and expecting an infant to sit through it, however, is unlikely to bear fruit. Stimuli should be designed in accordance with what is known about a particular age group's perceptual preferences and abilities. Young infants enjoy watching high contrast, colourful, moving stimuli. Small geometric stimuli on grey backgrounds work well with undergraduates who can be told to sit still and bribed with money or course credit, but an infant will lose interest almost immediately.

Changing the low-level visual features of stimuli such as colour and pattern between blocks, while keeping the underlying structure such as the spatial and temporal arrangement constant, can significantly increase the amount of time an infant will attend to a screen. Trial numbers should be kept to the absolute minimum necessary and rather than presented in one long block they can be interspersed with short, engaging attention-getters, such as a few seconds of pictures or video.

The pacing of stimulus presentation is important, too. Younger infants will take longer to disengage from stimuli and so will be unable to keep up with a fast rate of change. Toddlers, on the other hand, will rapidly grow bored of a slowly changing screen, and will readily direct their attention to running around, pulling on cables or throwing a tantrum.

Many researchers run more than one experiment in any particular session. For example, the learning and recognition stages of a language task could be separated by an unrelated habituation task. This can work effectively, but significantly improves the complexity and number of factors that need to be controlled for. Interspersing blocks of several different tasks can buy an increase in overall attention, but at the expense of not collecting enough data to analyse any of the individual tasks if the infant becomes fussy halfway through the session. Some infants (particularly those that are developing atypically) may strongly dislike certain tasks. This may have a negative effect on other tasks in the same session, so it is strongly advised that you ensure you have the ability to skip or exclude these tasks in such a situation.

Finally, it is vital to pilot all experimental tasks with the target age group. You will make numerous assumptions and balance a variety of constraints when putting together an experimental task, and even very experienced infant researchers are often unable to predict accurately how well a particular task will work. Piloting ensures first that an infant will sit through your task, second that the task produces suitable data from an infant population, and also that you are well practised at running the task so valuable infant participants aren't lost to experimenter error.

1.3 Classical behavioural methods

Infant research began with Jean Piaget in the 1920s. Piaget took detailed observations of his own children and tried to make them repeatable and interpretable. Typical of this approach was his demonstration of *object permanence*, whereby infants under 9 months will fail to retrieve a ball hidden under a blanket (Piaget, 1954). The experiment aims to show that for younger infants 'out of sight is out of mind'. But the task itself does not lend itself to investigating other aspects of infant cognition. Despite his influence on the field, Piaget didn't introduce systematic methods for understanding infancy.

1.3.1 Looking time methods

A more general approach came about with the introduction of looking time measures by Robert Fantz (Fantz, 1958). The amount of time an infant looks at a stimulus provides a measure of how interesting the infant finds it. This opened up a means of investigating numerous different questions with the same standard methods. Visual preference methods provided a simple means of demonstrating infant discrimination abilities. Habituation allowed for the demonstration and investigation of online learning while violation of expectation probed infants' beliefs about the world. These methods can also be adapted for use with auditory and cross-modal stimuli. They are represented schematically in Figure 1.1. In visual paradigms it is important to ensure the infant is looking at the screen at the start of each trial. It is usual to use a central flashing object and accompanying sound effect to draw attention back to the screen before each trial begins.

1.3.2 Visual preference

The simplest of these methods is the visual preference test (Fantz, 1958; Teller, 1979). Infants are shown two items, either sequentially or side-by-side (Figure 1.1a and b). Each item or pair is presented for a fixed amount of time (between 8–20 seconds) and for several repetitions with order or side of presentation counterbalanced. Because of infants' limited working memory, side-by-side presentation is preferable (see Oakes & Ribar, 2005). A camera positioned below the screen and pointing at the infant records the infant's response. The items must be sufficiently far apart that it is easy to tell which one the infant is looking at. Preferences are determined by offline coding whereby a researcher watches the video recording to count how long the infant looked at each item. Typically, these are expressed as a proportion score (looking time to a target item divided by total looking time to both items). Preferences are determined at the group level.

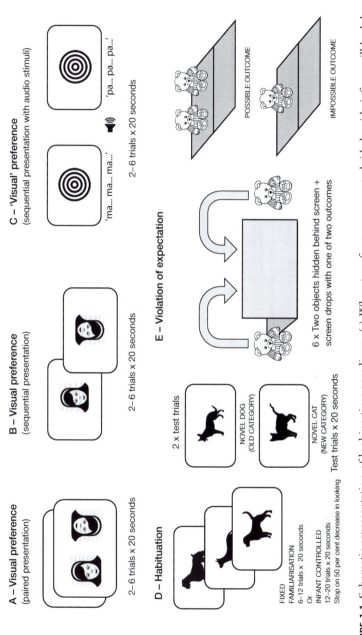

FIGURE 1.1 Schematic representation of looking time paradigms. (a) When two faces are presented side by side infants will look longer at upright face. (b) If faces presented sequentially infants may look longer on upright trials. (c) Preferential looking to the same visual stimulus can vary with different auditory accompaniment. (d) Infants are habituated to one image or category sequentially and looking times to two test items are compared. (e) Infants see two objects hidden behind a screen and then one of two outcomes. Infants look longer at the impossible outcome when screen is lowered to reveal only one object

Using this method, researchers have shown that infants have a preference for their mother over a stranger, for female faces over male (Quinn, Yahr, Kuhn, Slater, & Pascalis, 2002) and even that newborn babies have a preferences for faces with a direct gaze (Rigato, Johnson, Faraguna, & Farroni, 2010). Interestingly, the method can be used for testing auditory stimuli. Horowitz (1975) discovered that when different sounds accompanied the same neutral visual stimulus (a flashing light or simple picture) infants would show systematic preferences (Figure 1.1c). This greatly extends the range of this technique for studying early language acquisition (e.g., Cooper & Aslin, 1990). For a detailed summary see Johnson and Zamuner (2010). Visual preference is a limited method but is often a necessary prerequisite to establish that infants have no baseline preferences that might bias outcomes in more complex looking time tasks.

1.3.3 Habituation

The next major innovation came with the discovery that infant preferences can be manipulated. In habituation paradigms infants are first familiarised to one item or category reducing their interest in it, a test phase then compares looking times to a familiar item and a novel comparison object. The key insight (Cohen, 1973) is that reduced looking times are not due to fatigue but a sign that the infant has processed the stimulus. Recovery happens when the infant considers the comparison item novel in some way and regains interest in the stimulus. Habituation has become the main method within cognitive and perceptual research with infants (see Oakes, 2010; Colombo, Brez, & Curtindale, 2012).

There are two basic approaches to habituation. In the *fixed* or *familiarisation* protocol the learning phase consists of a fixed number of trials (typically 6–20) each of fixed length (8–20 seconds). This standardises presentation and is easier to run but does not allow for the fact that some infants might process the stimuli faster than others. In the *infant controlled* or *habituation* protocol, each trial in learning phase has a maximum length (20 or 30 seconds) but can also terminate early if the infant looks away for 2 continuous seconds. Learning continues until the infants reach a *habituation criterion*, typically a 50 per cent decrease in looking averaged over the last three trials compared with the first three. Infants who do not reach this criterion within a maximum number of trials (fifteen is recommended) are said not to have habituated and are often excluded from analysis. In both protocols, the test phase compares a familiar item, a novel in-category item and a novel out-of-category item for a total of two to six test trials (Figure 1.1d). Many short trials are better than fewer long ones. Infants under 5 months can demonstrate 'sticky fixation' where on some trials they look for very long periods and have difficulty disengaging.

Habituation has been particularly useful in investigating infants' category knowledge (Mareschal & Quinn, 2001). It allows researchers to probe infant discrimination in more detail than is possible with visual preference. For example, young infants would not be expected to have a particular prior preference for either dogs or cats but may well discriminate them. Quinn, Eimas, and Rosenkrantz (1993) familiarised one group of infants to six pairs of pictures of cats while a second group were familiarised with pictures of dogs. Both groups were tested in identical conditions with six new pairs composed of a novel cat and a novel dog. Infants in the first group looked longer to the novel dog images while infants in the second group did not discriminate, leading to the surprising asymmetry that for 4-month-old infants 'cats are dogs but dogs are not cats'. French, Mareschal, Mermillod, and Quinn (2004) were able to reverse this asymmetry by manipulating the variability of the habituation items. These subtle results demonstrate the power of the habituation method and provide a clear warning that infant categories are not equivalent to our adult intuitions. It also reminds us that the null result should not be over-interpreted, a common limitation for looking time studies (Aslin, 2007).

As long as infants show consistent preferences, the interpretation of habituation results is relatively straightforward, as discrimination has been demonstrated. But there are some caveats. Infants generally show an initial familiarity preference followed by a later novelty preference (Hunter & Ames, 1988). Even after habituation, novelty and familiarity preferences are both possible. Additionally, so-called 'fast' and 'slow' habituators can show different patterns of responding, something that is thought to be related to their speed of processing and cognitive ability (see Colombo, Brez, & Curtindale, 2012). Finally, infant controlled paradigms are technically demanding, as they require online judgment of whether an infant is looking at the screen. Learning to do this takes practice and ought to be validated with offline coding. A camera positioned above or below the monitor or stage pointing directly at the infant gives a sufficiently reliable signal. Eye-trackers aren't yet reliable enough to automate the process. We recommend controlling the experiment with a MATLAB script (e.g., Addyman, 2015). Datavyu provides software for offline coding videos from infant experiments (www.datavyu.org).

1.3.4 Violation of expectation

Baillargeon, Spelke, and Wasserman (1985) introduced the violation of expectation (VOE) paradigm that combines online learning and infants' pre-existing knowledge. In their experiment infants were familiarised with a horizontal barrier that rotates 180 degrees from flat to vertical to flat moving away from the infant. An object was then placed behind the screen. In one condition the screen now stops rotating when it encounters the object. In another the screen continues on its original trajectory apparently flattening the supposedly solid object. Five-month-old infants looked longer at this second impossible outcome, implying they have an understanding of object permanence, much younger than Piaget had claimed.

VOE has been used to demonstrate that infants understand basic 'naive physics' and possess other types of innate 'core knowledge' (Spelke & Kinzler, 2007). One example is an ability to count very small numbers (Wynn, 1992). In this experiment (Figure 1.1e) an infant sees two toys placed behind a screen that is removed to reveal only either one (impossible outcome) or two (possible outcome) items. The experimental set up is novel to the infant but interpreting the outcomes requires the infant to recruit their existing knowledge. Jackson and Sirois (2009) point out that this cognitive interpretation is not without difficulty. The impossible condition is often perceptually familiar, confounding surprise with a potential familiarity preference. VOE studies require careful control conditions to rule out this possibility, such as ensuring that the familiarisation phase is long enough for infants to develop a clear novelty preference.

1.3.5 Physical tasks

The study of infant motor development is a field in itself (see Piek, 2006). But researchers sometimes use physical tasks to investigate infant cognition. DeCasper and Fifer (1980) used a pacifier attached to a sensing device that played back a sound recording. They found that newborn babies could increase or decrease their baseline sucking-rate to hear a recording of their mother's voice rather than a stranger's. Rovee-Collier and Sullivan (1980) found that infants as young as 2 months would learn to move an overhead mobile attached to their legs by a ribbon in just 15 minutes. They would retain this knowledge one week later demonstrating that they possessed some long-term memory. Both cases are examples of operant conditioning where researchers selectively reinforced infants' natural physical activity.

Even if infants have the physical ability to interact with objects, their limited executive control means they may fail to act in the way that they want to. In particular, researchers must be very aware of perseveration. The classic example of this is the A not-B error. Infants see an object repeatedly hidden in one location A and are able to successfully retrieve it. The object is then hidden in a second location B and although infants look to this location, they reach to the old location. Researchers are therefore advised to use non-motor paradigms with infants under 1 year.

1.3.6 Standardised assessments of infant development

In longitudinal or other large scale cohort studies with at risk populations a standard measure of infant motor and cognitive development is often desirable. The most widely used are the Bayley Scales of Infant Development (BSID-III) for use from 1–42 months (Bayley, 2005) and the Mullen Scales of Early Learning (MSEL) for use from 1–68 months (Mullen, 1995). These are carefully controlled assessments with high inter-rater reliability. They take between 15 and 60 minutes to administer depending on the age of the child, in that younger infants take less time because there is less they can do. They are expensive to license and require training to administer correctly. They do not in general predict later cognitive ability. Researchers should think carefully if their research question really needs to include these measures. An exception is the Macarthur-Bates communicative development inventory (CDI, Fenson *et al.*, 2007), a parental questionnaire that gives a quick, easy and reliable measure of language development.

1.4 Eye-tracking

Eye-tracking methods in infancy research have great potential to efficiently gather data that is difficult or impossible to acquire in any other way. Eye-tracking is a window into the mind's eye, making it invaluable for research with preverbal infants who cannot or will not respond using the traditional tools of experimental psychology. Gathering high-quality data from infants, however, is far from trivial. We will first outline some of the eye-tracking paradigms used with infants, before touching on some relevant practical and methodological issues. This section will be fairly brief as a lot of the important issues are covered in much more detail in Chapter 2 by Wass.

1.4.1 Eye-tracking paradigms used with infants

Eye-tracking experiments in infancy can be considered as belonging to one of three broad classes of paradigm. The first involves similar or identical designs to those used in eye-tracking studies of older children and adults. The second class of paradigms measures the control of eye movements themselves or physiological changes in the eye, and relates these to cognitive processes. For example, changes in pupil diameter can be used as a measure of cognitive load (see Addyman, Rocha, & Mareschal, 2014; Jackson & Sirois, 2009). While the third and final class are those specific to infants and revolves broadly around using eye movements as a response modality, akin to button presses or verbal responses.

In these infant-specific paradigms responses may reflect a preference for one stimulus over another, following identical logic to the visual preference designs described earlier in this chapter (e.g., Di Giorgio, Meary, Pascalis, & Simion, 2013). These designs exploit the fact that infants develop accurate control over their eye movements long before they have the manual dexterity to respond by other means and allow us to adapt traditional cognitive psychology experiments for use in a much younger population (e.g., visual search, Frank, Amso, & Johnson, 2014). Gaze contingent paradigms take this a step further by coding eye movement responses online and adapting the pace of future stimulus presentation according to the infant's behaviour. As a result infants find these designs very engaging. An example is the gap/overlap task (originally performed with manual video coding: Landry & Bryson, 2004, now commonly performed with an eye-tracker: e.g., Elsabbagh *et al.*, 2013), in which a centrally presented stimulus is followed by a peripheral stimulus presented unpredictably at either the left or right hand side of the screen. The time taken for the infant to saccade from the central to the peripheral

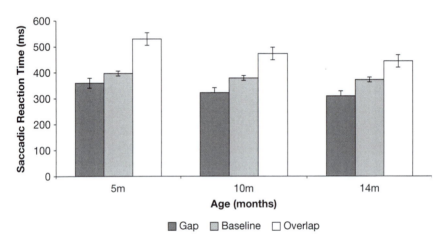

FIGURE 1.2 Saccadic reaction times (SRTs) from the gap overlap task at five, 10 and 14 months of age, calculated from eye-tracking data. Time taken to shift attention from a central (CS) to a peripheral (PS) stimulus is measured in three conditions, baseline: the CS disappears at the moment the PS appears; gap: the CS disappears 200ms before the PS appears (reducing competition between stimuli and aiding disengagement); overlap: the CS remains on screen after the PS appears (increasing competition between the stimuli with concomitant effects on SRTs). Note that overall SRTs reduce across development as shifts of attention become faster, and that the benefits of the gap condition increase while the costs of the overlap condition decrease with age

stimulus is recorded under conditions that manipulate the ease of disengagement from the central stimulus (see Figure 1.2). For more examples of gaze contingent paradigms in infancy, see Wang *et al.* (2012) or Wass, Porayska-Pomsta, and Johnson (2011).

1.4.2 Practical considerations and methodological challenges

Eye-trackers work by rapidly photographing the eye, and relating the angle of rotation of the eye to a point of gaze on screen. In order to do this accurately, the software must be calibrated by presenting small stimuli at known points on the screen (usually one at each corner, and one in the centre). What is a straightforward procedure in adults and children is less so in infants, who may not fixate on the calibration stimuli for long enough (if at all). The timing of these stimuli is important – if they stay on screen for too long, the infant may grow bored and look away; too short and the infant may not manage to focus on the stimulus in time for the measurement to be taken. A balance must be struck between a short calibration sequence, and an effective one that does not need to be repeated multiple times.

Even once successfully calibrated, eye-tracking data acquired from an infant will not be as clean as that from an adult. As a general rule the younger the infant, the more difficult it is to acquire usable raw eye-tracking data. Below 2 months of age, infants may not have good enough control of their eye movements for eye-tracking to provide meaningful information about cognition. At this age stimuli should be large, and researchers should have no expectation of resolving infants' gaze to small stimuli with any degree of accuracy. You may also encounter 'sticky fixation' whereby infants struggle to disengage from one stimulus and engage with another. By 6 months, eye-tracking is considerably more viable, although attrition rates may still be fairly high, since eye-trackers can fail to detect the eyes of some young infants, or the accuracy may be so poor that the data are unusable. By a year of age data quality is much higher, and by an infant's second year the data acquired will begin to approximate that of adults.

Infant eye-tracking data will be noisier (points of gaze reported by the eye-tracker are smeared out across time) and less accurate (estimated points of gaze are offset from actual gaze location) than that acquired from adults. In visual preference experiments, increasing the spacing between stimuli can ameliorate this. Noise is a particular problem for gaze contingent experiments where a trial may not move on until gaze is registered in an area of interest (AoI), leading to very long drawn-out blocks in which the baby quickly loses interest in the screen. A solution to this problem is to make AoIs larger than the stimuli upon which they are placed, ensuring that even when the accuracy of incoming data is low, the AoI is still triggered. Care must also be taken when measuring reaction times (RTs) to stimuli with oversized AoIs, since this will lead to artificially low RTs. This can be somewhat mitigated by averaging across neighbouring samples of data, at the expense of some temporal specificity.

1.5 Electroencephalography (EEG)

EEG involves recording the electrical activity of the brain by placing electrodes on the scalp (Figure 1.3). EEG has many advantages over other methods that measure brain activity, being non-invasive (and therefore able to be used in awake infants), relatively inexpensive and reasonably well tolerated, particularly in the first 6 to 12 months of life.

Electrical activity recorded by EEG originates in the postsynaptic potentials of cortical pyramidal cells, and from here conducts through the brain, skull and scalp, where it is recorded by an array of electrodes placed upon the head. Raw EEG data contains a mixture of brain activity and noise from physiological artefacts such

FIGURE 1.3 A 2-month-old infant wearing an EEG net

as muscular and eye movements, and from environmental electrical interference such as 50/60Hz mains supply noise. The challenge in analysing EEG data is to maximise the signal-to-noise ratio (SNR), which can be achieved by recording the cleanest data possible in the first instance, and then by a combination of statistical approaches (e.g., filtering, independent components analysis – ICA) and manually or algorithmically identifying and excluding noisy periods from analysis (see Fujioka, Mourad, He, & Trainor, 2011 for a comparison of several methods on infant EEG data).

The spatial resolution of EEG is considerably less than that of other functional imaging methods such as functional magnetic resonance imaging (fMRI) or positron emission tomography (PET) (see Chapter 3 for a discussion of MRI with children), meaning that we cannot precisely localise the origin of EEG activity to a particular part of the brain (although mathematical techniques can help, see Reynolds & Richards, 2009). The temporal resolution, however, is far superior to most other imaging methods, and therefore EEG is better suited to asking questions about the order and sequence of neural activity than about where it originates (e.g., processing of speech sounds, Kushnerenko, Teinonen, Volein, & Csibra, 2008).

Two of the most common ways to analyse EEG data are event related potentials (ERPs) and analyses of neural oscillations. ERPs rely upon the fact that repeated presentations of a stimulus will elicit repeated brain responses that are reliably time locked to the stimulus onset, unlike the noise which is distributed randomly across time and across trials. Averaging the brain's response to many trials will therefore increase the signal-to-noise ratio, by averaging out the noise, and 'averaging in' the neural response. For a detailed review and tutorial on ERPs in infancy see Hoehl and Wahl (2012). Many ERPs in adults are well studied and their functional significance, and often their neural origin, well understood. This is not the case in infancy, and the relationship between adult ERPs and their putative infant counterparts is not always straightforward (see Coch & Gullick, 2012 for a review).

While ERPs focus on the time domain of the EEG signal, analyses of neural oscillations are concerned with the frequency domain. One of the most striking aspects of EEG activity is the pattern of rhythmic oscillations seen at certain frequencies. In adults these frequencies are divided into functionally significant frequency bands: delta (0.5–4Hz), theta (4–8Hz), alpha (8–13Hz), beta (13–30Hz) and gamma (from around 30Hz up to 100Hz), although the borders of these bands may be lower in infants (see Saby & Marshall, 2012). Neural oscillations may be studied in relation to an experimental event (event related oscillations – EROs: e.g., while infants observe and execute actions, see Southgate, Osborne, Johnson,

& Csibra, 2009), or recorded during a longer time period (tens of seconds to minutes) while watching a video or playing (e.g., relating EEG power to working memory performance, see Bell & Wolfe, 2007).

Regardless of the analysis that you plan to carry out it is vital that you are aware of and able to meet the practical challenges of recording EEG from infants. The choice of EEG system is important since application times must not exceed a few minutes, and many EEG products that work well with adults are unsuitable for infants due to a long setup time. Precise placement of the electrodes is extremely important so that the array covers all possible brain regions, and so that data is comparable across participants and experiments. Researchers who apply the electrodes to infants must understand the importance of good placement, and be practised in achieving it rapidly and with the minimum distress to the participant.

Attrition rates are higher than in other methods – up to 50 per cent – since some infants will refuse to wear an EEG net or cap. Younger infants can often be distracted while the cap is applied by playing with toys. Older infants and toddlers often benefit from playing a game before they come to the lab in which various hat-like objects are put on their head, or on the head of a teddy bear or doll, working up to an EEG net. Once the electrodes are applied, many infants will reach up and grab at them, causing large artefacts in the data and shifting the position of the electrodes. To prevent this, parents can be asked to hold their child's hands, or the infant can be given small toys to hold so long as they are not noisy or distracting. It may be tempting to give snacks or a pacifier to infants during an EEG session but this should be avoided due to the muscle artefacts they introduce into the recording.

Trial numbers will be low in infant EEG work, particularly for ERP designs where stimuli need to be repeated many times. As the number of conditions in a design increases the number of trials per condition goes down, so keep things simple. The longer an infant can be kept engaged in an experimental task, the more clean EEG data will be available for analysis, so pay attention to stimulus related factors that increase attention, as described earlier in this chapter. For an empirical review and advice on factors leading to attrition in infant EEG, see Stets, Stahl, and Reid, 2012.

Variability in neural responses is higher across infants than adults. In ERP data this leads to 'temporal smearing' in which the latency of the peak of a single trial ERP varies across trials and participants. When these data are averaged, the ERPs are more rounded and less 'peaky'. Variability is also evident within an individual across development as myelination occurs and increased experience of the world leads to greater cortical specialisation, meaning that brain responses between ages may differ in latency, amplitude and scalp distribution.

1.6 Emerging methods

We do not have the space to give meaningful advice on newer methods but we would like to draw your attention to some promising possibilities. Be aware that these are not for beginners. One of the most rapidly spreading tools is functional Near Infrared Spectroscopy (fNIRS). An array of fibre optic sensors on the scalp measures scattered light from an array of light sources (Lloyd-Fox, Blasi, & Elwell, 2009). The wavelength of the light is such that it is absorbed by blood flowing near the surface of the brain providing a proxy for cortical activation, analogous to the BOLD measure of fMRI (see Chapter 3 and Aslin, Shuka, & Emberson, 2015). Using fNIRS allows researchers to localise cortical activity during cognitive tasks (Lloyd-Fox, Blasi, Mercure, Elwell, & Johnson, 2012). It has lower temporal resolution than EEG but better localisation and is much more portable.

Another growing area involves the collection of richer 'ecological' data. This can involve recording physiological data like heart rate and skin conductance as secondary measures during behavioural tasks (e.g., Colombo *et al.*, 2001). Or studying infants in their homes or naturalistic lab settings to investigate things like sleep patterns (see Chapter 13 for a discussion) or how infants learn to walk (Adolph *et al.*, 2012). The most extreme example is the 'Human Speechome project', which collected audio and video almost continuously for the first few years of life of the researcher's first child (Roy *et al.*, 2006). Activity trackers and head mounted cameras can give an infant's-eye view of the world (Aslin, 2009; Smith, Yu, Yoshida, & Fausey, 2014; see also Chapter 2 for a detailed discussion). But these have yet to make a big impact. Likewise, in the near future smartphones and tablets will undoubtedly allow more home-based research such as parent experience sampling but this has yet to happen (see Chapter 14 for a detailed discussion of new technologies).

An important design for understanding developmental disorders such as Autism Spectrum Disorders and ADHD are prospective infants-at-risk designs, often referred to as 'sibs studies'. If 100 infants are selected at random only one is likely to develop the disorder. But by studying infants who have an older sibling with an existing diagnosis, this can be reduced to one in five (Ozonoff *et al.*, 2011). Sibling studies allow us to study emerging symptoms of the disorder and to understand what protective factors are at play in the four out of five infants with a high genetic risk but who do not go on to develop the disorder. These studies are highly complex, often using extensive multimodal batteries of experimental measures collected by experienced researchers, as well as a thorough behavioural and clinical characterisation, at multiple time points. Even when testing a large sample of high-risk infants, the subset who develop a disorder is still small, and so there is a growing emphasis on spreading the load between multiple sites.

Finally, reflecting a wider trend in psychology, infancy researchers are encouraged to adopt more sophisticated statistical methods. Bayesian data analysis lends itself well to infant data (Kruschke, 2010; Piantadosi, Kidd, & Aslin, 2014). For classical statistics, reporting confidence intervals and effect sizes is important (Cumming, 2014). Be aware that Cohen's original guidelines on interpreting effect sizes do not apply to smaller, noisier samples found in infant studies. Recent meta-analysis of infant studies recommends the partial eta-squared cut-offs of .11, .25 and .50 for small, medium and large effects respectively (Mills-Smith, Spangler, Panneton, & Fritz, 2015).

1.7 Conclusion

In closing we offer you a few final words of advice. First, one thing that gets forgotten surprisingly often in infancy research is the role of development. Much research is content with describing the earliest age at which a competence is shown but doesn't attempt to explain why. Early learning mechanisms are hard to understand but they are crucial and cumulative. This is why we study infants in the first place. However, avoid longitudinal studies if you can. It is tempting to imagine running a longitudinal infant study that could be completed in a year or two. But there is so much that can go wrong in infant experiments and the narrow time windows for age appropriate testing make longitudinal research with infants very difficult. Finally, do not be afraid to ask for advice. There is an art to the science of infant testing and many tricks of the trade that we have not been able to cover here. When thinking about a new study the advice of a more experienced researcher is truly invaluable. Infancy researchers are a friendly and supportive community who are happy to help. Infant research is deceptively hard. But it is also very rewarding. And, of course, we have the cutest participants in the whole of science.

Practical tips

1 'The baby is always right' – Work to the infant's own schedule.
2 'Parents know their babies' – Involve the parents and listen to them.
3 'Collect lots of data in parallel' – Prefer rich, multimodal data and always video your experiments.

References

Addyman, C. (2015). Infant-habituation-in-Matlab: Version 1. Zenodo.

Addyman, C., Rocha, S., & Mareschal, D. (2014). Mapping the origins of time: Scalar errors in infant time estimation. *Developmental Psychology, 50*(8), 2030–5.

Adolph, K. E., Cole, W. G., Komati, M., Garciaguirre, J. S., Badaly, D., Lingeman, J. M., . . . & Sotsky, R. B. (2012). How do you learn to walk? Thousands of steps and dozens of falls per day. *Psychological Science, 23*(11), 1387–94.

Aslin, R. N. (2007). What is in a look? *Developmental Science, 10*(1), 48–53.

Aslin, R. N. (2009). How infants view natural scenes gathered from a head-mounted camera. *Optometry and Vision Science, 86,* 561–5.

Aslin, R. N., Shukla, M., & Emberson, L. L. (2015). Hemodynamic correlates of cognition in human infants. *Annual Review of Psychology, 66,* 349–9.

Baillargeon, R., Spelke, E. S., & Wasserman, S. (1985). Object permanence in five-month-old infants. *Cognition, 20*(3), 191–208.

Bayley, N. (2005). *Bayley scales of infant development.* San Antonio, TX: Harcourt Assessment.

Bell, M. A., & Wolfe, C. D. (2007). Changes in brain functioning from infancy to early childhood: Evidence from EEG power and coherence working memory tasks. *Developmental Neuropsychology, 31*(1), 21–38.

Coch, D., & Gullick, M. M. (2012). Event-related potentials and development. In S. J. Luck, & E. S. Kappenman (Eds), *The Oxford handbook of event-related potential components* (pp. 473–511). Oxford, UK: Oxford University Press.

Cohen, L. B. (1973). A two-process model of infant visual attention. *Merrill-Palmer Quarterly of Behavior and Development, 19*(3), 157–80.

Colombo, J., Brez, C. C., & Curtindale, L. M. (2012). Infant perception and cognition. In I. B. Weinter, R. M. Learner, M. A. Easterbrooks, & J. Mistry (Eds), *Handbook of psychology, developmental psychology* (pp. 61–89). Hoboken, NJ: John Wiley & Sons.

Colombo, J., Richman, W. A., Shaddy, D. J., Follmer Greenhoot, A., & Maikranz, J. M. (2001). Heart-rate defined phases of attention, look duration, and infant performance in the paired-comparison paradigm. *Child Development, 72,* 1605–16.

Cooper, R. P., & Aslin, R. N. (1990). Preference for infant directed speech in the first month after birth. *Child Development, 61*(5), 1584–95.

Cumming, G. (2014). The new statistics: Why and how. *Psychological Science, 25*(1), 7–29.

Datavyu Team (2014). Datavyu: A video coding tool. Databrary Project, New York University. Retrieved from www.datavyu.org.

DeCasper, A. J., & Fifer, W. P. (1980). Of human bonding: Newborns prefer their mothers' voices. *Science, 208*(4448), 1174–6.

Di Giorgio, E., Meary, D., Pascalis, O., & Simion, F. (2013). The face perception system becomes species-specific at 3 months: An eye-tracking study. *International Journal of Behavioral Development, 37*(2), 95–9.

Elsabbagh, M., Fernandes, J., Webb, S. J., Dawson, G., Charman, T., & Johnson, M. H. (2013). Disengagement of visual attention in infancy is associated with emerging autism in toddlerhood. *Biological Psychiatry, 74*(3), 189–94.

Fantz, R. L. (1958). Pattern vision in young infants. *Psychological Record, 8,* 43–9.

Fenson, L., Marchman, V. A., Thal, D. J., Dale, P. S., Reznick, J. S., & Bates, E. (2007). *MacArthur-Bates Communicative Development Inventories: User's guide and technical manual* (2nd edn). Baltimore, MD: Brookes.

Frank, M. C., Amso, D., & Johnson, S. P. (2014). Visual search and attention to faces during early infancy. *Journal of Experimental Child Psychology, 118*(1), 13–26.

French, R. M., Mareschal, D., Mermillod, M., & Quinn, P. C. (2004). The role of bottom-up processing in perceptual categorization by 3- to 4-month-old infants: Simulations and data. *Journal of Experimental Psychology: General, 133*(3), 382–97.

Fujioka, T., Mourad, N., He, C., & Trainor, L. J. (2011). Comparison of artifact correction methods for infant EEG applied to extraction of event-related potential signals. *Clinical Neurophysiology, 122*(1), 43–51.

Hessels, R. S., Cornelissen, T. H. W., Kemner, C., & Hooge, I. T. C. (2014). Qualitative tests of remote eyetracker recovery and performance during head rotation. *Behavior Research Methods, 47*(3), 848–59.

Hoehl, S., & Wahl, S. (2012). Recording infant ERP data for cognitive research. *Developmental Neuropsychology, 37*(3), 187–209.

Horowitz, F. D. (1975). Visual attention, auditory stimulation, and language discrimination in infants. *Monographs of the Society for Research in Child Development, 39*, 1–140.

Hunter, M. A., & Ames, E. W. (1988). A multifactor model of infant preferences for novel and familiar stimuli. In L. P. Lipsitt (Ed.), *Advances in child development and behaviour:* Vol. 4. (pp. 69–95). Norwood, NJ: Ablex.

Jackson, I., & Sirois, S. (2009). Infant cognition: Going full factorial with pupil dilation. *Developmental Science, 12*(4), 670–9.

Johnson, E., & Zamuner, T. (2010). Using infant and toddler testing methods in language acquisition research. In E. Blom & S. Unsworth (Eds), *Experimental methods in language acquisition research* (pp. 73–94). Philadelphia: John Benjamins.

Kruschke, J. (2010). Bayesian data analysis. Wiley Interdisciplinary Reviews: *Cognitive Science, 1*(5), 658–76.

Kushnerenko, E., Teinonen, T., Volein, A., & Csibra, G. (2008). Electrophysiological evidence of illusory audiovisual speech percept in human infants. *Proceedings of the National Academy of Sciences of the United States of America, 105*(32), 11442–5.

Landry, R., & Bryson, S. E. (2004). Impaired disengagement of attention in young children with autism. *Journal of Child Psychology and Psychiatry, 45*(6), 1115–22.

Lloyd-Fox, S., Blasi, A., & Elwell, C. E. (2009). Illuminating the developing brain: The past, present and future of functional near infrared spectroscopy. *Neuroscience Biobehavioral Reviews, 34*(3), 269–84.

Lloyd-Fox, S., Blasi, A., Mercure, E., Elwell, C. E., & Johnson, M. H. (2012). The emergence of cerebral specialization for the human voice over the first months of life. *Social Neuroscience, 7*(3), 317–30.

Mareschal, D., & Quinn, P. C. (2001). Categorization in infancy. *Trends in Cognitive Sciences, 5*(10), 443–50.

Mills-Smith, L., Spangler, D. P., Panneton, R., & Fritz, M. S. (2015). A missed opportunity for clarity: Problems in the reporting of effect size estimates in infant developmental science. *Infancy, 20*(4), 416–32.

Mullen, E. M. (1995). *Mullen scales of early learning*. Circle Pines, MN: American Guidance Service.

Oakes, L. M. (2010). Using habituation of looking time to assess mental processes in infancy. *Journal of Cognition and Development, 11*(3), 255–68.

Oakes, L. M., & Ribar, R. J. (2005). A comparison of infants' categorization in paired and successive presentation familiarization tasks. *Infancy, 7*, 85–98.

Ozonoff, S., Young, G. S., Carter, A., Messinger, D., Yirmiya, N., Zwaigenbaum, L., . . . & Stone, W. L. (2011). Recurrence risk for autism spectrum disorders: A baby siblings research consortium study. *Pediatrics, 128*(3), e488-e495.

Piaget, J. (1954). *The construction of reality in the child.* New York: Basic Books.

Piantadosi, S., Kidd, C., & Aslin, R. N. (2014). Rich analysis and rational models: Inferring individual behavior from infant looking data. *Developmental Science, 17,* 321–37.

Piek, J. P. (2006). *Infant motor development:* Vol. 10. Champaign, IL: Human Kinetics.

Quinn, P. C., Eimas, P. D., & Rosenkrantz, S. L. (1993). Evidence for representations of perceptually similar natural categories by 3-month-old and 4-month-old infants. *Perception, 22,* 463–75.

Quinn, P. C., Yahr, J., Kuhn, A., Slater, A. M., & Pascalis, O. (2002). Representation of the gender of human faces by infants: A preference for female. *Perception, 31,* 1109–21.

Reynolds, G. D., & Richards, J. E. (2009). Cortical source localization of infant cognition. *Developmental Neuropsychology, 34*(3), 312–29.

Rigato, S., Johnson, M. H., Faraguna, D., & Farroni, T. (2010). Direct gaze may modulate face recognition in newborns. *Infant and Child Development, 20*(1), 20–34.

Rovee-Collier, C., & Sullivan, M. W. (1980). Organization of infant memory. *Journal of Experimental Psychology: Human Learning and Memory, 6,* 798–807.

Roy, D., Patel, R., DeCamp, P., Kubat, R., Fleischman, M., Roy, B., . . . & Gorniak, P. (2006). The human speechome project. In *Proceedings of the 28th Annual Cognitive Science Conference* (pp. 2059–64). Mahwah, NJ: Lawrence Erlbaum.

Saby, J., & Marshall, P. (2012). The utility of EEG band power analysis in the study of infancy. *Developmental Neuropsychology, 37*(3), 253–73.

Smith, L. B., Yu, C., Yoshida, H., & Fausey, C. M. (2014). Contributions of head-mounted cameras to studying the visual environments of infants and young children. *Journal of Cognition and Development, 16*(3), 407–19.

Southgate, V., Johnson, M. H., Osborne, T., & Csibra, G. (2009). Predictive motor activation during action observation in human infants. *Biology Letters, 5*(6), 769–72.

Spelke, E. S., & Kinzler, K. D. (2007). Core knowledge. *Developmental Science, 10*(1), 89–96.

Stets, M., Stahl, D., & Reid, V. M. (2012). A meta-analysis investigating factors underlying attrition rates in infant ERP studies. *Developmental Neuropsychology, 37*(3), 226–52.

Teller, D.Y. (1979). The forced-choice preferential looking procedure: A psychophysical technique for use with human infants. *Infant Behavior and Development, 2,* 135–53.

Wang, Q., Bolhuis, J., Rothkopf, C. A., Kolling, T., Knopf, M., & Triesch, J. (2012). Infants in control: Rapid anticipation of action outcomes in a gaze-contingent paradigm. *PLoS One, 7*(2), e30884.

Wass, S. V., Porayska-Pomsta, K., & Johnson, M. H. (2011). Training attentional control in infancy. *Current Biology, 21*(18), 1543–7.

Wynn, K. (1992). Addition and subtraction by human infants. *Nature, 358*(6389), 749–50.

2

THE USE OF EYE-TRACKING WITH INFANTS AND CHILDREN

Sam V. Wass

2.1 Introduction

Eye-tracking is the principle of tracking participants' eye movements as they look around a scene. Fundamentally, it can be done in two ways: first, in screen-based tasks, in which viewing materials are presented on a computer monitor, and second, in naturalistic contexts.

In the first part of this chapter we discuss methodological issues associated with eye-tracking. We describe how eye-tracking works, the different types of eye-tracker available (screen-based and head-mounted), and different stimulus presentation and software packages. Finally, we discuss the challenges of variable data quality, and different factors to be borne in mind while designing an eye-tracking experiment. We also provide a glossary, including definitions of key eye-tracking terms. As with any scientific method, it is vitally important to remember at all times that eye-tracking is not perfect. Caution, and healthy scientific scepticism, should be used at all times in interpreting results.

Eye-tracking is a versatile method. In the second part of this chapter we discuss, with illustrative examples, the different types of eye-tracking study. First, we discuss studies that examine *how we use our eye movements* to construct a representation of the outside world. Second, we discuss studies that use eye-tracking to measure *individual differences* – for example in our ability to remember items of information for short periods of time. Third, we discuss studies that use eye-tracking to examine more 'high-level' aspects of cognition, such as whether young children are able to make mental state attributions to others. Fourth, we discuss uses of eye-tracking to provide targeted *cognitive training* for infants and young children. Fifth, we discuss 'naturalistic' eye-tracking that measures eye movements 'in the wild', away from traditional experimental settings. A glossary of key eye-tracking terms is provided in an Appendix at the end of this chapter.

2.2 Methodological issues in eye-tracking

2.2.1 How eye-tracking works

The principles of all of the eye-trackers discussed below are very similar. Eye-tracking works by identifying two separate elements: the position of the pupil, and the corneal reflection – i.e., the reflection of a point-light that is shone from the eye-tracker onto the participant's eyeball (e.g., Holmqvist *et al.*, 2011; see also Figure 2.1). As the participant's eye moves, the pupil moves, but the position of the corneal reflection remains constant. Calculating the distance between these two points allows us to estimate, therefore, the position of the eyeball within the head.

All eye-tracking starts with a calibration sequence, in which stimuli are presented at set, known positions within the scene. At each location, the distance between the pupil and the corneal reflection is measured. In this way the eye-tracker 'learns', for example, that when the participant is looking at 'point x' (e.g., the middle of the screen), the distance between the pupil and corneal reflection is 'vector y'. If subsequently, at any point during the recording, the distance between the pupil and corneal reflection is found to be vector y, then we conclude that the participant must be looking at point x. In this way, following a calibration, it is possible to estimate, based on the calibration points obtained, where within the scene the participant is looking.

FIGURE 2.1 Left shows an eye image obtained during recording, with the square showing the pupil, and the cross-hairs showing the corneal reflection. Middle shows an infant positioned in front of a Tobii T120 eye-tracker. Right shows 16 seconds of raw gaze data obtained from an infant during the viewing of the scene

Figure adapted from Wass, Forssman, and Leppanen (2014). Reprinted with permission

2.2.2 Types of eye-tracker

Screen-based eye-trackers – 'chin-rest' or 'head-free'

Screen-based eye-tracking involves presenting stimuli on a computer screen, and measuring where within the screen the participant is looking. Within screen-based eye-tracking, two approaches are widely used. The first, called 'chin-rest' eye-trackers, require the participant to use a chin-rest during tracking, in order to maintain the eye at a constant distance from the screen. Although chin-rest eye-trackers (such as the SMI 1000) offer the best temporal and spatial resolution, they are not widely used in developmental research due to the difficulty of encouraging young children to maintain their head on a chin-rest.

'Head-free' eye-trackers, in contrast, allow the participant to move their head freely in 3-D space during tracking. They do this by tracking the position of the head during tracking, and including information about the distance of the head from the screen into the calculations based on the location of the pupil and corneal reflection. It should be noted that, although they give more freedom of movement, participants are not allowed to move their heads *completely* freely, but are still required to maintain their head within a 3-D 'head box' due to limitations on the range and accuracy of the cameras. The size of the head box is approximately 40cm in each dimension, starting about 60cm away from the screen. All models from the manufacturer Tobii are heads-free (including the TX300 and smaller, portable eye-trackers such as the X2–60), as well as the SMI Red and the EyeTribe. Tobii products tend to be most widely used within developmental research, although these devices have the disadvantage that they do not allow the user to see the eye image (Figure 2.1). This can make it much harder to identify and eliminate problems encountered during eye-tracking (see Holmqvist et al., 2011).

Different types of tracker typically vary on two parameters. The first is spatial resolution – i.e., how accurately the eye-tracker can report where an individual is looking. Manufacturers often report, for example, that their eye-tracker is accurate to 1° of visual angle – meaning that when the participant is positioned approximately 60cm from the screen, the eye-tracker can accurately report where on the screen they are looking to within a few centimetres (although our experience suggests that these estimates tend to be over optimistic). The second parameter is temporal resolution – i.e., how frequently the gaze data are recorded. A 50Hz tracker records 50 data points per second (i.e., one every 20 milliseconds), whereas a 1000Hz tracker records 1000 data points per second (i.e., one every 1 millisecond). Differences in temporal resolution tend only to be important in cases where a researcher is planning to report on individual differences in fine-grained eye movements such as fixations and saccades, although increased resolution brings with it generally greater accuracy.

Head-mounted eye-tracker

Head-mounted eye-tracking does not require participants to view stimuli on a computer screen. Rather, the child wears a headpiece featuring two cameras. The first, which is positioned in the middle of the forehead, is a 'scene camera', which records what the child is seeing. The second, which is positioned in front of the child's eye, records the position of the pupil and (via a small infra-red emitter positioned next to the eye) and the corneal reflection (see Figure 2.2).

The most widely used head-mounted eye-tracker in infant research is the Positive Science eye-tracker (see Figure 2.2). The Positive Science eye-tracker can reliably be used with young infants (below 12 months in age), and with older children (above 3 years of age). However, as with other techniques such as electroencephalography (EEG), taking recordings in 12 to 36-month-olds can be challenging. The eye camera, which of necessity is positioned immediately in front of the eye, is often distracting for toddlers, and if it gets jogged or moved at all during recording a recalibration must be performed. Although similar devices from other manufacturers are available (including Tobii and SMI), these typically require the participant to wear glasses with built-in cameras, which tend to be adult size and to slip off children's smaller noses.

As we discuss in more depth below, there are a variety of advantages to naturalistic eye-tracking. However, it is also important to bear certain limitations in mind. For example, one challenge with head-mounted eye-tracking is that it is generally necessary to hand-code results. This requires watching a replay of the data collected, onto which has been superimposed the child's position of gaze (see Figure 2.2) and coding, frame by frame, where the child is looking. When large amounts of data are recorded, this can be labour intensive. In screen-based tracking, in contrast, this procedure can generally be automated based on the position of gaze relative to certain, pre-defined Areas of Interest (AOIs). Some experimenters have, however, found ways round this problem (see Smith, Yu, & Pereira, 2011, discussed below).

As an alternative to head-mounted eye-trackers, some researchers just use the scene camera positioned on the forehead, without the additional eye camera (e.g., Yu & Smith, 2012). This has two advantages: first, it is cheaper, since any lightweight camera can be used, reducing the cost from several thousand dollars to approximately $100. Second, it is less distracting for children (since the eye camera is absent, rendering the whole device invisible to children once they have it on

FIGURE 2.2 Left shows an image of a child wearing a head-mounted eye-tracker
(from Positive Science). Right shows an example of data recorded from
this tracker. The image shows the scene camera. The cross-hairs show an
estimate of where within that scene camera the child is looking. The eye
image recorded from the child can be seen in the top right hand corner
of the screen

their head). The disadvantage, however, is that the spatial resolution is much lower:
the experimenter sees the 'scene view' (i.e., the same image as shown in Figure
2.2b), but without the cross hairs that indicate where *within the scene* the child is
looking.

2.2.3 Stimulus presentation and analysis packages

Most commercially available eye-trackers come with built-in software to allow for
stimulus presentation and data analysis. The Tobii Studio package, for example, is
available for purchase with a Tobii eye-tracker. It allows the user to design
experiments using text elements, images, PDFs, movies, sound files, scene camera
and external video sources. It also allows the user to visualise and to replay eye-
tracking sessions, and to provide summary raw statistics, such as heat maps. Finally,
it automatically parses data into fixations and saccades (see 2.3.1 below), and by
tracking eye movements relative to certain, user-defined AOIs (see e.g., Figure
2.4a). Of note, however, our experience suggests that most of the commercial data
analysis packages available have been designed for use with adult data, and may
perform sub-optimally with some of the lower and more variable data quality that
is typically obtained from developmental populations – as we discuss further below
(see also Wass, Forssman, & Leppanen, 2014; Wass, Smith, & Johnson, 2012).

As an alternative to off-the-shelf, commercial products, therefore, many users prefer to design their own stimulus presentation and analysis packages, using programming tools such as E-Prime, Matlab and Python. These allow for far greater user control over all aspects of stimulus presentation and data analysis. During stimulus presentation, for example, it is possible to design experiments in which different events take place contingent on where on-screen a participant is looking. During data analysis, it is possible to program a greater range of analyses to those available to users of commercial products. Furthermore, certain aspects of the data recorded during eye-tracking, such as pupil size and head position, can only be analysed using user-defined analysis packages.

2.2.4 Data quality

As with any scientific technique, it is essential for users to evaluate the quality and the reliability of the data they have recorded before they draw any conclusions based on that data. Our analyses suggest that the quality of eye-tracking data obtained during recording is *not* always reliable. For example, we have found that systematically lower-quality eye-tracking data tends to be obtained from younger (relative to older) participants, and from individuals who are more fidgety during recording (Wass *et al.*, 2014). Other research has found that worse-quality data is obtained from individuals with bluish (compared with brownish) eye colour, and from infants who are seated freely on their parent's lap during recording (as opposed to seated in a special infant chair) (Hessels, Andersson, Hooge, Nystrom, & Kemner, 2015).

In evaluating data quality, three parameters are generally considered important. Two of these are illustrated in Figure 2.3. First, *precision* – i.e., sampling error ('jitter') in the reporting of the infant's position of gaze. The second parameter of data quality is *robustness* – i.e., the proportion of samples in which gaze location information is missing completely. The third parameter of data quality, which we do not illustrate in Figure 2.3, is *offset* or *spatial accuracy*. This is the disparity between where a child is *actually* looking and where the eye-tracker *reports* that the child is looking – most probably due to an inaccurate calibration. Our investigations and those of others suggest that all three types of error are relatively common during eye-tracking recording.

Figure 2.4 shows two simulations that were conducted to examine how poor data quality can affect eye-tracking results. The panel on the left shows data recorded during an experiment designed to measure whether infants look to the eyes, mouth or nose while viewing a face. Gaze data obtained during the presentation of the face is recorded (Figure 2.4a), and coded as to which of the AOIs it is within

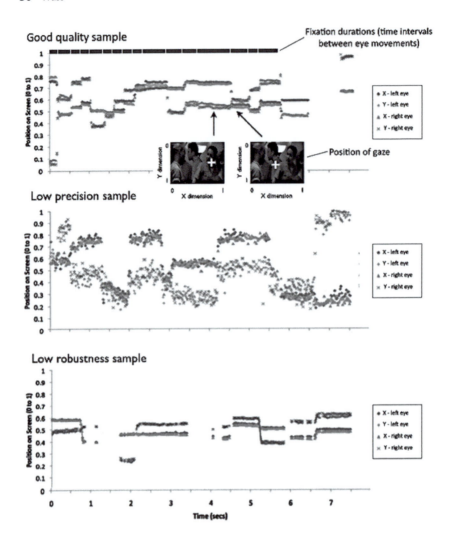

FIGURE 2.3 Three samples of viewing data recorded from a Tobii 1750 tracker recording at 50Hz. Data is from 11-month-old typically developing infants. The time (in seconds) is shown on the x axis and the gaze coordinates are both drawn on the y axis. Two illustrative frames are shown, to indicate how these data are converted into screen gaze positions. The top sample illustrates high-quality data, with continuous data. The second sample illustrates low precision data. In this sample, there is increased measurement error (due to inaccurate eye-tracking). Unlike in the previous sample, individual fixations are not clearly discernible. The third sample illustrates low robustness. Here, tracking is generally reliable but is interspersed with periods of missing data ranging from one iteration to several hundred msecs

Figure reproduced from Wass, Forssman, and Leppanen (2014). Reprinted with permission

(Figure 2.4b). Figure 2.4c shows the same data, but subjected to a 'low precision' simulation by adding Gaussian noise. An identical analysis has then been conducted (Figure 2.4d). It can be seen that, in the 'low precision' sample, the participant appears to be looking less to the eyes and more to the nose and mouth. This is despite the fact that the two samples were originally identical, and the only manipulation made has been to add random noise to the data obtained during tracking. This illustrates the danger of drawing conclusions based on gaze location, without first analysing how data quality varies within the sample (Hessels *et al.*, 2015; Wass *et al.*, 2014).

The right panel of Figure 2.4 shows data collected during an experiment to measure saccadic reaction times. Figure 2.4e shows the position of a target (drawn

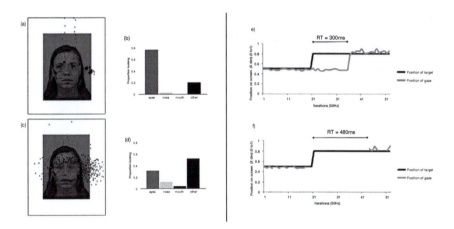

FIGURE 2.4 Two simulations conducted to illustrate how differences in data quality can affect the results of eye-tracker experiments. The left panel shows 10 seconds of viewing data from a 9-month infant. The experiment is designed to examine which area of the face – eyes, mouth, or nose – infants look to most. Figure 2.4 (a, b) shows the original data sample, (c, d) shows the same gaze data sample, but subjected to a 'low precision' simulation by adding Gaussian noise. Looking time to different areas of interests (AOIs) has been coded (b, d). The right panel shows an experiment designed to measure saccadic reaction time. (e) shows gaze data from a typically developing 12-month-old infant during a 1-sec gaze window. The black line shows the position of the target, and the grey line the position of gaze of the infant viewing the target. The latency between the shift in the target location and the first valid position of gaze recorded within the areas of interest is the oculomotor reaction time (in this instance 300msec). (f) Shows the same data sample, but subjected to a robustness simulation

Figures taken from Wass, Forssman, and Leppanen (2014). Reprinted with permission

in black), which shifts in location. The position of gaze is drawn in grey. It can be seen that a short time after the target shifts location the participant's gaze shifts location too. The latency between these two events can be used to index saccadic reaction times – in this case, 300msecs. Figure 2.4f shows identical data that have been altered to simulate the effect of low robustness (as illustrated in Figure 2.3). An identical analysis has been conducted as in Figure 2.4e. Reaction time has been coded as the time interval between the target shifting position and the first instance in which gaze is recorded within the new target position. It can be seen that the reaction time recorded is longer in the 'less robust' data – because eye-tracking data were missing at the critical time when the eye movement took place.

Data quality issues are particularly dangerous in two areas. The first are instances in which a paradigm is applied to individuals of different ages. In this case, eye-tracking data obtained from younger individuals generally tends to be lower in quality (Wass et al., 2014), and this may cause the false appearance of observed differences in key measures. Second, instances in which gaze behaviour is compared between two populations. This applies to studies comparing clinical and typical populations, to studies comparing 'high-risk' and 'low-risk' groups (such as infants from low socioeconomic status backgrounds, or infants with clinical diagnoses in the family), as well as to studies comparing groups defined by some other behavioural characteristic, such as good and poor learners. In each case, the danger is that between-group differences in fidgetiness or irritability may lead to differences in eye-tracking data quality, which can cause the false appearance of differences in gaze behaviour. For this reason it is important to measure data quality, and to report it when reporting results (e.g., Wass et al., 2015).

2.2.5 Home or laboratory-based studies

The increasing availability of low-cost, portable eye-trackers such as the EyeTribe has led to interest in running eye-tracking experiments in non-lab-based settings – such as in homes and schools.

Running studies in this way has a variety of practical advantages, such as reducing the requirement for lab space, as well as making it possible to access hard-to-reach populations such as low socioeconomic status (SES) and clinical populations. However, it should be noted that such research also has disadvantages. The behaviour of participants, as well as the quality of the eye-tracking data obtained, are heavily contingent on extraneous factors, such as the amount of ambient lighting in the room. Laboratories generally have blacked out windows and tightly controlled lighting, which allows the experimenter to ensure that lighting conditions for all individuals are identical. In non-lab situations, however, it is often impossible to control these. For example, if windows cannot be blacked out completely, then substantial differences are likely to subsist between data recorded on sunny and cloudy days. Our analyses suggest that the data quality recorded in community settings such as schools tends to be much lower than that recorded in lab-based settings (Ballieux *et al.*, 2016). This can lead to difficulties in interpreting certain measures, as discussed above.

2.3 Different types of eye-tracker paradigm

In this section we provide an overview of five different types of eye-tracking paradigms. Although far from exhaustive, this list has been selected to illustrate the range of possibilities that eye-tracking has to offer.

2.3.1 Basic eye parameters

Fixations and saccades

The most basic type of eye-tracking paradigm involves showing static or dynamic images on a computer screen to participants and measuring their spontaneous eye movements. Figure 2.3 shows an example of data recorded using one such type of paradigm that was intended to look at individual differences in eye movement frequency in infants. Data shown was recorded during a single 8-second static scene that was shown to infants. It can be seen that the data shows both a) moments where the eyeball is still, which are called fixations, and b) moments where the eyeball moves from one point to another, which are called saccades. In addition to fixations and saccades, there are other types of eye movements such as smooth pursuit (in which the eye moves continuously to maintain an object at fixation), vergence eye movements (in which the eyeballs rotate towards one another in order to maintain fixation on an object as it moves closer to us), vestibular-ocular reflex movements (in which the eyes make compensatory eye movements as the head moves, in order to keep the eyes stably oriented) and optokinetic nystagmus movements (which keep the eyes stably oriented over large-scale movements of the environment) (see Henderson, 2006). Although these latter parameters are important, and disruptions to any part of them can reveal cognitive abnormalities, the majority of published research has examined fixations and saccades.

Research suggests that there are marked differences between individuals in average fixation duration – i.e., how frequently we move our eyes. These individual differences are consistently observed across different types of viewing material (Castelhano & Henderson, 2008). It is currently unclear, however, exactly what factors influence individual differences in average fixation duration (Wass & Smith, 2014a). However, we do know that abnormal patterns of fixation durations may serve as a marker during early development – for example, we recently reported that infants in early stages of developing autism show shorter fixation durations during the viewing of static scenes (Wass *et al.*, 2015).

Research with adults has also revealed, however, a variety of ways in which fixation durations can be influenced both by what we are looking at (known as exogenous, or stimulus-driven factors), as well as what we have in mind while we are looking (known as endogenous, or participant-driven factors). Thus, for example, fixation durations are influenced by aspects such as how much 'visual clutter' there is at the point in the scene were are looking at (Henderson, Chanceaux, & Smith, 2009). Endogenous factors investigated include the nature of the viewing task given to participants (Tatler & Vincent, 2008).

Pupil size

In addition to the location and movement patterns of the eyes, eye-tracking also provides information about the size of participants' pupils (Laeng, Sirois, & Gredeback, 2012). Pupil size is influenced by a variety of factors. The first, and strongest, influence on pupil size is luminance – the pupil contracts and expands rapidly along with changes in luminance at the point fixated (Beatty & Lucero-Wagoner, 2000). Additionally, however, pupil size is thought to be more weakly influenced by other factors, such as autonomic arousal (higher arousal associated with larger pupil size) (Aston-Jones & Cohen, 2005) and cognitive load (higher cognitive load associated with larger tonic pupil size) (Karatekin, 2007).

Although these factors are of considerable interest to a range of researchers (Laeng *et al.*, 2012), it is important to emphasise that extreme caution should be exercised in interpreting pupil data. The influence of luminance on pupil size is considerably larger than the influence of other factors (Beatty & Lucero-Wagoner, 2000). When saccading from a brightly lit area of the screen to a darkly lit area, the pupil changes size. It is, therefore, necessary to ensure either that stimuli are isoluminant, or that all participants were viewing identical areas of the screen, before pupil size can be reported. It is also important to ensure that lighting conditions in the testing room are tightly controlled between participants.

2.3.2 Uses of eye-tracking in psychometrics

Eye-tracking paradigms are used in psychometrics to measure a range of factors. These include an individual's ability to exercise inhibitory control over their eye movements, to use temporarily stored memory traces to guide eye movements, as well as to measure their reaction time.

Figure 2.5 gives an illustrative example of one such paradigm. This is a task used to assess anticipatory eye movements during sequence learning in infants. The participant views a series of events, which are shown in schematic form on the left of the figure. First, a fixation target (the grey circle in the centre of the screen) appears, which disappears as soon as the participant looks to it. Then only two blank windows remain on screen. After 2000msec a reward appears in one of the windows (e.g., left). It remains there for 4000ms. The same sequence then repeats, starting from the fixation target and ending with the target appearing on the opposite side to the previous trial. This entire left–right (LR) sequence then repeats nine times (LRLRLRLRLRLRLRLRLR). The aim of the experiment is to measure participants' eye movements during the 2000msec window before the target appears. Do they look to the side where the target is going to appear, before it actually appears? If so, this would indicate that they have learnt the sequence.

Figure 2.5b gives an illustrative example of the data obtained for a single trial. Time is drawn on the x-axis, and the key stimulus presentation events are shown on the x-axis. The eye gaze trace obtained during the trial is drawn (x dimension only). It can be seen that the trial starts with the participant looking at the middle of the screen (0.5) on the x dimension (corresponding to the middle of the screen, which is where the fixation target is). Approximately 1300msec into the trial, it shifts to the right hand box on the screen (0.73 on the x dimension). This is the 'incorrect' side – i.e., the opposite side to where the target will appear. It then shifts, later in the trial, to the other side of the screen (the 'correct' side). A custom-built processing script has automatically coded the time latencies of these eye movements. In this case, the trial has been classified as an incorrect anticipation, since the first saccade was towards the opposite side to that where the target is going to appear.

Figure 2.5c gives an illustrative example of the final, summary data presented for this experiment. (The data are not genuine and used for illustrative purposes only.) The x-axis shows the trial number, and the y-axis the mean proportion of correct anticipations recorded across all participants. It can be seen that the graph trends upwards, indicating that over the course of eighteen trials, participants are correctly learning to make anticipatory eye movements based on the LRLR sequence.

A variety of other psychometric parameters can also be assessed using similar types of paradigm. These include: a) oculomotor delayed response – i.e., the ability to initiate a saccade based on temporarily stored information (e.g., Gilmore & Johnson, 1995); b) pro- and anti-saccades – i.e., the accuracy, and the latency, of initiating a saccade following a cue, both in the same (pro-) and the opposite (anti-) direction to that in which the cue was presented (Michel & Anderson, 2009);

c) attentional disengagement latencies – i.e., the latency to disengage attention from a central target to reorient towards a peripheral target (e.g., Leppanen *et al.*, 2011); d) visual search – i.e., the latency to look towards a target presented among an array of distractors (e.g., Frank, Amso, & Johnson, 2014). For an excellent review of previous studies that have used eye-tracking to measure individual differences in these ways, see Karatekin (2007).

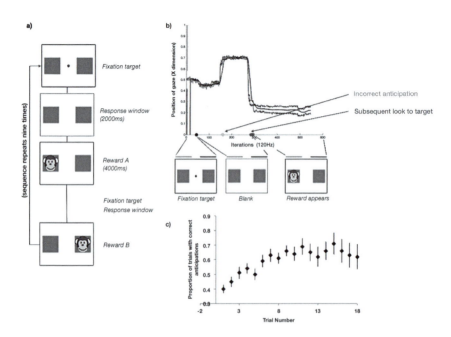

FIGURE 2.5 Example of a paradigm used to assess sequence learning abilities in human infants. a) shows the stimulus presentation sequence. A fixation target was presented, followed by a blank response window for 2000ms, followed by a reward in one rectangle for 4000ms. The same sequence then repeated, with the reward in the opposite window. The entire sequence then repeated nine times. b) shows an example of a single trial of data obtained during the presentation of this experiment. Just the x dimension (i.e., the left–right coordinates) of the eye-tracking data is shown. Timings of key events are indicated on the x axis. In the trial illustrated, the participant first makes a saccade to the incorrect side, followed by a subsequent saccade to the correct side. c) shows a simulated example of the final summary data. In this dataset, the proportion of correct anticipations has increased over the course of the 18-trial block. This would suggest that participants are learning to perform correct anticipatory eye movements based on the sequence presented

Figure taken from unpublished work

2.3.3 Higher-level aspects of cognition

In addition to more basic psychometrics, other researchers have used eye-tracking paradigms to investigate aspects of higher-level cognition. One example that can be used as an illustration of this approach comes from an experiment by Southgate and colleagues (Southgate, Senju, & Csibra, 2007) (see Figure 2.6). They devised a task in which 2-year-old children were familiarised to video sequences in which a puppet, watched by a human actor, reached up and hid a ball inside one of two boxes. The human actor then reached and removed the ball from the box in which it had been hidden. In certain trials, however, the actor looked away, and the puppet, unseen, moved the ball between boxes. They then measured children's looking behaviour after the actor had reappeared. Did the child look towards the box in which the ball *actually* was, or towards the box where the actor *thought* that the ball was? Their results suggested the latter, which they interpreted as indicating that 2-year-old children can correctly anticipate an actor's actions when these actions can be predicted only by attributing a false belief to the actor.

This experiment was designed in Clearview (a precursor to Tobii Studio). It involved presentation of a series of video clips that were each filmed separately. Within each video clip, the experimenters specified particular user-defined AOIs (corresponding to the purple windows through which the experimenter could be seen to reach) and a response period (i.e., the segment of the video during which responses should be measured). Figure 2.6b shows a segment from a single trial. (The data are not genuine and are used for illustrative purposes only.) The eye-tracking data recorded within the 3-second response period are drawn onto the screen. The locations of the two user-defined AOIs are also drawn onto the screen. The total number of samples of eye-tracking data within the target AOI is calculated, and divided by the number of samples of eye-tracking data available across both AOIs. Gaze data that are not within one of the two AOIs are excluded. Figure 2.6c shows the summary, average data recorded across all trials. The dependent variable is the proportion of gaze data recorded to the correct target, and trials have been split according to whether or not a switch took place. The main analysis is: are looking data during the 'Switch' trials significantly above chance (i.e., 0.5)? If so, this would indicate that participants are successful in anticipating where the actor will reach based not on where the ball *actually* is, but on where the actor *thinks* the ball is.

Other research has used similar techniques to explore the same/different concept in infants (Addyman & Mareschal, 2010), as well as whether infants can track the reliability of potential informants (Tummeltshammer, Wu, Sobel, & Kirkham, 2014), can learn based on patterns of statistical regularities in sequences (e.g., Kidd, Piantadosi, & Aslin, 2012), and are able to maintain a representation of a temporarily occluded object (Johnson, Amso, & Slemmer, 2003).

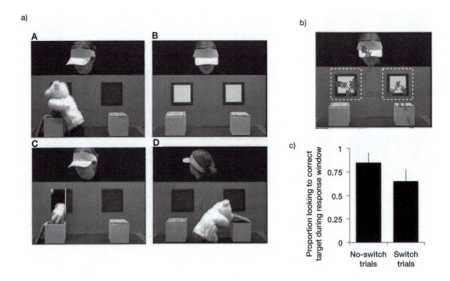

FIGURE 2.6 Example of an eye-tracking study examining high level aspects of cognition. a) shows selected scenes from the video clips presented. In familiarisation trials, participants were familiarised to an event in which (**A**) the puppet placed a ball in one of two boxes (**B**) both windows were illuminated and a chime sounded, and (**C**) an actor reached through the window above the box in which the ball was placed, and retrieved the ball. The participants were familiarised to the contingency between (**B**) and (**C**). In (**D**), a 'switch trial', the puppet moves the ball while the actor is looking away. This operation induces a false belief in the actor about the location of the ball. b) shows an illustrative example (using simulated data) of the raw eye-tracking data collected during the response window (**B**). All of the gaze data collected during the window has been drawn as red crosses onto the screen. Data is analysed based on the proportion of gaze data within the two AOIs (drawn as yellow dashed boxes) c) shows an example of summary data for this experiment. The proportion of gaze data to the correct vs the incorrect side is presented. The primary analysis concerns whether gaze data in the 'switch trials' is significantly above 0.5 (i.e., chance)

Figure adapted from Senju, Southgate, White, and Frith (2009)

2.3.4 Cognitive training

Recently, increases in the spatial accuracy of eye-tracking and in the temporal resolution have meant that researchers are able to design paradigms in which different events are triggered contingent on where on-screen a participant is looking. These types of paradigm are known as gaze-contingent paradigms.

One illustrative example of a use of gaze-contingent paradigms is to provide cognitive training for infants. For example, we (Wass, Porayska-Pomsta, & Johnson, 2011) designed a task in which an object was seen disappearing behind one of two windows, before the infant's gaze was distracted by a fixation target elsewhere on the screen. Once the fixation target had disappeared, the same two windows were re-presented. If the infant looked to the same window behind which the object had disappeared, they received an attractive animation as a reward. The task was designed to vary in complexity and difficulty contingent on performance. Better-performing infants were presented with a greater choice of possible locations (four or six windows instead of two), and the fixation target was also shown for a longer time period. In this way the difficulty of the training task varied contingent on performance. Thus, these approaches are analogous to the computerised, point-and-click interfaces used to train working memory in older children (Klingberg, 2010). This use of eye-tracking opens up the possibility of applying computerised training techniques to individuals who are too young, or who have too severe motor deficits, to operate a keyboard or mouse (Wass, 2014a).

2.3.5 Head-mounted tracking

One important limitation of all of the research described above is that it involves experiments presented in 2-D, on a computer screen, and featuring experimental stimuli that are highly artificial and 'pared-down'. This raises important questions about whether effects observed in these experiments might actually be observed in more 'real-world' contexts. One recent study assessed infants' peak look duration to novel stimuli, a measure of attention that has been extensively studied using screen-based stimuli (Colombo & Mitchell, 2009), and examined whether individual differences observed on screen-based versions of this paradigm could be replicated if the same measure were assessed in more naturalistic contexts (Wass, 2014b). Strikingly, results for all four screen-based task assessments administered showed high inter-correlations with each other, but showed no relationship at all to performance on the same task, when assessed in naturalistic contexts. This questions the ecological validity of individual differences observed on screen-based tasks. Similar concerns pertain to many of the tasks used, for example, to measure attention to social cues, since many of the 'social cues' used in these tasks (e.g., 4cm-tall head shots of an actor, filmed against a black background – Wu, Gopnik, Richardson, & Kirkham, 2011) bear little or no resemblance to the kinds of social cues actually encountered in ecologically valid contexts.

As a result of these concerns an increasing number of researchers are starting to use head-mounted eye-tracking to measure infants' spontaneous eye movements in genuinely naturalistic contexts, featuring live stimulus presentation, away from a computer screen (e.g., Land, 2009).

One illustrative example of an experiment that used head-mounted tracking comes from Smith and colleagues (Smith *et al.*, 2011). This study just used a head camera, rather than a full head-mounted tracker (which includes both a head and eye camera). In this experiment, the researchers wished to explore how the types of visual information that we naturally encounter differ between infants and adults. The experimental protocol was designed to allow for automated coding of the results. Parent and child were seated either side of a table, on which three coloured objects were placed (see Figure 2.7). All available surfaces were coloured white. Six 1-minute spontaneous play sessions were recorded. After the experiment, data were analysed frame by frame, to examine what proportion of the total available visual field was occupied by each of the objects, for parent and child respectively. Summary results (Figure 2.7c) showed that, for the children, a greater proportion of frames contained situations in which one object was visually dominant over the

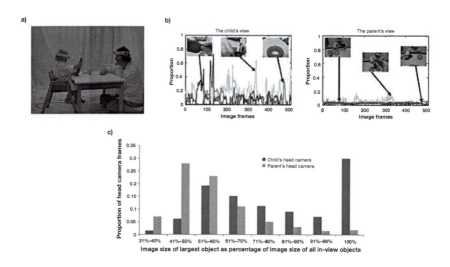

FIGURE 2.7 Example of a head-mounted tracking study. a) shows the experimental set-up. Mother and child are positioned either side of a table, both wearing head cameras. White surrounds are used so that the position of the toys within the participants' field of view can be automatically coded, using colour- and object-recognition algorithms. b) shows the raw data obtained for child and parent. The three lines indicate the proportion of the participant's field of view that was occupied by that object. c) shows a histogram derived from b)

Figure adapted from Smith, Yu, and Pereira (2011)

others (occupying a large proportion of the total field of view). For the adults, in contrast, there were almost always multiple objects present within the visual field at once. In other words, infants tend to get closer to the objects that they are looking at. This suggests that infants may learn to perceive by starting from situations in which the visual information is 'easier' (signal-to-noise ratios are higher) and then proceed step-wise towards full adult cognition (see Rost & McMurray, 2010; Wass & Smith, 2014b).

Other researchers have used head-mounted eye-tracking in a range of different ways. For example, some have used these techniques to study how infants use eye movement to coordinate aspects of their motor development and learning (e.g., Franchak & Adolph, 2010) and during language learning (e.g., Yu & Smith, 2012; Yurovsky, Smith, & Yu, 2013). Future years will likely see a considerable increase in the use of these kinds of techniques to address a range of new research questions.

Head-mounted eye-trackers can also be used to present more 'traditional' experimental paradigms, similar to those described above. In each case, an experimental paradigm can simply be transported from a screen-based task into a naturalistic one. For example, the screenshot shown in Figure 2.2 is from a language learning experiment run in our lab. This is a forced choice word learning paradigm, in which verbal labels are spoken by the experimenter while two objects are present, and responses are coded based on which of the two objects the child looks to. Virtually identical paradigms can be presented on a computer screen (Smith & Yu, 2012). Although presenting such an experiment within a naturalistic context has a number of advantages, there are also disadvantages such as the increased time requirement for coding results, as discussed above (see section 2.2.2).

2.4 Conclusion

In part 2 of this chapter we have reviewed a number of different *types* of research questions that can be addressed using eye-tracking. In 2.3.1 we discussed studies that have examined how we use our eye movements to construct a representation of the outside world. In 2.3.2 we discussed research that has used eye-tracking to measure individual differences, for example in our ability to remember items of information for short periods of time. In 2.3.3 we discussed uses of eye-tracking to examine more 'high-level' aspects of cognition, such as whether young children are able to make mental state attributions to others. In 2.3.4 we discussed uses of eye-tracking to provide cognitive training. In 2.3.5 we discussed naturalistic eye-tracking, and its pros and cons relative to more traditional, experimental protocols.

As with all scientific methods, it is vital that at every stage of the process, from project conception through to experimental design through to data analysis, caution and scepticism are exercised. A good scientist never fully trusts the method (s)he is using. This is true for eye-tracking as it is for any method. In part 1 of this chapter, therefore, we discussed a variety of methodological challenges in eye-tracking, such as the importance of data quality and its potential role in influencing results. It is important that these methodological caveats are always borne in mind.

Practical tips

1 First, consider what type of eye-tracker to use (naturalistic vs. screen-based).
2 Pilot your experiment and analyse results all the way through to the final stage, before commencing the final study.
3 Try to visualise your results at every step of the analysis, by plotting samples of raw and analysed data obtained from several different individuals. Eye-tracking data tends to vary substantially from one individual to another – so don't assume that what works well for one individual will work well for all.

Conflict of interest

The author declares that he has no financial involvement in any of the commercial manufacturers mentioned in this chapter.

Appendix: Glossary of key eye-tracking terms

More detailed descriptions of these terms can be found in Holmqvist *et al.* (2011).

Areas of Interest (AOI) – Participant's gaze is typically analysed relative to certain user-defined Areas of Interest (AOIs) within the stimulus presentation screen.
Calibration – a series of targets are presented at predetermined locations on the screen, which the participant's position of gaze is recorded. All subsequent gaze data have a correction that was calculated during calibration.
Corneal reflection – all commercial eye-trackers work by tracking the position of the participant's pupil (which moves as the eye moves) relative to the position of an infra-red light reflected from the participant's cornea (which remains still as the eye moves). Both corneal reflection and pupil must be detectable in order for tracking to take place.
Fixation duration – when viewing a visual array we spontaneously manifest a sequence of eye movements in order to ensure that light from objects of interest is projected onto the fovea. Our eyes alternate between periods in which the eye is static and visual processing occurs (fixations) and rapid eye movements (saccades) during which visual processing is suppressed.

Interpolation – the process of 'filling in' missing sections of eye-tracking data.

Look/visit durations – these are typically reported as the time interval elapsed between gaze entering an AOI and leaving it. A number of fixations can therefore be contained within a look.

Position of gaze (POG) – eye-trackers typically return the participant's position of gaze (POG) relative to a 2-D area (i.e., a computer screen, or a scene camera). POG is typically returned in X (horizontal) and Y (vertical) screen coordinates.

Precision – a measure of data quality, indexing the degree to which reporting of POG is consistent between samples.

Proportion looking to AOIs – the proportion of gaze data within a particular AOI relative to the total gaze data available for that trial.

Robustness – a measure of data quality, indexing how broken or fragmented contact with the eye-tracker is during recording.

Saccadic reaction times – the time interval between an event taking place and the first recorded oculomotor response to that event.

Sampling frequency – the number of POGs returned by the eye-tracker per second. Commercial eye-trackers vary from c. 25Hz (i.e., 25 POGs returned per second) to 2000Hz.

Spatial accuracy – a measure of data quality, indexing the disparity between where the participant is actually looking and the POG reported by the eye-tracker.

References

Addyman, C., & Mareschal, D. (2010). The perceptual origins of the abstract same/different concept in human infants. *Animal Cognition, 13*(6), 817–33.

Aston-Jones, G., & Cohen, J. D. (2005). An integrative theory of locus coeruleus-norepinephrine function: Adaptive gain and optimal performance. *Annual Review of Neuroscience, 28*, 403–50.

Ballieux, H., Wass, S. V., Tomalski, P., Kushnerenko, E., Karmiloff-Smith, A., Johnson, M. H., & Moore, D. G. (2016). Training attention control outside the lab: Applying gaze-contingent training to infants from diverse SES backgrounds. *Journal of Applied Developmental Psychology, 43*, 8–17.

Beatty, J., & Lucero-Wagoner, B. (2000). The pupillary system. In J. T. Cacioppo, L. G. Tassinary & G. Berntson (Eds), *Handbook of psychophysiology* (pp. 142–62). Cambridge, MA: Cambridge University Press.

Castelhano, M. S., & Henderson, J. M. (2008). Stable individual differences across images in human saccadic eye movements. *Canadian Journal of Experimental Psychology, 62*(1), 1–14.

Colombo, J., & Mitchell, D. W. (2009). Infant visual habituation. *Neurobiology of Learning and Memory, 92*(2), 225–34.

Franchak, J. M., & Adolph, K. E. (2010). Visually guided navigation: Head-mounted eye-tracking of natural locomotion in children and adults. *Vision Research, 50*(24), 2766–74.

Frank, M. C., Amso, D., & Johnson, S. P. (2014). Visual search and attention to faces in early infancy. *Journal of Experimental Child Psychology, 118,* 13–26.

Gilmore, R. O., & Johnson, M. H. (1995). Working memory in infancy – 6-month-olds' performance on two versions of the oculomotor delayed response task. *Journal of Experimental Child Psychology, 59*(3), 397–418.

Henderson, J. M. (2006). Eye movements. In C. Senior, T. Russell & M. S. Gazzaniga (Eds), *Methods in Mind* (pp. 171–191). Cambridge, MA: MIT Press.

Henderson, J. M., Chanceaux, M., & Smith, T. J. (2009). The influence of clutter on real-world scene search: Evidence from search efficiency and eye movements. *Journal of Vision, 9*(1), 1–8.

Hessels, R. S., Andersson, R., Hooge, I. T. C., Nystrom, M., & Kemner, C. (2015). Consequences of eye color, positioning, and head movement for eye-tracking data quality in infant research. *Infancy, 20,* 1–33.

Holmqvist, K., Nyström, M, Andersson, R., Dewhurst, R., Jarodzka, H., & van de Weijer, J. (2011). *Eye-tracking: A comprehensive guide to methods and measures.* Oxford, UK: Oxford University Press.

Johnson, S. P., Amso, D., & Slemmer, J. A. (2003). Development of object concepts in infancy: Evidence for early learning in an eye-tracking paradigm. *Proceedings of the National Academy of Sciences of the United States of America, 100*(18), 10568–73.

Karatekin, C. (2007). Eye-tracking studies of normative and atypical development. *Developmental Review, 27*(3), 283–348.

Kidd, C., Piantadosi, S. T., & Aslin, R. N. (2012). The Goldilocks effect: Human infants allocate attention to visual sequences that are neither too simple nor too complex. *PLoS One,* 7(5), e36399 36391–8.

Klingberg, T. (2010). Training and plasticity of working memory. *Trends in Cognitive Sciences, 14*(7), 317–324.

Laeng, B., Sirois, S., & Gredeback, G. (2012). Pupillometry: A window to the preconscious? *Perspectives on Psychological Science,* 7(1), 18–27.

Land, M. T. B. (2009). *Looking and acting: Vision and eye movements in natural behaviour.* Oxford, UK: Oxford University Press.

Leppanen, J. M., Peltola, M. J., Puura, K., Mantymaa, M., Mononen, N., & Lehtimaki, T. (2011). Serotonin and early cognitive development: Variation in the tryptophan hydroxylase 2 gene is associated with visual attention in 7-month-old infants. *Journal of Child Psychology and Psychiatry, 52*(11), 1144–52.

Michel, F., & Anderson, M. (2009). Using the antisaccade task to investigate the relationship between the development of inhibition and the development of intelligence. *Developmental Science, 12*(2), 272–88.

Rost, G. C., & McMurray, B. (2010). Finding the signal by adding noise: The role of noncontrastive phonetic variability in early word learning. *Infancy, 15*(6), 608–35.

Senju, A., Southgate, V., White, S. & Frith, U. (2009). Mindblind eyes: An absence of spontaneous theory of mind in Asperger syndrome. *Science, 325,* 883–5.

Smith, L. B., & Yu, C. (2012). Visual attention is not enough: Individual differences in statistical word-referent learning in infants. *Language Learning and Development, 15*(3), 113–45.

Smith, L. B., Yu, C., & Pereira, A. F. (2011). Not your mother's view: The dynamics of toddler visual experience. *Developmental Science, 14*(1), 9–17.

Southgate, V., Senju, A., & Csibra, G. (2007). Action anticipation through attribution of false belief in two-year-olds. *Psychological Science, 18*, 587–92.

Tatler, B., & Vincent, B. (2008). Visual attention in natural scenes: A probabilistic perspective. *International Journal of Psychology, 43*(3–4), 37–37.

Tummeltshammer, K. S., Wu, R. W., Sobel, D. M., & Kirkham, N. Z. (2014). Infants track the reliability of potential informants. *Psychological Science, 25*, 1730–8.

Wass, S. V. (2014a). Applying cognitive training to target executive functions during early development. *Child Neuropsychology, 21*(2), 150–66.

Wass, S. V. (2014b). Comparing methods for measuring peak look duration: Are individual differences observed on screen-based tasks also found in more ecologically valid contexts? *Infant Behavior and Development, 37*(3), 315–25.

Wass, S. V., Forssman, L., & Leppanen, J. (2014). Robustness and precision: How data quality may influence key dependent variables in infant eye-tracker analyses. *Infancy, 19*(5), 427–60.

Wass, S. V., Jones, E. J. H., Gliga, T., Smith, T. J., Charman, T., Team, B., & Johnson, M. H. (2015). Shorter spontaneous fixation durations in infants with later emerging autism. *Nature Scientific Reports, 5*(8), 1–8.

Wass, S. V., Porayska-Pomsta, K., & Johnson, M. H. (2011). Training attentional control in infancy. *Current Biology, 21*(18), 1543–7.

Wass, S. V., & Smith, T. J. (2014a). Individual differences in infant oculomotor behavior during the viewing of complex naturalistic scenes. *Infancy, 19*(4), 352–84.

Wass, S. V., & Smith, T. J. (2014b). Visual motherese? Signal-to-noise ratios in toddler-directed television. *Developmental Science, 18*(1), 24–37.

Wass, S. V., Smith, T. J., & Johnson, M. H. (2012). Parsing eye-tracking data of variable quality to provide accurate fixation duration estimates in infants and adults. *Behavior Research Methods, 45*(1), 229–50.

Wu, R., Gopnik, A., Richardson, D. C., & Kirkham, N. Z. (2011). Infants learn about objects from statistics and people. *Developmental Psychology, 47*(5), 1220–9.

Yu, C., & Smith, L. B. (2012). Embodied attention and word learning by toddlers. *Cognition, 125*(2), 244–62.

Yurovsky, D., Smith, L. B., & Yu, C. (2013). Statistical word learning at scale: The baby's view is better. *Developmental Science, 16*(6), 1–7.

3

IMAGING THE DEVELOPING HUMAN BRAIN USING FUNCTIONAL AND STRUCTURAL MAGNETIC RESONANCE IMAGING

Methodological and practical guidelines

Stephan E. Vogel, Anna A. Matejko and Daniel Ansari

3.1 Introduction

Do adults and children process information in the same way? How does the human brain mature over development? And how does learning change the structure and function of a child's brain? These are just a few of the questions that can be addressed through the use of non-invasive neuroimaging methods. Developmental cognitive neuroscience is an interdisciplinary field that uses neuroscientific methods to examine how changes in brain structure and function relate to cognitive, social and perceptual development. In the last thirty years, the field of developmental cognitive neuroscience has blossomed with the advent of many different neuroimaging techniques (see Figure 3.1).

The invention of magnetic resonance imaging (MRI) in the 1970s allowed for more detailed analyses of brain structure, but it was not until the discovery of the blood oxygen level dependent (BOLD) response in 1990 that brain activity could be assessed non-invasively with high spatial resolution (Ogawa, Lee, Kay, & Tank 1990). The BOLD signal reflects relative changes in blood oxygenation and can be used to make inferences about neuronal activity because blood oxygenation increases in regions where neurons are more active. Functional magnetic resonance imaging (fMRI) utilizes the BOLD signal to infer regional changes in brain activity and has been used to understand the neurobiological processes that underlie the development of human cognition and perception (Figure 3.2). The first study to use fMRI with children was conducted by Casey and colleagues (1995) who examined brain regions involved in verbal working memory. Since this time, neuroimaging has become ubiquitous in developmental research and has been used to understand many different processes from perception to decision making (Johnson, 2011a).

Neuroimaging provides an additional level of analysis that complements more conventional behavioural measures such as reaction time or accuracy. For example, neuroimaging has substantially added to our understanding of how children acquire maths and reading skills. Recent research has demonstrated that brain function is a better predictor of how well children will benefit from maths intervention than any behavioural measure (Supekar *et al.*, 2013). Brain structure and function have

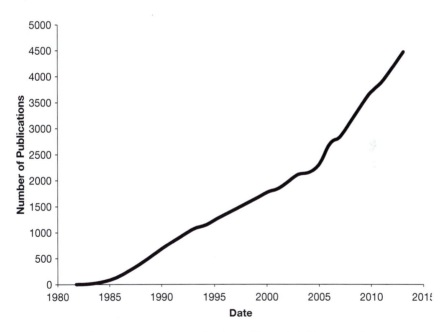

FIGURE 3.1 Publishing trends of research using MRI and children. Medline trend was used to retrieve the yearly statistics for publications that have key terms 'children' and 'MRI' in PubMed (www.dan.corlan.net/medline-trend.html)

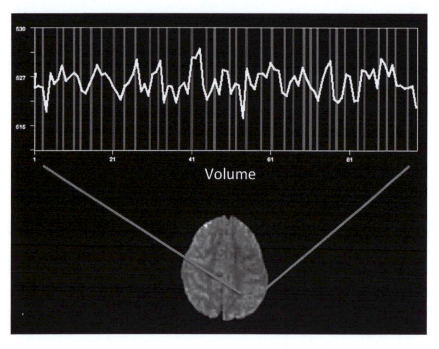

FIGURE 3.2 Fluctuations in the BOLD signal from a region in the parietal cortex during an experimental run. The horizontal lines in different shades of grey indicate trials from different conditions in the experiment

also been shown to be important predictors of dyslexia outcomes. In a longitudinal study of dyslexic children, individual differences in brain structure and function were much better predictors of children's reading gains over a 2.5-year period than any standardized tests of reading achievement (Hoeft *et al.*, 2011). These provide just two of many studies where neuroimaging has extended our understanding of how children acquire new skills. Much neuroimaging research is being used to understand how changes in the brain relate to changes in behaviour, and is pushing the boundaries of our knowledge on child development.

Though MRI has proved to be an important tool to understand human development, there are many special considerations that need to be made when conducting MRI research. In this chapter, we will discuss how functional and structural MRI can be applied to paediatric populations and we will review some of the best practices when conducting fMRI research with children. Overall, this chapter provides an introduction to MRI neuroimaging with children, and presents practical guidelines on how to design, analyse and interpret developmental neuro-imaging data.

3.2 Imaging children – experimental design

Developmental neuroimaging studies entail unique considerations regarding the research design and the experimental protocols. Simple experimental designs are generally preferable to complex designs, which can be overwhelming or too strenuous for some children (Luna, Velanova, & Geier, 2010). The scanning procedure is often a new and unusual experience, therefore, reducing task demands can help children to be more comfortable and willing to participate. Making the scanning procedure a comfortable experience becomes a central concern when working with children. In the next section, we will discuss several considerations that can help construct a design that is child-friendly and also meets the necessary methodological requirements.

3.2.1 Imaging designs

When designing an fMRI study, one needs to decide whether to use a *block, event-related, rapid event-related, mixed* or *self-paced* design (see also Amaro & Barker, 2006). Though all designs have previously been used in developmental neuroimaging studies, *block designs* and *event-related designs* are most commonly used with children. In a *block design*, a series of trials from the same condition are rapidly presented within a block followed by a rest or fixation period. The average brain activity from the blocks is then statistically compared to each other. In *event-related designs*, stimuli are not clustered into one block of trials, but dispersed in a continuous random sequence (see Figure 3.3). There are two types of *event-related designs*. In *slow event-related designs* the inter-trial-intervals (ITIs) last about 12 to 18 sec. The long duration of the ITIs allows for a full recovery (return to baseline) of the BOLD signal. Because of the slow presentation time, only a limited number of trials can be presented in this design. In contrast, *rapid event-related designs* use brief ITIs (between 5 to 9 sec), which allows for a more frequent trial presentation. Critically, while individual events (e.g., error trials) can be modelled in *event-related designs*, *block designs* only afford the ability to measure the average activation correlated with specific event types.

The most important advantages of *block designs* are their robustness (Rombouts et al., 1997) and statistical power (Aguirre & D'Esposito, 1999; Friston, Holmes, Price, Büchel, & Worsely, 1999). *Block designs* have high statistical power due to the additive effect of rapid trial presentation on the BOLD signal. The rapid trial presentation in a *block design* also reduces the overall scanning time in comparison with *event-related designs*. Consequently, *block designs* are particularly useful for paediatric neuroimaging studies due to their good signal-to-noise ratio and short overall run times.

a)

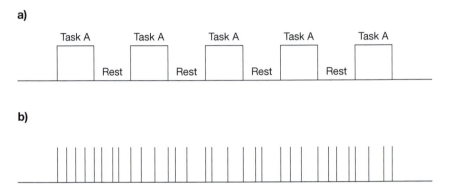

b)

FIGURE 3.3 Illustration of a) a *block design* and b) an *event-related design*

   Though there are many advantages of *block designs*, certain caveats should be addressed. One of the caveats is the increased risk of cognitive strategy adaptation (Goebel, 2015; Luna *et al.*, 2010). Cognitive strategy adaptation refers to systematic changes in the extent to which cognitive mechanisms are engaged over the course of an experiment. For instance, cognitive control mechanisms (e.g., maintaining task goals) may be reduced over the course of a scan as a consequence of task familiarisation. If cognitive strategy adaptation differs as a function of age or group (e.g., between typical and atypical developing children), a confound that is unrelated to the dimension of interest is introduced. The very nature of a *block design* (i.e., the high frequency of repeated presentation within a short amount of time) increases the probability that cognitive strategy adaptation will occur. Another disadvantage of *block designs* is that error trials cannot be removed (Murphy & Garavan, 2004). Younger children tend to be more error-prone than older children on many tasks. Differences in brain activation may therefore be related to differences in error processing instead of differences in the cognitive processes of interest. Thus, an advantage of *event-related designs* is that individual trials can be removed or sorted for post-hoc analyses. In other words, statistical analyses can focus on correct trials, which can mitigate some of the age-related confounds in behavioural performance (for a discussion about performance differences see section 3.5).
   Mixed designs combine features of the *block design* and the *event-related design* and are often used to investigate developmental changes in brain activation (see also Peterson & Dubis, 2012). *Mixed designs* can be used to investigate brain activity associated with single events (i.e., transient activation) as well as sustained brain activation elicited during a task period. Thus, brain activation related to single trials can be analysed at the same time as investigating the sustained activity of the blocked presentation.

3.2.2 Active versus passive task designs

Many developmental fMRI studies use 'active' paradigms where participants are instructed to make overt responses related to a dimension of interest (e.g., choosing one stimulus over another). Paradigms that require no overt response (passive designs such as fMRI adaptation; fMRI-A), or paradigms in which response selection is not directly related to the dimension of interest (implicit designs) are alternative designs. Passive or implicit designs have the advantage that potential performance confounds, which are frequently found in developmental neuroimaging studies (see section 3.5), are eliminated or at least reduced.

For example, implicit-reading-tasks have been shown to elicit similar brain activations as explicit-reading-tasks in which participants are instructed to consciously engage in word reading. Turkeltaub and colleagues (2003) used an implicit word-processing task that involved the detection of a 'tall letter' (e.g., the letter 'l' in 'alarm' compared with 'sauce') within words and artificial non-words (e.g., ). By contrasting the brain activation related to the presentation of words compared with non-words, the authors demonstrated regional differences in brain activation related to implicit word reading in the superior temporal cortex between children and adults. Since task performance was not related to the dimension of interest (i.e., the task was to detect a 'tall letter' and not to read the word), age-related brain activation differences could not be attributed to performance differences between ages. Implicit tasks are therefore a useful tool to investigate developmental changes in brain activity, while controlling age-related performance differences.

Another paradigm that has been used in developmental neuroimaging studies is fMRI-A (e.g., Vogel, Goffin, & Ansari, 2015). fMRI-A utilizes the inherent property of neural populations to attenuate their neural response to the repeated presentation of a stimulus. Specifically, neuronal populations (i.e., an ensemble of neurons) that process a particular stimulus will show a steady decrease in brain activity with repeated stimulus presentation (see also Grill-Spector & Malach, 2001). After neural adaptation has occurred, a new stimulus dimension is briefly introduced. If a particular region is sensitive to the new stimulus, a neural signal recovery from adaptation can be measured and investigated. One of the advantages of fMRI-A is that no overt response is required and that the design is purely passive; participants are solely instructed to monitor stimuli presentation.

For example, Vogel and colleagues (2015) used fMRI-A to measure developmental changes in the neural representations of number symbols. Children's brain response was adapted to the number 'six' by presenting the Arabic digit '6' repeatedly on a screen. After an adaptation phase, a new numeral deviating from the adaptation number '6' was presented and the brain response associated with the deviant was investigated. Children were instructed to press a button whenever a Smurf appeared on the monitor in order to maintain attention on the task. The left Intraparietal Sulcus (IPS) showed an increase in signal recovery that varied as a function of age, indicating developmental changes in the representation of numerical symbols. The discussed examples demonstrate how implicit and passive tasks can be used in developmental imaging studies and how they reduce potential performance differences across age groups.

3.2.3 Multiple and short functional runs

In order to assure children's compliance during scanning, it is advisable that the whole procedure (including preparation) does not exceed 60–90 minutes and that the actual scanning time does not take longer than 60 minutes. Also, instead of designing an experiment in which tasks are integrated into one single run, one can divide the experiment into *multiple and short functional runs* (see Figure 3.4), which offers several advantages. First, children do not need to remember different task instructions and, therefore, can focus on one task at a time. Furthermore, using tasks with simple instructions controls for extraneous complexities (e.g., cognitive load) that are unrelated to the dimension of interest (Luna *et al.*, 2010). Obviously an experimental approach that separates conditions into different runs can only be used in studies in which the 'switching' process between different tasks is not the dimension of interest.

An advantage of *multiple runs* is that they provide natural breaks between different runs. These breaks can be used productively to give verbal feedback on behavioural performance and motion (see also section 3.3). Another advantage of *short runs* is that children are less likely to move in the scanner, since the breaks between functional runs allow children to recover and to refocus on the next task. During these breaks children can wiggle their toes and remove some of the stiffness and tension. Lastly, *short runs* allow the researcher to quickly re-administer a run in the event something goes wrong.

In sum, there are different designs that can be used to investigate developmental changes in brain activation. Choosing the right design relies on multiple dimensions. For instance, the length of a functional run may vary considerably as a function of participants' age. To make necessary adjustments, it is advisable to pilot the experiment prior to data collection.

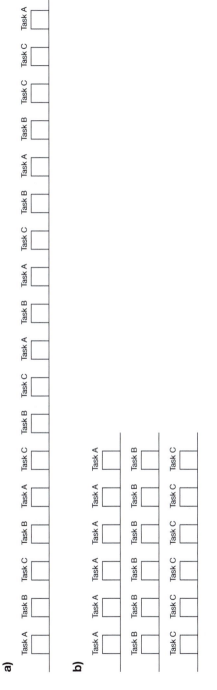

FIGURE 3.4 Illustration of a) a long run in which different task conditions are mixed, and b) of a simple design in which experimental tasks are separated into short runs

3.3 Scanning procedures with children

3.3.1 Scan preparation and motion prevention

The MRI is often an unusual and uncomfortable environment for children. Consequently, many research groups do a mock-scanning session to help increase the likelihood of good quality data from children during the real MRI, which is often very costly. The mock-scanning session helps familiarize children with the MRI environment by having them practise lying completely still while completing an fMRI task. Some research groups will also play a movie and monitor the child's movement using a head-tracking device; if the device detects motion the movie will stop playing. Motion-detecting devices that provide auditory feedback (e.g., beep sound) whenever movement is detected can also be incorporated into the mock-scanner while the child is completing a task (see Figure 3.5 below). MRI sounds are also typically played in the background to expose children to the sounds that an MRI makes. Scanner background noise can interfere with brain function and affect children's attention (Tomasi, Caparelli, Chang, & Ernst, 2005). Younger

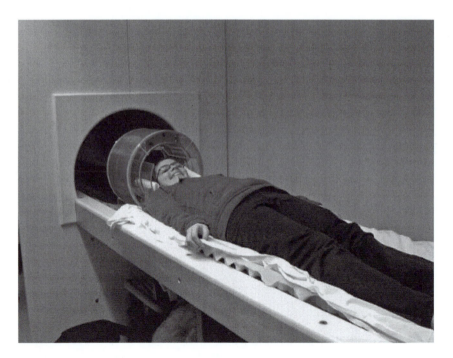

FIGURE 3.5 The mock-scanner at the University of Western Ontario is used to familiarize children with the MRI scanning environment

children may find it more difficult to inhibit the scanner noise during a cognitively demanding task (Raschle *et al.*, 2012). Therefore, age differences in brain activation could be attributed to differences in the ability to inhibit scanner background noise instead of changes in the construct that is being investigated. Thus, it is important for children to become accustomed to the kinds of sounds they will hear during the actual scan.

It is helpful to use child-friendly language and pictures when explaining the MRI procedures. For example, information about the scanning session can be presented in the form of a storybook. Comparing the MRI to a camera can often help children understand that the scanner is taking pictures, and the pictures will be blurry if the child moves. Some research groups also pretend the MRI is a spaceship and dress the participant in an astronaut suit to make the scanning more like a game. Overall, familiarizing children with the scanning procedures in simple language will make a significant difference in the child's comfort and cooperation during the real scan.

During the actual data acquisition, several techniques can be used to minimize discomfort and movement. Younger children may benefit from having someone in the MRI suite with them to reinforce staying still. A foam mattress on top of the scanning bed, extra padding around the head, and tape over the child's forehead and across the head coil can further reduce motion. There are also vacuum-pack systems designed for children that help reduce motion by providing a fitted shell that inflates with air after the head is positioned in the scanner (Huettel, Song, & McCarthy, 2009; e.g., vacuum immobilization bag from Med-Vac™).

At the MRI the examiner should also monitor movement and the child's accuracy while the scans are being acquired. Typically motion can be monitored while the scanner is running, and many scanners can determine the amount of rotation and translation (in the x-, y- and z- directions). The child's response accuracy can also be monitored online. Closely monitoring these two parameters during data collection can help determine whether any runs should be re-acquired. In between the runs, the experimenter can also provide the child with feedback and encouragement to help keep the child motivated. Often children are poor at determining whether they are moving or not, and thus, the experimenter should give them feedback on their motion.

Even though many of the techniques described above will help children be more comfortable in the MRI environment and will reduce motion, it is to be expected that a significant amount of data will be lost due to motion. As a result, a large amount of data collection is often required to have datasets with sufficient sample sizes that can be used for further analyses. Certain steps in the data pre-processing stage can help correct for the effects of motion (see section 3.4). However, it is important to take extra precautions when collecting MRI data with children to ensure that the best quality data are acquired.

3.3.2 Task familiarization

Extra time should be devoted to familiarising children with the experimental tasks. The researcher should explain the task in a child-friendly language to ensure that the child has understood the task accurately and should provide the child with several opportunities to practise the task. Unless the task is sensitive to training effects, a simple way to instruct children is to practise the task on a separate computer outside the scanner. Children often require more time and practice to understand a task compared with an adult.

3.4 Analysing functional imaging data

fMRI can detect small but meaningful changes in brain activity due to task-related changes in BOLD signal (Ogawa *et al.*, 1990; see introduction). Task-related changes in BOLD signal are, however, relatively small compared with other physiological factors such as breathing or a heartbeat (Huettel *et al.*, 2009). These sources of noise can potentially mask meaningful changes in task-related brain activity. Physiological effects that are associated with head motion can be particularly problematic because they can be correlated with aspects of the task design (e.g., with the onset of a stimuli) or with age. Another consideration relates to the issue of different brain sizes between age groups (Giedd *et al.*, 1999). In order to statistically compare the structure or function of different brain sizes, a common stereotactic space has to be defined. The next section will discuss how to address these issues.

3.4.1 Head motion

Changes in brain signal due to motion are common and difficult to correct (Friston, Williams, Howard, Frackowiak, & Turner, 1996). Over the course of a functional run, children may shift their head considerably. Even small head displacements can cause drastic changes in signal intensity, which are unrelated to the task. Head motion that correlates with age (motion is frequently larger in younger children) is of particular concern since it may explain age-related differences in brain activation. Scanning procedures that prevent head motion (see section 3.3) and motion-correction algorithms can reduce these differences.

All neuroimaging analysis software has some sort of motion-correction imple-
mented. These packages use mathematical algorithms (e.g., rigid-body transformation) to realign the collected images of a time series to the first image collected,
thus, correcting the spatial displacements of images induced by motion. However,
in many cases head motion may be substantial and can sometimes be so drastic that
the realignment procedures become inaccurate. Motion-correction algorithms
work fairly well for small spatial displacements (i.e., slow and steady drifts) but
become inaccurate when large displacements between images are corrected (i.e.,
large and sudden jumps; Huettel *et al.*, 2009). Since small displacements can be
corrected fairly well, a more liberal threshold inclusion criterion[1] can be applied.
Typical cut-off criteria for steady drifts are between 3mm and 5mm (see Figure
3.6), and cut-off values for sudden jumps are frequently between 1–2mm. Motion
estimates can also be entered as a covariate of no interest into the single-subject
general linear model to remove additional variance unrelated to brain activity.
Removing this error variance increases the sensitivity to real task-related changes
in brain activation (Johnstone *et al.*, 2006).

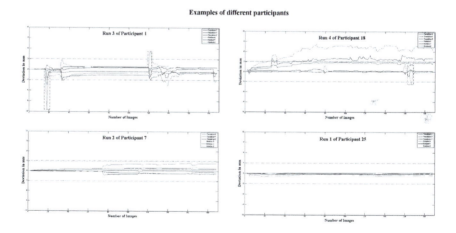

Examples of different participants

FIGURE 3.6 Motion displacement graphs of four functional runs from different
participants. According to motion criteria the functional runs on top
exceeded the motion threshold, whereas the functional runs on the
bottom met the predefined criteria. Dotted horizontal lines display the
cut-off criteria of 3mm for maximum overall displacement; dotted
rectangles display the cut-off criteria of 1.5 mm for max peak
displacements

Reprinted from Vogel *et al.*, 2015, with permission from Elsevier

3.4.2 Finding a common space

In order to statistically compare anatomical structures or functional regions of different brain sizes, a common stereotactic space has to be defined (Friston *et al.*, 1995). The Talairach (Talairach & Tournoux, 1988) and Montreal Neurological Institute templates (MNI; Evans *et al.*, 1993) are two stereotactic spaces that are frequently used in neuroimaging studies. Although small and consistent differences have been observed between the brain structures of 7 and 8-year-old children and adults, Talairach transformation (i.e., the process of warping anatomical data into Talairach space for group comparisons) appears to have minimal effects on differences in brain activation (Burgund *et al.*, 2002). However, experimenters should be aware that the Talairach transformations of brains from children younger than 7 years are less accurate. For instance, the contours of brain images (i.e., boundary between brain surface and Subarachnoid space) from a group of young children (2–6 years of age) were found to differ considerably more from images of adults and older children (7–14 years of age) after their heads were transformed into Talairach space (Muzik, Chugani, Juhasz, Shen, & Chugani, 2000). These findings suggest that more interpolations need to be made when transforming anatomical data from infants and younger children into standard space. As a consequence, an increasing number of brain templates are now available to improve statistical comparisons between infants, young children, and adults (e.g., Fonov *et al.*, 2011).

In addition to the stereotactic alignment approach, a number of new alignment techniques such as Cortex-based alignment (CBA) have been used to improve spatial alignment between individual brains (Goebel, Esposito, & Formisano, 2006). CBA uses anatomical high-resolution scans to determine curvature patterns of individual gyri and sulci (i.e., the boundary between grey and white matter is determined) in order to align individual brains based on anatomical patterns. The brains (i.e., sulci and gyri pattern of the cortex) are transformed into a 3D reconstruction and the individual curvature patterns are aligned onto an averaged cortical surface reconstruction. Functional imaging data are then mapped onto the surface of the averaged anatomical 3D reconstruction for statistical analyses. CBA has been shown to reduce the anatomical variability between individuals' brains and to improve statistical comparisons (Frost & Goebel, 2012). However, the process of brain reconstruction can be time consuming since the automatic segmentation procedure needs to be visually inspected and manually corrected.

3.5 Challenges in data interpretation

One of the great challenges in developmental neuroimaging studies is the frequent occurrence of performance differences between age groups. Younger children tend to be slower and more error-prone than older children and adults; making it difficult to disentangle developmental changes in task-related brain activation (i.e., the dimension of interest) from brain activation that is related to performance differences (Poldrack, 2000). Below, we outline a number of different experimental procedures that have been suggested to control for performance differences.

3.5.1 Equalizing task performance and investigating effects of task performance and age independently

One way to control for age-related differences in performance is to equalize task performance across age groups. Two different approaches have been used in the past to equate performance (Scerif, Kotsoni, & Casey, 2006). In the first method, performance differences are quantified in a behavioural pre-test. Based on the results of this pre-test, the difficulty levels of the task are adjusted so that task performance is equal across age groups (e.g., increasing the working memory load in an n-back task from a 1-back to a 2-back load). The second method evaluates performance during the task and adaptively adjusts the task difficulty online during scanning (task difficulty is adjusted based on previous trials). Although the procedure of these two approaches is different, they both aim to ameliorate performance differences between age groups.

Task performance from different age groups can also be matched after the scan, based on participants' performance in the scanner. Participants that are outside a specific performance range are either excluded from statistical analysis or put into an unmatched performance group. The advantage of including an unmatched performance group is that the independent influences of performance and age on brain activity can be investigated by examining brain activation differences between the matched and the unmatched subgroups.

For instance, a study by Schlaggar and colleagues (2002) used this approach to investigate the influence of performance and age differences on brain activation between a group of children and adults who performed a single-word language task. The authors divided participants into two subgroups in which performance was either very similar (matched group) or very dissimilar (unmatched group). Brain activation differences were compared between age groups (children vs. adults) and between the subgroups (matched vs. unmatched). Two regions of the brain showed activation related to task performance; brain activation was significantly different between children and adults in the unmatched group but similar in the matched group. Two regions of the brain were solely associated with age; significant differences between children and adults were found in both the matched and the unmatched subgroups. Finally, two regions were neither related to performance nor to age differences. Using this method, the authors were able to dissociate brain regions that were associated with performance and age-related differences from regions that were related to developmental changes in the task of interest. This study demonstrates the added value of controlling performance differences.

Another solution to mitigate performance differences is to use implicit or passive paradigms (see section 3.2.2). These kinds of designs entirely obviate the need to control for performance differences. Many empirical questions, however, may not be suitable for passive or implicit task designs and require active participation.

3.5.2 Appropriate control tasks

The use of appropriate control tasks is also important to ensure that brain activation differences are not due to task performance. Brain activity associated with the control task is subtracted from the brain activity associated with the experimental condition (e.g., Holloway & Ansari, 2010). The success of this approach rests on the assumption that the control task induces the same cognitive mechanisms and activates the same brain regions across groups (Poldrack, 2000). Consider an example in which brain activation associated with a control task (Task B) is subtracted from the brain activation associated with the experimental task (Task A) in a group of children and in a group of adults. Differences between these contrasts are then compared between the groups and activation differences are interpreted as meaningful developmental changes in the experimental task (Task A). This interpretation is valid under the premise that Task B, the control task, is the same across the two groups and does not elicit age-related brain activation differences. If this assumption is not true, observed differences in brain activation could be a result of differences in Task B (the control task) and not due to development changes in Task A (experimental task). One way to ensure that the control task is appropriate and does not differ between groups is to calculate a group contrast for the control task (e.g., Task B_{adults} − Task $B_{children}$). If this contrast does not reveal activation differences between the groups, then Task B can serve as an appropriate control condition because it is equal across both groups.

3.5.3 Developmental differences in the BOLD signal – an artefact of vasculature differences?

Though several aspects of task performance and the experimental design can lead to alternative explanations for developmental changes in brain activation, physio-logical factors could also contribute to observed age-related changes. More specifically, developmental differences in vascular physiology may explain observed age-related differences in the BOLD signal (Church, Petersen, & Schlagger, 2010). Presently, the precise nature of neurovascular coupling (the relationship between neural activity and the BOLD response) is not fully understood. Consequently, it is not possible to determine whether observed age-related differences in BOLD signal are associated with developmental differences in the underlying neurovascular physiology or with meaningful changes in neural information processing. However, a number of recent observations from the developmental neuroimaging literature speak against such an interpretation. For instance, similar modulation of the BOLD response has been observed when adults and children perform the same task (Church et al., 2010). In addition, studies have shown that one particular brain region may show larger brain activation in children for one task, while demonstrating larger brain activation in another task in adults (Church et al., 2010). These kinds of modulation would not be possible if age-related changes in brain activation were due to developmental changes in neurovascular coupling. If developmental changes in brain activation were solely attributed to neurovascular effects, one would predict task-independent activation patterns. The observation of task-dependent developmental changes in BOLD signal within a given region provides evidence that age-related differences reflect changes in neural information processing. Moreover, similar BOLD time course patterns have been reported for children and adults across regions with different vascular distribution (Kang, Burgund, Lugar, Petersen, & Schlaggar, 2003). Again, this pattern is difficult to explain with a neurovascular account. Although developmental differences in neurovascular coupling may contribute to developmental differences in the BOLD signal, increasing evidence suggests that developmental changes in activation reflect meaningful changes in neural processing.

3.6 Brain connectivity

Brain regions do not work in isolation of one another, but rather, form integrated networks (Bullmore & Sporns, 2009). Traditional fMRI methods (discussed above) examine regional changes in brain activation and do not typically discern whether regional changes in brain activation are part of an integrated brain network. An increasing number of studies have begun to use functional and structural connectivity analyses to understand how brain networks change over developmental time, and how they might be related to cognition. The 'Interactive Specialization' account of development is a framework for understanding functional brain development (Johnson, 2011b). This framework proposes that brain regions become more specialized through a process of activity-dependent interactions with other brain regions and that the functions of a brain region are partly determined by its connections to other regions. Understanding brain development in this context highlights how using measures of functional and structural connectivity may better explain developmental changes in the brain. In the following section, we review some of the methods that can be used to investigate functional and structural connectivity in children.

3.6.1 Functional connectivity

Functional connectivity is a method that examines how brain regions communicate with one another and connectivity is typically inferred when distributed brain regions show correlated patterns of activity (Stevens, 2009). It can be used to examine short-range connections (correlations between brain regions that are spatially close) as well as long-range connections (correlations between brain regions that are spatially distant). Functional connectivity analyses rely on functional MRI data where the participant is either completing a task or is at rest (resting-state fMRI). Some theories, such as the Interactive Specialization model discussed above, propose that cognitive development may be a process of brain networks becoming increasingly more inter-connected and functionally specialized (Stevens, 2009). Investigating functional connectivity has been helpful in explaining individual differences in mathematical (Emerson & Cantlon, 2012) and reading abilities (Koyama *et al.*, 2011), suggesting that functional integration likely has a role in cognitive development.

One notable concern when interpreting functional connectivity data is the effect of head motion, which can cause significant changes to the metrics of functional connectivity, and can result in erroneous inferences. It is especially a concern when comparing functional connectivity between age groups where motion may entirely explain developmental differences. Motion has been shown to cause decreases in long-distance connections and increases in short-distance connections (Power, Barnes, Snyder, Schlaggar, & Petersen, 2012; Van Dijk, Sabuncu, & Buckner, 2012). Indeed, developmental changes in network organization have been characterized by decreases in short-distance connections and increases in long-distance connections (Fair *et al.*, 2009), which can be entirely accounted for by age-related differences in head motion (Power *et al.*, 2012). Many of the motion-correction procedures described in the sections above can minimize the effects of motion. However, they do not entirely correct for motion-related effects in functional connectivity analyses (Power *et al.*, 2012). Recently, a new approach has been developed that uses *Independent Component Analysis (ICA) – Automatic Removal of Motion Artefacts* to decompose fMRI data so that motion-related artefacts can be identified and removed (Pruim, Mennes, Buitelaar, & Beckmann, 2015). This method more adequately controls for head motion and is better at preserving metrics of functional connectivity (Pruim *et al.*, 2015).

A second caveat to interpreting functional connectivity data is that functional connectivity analyses rely on correlations to interpret connectivity between regions. Therefore, it cannot be assumed that activity in one region causes activity in another region. In contrast, assessing effective connectivity relates to the causal relationship between brain regions and how activity in one region influences activity in another (Friston, 2011). Many methods have now been employed to assess effective connectivity, including Dynamic Causal Modelling or Granger causality (for a review of these methods see Friston, 2011).

3.6.2 Structural connectivity

Understanding brain function is essential to explaining developmental changes. However, structural connectivity also plays a critical role in learning and development. White matter tracts connect both proximal and distal regions of the brain, and they transmit and integrate information between these regions. Individual variability in the structural integrity of task-relevant pathways relates to individual differences in performance, which is likely a result of both genetic and experience-dependent changes (Johansen-Berg, 2010). White matter connectivity also relates to the strength of the correlations in both resting-state and task-related functional networks, implicating a strong structure-function relationship in brain networks (Hermundstad *et al.*, 2013).

Diffusion Tensor Imaging (DTI) is a technique used to assess white matter microstructures by measuring the movement of water molecules in the brain. The scan is like an anatomical scan (T1 weighted image) where the child lies still and does not need to complete a task. Several metrics can be used to make inferences about white matter, but fractional anisotropy (FA) is the most commonly used index of white matter integrity (Jones, 2008).

Several methods can be used to analyse DTI data that include whole-brain voxel-wise analyses to more targeted region of interest approaches. Whole-brain voxel-wise analyses are typically atheoretical and examine all white matter tracts, in contrast, region of interest approaches are more hypothesis driven and examine specific white matter tracts. Tractography is a 3D modelling technique that has become a popular method to visualize and identify white matter tracts, and can also be used to quantify white matter integrity along the modelled tracts. These methods have been employed to demonstrate developmental changes in white matter (Lebel & Beaulieu, 2011), relate individual differences in specific white matter tracts to individual differences in behaviour (Johansen-Berg, 2010) and to study microstructural plasticity following cognitive interventions (Keller & Just, 2009).

White matter tracts have systematically been related to reading abilities (Vandermosten, Boets, Wouters, & Ghesquière, 2012), mathematical processing (Matejko & Ansari, 2015), and neurodevelopmental disorders such as Autism Spectrum Disorders (ASD) (Ameis & Catani, 2014). An increasing number of studies are now using both structural and functional imaging to study developmental changes in brain networks.

3.7 MRI with special populations

3.7.1 Scanning infants

Scanning infants has a number of challenges and the procedures significantly differ from those discussed for children. Anatomical or resting-state scans are most commonly used with infants since visual or auditory tasks are difficult to acquire. Still, investigating task-based activity is becoming more common (for a review of infant fMRI research see Graham *et al.*, 2015). One obvious concern when collecting infant data is motion. Swaddling new-borns and young infants can help reduce motion, though this is often not as successful with older infants. Scheduling a scanning time during the infant's regular sleep time can facilitate sleeping during the scan. Caregivers are encouraged to bring anything that they usually use during their bedtime routine to replicate this routine as much as possible at the scanner (i.e., dimming lights, lullaby music, rocking chair, etc.). Once the infant is asleep, earplugs or a sound attenuation helmet can be used to reduce scanner noise, and the infant can then be placed into the scanner (Raschle *et al.*, 2012).

3.7.2 Scanning atypically developing children

Children with developmental disorders such as dyslexia, dyscalculia or ASD typically do not exhibit any gross brain abnormalities or lesions. Both structural and functional neuroimaging techniques are employed to examine how children with developmental disorders differ from typically developing children in the way they recruit brain regions or have relative differences in grey and white matter structures. MRI research with special populations often has its own challenges. The type of disability can often impact the kinds of tasks that can be used in the scanner and tasks may need to be catered to the population being studied. For example, typical button-pressing tasks may be difficult for children with motor disabilities such as Cerebral Palsy. Scanner background noise may also affect clinical populations differently (Raschle *et al.*, 2012), especially for populations such as children with ASD who have noise sensitivities (Stiegler & Davis, 2010). Thus, the scanning procedures and tasks need to be catered to the particular disorder or disability.

3.8 Conclusion

Functional neuroimaging is a remarkable tool to investigate developmental changes in cognition and perception. However, researchers face a number of challenges when investigating the brains of children and special paediatric populations. The present chapter has outlined some guidelines for designing and conducting neuro-imaging studies with children. Specifically, we have highlighted the importance of choosing a design that is best suited to the research question that is being studied. It is critical to design a task that is both age appropriate and will tap into the cognitive construct of interest. Children are less likely to endure long and complicated tasks. Therefore, it is important to use *multiple short runs* and to consider which design is suitable for the research question that is being asked. Children should also be carefully familiarised with MRI procedures prior to doing the experiment in order to ensure the best quality data. Special considerations often need to be made when analysing data from paediatric populations. Motion needs to be carefully examined and standard alignment procedures that are used for adults may not be appropriate for children. Several factors such as performance differences, control tasks and changes in vasculature can lead to different interpretations of paediatric neuroimaging data, therefore, these factors should be carefully considered when interpreting neurodevelopmental changes. We also discussed how novel brain imaging methods such as functional connectivity and diffusion tensor imaging can examine the functional and structural networks of the brain, and can be used to complement more conventional task-related fMRI methods. Finally, not all paediatric popula-tions are the same. The experimental design may need to be tailored differently to some groups such as infants and atypically developing children.

All of these considerations are fundamental to conducting neuroimaging research with children, and have successfully been used by many research groups. Though paediatric neuroimaging can be difficult, it is an invaluable tool to investigate cognitive development. Neuroimaging provides an additional level of analysis and complements behavioural methods. Indeed, neuroimaging results are often best understood in combination with behavioural methods. However, neuroimaging can also be a particularly useful tool when differences in cognitive processing are too subtle to detect at a behavioural level and become more evident once the process is examined at a neural level of analysis (e.g., Hoeft *et al.*, 2011). Neuroimaging has added to our knowledge of how representations change over developmental time, has helped inform biologically plausible models for how children learn, and has begun to elucidate how atypically and typically developing children differ. Though significant advances have been made in understanding the neural underpinnings of cognitive development, there are many questions that have yet to be explored.

Practical tips

1   Design a paradigm that balances methodological requirements with a child-friendly design.
2   Spend time preparing children for the MRI; this will help them be more comfortable and reduce movement.
3   Collect lots of data when conducting neuroimaging research with paediatric populations. Be prepared to lose a large amount of data due to motion artefacts and other difficulties during data collection.

Note

1   Functional time series that exceed a predefined threshold are often removed from further statistical analyses.

References

Aguirre, G. K., & D'Esposito, M. (1999). Experimental design for brain fMRI. In C. T. W. Moonen & P. A. Bandettini (Eds), *Functional MRI* (pp. 369–80). Berlin: Springer-Verlag.

Amaro, E., & Barker, G. J. (2006). Study design in fMRI: Basic principles. *Brain and Cognition*, *60*, 220–32.

Ameis, S. H., & Catani, M. (2014). Altered white matter connectivity as a neural substrate for social impairment in Autism Spectrum Disorder. *Cortex*, *62*, 158–81.

Bullmore, E., & Sporns, O. (2009). Complex brain networks: Graph theoretical analysis of structural and functional systems. *Nature Reviews Neuroscience*, *10*(3), 186–198.

Burgund, E. D., Kang, H. C., Kelly, J. E., Buckner, R. L., Snyder, A. Z., . . . & Schlagger, B. L. (2002). The feasibility of a common stereotactic space for children and adults in fMRI studies of development. *NeuroImage*, *17*, 184–200.

Casey, B. J., Cohen, J. D., Jezzard, P., Turner, R., Noll, D. C., Trainor, R. J., . . . & Rapoport, J. L. (1995). Activation of prefrontal cortex in children during a nonspatial working memory task with functional MRI. *Neuroimage*, *2*(3), 221–9.

Church, J. A, Petersen, S. E., & Schlaggar, B. L. (2010). The 'Task B problem' and other considerations in developmental functional neuroimaging. *Human Brain Mapping*, *31*(6), 852–62.

Emerson, R. W., & Cantlon, J. F. (2012). Early math achievement and functional connectivity in the fronto-parietal network. *Developmental Cognitive Neuroscience*, *2*, S139–S51.

Evans, A. C., Collins D. L., Mills S. R., Brown E. D., Kelly R. L., & Peters T. M. (1993). 3D statistical neuroanatomical models from 305 MRI volumes. In L. Klaisner (Ed.), *Proceedings of IEEE nuclear science symposium and medical imaging conference* (pp. 1813–17). The Institute of Electrical and Electronics Engineers.

Fair, D., Cohen, A. L., Power, J. D., Dosenbach, N. U. F., Church, J. A., Miezin, F. M., . . . & Petersen, S. E. (2009). Functional brain networks develop from a 'local to distributed' organization. *PLoS Computational Biology, 5*(5), e1000381.

Fonov, V., Evans, A. C., Botteron, K., Almli, R., McKinstry, D., & Collins, L. (2011). Unbiased average age-appropriate atlases for pediatric studies. *NeuroImage, 54*, 313–27.

Friston, K. J. (2011). Functional and effective connectivity: A review. *Brain Connectivity, 1*(1), 13–36.

Friston, K. J., Holmes, A. P., Price, C. J., Büchel, C., & Worsley, K. J. (1999). Multisubject fMRI studies and conjunction analyses. *NeuroImage, 10*(4), 385–96.

Friston, K. J., Holmes, A., Worsley, K. J., Poline, J. B., Frith, C. D., & Frackowiak, R. S. J. (1995). Statistical parametric maps in functional imaging: A general linear approach. *Human Brain Mapping, 2*, 189–210.

Friston, K. J., Williams, S., Howard, R., Frackowiak, R. S., & Turner, R. (1996). Movement-related effects in fMRI time-series. *Magnetic Resonance in Medicine, 35*(3), 346–55.

Frost, M. A., & Goebel, R. (2012). Measuring structural-functional correspondence: Spatial variability of specialised brain regions after macro-anatomical alignment. *NeuroImage, 59*(2), 1369–81.

Giedd, J. N., Blumenthal, J., Jeffries, N. O., Castellanos, F. X., Liu, H., Zijdenbos, A., . . . & Rapoport, J. L. (1999). Brain development during childhood and adolescence: A longitudinal MRI study. *Nature Neuroscience, 2*(10), 861–3.

Goebel, R. (2015). Revealing brain activity and white matter structure using functional and diffusion-weighted magnetic resonance imaging. In C. Stippich (Ed.), *Clinical Functional MRI: Presurgical functional neuroimaging* (2nd ed., pp. 13–57). Berlin Heidelberg: Springer-Verlag.

Goebel, R., Esposito, F., & Formisano, E. (2006). Analysis of functional image analysis contest (FIAC) data with BrainVoyager QX: From single-subject to cortically aligned group general linear model analysis and self-organizing group independent component analysis. *Human Brain Mapping, 27*, 392–401.

Graham, A. M., Pfeifer, J. H., Fisher, P. A., Lin, W., Gao, W., & Fair, D. A. (2015). The potential of infant fMRI research and the study of early life stress as a promising exemplar. *Developmental Cognitive Neuroscience, 12*, 12–39.

Grill-Spector, K., & Malach, R. (2001). fMR-adaptation: A tool for studying the functional properties of human cortical neurons. *Acta Psychologica, 107*(1–3), 293–321.

Hermundstad, A. M., Bassett, D. S., Brown, K. S., Aminoff, E. M., Clewett, D., Freeman, S., . . . & Carlson, J. M. (2013). Structural foundations of resting-state and task-based functional connectivity in the human brain. *Proceedings of the National Academy of Sciences of the United States of America, 110*(15), 6169–74.

Hoeft, F., McCandliss, B. D., Black, J. M. Gantman, A., Zakerani, N., Hulme, C., . . . & Gabrieli, J. D. E. (2011). Neural systems predicting long-term outcome in dyslexia. *Proceedings of the National Academy of Sciences of the United States of America, 108*(1), 361.

Holloway, I. D., & Ansari, D. (2010). Developmental specialization in the right intraparietal sulcus for the abstract representation of numerical magnitude. *Journal of Cognitive Neuroscience, 22*(11), 2627–37.

Huettel, S. A., Song, A. W., & Mccarthy, G. (2009). *Functional Magnetic Resonance Imaging* (2nd edn). Sunderland, MA: Sinauer Associates.

Johansen-Berg, H. (2010). Behavioural relevance of variation in white matter microstructure. *Current Opinion in Neurology, 23*(4), 351–8.

Johnson, M. H. (2011a). *Developmental Cognitive Neuroscience* (3rd edn). Malden, MA: Wiley-Blackwell.

Johnson, M. H. (2011b). Interactive specialization: A domain-general framework for human functional brain development? *Developmental Cognitive Neuroscience, 1*(1), 7–21.

Johnstone, T., Ores Walsh, K. S., Greischar, L. L., Alexander, A. L., Fox, A. S., Davidson, R. J., & Oakes, T. R. (2006). Motion correction and the use of motion covariates in multiple-subject fMRI analysis. *Human Brain Mapping, 27*(10), 779–88.

Jones, D. K. (2008). Studying connections in the living human brain with diffusion MRI. *Cortex, 44*(8), 936–52.

Kang, H. C., Burgund, E. D. D., Lugar, H. M., Petersen, S. E., & Schlaggar, B. L. (2003). Comparison of functional activation foci in children and adults using a common stereotactic space. *Neuroimage, 19*(1), 16–28.

Keller, T. A., & Just, M. A. (2009). Altering cortical connectivity: Remediation-induced changes in the white matter of poor readers. *Neuron, 64*(5), 624–31.

Koyama, M. S., Di Martino, A., Zuo, X.-N., Kelly, C., Mennes, M., Jutagir, D. R., . . . & Milham, M. P. (2011). Resting-state functional connectivity indexes reading competence in children and adults. *The Journal of Neuroscience, 31*(23), 8617–24.

Lebel, C., & Beaulieu, C. (2011). Longitudinal development of human brain wiring continues from childhood into adulthood. *The Journal of Neuroscience, 31*(30), 10937–47.

Luna, B., Velanova, K., & Geier, C. F. (2010). Methodological approaches in developmental neuroimaging studies. *Human Brain Mapping, 31*(6), 863–71.

Matejko, A. A., & Ansari, D. (2015). Drawing connections between white matter and numerical and mathematical cognition: A literature review. *Neuroscience & Biobehavioral Reviews, 48*, 35–52.

Murphy, K., & Garavan, H. (2004). Artifactual fMRI group and condition differences driven by performance confounds. *NeuroImage, 21*(1), 219–28.

Muzik, O., Chugani, D. C., Juhasz, C., Shen, C., & Chugani, H. T. (2000). Statistical parametric mapping: Assessment of application in children. *NeuroImage, 12*, 538–49.

Ogawa, S., Lee, T. M., Kay, A. R., & Tank, D. W. (1990). Brain magnetic resonance imaging with contrast dependent on blood oxygenation. *Proceedings of the National Academy of Sciences of the United States of America, 87*(24), 9868–72.

Petersen, S. E., & Dubis, J. W. (2012). The mixed block/event-related design. *NeuroImage, 62*(2), 1177–84.

Poldrack, R. A. (2000). Imaging brain plasticity: Conceptual and methodological issues – A theoretical review. *NeuroImage, 12*(1), 1–13.

Power, J. D., Barnes, K. A., Snyder, A. Z., Schlaggar, B. L., & Petersen, S. E. (2012). Spurious but systematic correlations in functional connectivity MRI networks arise from subject motion. *NeuroImage, 59*(3), 2142–54.

Pruim, R. H. R., Mennes, M., Buitelaar, J. K., & Beckmann, C. F. (2015). Evaluation of ICA-AROMA and alternative strategies for motion artifact removal in resting-state fMRI. *NeuroImage, 112*, 278–87.

Raschle, N., Zuk, J., Ortiz-Mantilla, S., Sliva, D. D., Franceschi, A., Grant, P. E., . . . & Gaab, N. (2012). Pediatric neuroimaging in early childhood and infancy: Challenges and practical guidelines. *Annals of the New York Academy of Sciences, 1252,* 43–50.

Rombouts, S. A., Barkhof, F., Hoogenraad, F. G., Sprenger, M., Valk, J., & Scheltens, P. (1997). Test-retest analysis with functional MR of the activated area in the human visual cortex. *American Journal of Neuroradiology, 18*(7), 1317–22.

Scerif, G., Kotsoni, E., & Casey, B. J. (2006). Functional neuroimaging of early cognitive development. In R. Cabeza & A. Kingston (Eds), *Handbook of functional neuroimaging of cognition* (2nd edn, pp. 351–78). Cambridge, MA: Massachusetts Institute of Technology.

Schlaggar, B. L., Brown, T. T., Lugar, H. M., Visscher, K. M., Miezin, F. M., & Petersen, S. E. (2002). Functional neuroanatomical differences between adults and school-age children in the processing of single words. *Science, 296,* 1476–9.

Stevens, M. C. (2009). The developmental cognitive neuroscience of functional connectivity. *Brain and Cognition, 70*(1), 1–12.

Stiegler, L. N., & Davis, R. (2010). Understanding sound sensitivity in individuals with autism spectrum disorders. *Focus on Autism and Other Developmental Disabilities, 25,* 67–75.

Supekar, K., Swigart, A. G., Tenison, C., Jolles, D. D., Rosenberg-Lee, M., Fuchs, L., & Menon, V. (2013). Neural predictors of individual differences in response to math tutoring in primary-grade school children. *Proceedings of the National Academy of Sciences of the United States of America, 110,* 1–6.

Talairach, J., & Tournoux, P. (1988). *Co-planar stereotaxic atlas of the human brain.* New York, NY: Thieme.

Tomasi, D., Caparelli, E. C., Chang, L., & Ernst, T. (2005). fMRI-acoustic noise alters brain activation during working memory tasks. *NeuroImage, 27*(2), 377–86.

Turkeltaub, P. E., Gareau, L., Flowers, D. L., Zeffiro, T. A., & Eden, G. F. (2003). Development of neural mechanisms for reading. *Nature Neuroscience, 6*(7), 767–73.

Van Dijk, K. R. A., Sabuncu, M. R., & Buckner, R. L. (2012). The influence of head motion on intrinsic functional connectivity MRI. *NeuroImage, 59*(1), 431–8.

Vandermosten, M., Boets, B., Wouters, J., & Ghesquière, P. (2012). A qualitative and quantitative review of diffusion tensor imaging studies in reading and dyslexia. *Neuroscience and Biobehavioral Reviews, 36*(6), 1532–52.

Vogel, S. E., Goffin, C., & Ansari, D. (2015). Developmental specialization of the left parietal cortex for the semantic representation of Arabic numerals: An fMR-Adaptation study. *Developmental Cognitive Neuroscience, 12,* 61–73.

4

STANDARDISED AND EXPERIMENTAL PSYCHOLOGICAL TASKS

Issues and solutions for research with children

Harry Purser and Jo Van Herwegen

4.1 Introduction

What children do and say provides us with important information about their development and wellbeing. However, there is only an indirect relationship between the former and the latter so that observing children alone cannot help us understand the underlying mechanisms. Experimental designs are there to explore specific hypotheses and examine the cause and effect relationship of different phenomena. This chapter will focus on how behavioural, experimental and standardised psychological tasks are used within experimental designs. In the first section, we will discuss the use of standardised tasks, focusing on selecting the appropriate task, issues that relate to the administration of the task, and how to correctly interpret the scores obtained from standardised tests. In the second part of the chapter, we will focus on experimental tasks. More specifically, we will discuss the advantages and disadvantages of designing your own experimental tasks and what confounding factors should be taken into account during the design stage. Next, the issue of validity as well as general issues when using tasks with children will be explored. Throughout the chapter, we will use examples from research with children who have neurodevelopmental disorders, not only because it includes our own research, which we know best, but more importantly, because working with children with additional needs reinforces certain issues when using experimental and standardised tasks.

The term 'test' is often used within psychology to refer to any type of assessment that participants complete, whether on paper or in real life. However, one of the difficulties for psychology as a field is that, in contrast to other sciences, the objects of study, psychological constructs such as 'theory of mind', are not directly observable, compared with, for example, temperature or weight. Therefore, it is better to refer to psychological assessments as 'tasks' or 'measurements' rather than 'tests', because often within psychology we cannot directly test the variables of interest. In addition, the term 'test' carries the connotation that there is a correct or incorrect answer and this may increase anxiety in children resulting in unreliable assessments. Therefore, for the remainder of this chapter we will use the word 'task' instead.

4.2 Using standardised tasks

4.2.1 Different types of standardised tasks

Standardised tasks are tasks that have been administered in a specific manner to a large group of people so that normed data has been obtained and the participant's score can be compared with that normed population when the standardised administration is employed. There are standardised tasks for all areas of psychology, including areas such as general intelligence, attention, memory, emotions, behaviours (actions) as well as all areas of achievement (mathematics, reading, language, etc.). Although both achievement and aptitude tasks are standardised, aptitude tasks are intended to predict the participant's future performance (such as intelligence tasks), whereas achievement tasks assess what a person has mastered or learned (such as the number of words one knows).

Standardised tasks are used with children for a variety of reasons. For example, standardised tasks are often used by educational and clinical psychologists to evaluate whether a specific child has special needs or qualifies for specialist education as well as to assess the child's mental or physical health. Within research contexts, standardised tasks are employed to evaluate whether training programmes and interventions have made an impact on a child's development or to match different groups. For example, participants with Williams syndrome (WS), a rare disorder that is caused by a genetic deletion on the long arm of chromosome seven (see Martens, Wilson, & Reuters, 2008 for a discussion), have overall learning difficulties with general IQ scores within the mild to moderate impairment range (50–70). This means that they rarely perform in line with their chronological age. Thus, within a research context their performance on experimental tasks (see below) is compared with children who are matched for mental age, i.e., children who have similar scores on a particular standardised task. For example, in our own research we have matched infants with WS to those with Down syndrome (DS) based on performance on the Bayley Scales of Infant and Toddler Development (Bayley, 1993; Karmiloff-Smith *et al.*, 2012; Van Herwegen, Ansari, Xu, & Karmiloff-Smith, 2008). Within forensic psychology, standardised tasks are often used within child custody evaluations to assess mental health or parent–child relationships (for a discussion see Gould, 2005).

Examples of standardised aptitude tasks include intelligence tasks such as Wechsler's Intelligence Scales, which include scales for infants (WPPSI-III: Wechsler, 2002), children (WISC-IV: Wechsler, 2003), adults (WAIS: Wechsler, 1997), and an abbreviated scale that can be used with children as well as adults (WASI: Wechsler, 1999). These scales are based on the view that intelligence is made up of a number of different abilities and thus they include several sub-tasks that measure different aspects of intelligence, including verbal and performance IQ. These tasks are administered on an individual basis in a quiet room, which means that they are time-consuming and therefore costly. On the other hand, the examiner has the opportunity to carefully observe what the child is doing or where the child is looking. This is very important as children might fail to answer correctly for a number of reasons. For example, children with language difficulties might find it difficult to understand the instructions. Children with developmental disorders also often show attention difficulties and need to be brought back to the task by the examiner. Finally, some of these tasks require the child to choose the correct answer from a number of different options. However, children who do not carefully look at the different options might fail the task, not because they do not have the aptitude or ability to do so, but because they just randomly chose an option. Although one has to follow the standardised procedure for scoring the task, individual administration of the tasks allows the examiner to take these possibilities into account when interpreting the child's performance.

Other aptitude tasks only include one type of assessment and thus, are easier to administer and score. In the Raven's Progressive Matrices (Raven, Raven, & Court, 2004), for example, children are shown a visual pattern that is missing a piece and they are asked to identify the missing piece from six options. There are different versions of the task available for use with different ages and groups, including Raven's Standard Progressive Matrices (RSPM; for use with the general population), Raven's Coloured Progressive Matrices (RCPM; for children and adults with special needs as well as elderly people and typically developing (TD) children aged 5 to 11 years old), and Raven's Advanced Progressive Matrices (RAPM; for adults and adolescents of above-average intelligence or gifted children). These tasks can be administered individually or as a group. In addition, it has been argued that this task is less culturally loaded, compared with some other aptitude tasks, as it contains minimal instructions and does not require any linguistic responses from the participant. Furthermore, the fact that this task can be administered to groups and scored automatically means that information from large numbers of children can be obtained quickly and relatively cheaply.

4.2.2 Choosing the appropriate standardised task

In order to obtain a score that reflects the participant's true abilities, it is important to choose the appropriate standardised task. The choice of which task to use might be based on the advantages and disadvantages of administering individual or group tasks. In addition, one has to take into account cultural and linguistic aspects. For example, the Wechsler's tasks are American: even the most able children in other countries might not know certain words or concepts. This is particularly problematic for the verbal sub-scales in which the child might be asked to provide a definition of a certain word or person that might be unknown to them. For this reason, in the UK the British Ability Scales III (BAS; Elliot & Smith, 2011) are often preferred instead because this task includes similar verbal and non-verbal sub-tasks to the Wechsler's scales, but it only includes concepts and words that British children are familiar with. Yet, in other countries there might not be an appropriate aptitude task available and one may have to use tasks that have been normed in the US or UK. In addition, when choosing a task one also has to consider the type of response that is required from the child. Some tasks require a timed response because it can be argued that intelligence is not only about finding the correct answer but also how fast one can find a solution. Such timed tasks might put children with motor difficulties and impairments at a disadvantage (for example, children with low attention span).

Another important factor when choosing what standardised task to use is the age of the participants, as normed data will only be available for a limited age range. This is rather straightforward when working with TD groups. However, when working with atypical groups this becomes a more tricky issue as participant groups will often show uneven cognitive profiles with better performance on certain abilities compared with others. For example, children with Autism Spectrum Disorders (ASD) often perform better on non-verbal tasks that rely on visuo-spatial abilities compared with tasks that tap into verbal abilities. Therefore, when assessing children with ASD on BAS sub-scales, they may perform at floor (i.e., the lowest age-equivalent norm available) on certain verbal tasks while being at ceiling for non-verbal tasks (i.e., highest age-equivalent norm available). This means that no appropriate IQ or age-equivalent score can be calculated and that the discrepancy between children's chronological age and mental age could have been larger should age-equivalent norms from younger and older children have been available. Therefore, floor and ceiling effects should be avoided and it is important to use tasks that have been standardised with children from a wide range of ages. For example, the WASI scales can be administered with participants aged 6 to 89 years old.

4.2.3 Administration of standardised tasks

One important aspect of standardised tasks is that, in order to compare the score of a particular participant with the normed data, specific instructions have to be followed and thus only a trained psychologist should administer the task. The fact that instructions are standardised means that different people can assess a child over the child's development and that these performance scores can still be compared. However, in our experience a rigid set of instructions does not automatically imply that testing outcomes are objective. For example, a 6½-old boy with severe language difficulties who took part in our research was assessed on his non-verbal abilities in order to confirm whether or not he met the inclusion criteria of specific language impairment for the study. He obtained a raw score of 16 on RCPM, which put him in the fortieth percentile for his age range. However, it transpired afterwards that when his educational psychologist had assessed him a few weeks before, he had only obtained a score within the first percentile for children of his age. Although one should not repeat standardised tasks within such a short time frame (usually not within 6 months) to avoid learning effects, it is unlikely that this difference in scores could be attributed to a learning effect or development between time one and time two alone. Through discussion with the parents and the educational psychologist, it was revealed that while the educational psychologist used a 'purist' view where she did not provide feedback, the experimenter in our research study had provided general motivational feedback ('keep going', 'good job') during the testing session. This suggests that motivation plays an important role when assessing children.

In our own experience in working with children with neurodevelopmental disorders, motivation is an important aspect of the assessment session and score. However, there is a debate as to whether praise should be used when assessing children. On the one hand, it has been shown that random reinforcement can have the opposite effect and decrease the motivation to respond (see Eisenberger & Cameron, 1998). In addition, one cannot ensure that different people will respond with the same motivation from reinforcement, which is why most manuals will verify what kind of feedback can be provided. On the other hand, children are used to receiving a lot of motivational feedback when performing tasks and might find it stressful when an examiner sits silently next to them. Furthermore, a review study that evaluated the impact of incentives, including praise, sweets, money, social reinforcement and tokens, did not find any consistent differences between studies that did and did not offer incentives (Sattler, 1988). While the debate continues, we recommend for now that researchers use motivational feedback because, other things being equal, this will be less stressful for children. It is also important that researchers remain consistent in their own testing and document the particular decisions that they made. In addition to what kind of motivational feedback is provided, one needs to take into account the mood and fatigue of the child, the length of the task to be administered, the time and day of the assessment, and the relationship between the examiner and examinee. Thus, the interpretation of the scores requires a thorough understanding of the task, the task-taker and the conditions of the assessment session. (See also Chapters 2 and 3 for further consideration of how the conditions of the assessment session can be influential in eye-tracking and brain imaging studies with children.)

Due to the fact that standardised tasks require test administrators to adhere to the instructions, as well as the type of feedback that can or cannot be provided, some test makers have started to develop computer-assisted tasks. For example, the New Group Reading Test Digital (2010), a task that assesses reading ability (phonology, word reading and passage comprehension) in children aged 7 to 16 years old, is an adaptive online achievement task that starts with the child's chronological age but is based upon the child's performance. The digital test is able to adapt the reading material during the session in order to reflect the child's actual reading ability. The fact that the task is administered on a computer means that the procedure is completely standardised, no task administrator is required, scoring happens online and automatically rather than off-line, and there is no experimenter bias involved. In addition, computerised testing also reduces the number of experimenter errors such as skipping items, not demonstrating certain items or not accurately assessing the basal and ceiling item for a particular child.

Standardised tasks are often used in research to compare or match groups, especially in research that includes atypical groups. In order to be able to match two groups, it is important to establish that both groups approach the task in a similar way because it is possible that two groups will obtain the same score through different strategies, so that similar scores might not reflect similar levels of underlying ability. For example, research has shown that children with DS make different types of errors on RCPM compared with TD children (Gunn & Jarrold, 2004). This means that even when you select younger TD children who are matched for the total number of errors the DS children make, you cannot assume that the groups are actually matched for non-verbal performance as the groups might rely on atypical

strategies. In contrast, children with WS have shown that they do make the same type of errors as younger TD children and you can meaningfully match the two groups for RCPM scores and ability (Van Herwegen, Farran, & Annaz, 2011). Thus, a thorough understanding of the task itself is required before a child's performance can be scored accurately.

One serious drawback related to standardised tasks is the fact that one should not usually test the same child twice within a short time span (often within 6 months) in order to avoid learning effects. This provides some constraints when evaluating an intervention programme where one might want to use standardised tasks to compare performance before and after a particular intervention. There are currently a number of standardised tasks that provide different lists of stimuli for the same sub-tasks. As both lists are standardised on the same population, one set of stimuli can be used pre-intervention and the other one at the end of the intervention programme. For example, the Early Numeracy Test (ENT; Van Luit, Van de Rijt, & Pennings, 1994) consists of forty items that evaluate different aspects of young children's numerical competence. It has two analogous versions – version A and version B – so that a different set can be used at two different time points (see for example Aunio & Niemivirta, 2010).

4.2.4 Scoring standardised tasks

Once the administration of the task is completed, there are different scores that can be calculated from standardised tasks. In the first instance, one can calculate the raw score of a certain task, which is the amount of correct answers a child has given. Raw scores have the disadvantage that one cannot always directly compare scores, as children of different ages often have different starting points and different tasks might have a different total amount of items that have been administered. Therefore, most tasks will provide age-equivalent norms or performance norms based on the standardised norms. Performance norms can include statistical metrics such as cumulative percentages, percentiles, z-scores, t-scores and IQ scores. The norms of a test are based upon the distribution of the scores of the people in the normed sample. It is beyond the scope of this chapter to discuss the differences between all these different scores but there are a few pointers one has to keep in mind when interpreting them.

First of all, one has to question how each norm has been obtained and who was included within the normed sample. Often, you will find that ethnic minorities are not represented within normed samples and thus, if one has tested a child from an ethnic minority and this child obtained a lower score, it is unclear whether this lower score is caused by some cultural differences or a true representation of that child's abilities. This is called 'mismatched norming'. In addition, there are very few standardised tasks that assess all relevant cognitive abilities within one type of task, so that often a battery of standardised tasks has to be employed in order to obtain a well-rounded psychological assessment of a child. However, different standardised tasks will be normed on different groups across different countries and cultures, which might make comparison between standardised tasks difficult (see Brock, Jarrold, Farran, Laws, & Riby 2007, for a discussion).

Second, one needs to consider the appropriateness of each score. Standardised tasks that contain multiple sub-tasks often provide an overall score as well as scales that combine scores across different sub-tasks. For example, the Wechsler's scales provide a full scale IQ score (FSIQ) as well as a verbal (VIQ) and performance intelligence quotient (PIQ). However, one has to be careful interpreting these scale scores in atypical groups that show uneven cognitive profiles. One such example is WS: although participants with WS have FSIQs between 50–70 on average, their VIQs are often better and develop at a faster rate compared with their PIQs. Therefore, FSIQs do not provide an accurate representation about their verbal or non-verbal abilities (Jarrold, Baddeley, & Hewes, 1998). In addition, even TD children have been found to show a discrepancy between their verbal and non-verbal abilities (Brock *et al.*, 2007).

Third, although as described above raw scores do not allow comparisons between tasks or different age groups, when working with particular groups normed scores might simply not be available. For example, in the BAS pattern construction sub-task, children are asked to copy a pattern from a book using either foam squares or 3-dimensional plastic cubes for the more advanced forms. Participants obtain a score based on the time it takes them to complete an item as well as the total number of items completed. Participants with WS are particularly weak on this task and, often, normed scores are not available for their low performance. Thus, any ability score lower than sixty-five renders an age-equivalent score of 3-years-old. In such cases no accurate comparisons can be made between groups and thus it might be better to use ability or raw scores (see Van Herwegen, Rundblad, Davelaar, & Annaz, 2011).

In sum, standardised tasks have the advantage that they allow performance scores of different children, or scores on different tasks, to be directly compared with one another so that one can assess how a child's performance score compares with the norm. However, the fact that normed scores are obtained from a specific sample from the population has its drawbacks when the tasks are used with ethnic minority or specific atypical groups. In addition, the fact that the content of standardised tasks is set in stone only allows the researcher access to a limited amount of information.

4.3 Experimental tasks

4.3.1 Using experimental tasks

As standardised tasks only allow you to answer questions that are tested within the scope of the task, researchers often develop their own experimental tasks in which they can carefully manipulate a particular variable of interest (i.e., the experimental variable) and control for confounding variables. For example, although the Early Number Concept task from the British Abilities Scales (Elliot & Smith, 2011) allows one to assess children's early mathematical abilities across a standardised population, it includes a wide variety of mathematical abilities, including children's understanding of cardinality (i.e., the understanding of counting), digit recognition knowledge, comparison of sets and understanding of mathematical concepts such as 'more'. Therefore, this task is too general to allow one to examine whether specific populations have issues with a particular mathematical concept only, say for example the understanding of counting.

Yet, although experimental tasks are often designed to answer a specific question, some experimental tasks have been used so often with children that, even though they are not standardised, they are considered good measures to answer that specific question. For example, the Sally–Anne task (Baron-Cohen, Leslie, & Frith, 1985) is a commonly used task to assess young children's theory of mind abilities. Therefore, it is always good to check the literature first to see what tasks are commonly used within the field before starting to design your own tasks as you may well find an established task that can help you answer your question.

The aim of matching on standardised tests or mental-age measures leads the researcher to indirectly equate the participant groups on their ability to perform the non-central aspects of the task. However, 'task-matching' is an alternative that achieves this equating of ability level directly. Task-matching is the use of a control condition that is the same as the experimental task differing only in the information required at test. For example, if the hypothesis is that Group X are more susceptible to background noise in memory tasks than Group Y, the groups could be matched for performance on the noiseless condition of the memory task. Performance on this control condition (noiseless) can then be used to match performance of the different groups before comparing performance on the experimental condition (with background noise). It is important, however, to ensure that the control task is sensitive for the groups being matched, i.e., that the lack of any group difference is not due to floor or ceiling effects (see Jarrold & Brock, 2004). Examples abound of control conditions that fulfil the criteria above in studies that match groups on standardised tests or mental-age measures, e.g., in studies that contrast social and non-social tasks in ASD research (e.g., Klin, 2000). However, it is hard to find examples of group matching at the outset of a study for participants' performance on the task-matched control condition, which would obviate any need for matching on these additional tasks (see Phillips, Jarrold, Baddeley, Grant, & Karmiloff-Smith, 2004).

4.3.2 Designing experimental tasks

Designing your own experimental task requires careful consideration of confounds at the design stage and one has to ensure that all confounding variables have been controlled for, so that any differences between groups or conditions are caused by differences of the variable in question. Variables that are particularly important when working with children include effects caused by limited motivation, administration of the task, working memory demands as well as the verbal and motor demands of a task. We will now turn to each of these issues in more detail.

Administration of the task

Before one starts the design of an experimental task, one should consider how the task will be administered and how the responses will be recorded. For example, children with ASD perform better on traditional executive control tasks that are administered on a computer, in contrast to face-to-face tasks with an experimenter, as computerised tasks require fewer social interactions (see Kenworthy, Yerys, Anthony, & Wallace, 2008 for a discussion). However, a recent study that has directly compared computer as well as experimenter-administered versions of executive functioning (EF) tasks in the same children with ASD has shown that there was no difference, and that problems with EF tasks observed in ASD cannot be attributed to a limited ability to engage with an experimenter or the extra social demands of such tasks (Williams & Jarrold, 2013).

Computerised tasks have the advantage that the administration can be standardised across different participants and that performance can be scored automatically. However, administering a task on computer can make it difficult for the experimenter to monitor the child's motivation carefully as the task progresses. Therefore, it is easier for the experimenter to encourage the child when enthusiasm wanes when the task is not administered on a computer. One solution could be to include regular breaks to keep the child motivated as well as giving the child a token or a reward picture after a certain number of trials have been completed. In addition, one should statistically compare performance at the end of the task with that of the start of the task or counter-balance stimulus lists across participants to ensure that motivation alone cannot explain the observed results.

Most computerised experimental tasks require children to press a certain key or button on a response pad or keyboard when viewing particular stimuli. This requires a number of abilities. First of all, the child needs to have appropriate motor skills to press that particular button or response key as well as good eye–hand coordination. More importantly, the child needs to keep in mind which button to press for a particular answer. For example, a child might be required to press the yellow button for when the stimuli on the left-hand side of the screen is correct and a red button when the answer on the right-hand side is correct (see Halberda & Feigenson, 2008 for an example). This means that the child needs to keep in mind the correct answer as well as which button to press. This can be very taxing for children's limited working memory abilities. Therefore, it might be better to use a touch screen so that children can respond by touching the correct answer on the screen itself, instead of having to link stimuli on the screen to a particular button on a response pad or keyboard. A related point is that unless memory is being assessed, it is always better to display any task-relevant stimuli until the response has been made, rather than altering the display to a 'response screen' that features only the possible responses. For example, a receptive vocabulary task might present an image for naming. If the image disappears before participants have responded, an incorrect answer might owe, at least in part, to forgetting aspects of the image, rather than to a lack of lexico-semantic knowledge.

Another alternative to response buttons might be to ask children to act out a response or to verbally provide an answer. Yet again, these methodologies have their own disadvantages in that young children have a limited vocabulary and grammar and might not be able to explain what they are thinking. Furthermore, verbal responses might disadvantage certain children with neurodevelopmental disorders. For example, children with language difficulties, but also very young children, might not elaborate as much as TD controls on their answers due to their limited language abilities, yet they may provide the correct answer when a non-verbal response is required.

Instructions of the task

Not only does one need to be careful with the type of response that is required from the children, but one also needs to carefully consider the instructions that the child is given. Ideally, instructions should be fairly short, and simple grammatical sentences should be used when working with children. In addition, one may want to consider adding a short task before the experimental tasks that assesses the child's understanding of the instructions or train the child on the type of response that is required from them. For example, it has been argued that a child's approximate number abilities (ANS) are related to their number word knowledge (Mussolin, Nys, Leybaert, & Content, 2012; Wagner & Johnson, 2011). Children's ANS abilities are often assessed by a task in which children are presented with two amounts of dots on a screen and they have to indicate whether there are more dots on the left or right-hand side of the screen. Recent research has shown that when only children who passed a training task that shows they understand the meaning of the word 'more' are included in the analyses, the correlation between ANS and exact number word knowledge disappears (Negen & Sarnecka, 2015).

Another example that shows that task instructions are important comes from our own studies in which we examined figurative language comprehension (including metaphors such as 'my teacher is a dragon') in children with WS. In these studies children listen to short stories that end with a figurative expression and children are asked to indicate what the speaker means by selecting the correct picture out of three options. This question is then followed by a memory question that asks about a fact that was mentioned in the story. Any child who fails the memory question is then removed from the final data to ensure that those who fail the question about the figurative expression do so because they do not understand the expression and not because they were not paying attention to the story (Van Herwegen, Dimitriou, & Rundblad, 2013).

Motivation

As we described before, motivation is an important aspect of children's perform-ance. Therefore, it is important to make the task relevant or interesting to children. For example, providing stimuli as part of a narrative might make the assessment more game-like and pleasant for children, which might impact positively on their performance. Instead of simply administering a digit span task, where the experimenter reads out a list of numbers to be repeated back by the participant in correct serial order, there could be a narrative wherein a 'secret agent' is imprisoned by a master criminal: the participant must listen to the secret codes and relay them to mission control, in order to break the security system and release the agent (as used in Purser *et al.*, 2012). It is possible that even simply framing tasks as 'games' when describing them to participants, rather than only describing what the task requires, would spark interest and engagement.

Reaction times

Finally, tasks are often administered on a computer in order to obtain reaction time (RT) measures from children as RTs can provide richer data than just the number of correct answers. For example, it has been argued that difficulties with making inferences about mental states in ASD would not only be reflected in number of incorrect responses but also in the time it takes people with ASD to make these inferences (Bowler, 1997). Indeed, adolescents with Asperger syndrome do take longer to process both mental states and physical state inferences in a story context. Yet, there is a large difference in the time it takes them to process mental states versus physical states which shows that, although they have general difficulties with making inferences about stories they have been told, they find inferences about mental states especially challenging (Kaland, Smith, & Mortensen, 2007).

However, one needs to be careful when interpreting RT data from children in that RTs in children are very variable. As noted by Lange-Küttner (2012), variability in children's RT data may be so large that it is not possible to detect differences between group means: within-group differences will be greater than between-group differences. This variability may be especially marked when children enter school (Kail & Ferrer, 2007), with large individual differences eventually diminishing because of the leveling effects of schooling. Unusually large variability in RT data seems to be associated with particular developmental disorders, such as attention deficit and hyperactivity disorder (ADHD). For example, Epstein *et al.* (2011) found elevated variability of RTs in children with ADHD relative to TD controls, across five neuropsychological tasks that tapped attention and executive function abilities. These effects were neither modulated by task, nor by ADHD subtype: irrespective of the task, children with ADHD demonstrated irregular patterns of RTs, featuring occasional long times. The authors pointed out that although these infrequent long RTs might reflect attentional lapses (e.g., Hervey *et al.*, 2006), the reason for these events is currently unknown.

4.3.3 Piloting and validation of new experimental tasks

Once the experimental task is set up it is important to take some time and pilot the task with some participants. This is important for all experimental tasks but especially when working with children as all adults, including experimenters who are experienced in working with children, have certain expectations of children's performance and behaviour that might be incorrect.

In addition, one needs to evaluate the validity of the task, which can be broadly defined as the ability of the task to measure the characteristics that it is designed to assess. Although the notion of validity is often subdivided into different types, they are unified in the sense that they form part of the overall justification for a particular test's application and interpretation. Messick (1980) highlighted the risk of thinking about these aspects of validity as subtypes, such as population validity, because this view might lead researchers to treat any single one of these, or even a small group, as the whole of validity. Messick suggested that if, instead, one were to use the more descriptive term 'population generalizability', it would guard against this confusion and emphasise that validity consists of various conditions that must be satisfied, each of which will be of differing importance, depending on the test in question.

In developing a new task, researchers might be queried about so-called concurrent validity, which might also be known simply as 'relation to existing measures'. In practice, concurrent validity tends to consist of a moderate degree of shared variance between performance on the new task and performance on any highly cited task that purports to assess a similar ability. There are at least two reasons why researchers developing a new task might not desire concurrent validity. First, many established tasks do not stand up to a cursory analysis of their own (multifaceted) validity (see Purser, 2015 for an example), so that concurrent validity in relation to these tasks might be undesirable. Second, the new task might not be intended to assess exactly the same type of ability that the reference task was designed to assess, rendering the comparison flawed. However, concurrent validity might rightly be considered as important under some circumstances. One example is developing a culturally neutral version of an existing task: in this case, at least when testing the population for which the original task was devised, high concurrent validity would be necessary to convince us that the new test is measuring the same construct as the original.

Another aspect of validity, which is often used to scrutinise new tasks, is face validity. This is simply whether the task appears to assess what it is intended to assess. Although this aspect of validity might appear, on the face of it (no pun intended), to be somewhat vague, it can be operationalised in terms of inter-rater reliability on metrics of relevance and relatedness to the ability intended to be probed by the task (see, for example Nevo, 1985). Practically, this would involve a study that evaluated the face validity of the task. In assessing the face validity of a new vocabulary task, say, participants (the raters) would rate the task on scales or questions assessing the degree to which the task appeared to measure vocabulary, or to address the specific aspect of vocabulary that the task was designed to measure (see also Chapter 5 for a detailed discussion of inter-rater reliability).

A further, and very important aspect of validity is construct validity, which concerns the degree to which a task actually assesses (rather than appears to assess) what it is intended to assess. It is beyond the scope of this chapter to discuss this in detail, but it is worth noting that good construct validity relies heavily on the quality of the underlying theoretical concepts on which the task is based (see Messick, 1995). For the researcher, ensuring construct validity essentially means ensuring that the scientific basis of the task is sound: the theoretical framework is empirically supported and internally consistent, and the characteristics of the measure are what the theoretical framework would predict. For example, if our theory of vocabulary acquisition entails a gradual accretion of known words over chronological age, then we would expect to see a steady increase of our vocabulary measure when plotted against age.

4.4 Conclusions

In this chapter we have discussed some practical aspects that are important when using either standardised or experimental tasks. Standardised tasks are often used when making a clinical diagnosis, to decide whether a child belongs to a certain experimental group or to match experimental groups to one another. As the procedure and instructions are standardised, the normed outcomes of these tasks can be compared between groups and testing sessions as well as over time.

Limitations of standardised tasks include the problem that they can only be administered by a trained professional and that often the standardised procedure and instructions do not take into account or allow permutations for cultural differences or language issues. More importantly, as with any task, they only provide information about the task at hand and thus often one is obliged to design a new experimental task in order to manipulate the dependent variable in question.

Designing your own experimental task can be time-consuming, especially when one has to control for many variables and one has to spend enough time piloting the task to ensure validity. However, if designed properly they can be used to match participants on non-central tasks demands, with the inclusion of an appropriate control condition that differs from the main experimental task only in the information required. The logic behind conventional matching procedures, based on standardised tasks or mental-age assessments, is to attempt to equate groups for these non-central demands, but these procedures approach this only indirectly.

Regardless of whether one uses a standardised task, or develops a new experimental task, there are a few issues one has to take into account when working with children. First and most importantly, when working with children one has to take development seriously. This means that one needs to use tasks that are age-appropriate and when one works with atypical groups this often requires tasks that span a large age range. This can be quite challenging both when it comes to finding a standardised task as well as when creating a new experimental task. Yet, this is very important in order to avoid floor and ceiling effects as we have discussed. Second, one needs to ensure that children pay attention to the task at hand. This can be done by monitoring where children are looking, allowing children to take breaks or by including motivational stimuli and stories when designing your own experimental task. Finally, those administering the tasks should be wary of their own eye movements and avoid looking at the correct answer, in order not to give the correct answer away as children in general look where adults are looking in order to learn new things.

Still, tasks, whether they are standardised or experimental, will only render information about the variables that are being tested. In addition, the tasks do not tell us anything about how children perform in their daily life. For example, performance on language tasks, whether standardised or experimental, does not inform us how children communicate within different social settings such as in the home or classroom. So some research questions will require a more qualitative or mixed approach which is discussed elsewhere within this volume (see also Chapters 10, 11, 13 and 14 for further discussion of mixed methods research).

Practical tips

1   Keep instructions simple and include a pre-test to check that children understand the wording used.
2   Motivation is an important aspect of children's performance. Therefore, when you design your task ensure that it includes a narrative or stimuli that children will enjoy.
3   Although reaction times (RTs) provide you with rich data sources, RTs are often very variable in children for a number of reasons (e.g., concentration during the task, motor abilities, distractability, etc.) and thus, unless one has a control task that matches the experimental task exactly except for the variable at interest, one has to question whether they should be used in research with children.

References

Aunio, P., & Niemivirta, M. (2010). Predicting children's mathematical performance in grade one by early numeracy. *Learning and Individual Differences, 20*, 427–35.

Baron-Cohen, S., Leslie, A. M., & Frith, U. (1985). Does the autistic child have a 'theory of mind'? *Cognition, 21*, 37–46.

Bayley, N. (1993). *Bayley Scales of Infant Development* (2nd edn). San Antonio, TX: The Psychological Corporation.

Bowler, D. M. (1997). Reaction times for mental-state and non mental-state questions in 'theory of mind tasks': Evidence against logico-affective states in Asperger's syndrome. *European Child and Adolescent Psychiatry, 6*, 160–5.

Brock, J., Jarrold, C., Farran, E. K., Laws, G., & Riby, D. M. (2007). Do children with Williams syndrome really have good vocabulary knowledge? Methods for comparing cognitive and linguistic abilities in developmental disorders. *Clinical Linguistics & Phonetics, 21*, 673–88.

Eisenberger, R., & Cameron, J. (1998). Reward, intrinsic interest, and creativity: New findings. *American Psychologist, 53*(6), 676–9.

Eliott, C. D., & Smith, P. (2011). *British Ability Scales* (3rd edn). BAS3. London: GL-Assessment.

Epstein J. N., Langberg, J. M., Rosen, P. J., Graham, A., Narad, M. E., Antonini, T. N., . . . & Altaye, M. (2011). Evidence for higher reaction time variability for children with ADHD on a range of cognitive tasks including reward and event rate manipulations. *Neuropsychology, 25*, 427–41.

Gould, J. (2005). Use of psychological tests in child custody assessment. *Journal of Child Custody, 2*, 49–69.

Gunn, D. M., & Jarrold, C. (2004). Raven's matrices performance in Down syndrome: Evidence of unusual errors. *Research in Developmental Disabilities, 25*(5), 443–57.

Halberda, J., & Feigenson, L. (2008). Developmental change in the acuity of the 'Number Sense': The approximate number system in 3-, 4-, 5-, 6-year-olds and adults. *Developmental Psychology, 44*(5), 1457–65.

Hervey, A., Epstein, J. N., Curry, J. F., Tonev, S., Arnold, L. E., Conners, C. K., . . . & Hetchman, L. (2006). Reaction time distribution analysis of neuropsychological performance in an ADHD sample. *Child Neuropsychology, 12*, 125–40.

Jarrold, C., Baddeley, A. D., & Hewes, A. K. (1988). Verbal and non-verbal abilities in the Williams Syndrome phenotype: Evidence for diverging developmental trajectories. *Journal of Child Psychology and Psychiatry, 39*(4), 511–23.

Jarrold, C., & Brock, J. (2004). To match or not to match? Methodological issues in autism-related research. *Journal of Autism and Developmental Disorders, 34*, 81–6.

Kail, R. V., & Ferrer, E. (2007). Processing speed in childhood and adolescence: Longitudinal models for examining developmental change. *Child Development, 78*, 1760–70.

Kaland, N., Smith, L., & Mortensen, E. L. (2007). Response times of children and adolescents with Asperger syndrome on an 'advanced' test of theory of mind. *Journal of Autism and Developmental Disorders, 37*, 197–209.

Karmiloff-Smith, A., D'Souza, D., Dekker, T., Van Herwegen, J., Xu, F., Rodic, M., & Ansari, D. (2012). Genetic and environmental vulnerabilities: The importance of cross-syndrome comparisons. *Proceedings of the National Academy of Sciences of the United States of America, 190*(2), 17261–5.

Kenworthy, L., Yerys, B. E., Anthony, L. G., & Wallace, G. L. (2008). Understanding executive control in autism spectrum disorders in the lab and in the real world. *Neuropsychology Review, 18*(4), 320–38.

Klin, A. (2000). Attributing social meaning to ambiguous visual stimuli in higher-functioning autism and Asperger syndrome: The Social Attribution Task. *Journal of Child Psychology & Psychiatry, 41*(7), 831–46.

Lange-Küttner, C. (2012). The importance of reaction times for Developmental Science: What a difference milliseconds make. Inaugural Issue, *International Journal of Developmental Science, 6*, 51–5.

Martens, M. A., Wilson, S. J., & Reutens, D. C. (2008). Research review: Williams syndrome: A critical review of the cognitive, behavioural, and neuroanatomical phenotype. *Journal of Child Psychology & Psychiatry, 49*(6), 567–608.

Messick, S. (1980). Test validity and the ethics of assessment. *American Psychologist, 35*, 1012–27.

Messick, S. (1995). Standards of validity and the validity of standards in performance assessment. *Educational Measurement: Issues and Practice, 14*(4), 5–8.

Mussolin, C., Nys, J., Leybaert, J., & Content, A. (2012). Relationships between approximate number system acuity and early symbolic number abilities. *Trends in Neuroscience and Education, 1*, 21–31.

Negen, J., & Sarnecka, B. W. (2015). Is there really a link between exact-number knowledge and approximate number system acuity in young children? *British Journal of Developmental Psychology, 33*(1), 92–105.

Nevo, B. (1985). Face validity revisited. *Journal of Educational Measurement, 22*(4), 287–93.

New Group Reading Test Digital. (2010). UK: GL-Assessment.

Phillips, C. E., Jarrold, C., Baddeley, A. D., Grant, J., & Karmiloff-Smith, A. (2004). Comprehension of spatial language terms in Williams syndrome: Evidence for an interaction between domains of strength and weakness. *Cortex, 40*(1), 85–101.

Purser, H. R. M. (2015). Experimental difficulties in neurodevelopmental disorders: Evidence from Down syndrome. In: J. V. Herwegen & D. Riby, (Eds), *Neurodevelopmental Disorders: Research challenges and solutions* (pp.199–218). Hove: Psychology Press.

Purser, H. R. M., Farran, E. K., Courbois, Y., Lemahieu, A., Sockeel, P., & Blades, M. (2012). Short-term memory, executive control and children's route learning. *Journal of Experimental Child Psychology, 113*, 273–85.

Raven, J., Raven, J. C., & Court, J. H. (2004). *Manual for Raven's Progressive Matrices and Vocabulary Scales*. San Antonio, TX: Harcourt Assessment.

Sattler, J. M. (1988). *Assessment of Children* (3rd edn). San Diego, CA: Jerome M. Sattler Publications.

Van Herwegen, J., Ansari, D., Xu, F., & Karmiloff-Smith, A. (2008). Small and large number processing in infants and toddlers with Williams syndrome. *Developmental Science, 11*(5), 637–43.

Van Herwegen, J., Dimitriou, D., & Rundblad, G. (2013). Development of novel metaphor and metonymy comprehension in typically developing children and Williams syndrome. *Research in Developmental Disabilities, 34*, 1300–11.

Van Herwegen, J., Farran, E., & Annaz, D. (2011). Item and error analysis on Raven's Coloured Progressive Matrices in Williams Syndrome. *Research in Developmental Disabilities, 32*(1), 93–9.

Van Herwegen, J., Rundblad, G., Davelaar, E. J., & Annaz, D. (2011). Variability and standardised test profiles in typically developing children and children with Williams syndrome. *British Journal of Developmental Psychology, 29*, 883–94.

Van Luit, E. E. H., van de Rijt, B. A. M., & Pennings, A. H. (1994). *Utrechtse Getalbegrip Toets (Early Numeracy Test)*. Doetinchem: Graviant.

Wagner, J. B., & Johnson, S. C. (2011). An association between understanding cardinality and analog magnitude representations in preschoolers. *Cognition, 119*, 10–22.

Wechsler, D. (1997). *Wechsler Adult Intelligence Scale* (3rd edn). San Antonio, TX: Psychological Corporation.

Wechsler, D. (1999). *Manual for the Wechsler Abbreviated Scale of Intelligence*. San Antonio, TX: The Psychological Corporation.

Wechsler, D. (2002). *Wechsler Preschool and Primary Scale of Intelligence* (3rd edn). San Antonio, TX: Psychological Corporation.

Wechsler, D. (2003). *Wechsler Intelligence Scale for Children* (4th edn). San Antonio, TX: Psychological Corporation.

Williams, D., & Jarrold, C. (2013). Assessing planning and set-shifting abilities in autism: Are experimenter administered tasks and computerised versions of tasks equivalent? *Autism Research*, 6(6), 461–7.

5

RESEARCHING CHILDREN'S CONVERSATIONS

Harriet Tenenbaum, Patrick Leman,
Ana Aznar and Cheryl To

5.1 Introduction

Developmental psychologists have long been interested in studying children's conversations as a window into children's development. Not only can analysis and understanding of children's conversations reveal what children know, think and believe about the world; conversation is also a central medium through which children develop, and come to learn about the world, themselves and others. Thus, from the perspective of developmental and social psychology, children's conversations are important to study for several reasons. First, children's conversations give us insight into children's thoughts and beliefs. Through language, children express their opinions. Imagine a 2-year-old girl who says, 'me like cheese, you no like cheese.' From this brief conversation excerpt, we can infer that this child has preferences and at least an implicit understanding of desire. Moreover, she understands that not everyone has the same preference. Were we, however, to interview her and ask her directly if people have different desires, we might assume that she would not understand the question nor be able to respond intelligently. Indeed, until age 3 years, in standard interviews children answer that two people cannot like different things (Pons, Harris, & de Rosnay, 2004). Rather than directly interviewing children about a topic that they have never considered before, researchers may choose to study children's conversations in a naturalistic or semi-naturalistic setting. Doing so may give them greater insight into what a child understands because in conversations children may respond and contribute more spontaneously than in an interview where they may feel inhibited by the formal question-and-answer structure.

Second, from such a conversation, we can learn about the syntactic competence of this child. Although only 2, this child's utterance follows the grammatical order of English (a subject-verb-object language, in which subjects come before verbs). However, at the same time we can also infer that this young child has not mastered adult grammar. Yet, we could conclude that this child has appropriated some understanding of adult linguistic conventions.

Third, studying children's conversations with parents, teachers and peers tells us about children's worlds. They provide us with information about the types of conversations in which children participate. Parents have beliefs about socialisation for their children. In everyday interactions, such as conversation, parents transmit these messages (Vygotsky, 1978), which children may appropriate and reproduce in their interactions with siblings, friends and playmates. Understanding these conversations can tell us about the socio-cultural milieu in which a child is raised, the expectations that others have for this child, and perhaps even give some insight into how this child will develop. Although conversations change with development, there are enduring patterns of interaction that are acquired in childhood and endure throughout the lifespan. For example, girls dyads tend to use more emotion words than boys dyads (see an example of a coded transcript in the Appendix to his chapter), and mothers tend to use more emotion words than do fathers when talking to their children (Tenenbaum, Ford, & Alkhedairy, 2011; Aznar & Tenenbaum, 2015). These gender effects are sometimes small and, in the case of use of emotion words in conversations, not mirrored by children's emotion understanding. However, the patterns of conversation indicate important differences in children's social behaviour and understanding of gender and relationships.

Researchers sometimes use qualitative analyses of conversations as a means to understanding detailed instances or case studies (see Part 2 for examples, particularly Chapters 6, 8 and 9). However, this chapter will discuss a quantitative approach to examining children's language and reasoning. Such an approach is important because it allows researchers to test hypotheses about conversation and development systematically, and to generalise these across a population to explain processes of developmental change more broadly. In this chapter we first consider methods for eliciting conversations between adults and children, and children with other children. Second, we will discuss a pre-existing database of conversations and the benefits and drawbacks to using this database compared with collecting one's own data. Third, we will explain how to develop a coding scheme and the need for inter-rater reliability when making systematic observations of interactions. Fourth, we will discuss how to analyse some types of data from conversations. Finally, we will provide three practical tips for research on child conversations. Throughout this chapter, we will use examples from our own research.

5.2 Eliciting conversations

Before you begin to plan your study, consider your research question. This question will guide how you think about your study. Imagine that you are interested in gender differences in emotion. Perhaps as a developmental psychologist, you think that parents might contribute to a gender difference. This question is exactly where we started (Aznar & Tenenbaum, 2013; 2015). How might you test this question? Simply asking parents whether they use more emotion words with their sons or daughters is not necessarily going to give you an accurate answer to your question. People do not always pay such close attention to the types of words they use in a conversation. To answer such a question, you would need to look at the conversations from a number of examples of mothers and fathers talking to children and then explore whether there are consistent patterns of difference in the ways in which parent talk affects boys' and girls' subsequent behaviour.

Once we had decided that we would investigate parent–child talk about emotion (Aznar & Tenenbaum, 2013; 2015), we were left with a few other questions before we could begin. We wanted to make sure that the different families in our study all had similar types of conversations. If not, our study would have a large confounding effect because we know that the type of context, even details as simple as the type of toys with which parents and children are provided, contributes to the way parents and children interact (Leaper & Gleason, 1996). While situation can influence conversations, the goal of this study was to explore the role of parental influence in the first instance. Our intention was, as far as possible, to rule out the possibility that features of a situation might cause differences in the way that parents and children spoke to each other. So we knew that we needed to make sure that the task parents and children engaged in for our study was the same for all participants. On this note, always remember to give all participants the same instructions. Keep this in mind, especially if there are a few researchers collecting data for the same project.

We chose to ask parents and children to discuss emotion-laden events. We had to decide whether we were interested in discussion of one's own emotion or other people's emotion through a play task. During play children reflect on emotions while parents guide children's ideas and beliefs about emotions (Fivush, 1993). Stories serve as an important cultural tool for expressing socio-cognitive understanding of emotions and beliefs (Fivush, 1989). Moreover, discussing someone else's emotion state may be easier for children to process because they distance themselves to focus on a cognitive understanding of emotion. In contrast, reminiscence gives children an opportunity to put emotions into perspective, which is more difficult than merely discussing present emotions (Fivush, 1989; Laible,

2004). For our study we decided to focus on both types of contexts (i.e., play and reminiscence) to see also if the contexts led to variations in how parents and children talked to one another. Because emotion words may be used rarely between parents and children, we needed to think of ways to induce conversations that would include a lot of emotion.

Based on Cervantes and Callanan (1998), we asked parents and children to tell a story together that involved four different events designed to elicit emotion: (i) the parents leave their children to go on an overnight trip, (ii) the child falls down and hurts himself, (iii) the dog runs away, and (iv) the parents return home. For the reminiscence task, we asked parents and children to discuss four events in the child's life that would elicit emotion (i.e., the first day of school, a visit to a doctor, a visit to the zoo and a time the child fell down). We videotaped parents and children in these two different conversational contexts so that we could later transcribe and code these conversations. Transcription involves typing out everything the participants say and then having a second transcriber make sure that nothing was missed. It is very time-consuming work. However, it is essential to have an accurate record of the conversation from which to start coding. On average, expect to spend eight times as long transcribing the conversations as the length of the conversation. We will discuss coding later on in this chapter.

Imagine, instead of parents, you were more interested in how emotion conversations between peers may vary with the gender of the child. Again, you would need to devise a situation in which all the children can engage in a similar way to avoid confounds based on the context. In our prior work (Tenenbaum *et al.*, 2011), we asked children between the ages of 5 and 8 years to create a story in pairs to accompany wordless picture books (Mayer, 1967). We asked girl–girl, boy–boy and boy–girl pairs to tell stories, which we recorded (see an example of a coded conversation in the Appendix to this chapter). There are many different tasks that you can use depending on what your interests are. For example, Leman and Björnberg (2010) asked children to discuss moral dilemmas (focusing on the appropriateness of different punishments) to understand how gender influenced children's conversations and whether they changed their moral views after discussions. In another study, Leman *et al.* (2011) explored how children from different ethnic groups talked when they built a Lego mosaic together to identify whether ethnicity influences conversations and task performance in collaborative settings in the classroom. What matters most is that the context of the task elicits the types of conversations you wish to analyse, and that there are no additional features (confounding variables) that could interfere with your ability to demonstrate a clear relationship between factors in a conversation.

Of course, everyday conversations are often spontaneous and rely on a host of additional factors such as whether people know one another, what their relationship is, and what they are discussing or trying to achieve with a conversation. While the need to control a task carefully is important to allow us to make inferences and generalisations, one concern with this approach is that these conversations may be viewed as contrived and not very naturalistic. Although the presence of a recording device will always alter conversations, one can choose tasks that approach the sort of naturalistic flavour of everyday conversations. We usually set up the camera before we explain the task to the participants so that by the time they start completing the tasks they are used to the camera. With the same effect, it is also useful to ask participants to do a warm-up task. And, needless to say, such conversations are almost always less contrived or artificial than formal interviews or many experimental approaches. For ethical reasons, in our opinion, researchers must always inform participants that they are in a research study. Participants need to be given enough information about the study to make an informed decision about whether they want to participate in the research. In the case of young children, we always explain in terms that they can understand what we are going to do, we ask them if they understand what they are required to do and if they want to participate. We always tell them that they can stop at any time and that they are not required to participate. We also assure them that everything they say will be confidential and that no one else will hear what they say. While some individuals may self-monitor their behaviour when they know they are under observation, it is important always to obtain consent from participants to ensure that the research process is open and transparent (for a detailed discussion on ethical procedures when working with children see Chapter 15).

However, semi-naturalistic studies can also yield important research information. Let us give you an example of a more naturalistic parent–child study. To and Tenenbaum (under review) videotaped parents and children as they visited exhibits at a natural history museum. We followed a protocol developed by Crowley and Callanan (1998). As participants entered the main exhibit, parents were told that the researchers were interested in how parents and children typically converse when visiting exhibits. They were asked to provide written consent and the researchers placed a sticker on their child's back so that we could distinguish those families who had given consent from those who had not. Families who did not give consent did not participate in the study. Other than a signature, the only information we requested from parents was their child's age and gender. Video-recorders with external microphones were placed at exhibits to record the conversations.

Because we did not tell families what to discuss, these conversations are more naturalistic than the studies we previously discussed. A great advantage to the naturalistic setting is that it may lead to more spontaneous conversations, and exploring what individuals talk about in less constrained or controlled circumstances is also an important issue for developmental and social psychologists.

5.3 Using conversations from extant datasets

One thing you need to remember is that collecting data from participants is a lot of work! It is not easy to find the participants, visit them in their homes and schools, and transcribe all the conversations. Moreover, it is extremely difficult to collect longitudinal data from different children, and even more difficult to collect truly naturalistic data. Fortunately, Brian MacWhinney and Catherine Snow set up a way for researchers in child language to share their data on the Child Language Data Exchange System (CHILDES, MacWhinney, 2000a) which can now be accessed from www.childes.psy.cmu.edu/. This database has over 100 different corpora of child language samples that a number of researchers have donated. Over 1500 articles have been published using these datasets since they were uploaded to CHILDES. Because the website for CHILDES extensively lists and describes the different corpora, and explains how to download these databases, the transcription standardisation (CHAT), and the computer program that can be used to analyse these transcripts (CLAN), we will not explain them in detail here. Instead, we will give a flavour of the types of corpora that can be downloaded from CHILDES, but we urge the reader to look at this impressive website.

The CHILDES database includes transcripts of children with friends, peers, teachers, parents and researchers. It includes conversations as well as narratives. Corpora have been donated from children speaking English (e.g., US, UK), German, Basque and many other languages. There are corpora from bilingual children, clinical samples (e.g., children with Down syndrome), and narrative samples from children telling stories (mostly frog stories; Mayer, 1967). Although the database was envisioned to examine child language and, as a result, the database tends to focus on language acquisition and on younger children, researchers have used this database to answer many other research questions.

Let's describe two corpora from CHILDES to give examples of the database and what can be done with it. One example, the Home-School Study of Language and Literacy (Dickinson & Tabors, 2001), recruited low-income families from Head Start facilities and day-care centres in the greater Boston metropolitan area. Family incomes varied substantially within the low-income range. Eighty-three children participated in the first wave of data collection when children were 3 years of age. Children and their mothers engaged in book reading when children were 3, 4 and 5 years of age. Conversations during family mealtimes were recorded at each of these ages. Mealtimes were chosen because this is a typical activity conducted by most families during which conversations take place. Parents and children also played together and the children narrated stories. Researchers have used this database to examine topics such as the frequency of explanation during mealtimes in low-income families (Beals, 1997), the types of advanced vocabulary low-income parents use with their children (Beals & Tabors, 1995), mothers' explanations about magnets (Tenenbaum, Snow, Roach, & Kurland, 2004), and literacy development (Dickinson & Tabors, 2001). However, there are plenty of other topics that could be investigated. For example, one could examine how parents explain nutrition and healthy eating to young children. Thus, these data sets form rich resources for many research questions and also for longitudinal examinations.

A great advantage for developmental researchers is that, within CHILDES, there are many longitudinal data sets of a few or even one child that can be combined to look at a particular topic in depth. For example, there are repeated recordings of Brian MacWhinney's sons, one from when he was 7 months to 5:11, and the other from 2:6 to 7:10, taken every few weeks (MacWhinney, 2000a). Combined with other corpora, Bartsch, Horvath, and Estes (2003) investigated children's and adults' use of learning. Using the CLAN program, the authors were able to search for specific words such as learn and teach.

There are limitations to using an extant dataset. A key limitation is that the data may not be designed to answer the exact question you want to ask. For example, you may be interested in whether the use of rare vocabulary may be related to children's standardised vocabulary scores. Perhaps the researchers did not ask participants to complete a measure. Second, it could be that the sample size, children's ages or participants' demographic characteristics do not exactly suit your research questions. You are therefore limited to the information the researchers have collected. However, the main advantage is the time and costs saved so you need to weigh up the costs and benefits involved and decide whether to use extant data or to collect your own. Either way, we recommend that you look at CHILDES before collecting your own data.

5.4 Coding schemes

Whether you decide to collect your own data or use a pre-existing dataset, after transcription, the next step will be to code the data. Before you start coding you will need to make a few decisions. For example, will you code the entire conversation? Will you code conversations during which participants go off topic? Or will you code the warm-up task in case you asked participants to complete one? This will largely depend on your research question, but remember to be consistent across your sample. Coding aspects of conversations into different categories allows you to identify themes and ideas in the data, and allows you to assess different features in an objective, systematic way. A category is an operational definition of the ideas that you want to analyse (i.e., valence of emotion word: positive, neutral or negative). Sometimes an existing coding scheme may be appropriate, but often you will need to develop one yourself. Bakeman and Gotmman (1997) have written an excellent book that provides a detailed analysis of how to create a coding scheme. We will briefly summarise five main points, but we urge you to read the book before developing a coding scheme. First, similar to collecting data, you need to begin with your research question. You will want to keep this in mind the entire time you are developing your coding scheme and as you modify it. You want to make sure that whatever coding scheme you develop answers your research questions. What good would it be to code instances of pretend play, however interesting, if you were interested in emotion? Of course it would not help answer your research question at all; the point is that it is important to make sure you have a match between your coding scheme and your research question. The second is that you need to keep your coding scheme simple enough that you and another researcher could understand, remember and use it. The number of categories is up to you.

Let us give a concrete example. Suppose you were interested in whether children with Williams syndrome or typically developing children use more emotion words, whether the emotion words occur as labels (descriptive) or explanations, and how parents respond to their use of emotion (Van Herwegen, Aznar, & Tenenbaum, 2014). You have collected videotapes of both sets of children reading wordless picture books with their parents and their conversations have been transcribed. In reality, you have three separate research questions. To a certain extent, you will want to develop a coding system for each question. You would need to decide for your coding scheme what constitutes an emotion word. Is it a word, such as 'happy'? Does 'like' count? What about emotion behaviours, such as kiss? There are two main methods researchers use to develop coding schemes. The first is to look at a pre-existing coding scheme, such as the one used by Cervantes and Callanan (1998). For the first two research questions in this example, using an existing coding scheme would be sufficient. They also have one for distinguishing labels and explanations. However, the third research question focusing on how parents respond is more open-ended. You could use the second method of developing a coding scheme for this research question. In this method, you read the transcripts over and over until you start to see patterns emerge from the data. Maybe you notice that parents have a tendency to change the subject, add to the child's example, respond with a question, etc. You would then develop a coding scheme to classify each one of the parents' utterances as such. A third point from Bakeman and Gottman (1997) concerns the splitting and lumping of codes. For example, let's say you have coded each instance of different emotion words (e.g., chuffed, happy, sad, gutted, etc.) into a separate category based on main categories (e.g., happy, sad, etc.). Now, let's say you are not interested in whether children use the word sad more than happy, but you are interested in whether they use more positive or negatively valenced words. You simply need to add up all the positively valenced words. You then add up all the negatively valenced words into a negative category. This process can be computed in a software package. But what if you want to look at whether the words are formal (e.g., happy) or informal (e.g., chuffed)? Because you coded the words into the larger categories, you would not have this information and would have to begin coding again. What this suggests is that you need to decide from the beginning how narrow you want your coding scheme to be and how many categories you want.

Fourth, you will need to decide if you want your coding scheme to be mutually exclusive or whether each unit can include more than one code (Bakeman & Gottman, 1997). For example, maybe you are interested in how parents explain everyday science to children. Maybe you are interested in the use of analogies and explanations. You define an explanation as using causal language, such as 'since' or 'because'. An analogy is defined as when the current situation is compared with another event. Can a sentence be both an analogy and an explanation? When referring to pictures in a zoetrope (a slotted cylinder that could be used as an animation device), what if someone said, 'We can see the horse moving because it's like how they made cartoons'? Like many issues in coding, you need to decide. Whichever way you decide fits your scheme is acceptable, but you need to be consistent.

Finally, Bakeman and Gottman (1990) argue that coding schemes evolve and change. Even if you use a pre-existing scheme, as you read your transcripts, you will need to amend your scheme. Perhaps some codes never occur. Perhaps you notice that instead of just one kind of explanation, there are numerous types. If a parent says, 'If you drop that, it will go fast', such a sentence explains a causal relation so you may decide to add such types of constructions to your coding scheme. You need to be sensitive to patterns in your data. Coding schemes should change and evolve to fit the data.

In our experience, there are a few other decisions you will need to make. One thing to remember is that you need to decide on your unit of analysis. Are you coding at the sentence level where each sentence receives a code? Or do you only code when you have something of interest? These questions are answered based on what your research questions are. So if you are interested in how frequently a code occurs in relation to other codes, then you will need to code each line. If you are interested in frequency alone (how many times the child used a certain code), you will not need to code each line, but rather the number of times the word or theme occurs. Another decision you will need to make is what will constitute your unit of analysis. Is it every time an utterance is spoken? If so, you will also need to figure out what an utterance is. You could decide that it is a sentence or a thought unit. A sentence follows typical structure, whereas a thought unit is every time an idea is mentioned, in which case you could have many thought units in a sentence. The decision is yours, but you need to be clear and consistent.

5.5 Inter-rater reliability

Given that there are many decisions you need to make, how can you guarantee you were consistent across all your transcripts? This point is where inter-rater reliability becomes important (Bakeman & Gottman, 1997). Inter-rater reliability is simply the idea that two coders agree on the codes they 'score' from a transcript, based on the coding scheme used. It is extremely important to conduct inter-rater reliability because if not, your coding could simply be your idiosyncratic view of the world. In addition, we know that people have many biases. So you could unconsciously code based on your stereotypes. Research from implicit attitudes indicates that we have biases based on gender and ethnicity (Greenwald, McGhee, & Schwartz, 1998). If you were to code conversations from children who were from an ethnic minority and majority background without inter-rater reliability, there is a chance that you might give more positive codes to ethnic majority than minority children without realising it. Or you might code in a way that is congruent with your hypotheses. Inter-rater reliability serves as a check against these possibilities.

It can be quite a process to attain inter-rater reliability. It can involve many iterations and changes to the coding scheme. Most methodologists recommend that you achieve inter-rater reliability on a sample of 20 per cent of the transcripts. This percentage is recommended by Bakeman and Gottman (1997) in developmental psychology, Thorndike and Thorndike-Christ (2011) in education research, and Neuendorf (2002) in media content analysis. Neuendorf (2002) argues that *at least* 50 units or 10 per cent should be coded by both raters for checking.

Does this sound simple? It is not always. There are a few steps coders need to take to achieve inter-rater reliability. We will explain our practice in gaining inter-rater reliability, but there are certainly other ways. The first step is to develop a very explicit, written coding scheme. Next, the coder who devised this scheme meets with a second coder and explains the coding scheme. They may code a few transcripts together to make sure that they have similar understandings of the coding scheme. Second, each person codes a few separately. The two coders return to compare and discuss their coding. At this point, we would not expect the coders to be reliable. This step is used for looking for ways in which the coding scheme is not clearly operationally defined. This meeting is important because it allows a discussion for how the coding scheme needs to adapt. In addition, the coders may have noticed something that occurs in the transcripts that might be of interest, but is not yet captured by the coding scheme. Let's say you are interested in the cognitively demanding language parents use and your coding scheme includes analogies and explanations. Perhaps in this iteration you notice that parents also ask lots of 'why' questions. Maybe you decide to add them to the coding scheme. Your coding scheme has now evolved. You would now have each person code a few transcripts to see if you agree.

This process can go through many iterations. What you must keep in mind is that you need to gain inter-rater reliability on around 20 per cent of your data set. These transcripts must be ones that you have never discussed together. It is often good to keep two times this percentage to the side until you are absolutely certain you are ready to gain inter-rater reliability. Remember that you will need to gain inter-rater reliability on anything in your data that could be perceived as subjective. This includes all coding schemes, what constitutes a sentence or a unit of analysis, and so on.

One other benefit of inter-rater reliability is that it forces you to define your categories very explicitly. If these categories and codes are not explained clearly, then it will be extremely difficult for the second coder to gain reliability. How do you assess whether you have gained inter-rater reliability? One way might be to calculate the number of times you agree divided by the total number of codes. This would be a simple percentage agreement (Bakeman & Gottman, 1997). However, it is better to use a stricter criterion. We use a Cohen's kappa, which controls for the level of chance agreement. If you have two coding categories, by chance it is expected that you to agree 25 per cent of the time. The Cohen's kappa takes the percentage agreement and subtracts out the chance agreement. Thus, it is more stringent than a simple percentage agreement. Any commercially available statistics package can calculate the kappa for you. Fleiss (1981) considers kappas between .60 and .75 (60 per cent to 75 per cent) as good and over .75 (75 per cent) as excellent.

If you attain a reliability that is good rather than excellent, it means that you still have substantial disagreement. What should you do with those cases? Typically, the two coders would meet to discuss these cases and come to an agreement. Once all of these steps are followed and you have achieved inter-rater reliability, one of the coders would then go through all the transcripts and code all the remaining cases. It is best to do this in a short space of time because of concerns about reliability drift or decay, which occurs when a coder is no longer reliable with oneself (see Cooper, Copeland, Brown, Harris, & Gourlay, 1977, for an example of reliability drift).

One important point to remember about inter-rater reliability is that it can take a long time and go through many iterations to attain excellent inter-rater reliability. Yet very little of a method section is devoted to this process. Instead, most articles devote about five lines at the most to this process including the reporting of the Cohen's kappa coefficient. When writing your method section, you need to refer to the process by which categories were defined and agreement achieved. A good coding scheme will possess a clear rationale and would be easily replicable by a new researcher, should she or he wish to use it.

Another method, which we see less frequently in the literature, is when two coders code all of the data separately and then report a percentage agreement on different categories. As we mentioned, this method may be less stringent because it overcompensates for chance agreement. Most journals prefer a kappa value on a selected amount of data, but you will need to follow the conventions in different fields.

There is one more precaution you should take to weed out biases both in your reliability and again in your final coding. You must be blind to the factors of interest at both stages. As previously mentioned, we all have biases. Suppose that your hypothesis was that girls would use more emotion words than boys would. When coding both for reliability and in the final coding stage, you should assign each transcript a number rather than a name so that you do not know whether the child in the transcript is a girl or a boy. Such a procedure will guard against some accidental bias. During the reliability stage, it is best if you can find someone with whom you can conduct your inter-rater reliability who is blind to the hypotheses, that is, they do not know what the hypotheses are. Using this method, you can avoid confirming your biases (confirmation bias), which can pose a threat to internal validity.

5.6 Analysis of data

At this stage, you have completed your reliability and your final coding. You need to answer one more question before you can begin to examine your data. This question is whether you want to analyse your data as frequencies or proportion scores. The answer to this question will depend on your research question, your design and conventions in the field. Are you more interested in how many of each category a participant uses or the general richness or proportion of the conversation dedicated to that category or topic? For example, imagine you are interested in whether low-income or middle-income children use more rare vocabulary (low frequency words). Are you interested in the frequency count of these words or the amount per utterance? You will need to consider whether you allowed the data collection to be determined by the participant or researcher. In some cases, the length of time devoted to a task is determined by participants (e.g., Cervantes & Callanan, 1998; Fivush, Brotman, Buckner, & Goodman, 2000; Kuebli & Fivush, 1992; Leman *et al.*, 2011) because of arguments that conversations occur more naturalistically this way. However, if some conversations were twice as long, it would come as no surprise if children who talk more use twice as many rare words. In this case, you may wish to use proportion scores (see Brownell, Svelotva, Anderson, Nichols, & Drummond, 2013; Garret-Peters, Mills-Koonce, Zerwas, Cox, & Vernon-Feagans, 2011; Sales, Fivush, & Peterson, 2003, for examples). Using proportions rather than total frequencies controls for participants' total amount of talk. Proportions can be calculated as the total number of items of interest divided by the total number of utterances or sentences. These need to be calculated separately for each participant.

Now you can begin to enter your data into a statistics package and start to analyse it. If you plan to use ANOVA or regression models, you will need to carefully screen your data to make sure it is normally distributed. Methods for transforming data and winsorization (a transformation of statistics of a batch or sample by transforming extreme values) are beyond the scope of this chapter. The reader is referred to Tabachnick and Fidell (2011). You now tabulate the scores for each variable of interest (e.g., emotion words). You could conduct a one-way ANOVA with the number of emotion words (or proportion) as your dependent variable. Or perhaps only about half of the children in your study used an emotion word, and you want to dichotomise your data on whether children used an emotion word or not and conduct a chi square to see if girls or boys were more likely to use an emotion word. Your analyses will be led by your research questions.

5.7 Some limitations

It would be remiss not to discuss some of the limitations of these methods, such as ecological validity. One way in which this may manifest is when people change their behaviour because they know that they are being recorded. We would expect this to happen, but less so for young children who are less concerned about demand characteristics. For example, parents could become more polite or restrained because they know they are being observed.

In actuality, people's interpretation of the task can also influence their behaviour. In a study examining parents and their preschool-aged children completing models, Renshaw and Gardner (1990) interviewed parents about what they thought the task was designed to assess. About half of the parents had a process interpretation, in that they reported that the task was designed to examine teaching and learning between parents and children. The other half thought that the task was focused on product, that is, with the child's ability to complete the task in comparison with other children. These different interpretations were related to differences in behaviour. Parents who had a process orientation used more indirect strategies, such as asking questions, to guide their children. Parents who had more of a product orientation tended to be more direct, such as completing some of the model for the child. What these findings suggest is that researchers need to be careful in assuming that the participants share inter-subjectivity with the researcher and that they interpret the task in the same way that researchers do. Researchers also need to decide carefully how they will explain the tasks to participants because slight differences in wording may influence the way in which participants interpret tasks with a significant influence on subsequent conversations.

In sum, there are benefits and disadvantages of using children's conversations as a method of studying development. Studying children's conversations in everyday situations helps us understand learning in a real-world context. Children's talk gives us insight into their thoughts and beliefs. These conversations also give us insight into the context of development. By looking at children's conversations rather than interviews, the data are protected from inaccurate recall (Ericsson & Simon, 1980). On the negative side, however, is that conversations may not be appropriate for specific research questions (e.g., do children show implicit ethnic bias?). In addition, studying conversations is time-consuming work. We recommend that researchers carefully consider different factors in finding the method that best answers their research question.

Practical tips

1   Adults and children may feel uncomfortable when being recorded. It is clear that knowing that you are being observed may alter your behaviour, but we argue that in this day and age we are more used to being constantly surrounded by cameras and being exposed to social media, especially in the case of young children. To ease participants' discomfort, it helps to place the camera and turn it on while you get to know each other and explain the tasks to them, so that by the time they start they are used to the camera. With the same

purpose, some researchers set up a warming-up task. Finally, always remind participants that no one but the research team will have access to the video files and that you are interested in everyday parent–child or peer interactions.

2   A good idea, when developing a coding scheme, is to take note of the changes that you have made to the original coding scheme along the way. As mentioned earlier in this chapter, the finalised coding scheme needs to reflect the conversations of the participants in your study. Any changes that you have made to an original coding scheme need to be justified in the writing of the methodology section. Because there may be a time delay between the creation of your coding scheme and the writing up of your methodology, keeping a short diary of the changes and the reasons for those changes may help jog your memory when it comes time to writing up findings.

3   Always make sure that your research questions guide every step of the research, from the selection of the participants and development of the coding scheme, to the analysis plan.

References

Aznar, A., & Tenenbaum, H. R. (2013). Spanish parent-child emotion talk and their children's understanding of emotion. *Frontiers in Psychology, 4*, 670.

Aznar, A., & Tenenbaum, H. R. (2015). Gender and age differences in parent–child emotion talk. *British Journal of Developmental Psychology, 33*, 148–55.

Bakeman, R., & Gottman, J. M. (1997). *Observing interaction: An introduction to sequential analysis* (2nd edn). New York: Cambridge University Press.

Bartsch, K., Horvath, K., & Estes, D. (2003). Young children's talk about learning events. *Cognitive Development, 18*, 177–93.

Beals, D. E. (1997). Sources of support for learning words in conversation: Evidence from mealtimes. *Journal of Child Language, 24*, 673–94.

Beals, D. E., & Tabors, P. O. (1995). Arboretum, bureaucratic, and carbohydrates: Preschoolers' exposure to rare vocabulary at home. *First Language, 15*, 57–76.

Brownell, C. A., Svetlova, M., Anderson, R., Nichols, S. R., & Drummond, J. (2013). Socialisation of early prosocial behaviour: Parents' talk about emotions is associated with sharing and helping in toddlers. *Infancy, 18*, 91–119.

Cervantes, C. A., & Callanan, M. A. (1998). Labels and explanations in mother-child emotion talk: Age and gender differentiation. *Developmental Psychology, 34*, 88–98.

Cooper, J. E., Copeland, J. R. M., Brown, G. W., Harris, T., & Gourlay, A. J. (1977). Further studies on interviewer training and inter-rater reliability of the Present State Examination (PSE). *Psychological Medicine, 7*(3), 517–23.

Crowley, K., & Callanan, M. (1998). Describing and supporting collaborative scientific thinking in parent-child interactions. *The Journal of Museum Education, 23*, 12–17.

Dickinson, D. K., & Tabors, P. O. (Eds) (2001). *Beginning literacy with language: Young children learning at home and school*. Baltimore: Paul Brookes Publishing.

Ericsson, K. A., & Simon, H. A. (1980). Verbal reports as data. *Psychological Review, 87*, 215–50.

Fivush, R. (1989). Exploring sex differences in the emotional content of mother-child conversations about the past. *Sex Roles, 20*, 675–91.

Fivush, R. (1993). Developmental perspectives on autobiographical recall. In G. S. Goodman & B. L. Bottoms (Eds), *Child victims, child witnesses: Understanding and improving testimony* (pp. 1–24). New York, NY: Guilford.

Fivush, R., Brotman, M. A., Buckner, J. P., & Goodman, S. H. (2000). Gender differences in parent-child emotion narratives. *Sex Roles, 42*, 233–52.

Fleiss, J. L. (1981). *Statistical methods for rates and proportions.* New York: Wiley.

Garrett-Peters, P., Mills-Koonce, R., Zerwas, S., Cox, M., & Vernon-Feagans, L. (2011). Fathers' early emotion talk: Associations with income, ethnicity, and family factors. *Journal of Marriage and Family, 73*, 335–53.

Greenwald, A. G., McGhee, D. E., & Schwartz, J. K. L. (1998). Measuring individual differences in implicit cognition: The Implicit Association Test. *Journal of Personality and Social Psychology, 74*, 1464–80.

Kuebli, J., & Fivush, R. (1992). Gender differences in parent-child conversations about past emotions. *Sex Roles, 27*, 683–98.

Laible, D. J. (2004). Mother-child discourse surrounding a child's past behaviour at 30 months: Links to emotional understanding and early conscience development at 36 months. *Merrill-Palmer Quarterly, 50*, 159–80.

Leaper, C., & Gleason, J. B. (1996). The relation of gender and play activity to parent and child communication. *International Journal of Behavioral Development, 19*, 689–703.

Leman, P. J., & Björnberg, M. (2010). Gender, conversation, and development: A study of children's conceptions of punishment. *Child Development, 81*, 958–72.

Leman, P. J., Macedo, A. P., Bluschke, A., Hudson, L., Rawlings, C., & Wright, H. (2011). The influence of gender and ethnicity on children's peer collaborations. *British Journal of Developmental Psychology, 29*, 131–37.

MacWhinney, B. (2000a). *The CHILDES project: Tools for analyzing talk.* Mahwah, NJ: Lawrence Erlbaum Associates. 3rd edn. Vol 1: The Format and Programs.

MacWhinney, B. (2000b). *The CHILDES project: Tools for analyzing talk.* Mahwah, NJ: Lawrence Erlbaum Associates. 3rd edn. Vol 2: The Database.

Mayer, M. (1967). *Frog goes to dinner: A boy, a dog, and a frog.* New York: Dial Books for Young Readers.

Neuendorf, K. A. (2002). *The content analysis guidebook.* Thousand Oaks, CA: Sage.

Pons, F., Harris, P. L., & de Rosnay, M. (2004). Emotion comprehension between 3 and 11 years: Developmental periods and hierarchical organizations. *European Journal of Developmental Psychology, 1*, 127–52.

Renshaw, P. D., & Gardner, R. (1990). Process versus product task interpretation and parental teaching practice. *International Journal of Behavioral Development, 13*, 489–505.

Sales, J. M., Fivush, R., & Peterson, C. (2003). Parental reminiscing about positive and negative events. *Journal of Cognition and Development, 4*, 185–209.

Tabachnick, B., & Fidell, L. (2011). *Using multivariate statistics.* Boston, MA: Pearson.

Tenenbaum, H. R., Ford, S., & Alkhedairy, B. (2011). Telling stories: Gender differences in peers' emotion talk and communication style. *British Journal of Developmental Psychology, 29*, 707–21.

Tenenbaum, H. R., Snow, C. E., Roach, K. A., & Kurland, B. (2005). Talking and reading science: Longitudinal data on sex differences in mother–child conversations in low-income families. *Journal of Applied Developmental Psychology, 26*, 1–19.

Thorndike, R. M., & Thorndike-Christ, T.N. (2011). *Measurement and evaluation in psychology and education* (8th edn). Upper Saddle River, NJ: Prentice Hall.

To, C., & Tenenbaum, H. R. (under review). What do parents and children talk about at a natural history museum?

Van Herwegen, J., Aznar, A., & Tenenbaum, H. R. (2014). The use of emotions in narratives in Williams Syndrome. *Journal of Communication Disorders, 50*, 1–7.

Vygotsky, L. (1978). *Mind in society*. Cambridge, MA: Harvard University Press.

Appendix: Coded transcript of two children telling *Frog goes to dinner* (Mayer, 1967)

*CH1: Erm, they are deciding what to eat while some people are playing some music.

*CH2: The band keeps on playing the music until the frog got stuck into the instrument.

*CH1: Erm, the man, they've stopped playing the music and the man's looking what's inside.

*CH2: He keeps on looking and suddenly the frog jumped on his face.

*CH1: And then he, and then they cheered.

*CH2: And then he fell into the drum.

*CH1: Erm, now there was a big hole in the drum.

*CH2: And it, and they were all laughing and upset.

%spa: $DL

*CH1: Erm, the waiter's col, got some food and the frog's trying to get the food.

*CH2: The waiter came to this lady, but the frog was inside her food.

*CH1: And the lady ate the food and she saw the frog.

*CH2: The lady got out of her chair and, and she knocked everything over.

*CH2: And the frog went flying.

*CH1: And she screamed, and then the frog went into a man's drink.

*CH2: And then the lady got really cross because she went with the, the people that were playing the instruments and they.

%spa: $NE

*CH2: they were upset as well about the frog.

%spa: $DE

*CH1: Erm then, and then the man saw the frog and with the lady, with the lady and I think he tried to kiss.

*CH2:	The man.
*CH1:	The man.
*CH2:	Everybody, everybody was trying to get the frog and, and everybody was feeling fantastic.
%spa:	$PL
*CH1:	Erm and then the man found, the little boy then pointed at the man and the mum said ssh be quiet.
*CH2:	And then he went to the fire exit and they, and the little boy pointed at him and said that's, that's my frog.
*CH1:	And then he, and then he went, he, the man went like that, he pointed and the, at somebody and he took his frog home.
*CH2:	The sister and brother were, the sister was very cross and so was, and, because they, they let the dinner go down and he got the frog back.
%spa:	$NE
*CH1:	Erm, the mum looked round and had a really bad face on her.
*CH2:	They got home and the dad got really stressed because he got his frog back and he really wasn't, he really wasn't meant to because he's leant a bad lesson and everybody was laughing poking their tongue out.
%spa:	$AE
*CH1:	And the dog went, had his, his head near the door and the boy was sad.
%spa:	$DL
*CH2:	The frog and the boy were playing together.
*CH1:	And the dog was laying on the bed.
*CH2:	With the tortoise.

Note. *CH1 is the first child, *CH2 is the second child. Lines beginning with %spa are codes. D, N, P, F following the $ denote the type of emotion coded with D standing for distress (e.g., sad, upset), N for anger (e.g., cross, mad), P for pleasure (e.g., happy, fantastic), and F for fear (e.g., stressed, afraid). A %spa line ending with an L denotes an emotion label, whereas one ending with an E denotes an emotion explanation. This conversation was transcribed in minCHAT and coded using the CLAN program (MacWhinney, 2000b).

PART 2

Qualitative methods in research with children

6

THE USE OF SEMI-STRUCTURED INTERVIEWS WITH YOUNG CHILDREN

Jess Prior

6.1 Introduction

In the past children's lives were often explored by examining the views and perspectives of adult caretakers, rather than by asking the children themselves (Kirk, 2007). However, parents can be inaccurate reporters on the lives of their children, because their answers will reflect their own concerns and issues, they may be unaware of some aspects of their children's lives such as when they are at school or with friends, or they haven't fully appreciated how their child is feeling about a particular issue (Eiser & Twamley, 1999). More recently researchers have sought to elicit responses directly from the child participants, and this has been summarised as a shift from researchers seeking information *about* children, to seeking information *from* children (Doherty & Sandelowski, 1999).

Interviews can vary in their structure from structured, through to semi-structured and unstructured interviews. Choosing an appropriate type of interview will be dependent on the research question and the approach used by the researcher (Flewitt, 2013). Structured interviews have pre-determined questions and the researcher then reads the questions in a set order and records responses. In contrast, an unstructured interview will allow the topics to be generated by the interviewee. The most common type of interview used in qualitative research is the semi-structured interview, where the researcher has some planned questions and prompts that provide an overall framework, but there is some scope for flexibility and for the interview to vary for each individual as it unfolds. The interviewer is able to vary the order of the questions or add new questions if appropriate (Flewitt, 2013; Greig, Taylor, & Mackay, 2013).

In this chapter I will consider and reflect on semi-structured interviews with children who 'look and feel different'. I will include personal reflections from my own research as a Social Developmental Psychologist with children with visible differences of the face, alongside research evidence from the diverse disciplines of Children's Nursing, Medicine, Dermatology, Social Work, Sociology and Psychology. Visible differences, conditions which include a component which is visible to others, such as a facial scar, loss of an eye or skin condition, are stressful for children and adults because the visibility can trigger negative reactions from others, can be stigmatising and can result in fewer choices about when or how the person chooses to disclose their condition to others (Joachim & Acorn, 2000). It is important that qualitative research is conducted on 'living with' chronic illnesses, disabilities or conditions, and that qualitative researchers understand how children are active in constructing and determining their own social lives (Sartain, Clarke, & Heyman, 2000). The children who have a visible difference are the experts in what it means to be a child, and indeed what it means to look different as a child, and how their appearance impacts on their daily lives and interactions at home, school and in other groups to which they belong. It is the knowledge and experiences of these children that can be understood in using qualitative research methods in general, and semi-structured interviews in particular (see Mayall, 2008, for a further discussion of how researchers can learn about children's knowledge).

The title of the chapter refers to semi-structured interviews with 'young children', which for the purposes of this chapter will refer predominantly to children in the life-stage of middle childhood (from 6–12 years). However, I have also included some studies with early adolescents where I felt it would elucidate some aspects of interviewing children with a visible difference. It is worth noting that there is a long-standing debate concerning contended views about the age at which children are competent to give accurate interviews (see Docherty & Sandelowski, 1999; Kortesluoma, Hentinen, & Nikkonen, 2003). While many published studies only to tend to recruit children over the age of 6 or 7 years, competence should not be defined by the chronological age of the child (Kortesluoma et al., 2003) but rather it is wise to consider their age alongside their broader competencies to answer the interview questions. In fact the idea of 'competence' is not straightforward, since it relates closely to the way that the meaning is constructed by the interviewer and the child as well as to the situation and context of the interview. It is always possible that inexperience can be mistaken for immaturity or incompetence in an interview with a child (Westcott & Littleton, 2005). My experience concurs with D'Auria, Christian, and Richardson (1997) that by middle childhood children are able to report their experiences of daily life, as well as their stresses and coping strategies and are the 'experts' in what it is like to grow up with a visible difference, even though they are still developing their cognitive and social skills and broad knowledge base about the world and their sense of self.

In this chapter I will first consider semi-structured interviews as a qualitative method that can be used in research with children, including the advantages and disadvantages. Second, I will discuss some key issues for the researcher who is planning to use this method with children, including establishing rapport, designing and asking questions, and including tasks or activities in the interview. Third, I will reflect on my own experience of using dyadic interviews with both young children who have a visible difference of the face and their mothers. Finally, I will provide three practical tips for research on child conversations. Throughout this chapter, I will use examples from my own research conducted with Dr Lindsay O'Dell with children who look and feel 'different'.

6.2 Semi-structured interviews

Semi-structured interviews are a useful qualitative method that can be used for collecting data with children. Kortesluoma *et al.* (2003) suggest that interviews can allow a skilled researcher to gain access to children's experiences and perceptions of the world. Semi-structured interviews are therefore suitable for researchers who are seeking to explore the child's 'world of experiences' (Kortesluoma *et al.*, 2003, p. 435), including their subjective experiences and interpretations of events, their feelings and emotions, and how they conceptualise important events in their lives.

The use of open-ended questions in semi-structured interviews with children can allow them to describe their views, beliefs and experiences in their own words, and to explain their point of view, which may differ in important ways from those of the adults around them (Kortesluoma *et al.*, 2003). As a qualitative method, the semi-structured interview allows the child space and time to express their views, without limiting their responses to a narrower range of categories, scales or coding frames that have been designed by the adult researcher. The semi-structured nature of the interviews allows flexibility for the researcher to ask questions that are appropriate for the child, in a sensitive and personalised way (Eiser & Twamley, 1999). Galletta (2013) highlights the 'unique flexibility' (p. 2) of the semi-structured nature of the interview, which has the advantage of having sufficient structure to allow the researcher to explore key concepts relating to their research question, while allowing space in the interviews for participants to reflect on new ideas. The flowing interaction between the child and the researcher can allow the researcher to pick up on issues that are important for the child, and discover what matters most to them about the topic being researched (Greig *et al.*, 2013). In the reciprocal relationship created between the researcher and participant, it is possible to gain a good understanding of their lived experiences and their views concerning the phenomenon being studied (Galletta, 2013). This ability for the researcher to 'unpack' complex ideas, and explore the textures and nuances contained in semi-structured interviews allows the researcher to closely attend to the complexity of the phenomenon under study (Galletta, 2013). In comparison with focus groups, semi-structured interviews have advantages such as: allowing a more bespoke and tailored setting suitable for the individual child to talk about sensitive issues or several issues; facilitating children who are more shy or anxious to participate; allowing flexibility in making arrangements to conduct the interview to suit the individual rather than coordinate with a group of people (see Hennessy & Heary, 2005, for further comparisons between focus groups and semi-structured interviews. See also Chapter 8 for a detailed discussion of the use of focus groups).

There are some challenges that adults can face when conducting research with children. Kortesluoma *et al.* (2003) make the point that as adults 'we will never see the world through a child's eyes, rather we will see it through various layers of experience' (p. 437). The knowledge that the adult researcher holds about children, as well as their a priori assumptions about children and childhood will influence their orientation and approach to research. There are assumptions made by the researcher about children's competencies and their ability to give an account of their thoughts and beliefs, and the linguistic abilities and skills that this would necessitate. Researchers will also have beliefs about how children differ from adults, their vulnerabilities, and social and emotional worlds. As with many other forms of qualitative research, the researcher will need to endeavour to set aside their own beliefs (as far as this is possible) and work reflectively so as not to impose their own assumptions and beliefs on the children or their interview data. (This is a process commonly called *bracketing*. Please see Ahern, 1999, for more practical tips on how to do this, for example, by identifying issues one takes for granted such as one's motivations for conducting research, or by reflecting on your own value systems and beliefs.)

Conducting interviews can be challenging for the researcher, and it requires a high level of skill by the researcher wishing to use this method as a research tool. The circumstances of interviewing children are highly sensitive to various 'interferences' (Kortesluoma *et al.*, 2003), some of which relate to the demands of the interview situation. Some of these 'interferences' include children's ability to respond to questions, their developmental capabilities, and how well they are able to negotiate the interview and cope with the questions that are being asked of them (Greig *et al.*, 2013). In addition, the child's vocabulary may limit their ability to fully answer some questions, or to abstract their feelings and beliefs in order to answer a question (Eiser & Twamley, 1999). A number of suggestions for collecting high quality interview data with young children will be explored later in this chapter, (see section 6.2.2).

Equally, there are some challenges for the child who is working with the adult researcher. Children may be wary of the adult interviewer and may try to give the 'correct' response to a question, rather than their own opinion. Bricher (1999) highlights the problem that in everyday life we ask children many questions that have a correct answer such as 'have you cleaned your teeth?' Thus, children may quite reasonably conclude that the adult interviewer is looking for a particular response. Kellett and Ding (2004) note that during their primary school years children have been taught to answer questions, and to respond even when they do not know the answer. Kellett and Ding summarise the problem succinctly when they say 'to answer "I don't know" risks being thought cheeky, awkward, or inattentive' (p. 166). This also relates to the issue of power. Bricher (1999) suggests that it is important that the researcher who is planning to use interviews gives some attention to the power imbalance that exists between adults and children. For example, if the role of the researcher is seen as similar to that of a teacher, then the child may seek further guidance and advice during the interview (Kellett & Ding, 2004). Flewitt (2013) suggests that using activities during interviews can help to diffuse some of the potential tensions that can arise between the child and the researcher, and more discussion of this can be found in section 6.3 below.

6.2.1 Considerations when using semi-structured interviews with children

If a researcher chooses to use semi-structured interviews, it is a basic requirement that they are interested in listening to the stories of children, and have designed a research question that may usefully be answered using qualitative interviews. Examples of some of the research aims/questions that have been used by researchers employing interviews with children who look and feel different include 'to explore the unfolding of the chronic illness experience for children with cystic fibrosis during middle childhood' (D'Auria et al., 1997, p. 100); 'What problems do children with Epidermolysis Bullosa actually experience as the most difficult and what is the impact of these difficulties on their daily life?' (van Scheppingen, Lettinga, Duipmans, Maathuis, & Jonkman, 2008, p. 144). In our own research we aimed to expand the existing literature by exploring the experiences and perspectives of children living with a facial disfigurement as they entered adolescence, and the issues that appeared to be important and significant to them (Prior & O'Dell, 2009). In the following section I will consider establishing rapport, and designing interview questions for use with semi-structured interviews with young children.

Establishing rapport: Setting and place

Before starting to interview the child, careful consideration should be given to establishing a rapport with the child. Researchers need to present themselves as friendly and welcoming, and allow the child some time to settle in, especially in an unfamiliar environment (Greig et al., 2013). For example in a semi-structured interview study with 6–19 year olds, van Scheppingen et al. (2008) describe a period of getting to know each other, and allowing the atmosphere to 'warm up'. The researcher needs to take care to explain to the child why they are there, and what will happen during the interview (Greig et al., 2013). One useful suggestion made by van Scheppingen et al. (2008) to help establish a rapport was to reassure the children that they were experts in their story and the interviewer didn't know the answers already.

Some researchers choose to interview a child participant in their own home because this is an environment that is familiar to the child and where the child can see that the researcher has been accepted by the parents, and the parents are in the house for the duration of the interview (Aldgate & Bradley, 2004). However, it may not always be desirable, or indeed practical, to interview children in their own home. Often interviews are conducted in a public space such as a school or hospital where the researcher can perhaps arrange more than one interview on a single day, and which may be convenient for the child and their parent(s) if they already have another appointment at the chosen venue.

Some studies, such as the van Scheppingen et al. (2008) study outlined above, conduct interviews in different settings (such as the home and the hospital) to accommodate the needs of the individual family. It may also be possible for some researchers to give children a choice over the place where they wish to be interviewed. In a study by Woodgate (1998) twenty-three adolescents aged 13–16 years were recruited from a paediatric hospital in Canada. They had been diagnosed with a range of conditions including Diabetes, Asthma, Arthritis, Crohn's disease or Ulcerative Colitis. These were all conditions that required daily treatment regimens, and where symptoms fluctuated from day to day and often included periods of stability and flare-ups. Woodgate (1998) suggested that giving participants some choice about where they wanted to be interviewed is one way of developing rapport and trust between the researcher and the participant. Of the twenty-three adolescents, seventeen chose to be interviewed in their own home and six chose to be interviewed in the researcher's office. It may not always be practicable, or perhaps desirable, to offer this kind of choice, for example if geographical distance, time or money prevents it. But, it is interesting that the children preferred different places where they felt more comfortable to be interviewed.

Another important point is to allow the child to take the interview at its own pace. Any signs of impatience can inhibit the child's responses during the interview (Kellett & Ding, 2004). Flewitt (2013) notes that interviewing is a skill that requires practice. As is the case in any social situation, the researcher should pay close attention to the child's body language to see if they are getting tired or are distracted (see also Chapters 7 and 9 for further discussion of body language). The researcher can also consider the ambience and atmosphere of the interview, to see if the child (and interviewer) is calm and relaxed, and are both feeling comfortable. Flewitt (2013) makes an important point that comfortable silences are very important in interviews to allow spaces where participants can think before they respond.

A further important suggestion about establishing and maintaining rapport comes from Bricher (1999) who reflects that in practice there are considerable individual differences between children when they are being interviewed. Some are more 'chatty' and confident, while others will need a little more time to feel comfortable with the researcher. One practical idea outlined by Flewitt (2013) is to have something to share, which the adult interviewer and the child are both interested in. The shared engagement in a task, activity or topic of conversation can help to establish a bond of communication (for example, discussing a photograph or a child's drawing. See section 6.3 below on using activities in interviews with children) that helps the child to engage with the interview.

Designing the interview questions

One of the most important practical issues facing the researcher is the necessity to design a set of interview questions that can be used as a guide during the interviews – sometimes called an interview schedule. This stage of the research process requires a lot of time, care and attention and should not be rushed. Take some time to develop your ideas and design questions that you feel will help you to answer your research question. This will require a number of drafts until you feel entirely happy with the questions, the wording and the order. The number of questions that you will include will vary between studies, and will depend on the age of the child, as well as the number of topics that need to be discussed, but it is self-evident that including more questions will add to the length of the interview.

Kortesluoma et al. (2003) suggest that the challenge is to formulate questions about the theoretical issues that are of interest to the researcher, while making sure that the questions are phrased using language that the child can understand and respond to. There is a risk that over-simplistic language could be viewed with suspicion by the child, who may then think the adult is being patronising or doesn't have a clue about what their lives are really like. Questions need to be clear and concise, not overly long or complicated because otherwise children will tend to answer a part of the question relating only to the part they understand (Bricher, 1999). Make sure your questions are jargon free and written in clear and straightforward language. Prompts and probes are useful to clarify children's meaning, but van Scheppingen *et al.* (2008) suggest it may be preferable to make careful use of probes and action words to ask what the children would do, rather than how they felt. (See also section 6.2.2 below for practical examples of how to use prompts during the interview.) Abstract concepts are likely to be very difficult for children to discuss, and Kortesluoma *et al.* (2003) suggest that concentrating on here and now situations can facilitate better responses from children. For example, in their interviews children aged 4–11 years found it difficult to answer the question 'what does pain feel like?' However they were more able to answer questions about a personal experience of pain such as 'Can you tell me how that headache felt like?' (p. 438). Furthermore, Kortesluoma *et al.* (2003) suggest that even if you are interested in children's feelings, it is still a good idea to ask them what they would do. For example 'now tell me what you would do when you have pains and it hurts' (p. 439).

In a useful discussion of some of the kinds of questions that can be used with children and young people, Greig *et al.* (2013) suggest that very young children can answer who, what and where questions, but by primary school age, children are more consistently able to reply to questions that require an explanation such as why, when and how questions. Temporal questions can be challenging, and for younger children questions about the past, present and future may be tied to their everyday routines. Scott (as cited in Noble-Carr, 2006) suggests that it is better to ask questions about activities or events in the present or very recent past for children aged 8–9 years (or younger). It is also possible for the researcher to use reflective techniques to check what the child has understood by particular terms or questions (Bricher, 1999). Interviews are also seen as an appropriate data collection method for teenagers, because they are regarded as being able to reflect on both hypothetical and personal experiences, and also because they have the capacity to arrive at a conclusion or make a judgement, and speculate about their thoughts (Woodgate, 1998). To some extent teenagers can also reflect back over their past experiences, and make comparisons with their present situation (for example, when did you first realise you were ill?) (Woodgate, 1998).

When you have finalised your interview schedule, it is very sensible to pilot it with some children and see how well it works as a research tool (after you have ethical clearance. See Chapter 15 for a discussion of ethics in relation to research with children). Consider if any of the questions are ambiguous or difficult for the child to understand. Are there any parts of the interview that are repetitive?

Did you notice anything that you had missed out? Did the child mention something that you could add as an additional question? It may be that you can make revisions to your interview schedule that will improve the clarity, ordering or focus of the interview questions, by reflecting on children's responses to your pilot interview questions. For example, were there questions that they didn't understand, or where the meaning was ambiguous, or which seemed in the wrong place in the interview? This reflective thinking is a difficult activity to do on your own, and I have found that it works much better if you can discuss your thoughts with a colleague, and together consider any changes that may be necessary to the interview schedule.

6.2.2 Conducting interviews with young children

Often interviews with children tend to be quite rapid, with short exchanges, and the interviewer will need to make frequent use of prompts and probes to understand the children's views and opinions (Noble-Carr, 2006). The use of prompts and probes will also help to slow the interview down a little and give the child some time to think. Some of these characteristically short exchanges can be seen in the interview extract shown below with Lucas,[1] an 11-year-old boy with facial scarring and a compromised immune system (his case is discussed further in Prior & O'Dell, 2009). Here, we were asking him about his experiences with his friends and peer group.

Interviewer:	'Tell me a bit about your friends, is there anything else you want to tell me that you didn't tell me earlier?'
Lucas:	'They're supportive and they don't bother me about my face or anything.'
Interviewer:	'They don't bother you about your face?'
Lucas:	'No. And once when I was ill, they wrote get-well cards for me. And they're fun and like funning around. There's . . . (lists the names of some of his friends).'
Interviewer:	'It sounds like you have a lot of good friends. Why do you like them?'
Lucas:	'They're very supportive and they don't bother me, and like, they don't look at the outside, they look on the inside. Like they see through the facial scarring.'
Interviewer:	'The inside is really important as well. What kind of things do you do with your friends?'
Lucas:	'We play games, jokes, we do judo. And we laugh together.'

Noble-Carr (2006) suggests repeating or re-phrasing what the child has said, and using prompts such as 'tell me more about that' can be very useful in interviews with children. These techniques can be seen in the extract above, when the interviewer repeats the phrase 'they don't bother you about your face . . .' where we sought to try to clarify the meaning of how or why he was being bothered. This relates to another important point, namely the use of reflective listening during the interview in order to understand the terms being used by the children. It is good practice to keep a research journal and jot down any important or striking aspects of the interview as soon as possible. For example, I noticed at the time of the interview that Lucas noted when friends were *not doing* anything negative, and this helped him to identify these children as his friends. He also considered their kind and positive behaviours such as having fun or making a card when he was unwell (see Prior & O'Dell, 2009 for further discussion).

Length of interviews

Flewitt (2013) suggests that asking how long an interview should be is 'rather like asking how long a piece of string is' (p. 23). Because of the semi-structured nature of the interviews, it is quite difficult to estimate how long an interview will take. Researchers with very little experience of talking to children may underestimate the length of time it takes them to answer questions (Kellett & Ding, 2004), and some interviews will last considerably longer than others. It is important not to over-run the length of time that you have agreed, because participants will have plans for the rest of the day. In our study interviews were sometimes conducted in private rooms at children's hospitals after routine appointments, and very often someone else waiting to use the room would rigidly enforce the 1-hour slot. However long the interview is, the researcher needs to be sensitive to the child feeling uneasy about answering a question, and the need to offer reassurance that they can choose not to answer a question, or stop the interview at any time (Aldgate & Bradley, 2004). Flewitt (2013) also reminds the researcher to pay attention to the social signals of children, such as appearing tired, and to attend to them by having a break or perhaps offering to continue the interview at a later point in time.

Be sure that you have left some time for the consent procedure, debriefing of the child (and parent) and for them to ask any questions they may have. Typically interviews with young children will last under an hour. However, your pilot study will help you to establish that the interview is manageable for the children and families you have recruited, and that every question is relevant and necessary to the research question, without unnecessary repetition.

Number of participants

How many children are recruited will depend on the availability of the sample, the aims and approach of the study, as well as a number of more pragmatic considerations such as how much money is available and how much time can be given to the data collection (Flewitt, 2013). This relates to the question of knowing 'how many interviews are enough' (Flewitt, 2013), and here the requirements of the research project (for example, university guidelines, the expectations of any funding organisation or stakeholders, peer review feedback, etc.) will also shape the ideas of the researcher.

The choice concerning the number of participants will also be influenced by the research design, and by other associated requirements. There are wide variations in the number of children who are interviewed in different studies (and indeed publications) using semi-structured interviews. For example, Sartain *et al.* (2000) employed a small number of case studies, and conducted semi-structured interviews with six children (and parents) who had chronic illnesses and explored their experiences of hospitals. These interviews lasted from 40–90 minutes and were augmented with a drawing technique (see section 6.3 for more details). The parental interviews were a little longer. These interviews were then analysed using *Grounded Theory*. In contrast, Roberts and Shute (2011) interviewed twenty-six young people aged 7–19 years who were living with a craniofacial condition (and twenty-eight parents). These interviews were shorter, ranging from 15–40 minutes long. These data were analysed using a *Thematic Analysis* (see Lyons & Coyle, 2007, for a full discussion of these methods).

It is important to note, therefore, that research that uses semi-structured interviews will show considerable heterogeneity in the interview design, length, number of participants and choice of method for analysis. This relates to the concept of *epistemology*, which is 'particular sets of assumptions about the bases or possibilities for knowledge' (Coyle, 2007, p. 11). There is not one particular blueprint for how many children to include, or how long to interview them for. Instead, the researcher is faced with a series of decisions and choices that are made as part of the research process, and shaped by considerations concerning the data that the researcher plans to collect (Coyle, 2007). (See Coyle, 2007 for a detailed discussion of epistemology and a broader introduction to qualitative research.) However many interviews are planned, it is important to be flexible, and collect more data if it is considered necessary, in order to have a strong evidence base for the analysis (Flewitt, 2013).

6.3 Using activities and task based methods in interviews with children

On some occasions researchers may decide to include an activity as part of the interview with a child (see also Chapter 9). There may be different reasons why asking the child to undertake an activity is seen as advantageous for the quality of the interview data and/or understanding the child's experience. For example, van Scheppingen *et al.* (2008) interviewed children with Epidermolysis Bullosa while they were going for a walk, playing a game or drawing. They did not offer an explanation for why they did this, other than the fact the children could participate in the interview alongside these other activities. However, Bricher's (1999) suggestion is that interviews that arise more informally during everyday activities including play or natural situations can provide the most significant data for researchers possibly because the child can talk more freely and less self-consciously.

One interesting development in qualitative research with children has been the use of photographs to promote discussion during an interview with children. For example, Boylan, Linden and Alderdice (2009) made use of photographs during interviews with children with an acquired brain injury. Photographs were included as means of promoting discussion, and to assist the child in understanding the question (for example, using a picture of a swimming pool to initiate discussion about a family swimming trip). In this study, Boylan *et al.* (2009) found that the technique was simple and effective, and helped to elicit very useful interview data. The use of photographs helps a young child to stay focussed on the topic, and provides a shared focus for the interview questions.

The use of drawings by children during a semi-structured interview may also be valuable. Sartain *et al.* (2000) conducted semi-structured interviews with six children who had chronic illnesses (such as Asthma, Cystic fibrosis or Rett's syndrome) and explored the experiences of being in hospital, and being 'at home'. They argued that including a drawing task could serve to augment the interview data, particularly for younger children (pre-adolescent) who are not too self-conscious about their drawings. Sartain *et al.* (2000) included a drawing task alongside an interview of up to 30 minutes, by asking the children to 'draw a picture about what it is like to be in hospital, compared with being at home' (p. 917). In this study this task was designed to help to draw the child into the interview, and act as a starting point for them to talk about themselves and their experiences of living with a chronic illness. The drawing also facilitated shared meaning making between the interviewer and child, in allowing the interviewer to refer to the picture and generate questions such as 'what's happening here' (p. 917). For example, one child, Nigel, drew a picture showing how he had created a niche for himself at the hospital, by moving furniture and some of his belongings to create a bespoke space that he felt more comfortable with (see Figure 6.1).

However, the researcher should be mindful that using any creative techniques or activities in interviews with children needs to be approached with caution (Punch, 2002). Certainly using 'child friendly' techniques may help the child to feel at ease during the interview, but they may also create particular challenges and difficulties. For instance, when asking a child to draw a picture, or discuss a photograph, the researcher could appear patronising, or create a feeling of pressure to deliver a performance during an interview – undermining their efforts to encourage the participants to relax and talk freely about their experiences (Boylan et al., 2009; Punch, 2002). Any task based activity will also need to be evaluated to ensure that it is assisting the child in expressing their ideas. Some children will respond more positively than others to tasks in the interview, and 'extra' tasks are rarely a substitute for carefully thought-out questions and skilled interviewing.

FIGURE 6.1 Creating a niche in the hospital. (Nigel, an 11 year old boy with cystic fibrosis)

Drawing reproduced from Sartain, Clarke, & Heyman, R. (2000) with permission from Wiley Publishers

6.4 Dyadic interviews

Bricher (1999) makes the point that any research project with children will also involve interactions with parents. The researcher will need to decide whether to interview the child on their own, or with a parent present, or whether to interview the parent and child together (called a dyadic interview). Interviewing a child on their own allows them space to talk without interruption and without a parent 'taking over' from a child. However, some children need the comfort of having a parent with them, and a researcher may need to be flexible to consider whether interviews with individual children are being constrained, or improved by the presence of a parent (Bricher, 1999). Whatever the researcher has planned in advance, it is advisable to ask the child and the parent(s) what they would prefer.

In our own research, we made use of dyadic interviews with four children, aged 11–13 years, and their mothers (Prior & O'Dell, 2009). All of the children had a visible difference of the face, which they had lived with since infancy. In each family the mother and child were interviewed together, asking the child some questions first, before asking the mothers additional questions. These dyadic interviews seemed to facilitate supportive and collaborative interviews, with both participants interjecting with comments and snippets of information whenever they chose to. During the course of the research we came to see these dyadic interviews as an extremely valuable research tool.

One of our participants, Ashley,[2] was extremely shy at the start of the interview and slightly unwilling to answer questions. When he was asked, 'Do you want to tell me anything?' he replied, 'Ask mum.' However, once the interview with his mother was underway, he was then able to find his own voice, make comments, clarify issues and 'chip in' to add to what she was saying. This created a joint meaning making between the child and the parent, and allowed us to gain rich and detailed data from the researcher and both participants as well as from the discussion *between* the two participants. Consider this example from the interview, where Ashley and his mum, Susan, are discussing the problems he encountered using public transport and feelings of being unable to attend a 'fun day' organised by the national charity Changing Faces.[3]

Susan:	'They've got a fun day in June, but we wouldn't be able to go, cos you know I can't take him on big trains. You know it's a bit . . .'
Interviewer:	'What happens if Ashley has to go on the big train?'
Susan:	'He's been on the big train, but you know people stare at him and he starts getting upset and screaming and shouting.'

Interviewer:	'What do you say to them when they stare at you, Ashley.'
Ashley:	'I just tell them.'
Susan:	'They (Changing Faces) told him to say, like, why are you staring at me? Hey don't look at me, let's talk about something else. Some days he couldn't cope with that, they'd catch him in a really bad mood. But other days he might say "Oh well, don't mind my eye, what football team do you support?" '
Ashley:	'It depends.'

We felt that without the support he gained from having his mother with him in this dyadic interview, it was very unlikely he would have been able to continue with the interview. His brief contributions added to his mother's more detailed explanation of why using public transport had created problems for Ashley in the past. In this example we can see how the use of open-ended questions in the interview helped to maintain the dialogue between the child, the mother and the interviewer, encouraging them to answer questions as fully as possible. The flowing interaction created a shared meaning making, and resulted in richer and more interesting data than could have been obtained by interviewing Ashley on his own.

6.5 Concluding the interview and analysing the data

When concluding an interview with a young child, the researcher needs to make sure that the child is aware that the interview is coming to an end, and has the opportunity to ask any questions they may have (Bricher, 1999). Children also need to be offered the right to withdrawal (Bricher, 1999) that extends to letting the child know that they can withdraw part or all of their data after the interview has ended. In the case of Lucas, I reminded him that his mum had my email address and he could get in touch after the end of the interview and say 'I want you to take that out'. Lucas then replied: 'There is one thing Jess. Can you change the list of names of my teachers?' I was then able to reassure him that all of his teachers' names would be changed (as is standard practice for all names to be changed when transcribing interview data to protect anonymity). Finally, give the child a little time and space to collect him/herself before leaving the interview room, especially if they have talked about personal feelings and experiences.

As a final comment, when planning your study you need to consider the method of analysis you will use to analyse your interview data. You need to be clear from the start what your aim is in using the interviews, and which method or approach you are adopting. A full discussion of interpreting and analysing qualitative data is beyond the scope of this chapter, but an excellent comparison of four main approaches in qualitative research, Narrative Analysis, Discourse Analysis, Inter-pretative Phenomenological Analysis and Grounded Theory can be found in Lyons and Coyle (2007).

6.6 Conclusions

Semi-structured interviews, as a research technique with young children, provide the researcher with a key to understanding the world from the perspective of the people who understand childhood experiences the best, namely the children themselves. As researchers we need to conduct interviews in ways that will best enable the child to convey their experiences. In this chapter we have seen how establishing trust and rapport, asking appropriate and sensitive questions, and using tasks and activities in interviews with young children, with or without a parent present, can improve the quality of the data that we collect. To be a competent researcher, you will need to remain curious and interested in the *world of experiences* (Kortesluoma *et al.*, 2003) of the child, and to try to find ways of understanding their point of view. In my own interviews with children who 'look different' I have sometimes felt, for a short while, that they have allowed me to step into their world during my interviewing, and collect information that it might not be possible to otherwise have discovered. This is the unique contribution of semi-structured interviews as a research tool for working with young children.

Practical tips

1   Sketch out your ideas for your interview questions and spend time discussing them with a colleague, collaborator or supervisor. Do not rush this stage. One useful tip is to read the questions to another person, because they often sound quite different when spoken out loud. Check if the wording of the questions is clear and comprehensible for children in the age group you plan to research, if possible by piloting the questions with a small sample of children. Make sure you allow time to reflect on your questions and make any changes that are needed to the final schedule of questions.

2   Pay considerable attention to establishing a rapport with the child you will be interviewing, so there is a feeling that you are a safe and trustworthy person to talk to. This is the corner stone of the interview. Make sure the child knows who you are, and why you are there, as well as what will happen next. I find that most young children like to explore the recording equipment that I have brought along, and record a small section of speech themselves and listen back

to their voice on the recorder. This is often the source of much amusement (as a useful by-product, this is also a good test that the recording equipment is working properly).

3   Remember that all research with children will inevitably involve adults such as their parents, carers and others. Take time to consider whether for the study you have planned, it is better to interview young children on their own, or with a parent or carer present (in a dyadic interview), and, if possible, ask the child what they would prefer.

Notes

1   A pseudonym has been used to protect the participant's identity.
2   Pseudonymns have been used to protect the participants' identity.
3   Changing Faces is a national charity based in London, UK. They are a charity for people and families who are living with conditions, marks or scars that affect their appearance. Their website is www.changingfaces.org.uk.

References

Ahern, K. J. (1999). Pearls, pith and provocation: Ten tips for reflexive bracketing. *Qualitative Health Research, 9*, 407–11.

Aldgate, J., & Bradley, M. (2004). Children's experiences of short-term accommodation. In V. Lewis, M. Kellett, C. Robinson, S. Fraser & S. Ding. (Eds), *The reality of research with children and young people* (pp. 67–93). London: Sage.

Boylan, A-M., Linden, M., & Alderdice, F. (2009). Interviewing children with acquired brain injury (ABI). *Journal of Early Childhood Research, 7*, 264–82.

Bricher, G. (1999). Children and qualitative research methods: A review of the literature related to interview and interpretive processes. *Nurse Researcher, 6*, 65–77.

Coyle, A. (2007). Introduction to qualitative psychological research. In E. Lyons & A. Coyle (Eds), *Analysing qualitative data in psychology* (pp. 9–29). London: Sage.

D'Auria, J. P., Christian, B. J., & Richardson, L. F. (1997). Through the looking glass: Children's perceptions of growing up with Cystic Fibrosis. *Canadian Journal of Nursing Research, 29*, 99–112.

Docherty, S., & Sandelowski, M. (1999). Focus on qualitative methods. Interviewing children. *Research in Nursing and Health, 22*, 177–85.

Eiser, C., & Twamley, S. (1999). Talking to children about health and illness. In M. Murray & K. Chamberlain (Eds), *Qualitative Health psychology: Theories and methods* (pp. 133–47). London: Sage.

Flewitt, R. (2013). Interviews. In A. Clark, R. Flewitt, M. Hammersley, & M. Robb (Eds), *Understanding research with children and young people* (pp. 136–53). London: Sage.

Galletta, A. (2013). *Mastering the semi-structured interview and beyond. From research design to analysis and publication.* New York: NYU Press.

Greig, A., Taylor, J., & Mackay, T. (2013). *Doing research with children. A practical guide.* (3rd edn). London: Sage.

Hennessy, E., & Heary, C. (2005). Exploring children's views through focus groups. In S. Greene & D. Hogan (Eds), *Researching children's experience: Approaches and methods* (pp. 236–52). London: Sage.

Joachim, G., & Acorn, S. (2000). Stigma of visible and invisible chronic conditions. *Journal of Advanced Nursing, 32(1),* 243–8.

Kellett, M., & Ding, S. (2004). Middle childhood. In S. Fraser, V. Lewis, S. Ding, M. Kellett, & C. Robinson (Eds), *Doing research with children and young people* (pp. 161–74). London: Sage.

Kirk, S. (2007). Methodological and ethical issues in conducting qualitative research with children and young people: A literature review. *International Journal of Nursing Studies, 44,* 1250–60.

Kortesluoma, R-L., Hentinen, M., & Nikkonen, M. (2003). Conducting a qualitative child interview: Methodological considerations. *Journal of Advanced Nursing, 42,* 434–41.

Lyons, E., & Coyle, A. (2007). (Eds). *Analysing qualitative data in psychology.* London: Sage.

Mayall, B. (2008). Conversations with children: Working with generational issues. In P. Christensen & A. James (Eds), *Research with children: Perspectives and practices* (pp. 109–24). Oxford: Routledge.

Noble-Carr, D. (2006). *Engaging children in research on sensitive issues.* Institute of Child Protection studies. Retrieved from www.dhcs.act.gov.au/__data/assets/pdf_file/0005/10301/Engaging_Children_LitReviewEngaging.pdf on 3 June 2015.

Prior, J., & O'Dell, L. (2009). 'Coping quite well with a few difficult bits': Living with disfigurement in early adolescence. *Journal of Health Psychology, 14,* 731–40.

Punch, S. (2002). Research with children. The same or different from research with adults? *Childhood, 9,* 321–41.

Roberts, R. M., & Shute, R. (2011). Children's experience of living with a craniofacial condition: Perspectives of children and parents. *Clinical Child Psychology and Psychiatry, 16,* 317–34.

Sartain, S. A., Clarke, C. L., & Heyman, R. (2000). Hearing the voices of children with chronic illness. *Journal of Advanced Nursing, 32,* 913–21.

Van Scheppingen, C., Lettinga, A. T., Duipmans, J. C., Maathuis, C. G. B., & Jonkman, M. F. (2008). Main problems experienced by children with Epidermolysis Bullosa: A qualitative study with semi-structured interviews. *Acta Dermato-Venereologica, 88,* 143–50.

Westcott, H., & Littleton, K. S. (2005). Exploring meaning through interviews with children. In S. Greene, & D. Hogan (Eds), *Researching children's experience: Approaches and methods* (pp. 141–57). London: Sage.

Woodgate, R. L. (1998). Adolescents perspectives of chronic illness: 'It's hard'. *Journal of Pediatric Nursing, 13,* 210–23.

7

ETHNOGRAPHIC STUDIES OF YOUNG CHILDREN

Eva Gulløv and Lisbeth Ljosdal Skreland

7.1 Introduction

Ethnographic research investigates the everyday lives of people. When studying children, the aim is to understand what kind of life children are part of, what values and understandings they grow up with, and how they perceive and make sense of their social and cultural surroundings. Carrying out an ethnographic study means to invest one's time and body in observing and interacting with the children of interest in order to get a deeper understanding of the culture the children are embedded in. The advantage of the approach is, thus, that it gives a richer and more varied material than passing out questionnaires or listening to people's narratives in interviews alone (Alvesson & Sköldberg, 2008).

To do so may sound easy. Yet, it demands a host of reflections, some of which we will address in this chapter. It is not enough to say 'I did fieldwork with twenty children', 'I carried out participant observation' or conducted 'semi-structured interviews'. Fieldwork, participant observation and interviews are not objective techniques to be carried out regardless of context and project (see also Chapters 6 and 8 for more detailed consideration of interviews, and observations and fieldwork with children). Any choice of method requires explicit reflections on the use of concepts and categories, the position of the researcher, and issues related to social, physical and cultural contexts. Also, ethical concerns are basic to any ethnographic research process, not least when the object of study is children (see Chapter 15 for a detailed discussion of ethical issues when working with children).

By exploring over time the ways in which children act and relate to their physical and social surroundings, the purpose of the approach is to understand the different conditions, obstacles and opportunities that characterise the life of individuals as well as groups of children. In this attempt, focus is directed equally at children and their social processes as well as at the material, discursive, cultural and social environments they interact with. Using an ethnographic approach represents an effort to understand what it entails to be a child in a given place, in terms of both experience and conditions. This will allow the researcher to be able to explain the interrelationship between children and contexts defining, and defined by, individual children and groups of children.

Thus, the ethnographer investigates children's everyday lives, their experiences, as well as their social and cultural surroundings. In this way, ethnographic child research is also social science in the sense that it explores more general aspects of society concerning categories, relationships, hierarchies and values, distributions and distinctions – all aspects of importance to individual children as well as society (see for example James & Prout, 1990; Hirschfeld, 2002).

7.2 What kind of knowledge is provided?

To study children's lives means selecting a site of study or following a specific group of children over a period of time, in order to become familiar with their perceptions, preferences and reasoning. But how can a study of a few children over time provide more general insight into the lives of children in a given society? Can we speak of a particularly 'child perspective', and if so, what does it mean? In any group of children there will be many co-existing perceptions, interests and positions, which cannot be summed up in a single perspective without ignoring variations, struggles and disagreements. Summarising the perceptions of a selected group of children runs the risk of presenting children as a more homogeneous social category than is actually the case.

While aware of this, we will, nevertheless, argue that a study of a small number of children can provide important contributions to our knowledge of children and childhood. However, rather than regarding such a 'child perspective' as a representational concept (reducing children's various understandings to a single perspective), we view it in relational terms, indicating the necessity of taking the child's position into account. Exploring children's various experiences and perceptions can add to existing knowledge on social relations and cultural values, as they speak from a specific position in the generational structure of society without, however, perceiving it in the same way. Examining how specific children experience their surroundings provides knowledge not only about their lives but also more generally about what it entails to be a child (and an adult) in the setting of investigation (see for example the seminal studies of Bluebond-Langner, 1980; Connolly, 1998; James, 1993; Thorne, 1993; Willis, 1977).

This relates to the fact that children are at the same time an invested social category and social actors. In all societies, there are forces engaged in adjusting and directing children for the sake of reproducing values, positions and legitimacy. Every society has institutional regimes, formed around various religious, political and educational interests, to ensure the upbringing and social incorporation of new members of society. It follows that exploring children's everyday lives may provide insight into more general societal values and priorities. Yet, as the growing body of childhood studies (most referring back to the pivotal works of James, Jenks, & Prout, 1998) over the last 25 years have documented, children do not passively reiterate structural and cultural determinants; rather, they participate actively in encounters with their environments on the basis of individual experiences and dispositions. Therefore, the interest of ethnographic child research is not directed at one-way processes of transmission in which children passively adopt the norms and purposes of others, but rather at understanding the complex social processes in which children actively take stock, appropriate or react against the norms and ambitions of their environments (e.g., Ferguson, 2001).

Analysing such complex processes requires time, and ethnographic observations are in fact characterised by their duration. The precise amount of time needed will of course depend on the specific research questions. However, as the aim is to get a deep understanding of children's lives in a specific social and cultural setting, it will rarely be advisable to spend less than 2 or 3 months on observing.

7.3 Researching a well-known category

A particular challenge when studying children and childhood is linked to the fact that the topic is bursting with meaning and significance long before the researcher enters the field. Statements about children are abundant in the public debate, and we are constantly fed new 'truths' about children and the risks to their wellbeing. As a scholar interested in exploring issues concerning children, it is necessary to challenge such basic assumptions about how children 'are' in order to produce new knowledge. It is, however, illusionary to believe that we can get rid of all preconceptions in order to view children more objectively. There is no neutral understanding of children. Rather, the goal is to become able to identify different personal and cultural perceptions of children and childhood in order to review these systematically.

The sociologist Pierre Bourdieu argues that a fundamental action for the researcher is to 'pre-construct the object', which means to identify and 'break with' commonplace understandings, as these are often implicit parts of the scientific object without the researcher realising (Bourdieu, Chamboredon, & Passeron, 1991, pp. 248–9). This is particularly true when it comes to the study of social groups (youth, alcoholics, the mentally ill, immigrants, elderly people) that are often predefined by demarcations taken for granted and associated with worries and problems (Bourdieu et al., 1991). The point is that such categories appear more unambiguous than they are, and therefore present an unrecognised risk of influencing the researcher's understanding and interpretations from the very outset of a project.

7.4 The problem with age

The need for a break with implicit pre-conceptualisations is particularly pertinent when it comes to the notion of age, as the relation between age and competencies varies enormously cross-culturally (Lancy, 2008; Montgomery, 2009). When a specific study chooses a particular group of children, such as 8-year-olds rather than 12-year-olds, the choice is often not motivated or based on ideas of a developmental structure, which are rarely explicated or investigated (see also Chapters 4, 5, 6 and 9 for further consideration of the age of the child in relation to specific research methods).

In their often-cited book on participant observation among children, Fine and Sandstrom (1988) argue for the need to operate with an age-defined phase classification of childhood. 'As children change, so do the demands of the researcher' (Fine & Sandstrom, 1988, p. 48), explain the authors; hence the examination in the book of three age groups: *preschoolers*, *preadolescents* and *adolescents*, and the various demands these age groups make on the researcher. They advocate that the researcher takes up what they call a 'friend role' in relation to children implicating to refrain from enforcing rules or reprimand in ways that other adults do (see Corsaro, 1985 for an elaboration on 'friend role'). The intention is to downplay adult authority, although the extent to which this is possible depends on the children's age and stage of development. Whereas an ethnographer would normally award adult informants 'equal status' regardless of social status, a researcher of children is not, according to Fine and Sandstrom, able to do the same (Fine & Sandstrom, 1988). In this way, they argue for a special 'children's edition' of ethnography, taking into account differences of authority between researcher and children.

As discussed elsewhere (Gulløv & Højlund, 2003), the question is, however, whether the challenges to the research role are principally different from those faced by researchers undertaking participant observation with any other group of participants who are different from the researcher's own social circles. Does not any participant observation require specific considerations and adjustments of roles? And is an ethnographer not always involved in questions of authority in relation to the people whose perspective they seek to portray? Commenting on this, the sociologist and childhood researcher Anne Solberg argues:

> Although one obviously has to approach a 4-year-old differently from a 14-year-old, in ordinary social interaction as well as in research encounters, I suggest a certain reluctance among researchers with respect to drawing conclusions about these differences, because this may maintain and strengthen our prior assumptions about how children 'are'.
>
> (Solberg, 1996, p. 54)

Anne Solberg suggests concentrating less on the age issue and more on the children's situational context. Solberg's argument is that, despite age being an unavoidable biological condition, the social construction of the meaning of age is a factor so decisive that one cannot help but become part of this construction when defining a 10-year-old as essentially different from a 14-year-old.

These concerns lead us to argue that a researcher should explicitly explain why a specific age group has been selected for study. It would be an illusion to believe that we are not subject to some – perhaps stereotypic – understandings of how children of different ages are. Yet, such understandings need to be made transparent in order to reflect their implications for the relation between children and researcher, and for the design and outcome of the study. This is not to ignore either biological differences or the way generational inequalities manifest themselves in children's everyday lives. Children are smaller, have less experience and do not typically have the same repertoire of vocabulary or the same privileges as adults. As adult researchers, we have to specify which age groups we work with. However, as soon as we begin to create guidelines for how this should be done in relation to specific age groups, we risk ending up with rigid assumptions about how children *are* and what needs they have. In a scientific context, these preconceptions must be part of the object of study, as they will inevitably have an impact on children's lives.

7.5 Studies in child institutions

Reflections on preconceptions become particularly urgent when studying children in institutional settings. Children in most contemporary societies spend many hours every week in different institutional arrangements, particularly schools. Child institutions are therefore commonly used when researchers want to investigate children's everyday lives. Here, many children arrive at the same time, it is fairly easy to get access and uncomplicated to follow children around, and opening hours and institutional schedules make planning relatively straightforward.

It is, however, not only the physical framework and schedules that are pre-organised; also the educational work and organisation of social life are bursting with ideas of what children are and need – ideas that slip into everyday organisation unnoticed (Albon & Rosen, 2013). The division of children into age-defined classes may serve as an example. Regardless of individual children's skills and competencies, they will often be classified according to age, affecting who they spend their time with, what tasks they are given, what they can do and what expectations they meet. Yet, the more rigid the age divisions and age-related requirements, the more the actions of children might confirm the relevance of age. If the researcher is not acutely aware of how the institutional organisation itself helps shape certain ways of being a child, the research project may unwillingly reaffirm rather than explore these perceptions. In this way, the institutional organisation may have a self-perpetuating impact on the object of study. As pointed out, the work of unravelling ideas about children is necessary preliminary work. Yet, paying close attention to the influence of predetermined understandings is not only part of the process of preparation, but a reflexive precondition that follows the ethnographer throughout the research process. When the fieldworker relates to children, their parents, siblings, caretakers or teachers, making observations in child institutions, homes or playgrounds, this need to reflect on preconceptions is urgent.

7.6 Children as informants

The last 25 years or so have witnessed an extended scholarly debate on the role of the adult researcher in relation to children (e.g., Christensen & James, 2000; Corsaro, 1985; Fine & Sandstrom, 1988; Lærke, 1998; Mandell, 1991; Mayall, 2000; Thorne, 1993). The scope of the present chapter does not allow for a detailed revision of the various positions. Instead, we will point out that the debate itself might have an essentialist tinge of which we are sceptical. Whether describing, like Fine and Sandstrom, the differences between researcher and child in biological terms, or more subtly presenting a 'least adult' or 'unusual type of adult' role, as several contemporary ethnographers do, there is, as discussed by Albon and Rosen (2013), a risk of naturalising socially and culturally established differences. Our experiences from fieldworks in early childhood settings have taught us the importance of not considering intergenerational relationships as different from any other relationships that we, as scientists, engage in. Children do not differ more from adults than other adults living in different social or cultural contexts can do, and it is, therefore, possible to handle the problem of children's 'strangeness' in ways completely comparable to those used by sociologists, anthropologists and journalists striving to familiarise themselves with the way in which other people experience their lives. It is a general requirement in any qualitative exploration that the researcher adjusts the methods to best suit the various informants' different competencies and circumstances.

Rather than developing a design based on pre-existing notions, we see it as one of the greatest challenges to become a person who children (and adults) can accept. It requires time and personal investment to become acquainted with informants and obtain confidence. In our research, both of us have experienced how being interested, patient and letting the children approach you in their own time are a fruitful way to gain confidence. And once accepted, it is possible, through daily conversations and observations, to get to know what is at stake for informants in the interactions they are involved in, what makes sense to them, what individual children are interested in, how social rules work, and which patterns of status and principles of inclusion and exclusion exist. This knowledge is a prerequisite for understanding children's various interpretations, reasoning and relations.

7.7 Making broad observations

Because ethnographic research addresses the ways in which people interact with and make sense of their surroundings, the social, physical and cultural contexts will always be part of the object. We cannot understand the way a child orients itself, prioritises its actions and makes sense of situations without knowing the social context. Who is present and who is not? Who has the power to define activities and manage time, and who are expected to follow the structure? What are the different perspectives of the actors? Are they in accordance, do they differ, and if so, do their divergences relate to different positions, roles and classifications? Such issues need to be pursued in order to know the social order that children relate to. Not only does this entail that the observations must include the actions of everyone present; it also requires more systematic knowledge of the situation observed, i.e., where it takes place and what that means for the actions. Also the time structure, the interior decor and the atmosphere of a place all have an impact on behaviour, providing opportunities and setting limitations for movement and performance. It makes a difference to a child's actions, interaction and display of competencies, whether they take place in a swimming pool, a classroom, on a public playground or at home, just as it matters what time it is in the day. So, observing in everyday settings involves careful consideration of the time and place of action, including awareness of social positions, roles and relationships, as these parameters will inevitably influence the behaviour and interpretation of a child (see also Chapters

8 and 9 for further consideration of place and context on research with children).

It is, furthermore, essential to pay attention to the material structure of a location. In many child institutions (schools and day-care centres), for example, it is noteworthy how chairs and tables vary in size and number, indicating two social categories: a mass of children and a single adult. Without anyone ever commenting on the organisation, the furnishing itself supports a certain categorisation, structure of authority and distribution of people. Also, the vertical organisation has social implications, evident, for instance, when costly or hazardous materials are placed high up on a shelf, while cheap crayons, paint and paper are placed near the floor. Without making it explicit, the distribution of things supports an age-based hierarchy with the grown-up as the one with the legitimate right to decide over activities and materials.

The examples indicate the way cultural notions of children, authority, development, learning and care frame the settings children are observed in. This is particularly true in child institutions established to ensure that children develop and learn in appropriate ways (see for example the discussion in Albon & Rosen, 2013). Moral judgments pertaining to right and wrong, clean and dirty, essential and unimportant, decent and inappropriate, etc. influence the way institutional life is organised and the way children's actions are met and interpreted. In order to capture such values it is necessary to make broad observations of interactions between all agents – human as well as non-human.

7.8 Reading children's bodies

Studying young children reminds us that it is necessary, when striving to understand other people's views and experiences, not only to listen to their speaking but also to focus systematically on the way they use language, their pauses and silences, their movements, gestures and facial expressions. Young children use their bodies a lot, and in a striking variety of ways. They run, jump, dance and climb; they twist and sway, toss and turn. These movements are part of the way they express themselves, deal with their physical and social environments, interact and communicate. Although the amount of movements is probably a distinctive characteristic of young children, it is obviously not reserved for children to use their bodies when relating to the surroundings. We all engage with the world through our bodies, communicating and interpreting through our senses (Schilhab, Juelskjær, & Moser, 2008). Noticing the various corporal expressions is, thus, a prerequisite for understanding human engagement. Yet, such an understanding will inevitably be based on an ascription of meaning reflecting the researcher's personal interpretation of bodily communication. In order to avoid an interpretation being too subjective, it is important to carry out very detailed observations. Video recordings have proven to be particularly useful in this regard.

Methods of recording have a tendency to focus on verbal interaction. Even when dealing with filmed material, the academic tradition of producing texts requires a transcription, which gives priority to the spoken word and risks overlooking or simplifying movements and gestures in the descriptions. As observers, we need to develop ways of grasping how children engage and express themselves through their bodies in specific kinds of 'choreography'. Also, we need to consider how to represent such complex bodily displays. This need became obvious to one of the authors, Eva, in a study exploring the social relations of preschoolers. Having observed interaction between the children on a daily basis for 2 months, she decided to replace the notebook with a video camera. Watching through the footage, she realised how little attention she had paid to the ever-present silent children who, like herself, sat close to the walls, watching the more influential children's organisation of themes, roles and course of play. In the notebook, she had minutely written down all linguistic statements and gestures by the defining children, but she had overlooked how the silent audience was also part of the interaction through tacit support, display of interest and enthusiasm, and availability as potential playmates for the more actively engaged children. Furthermore, Eva became aware how often the 'silent' children in contexts with equals would turn into definers themselves, using expressions and gestures they had picked up by observing the more experienced children. As the aim of the study was to investigate children's social relations, this distribution of roles, obviously, was of vital importance. In this case, the change in method allowed the researcher to recognise the bias of the spoken word and see aspects of interaction she had so far overlooked.

7.9 Interviewing children

In the same way that observing children does not, in principle, differ from observing other groups of informants, conducting interviews is not fundamentally different either. And yet there are some particular challenges when interviewing very young children (see also Chapter 6 and 9 for further discussion of interviewing with children). Most young children do not have the required experience to formulate in general terms reflections on life, and often they will find the organised interview situation rather strange, not knowing what is expected of them (Boyden & Ennew, 1997). We have both experienced awkward situations with children who either did not respond to questions or expressed their boredom unmistakably, often trying to divert the situation by use of some of the appealing materials in the unfamiliar room the interview was assigned to. Other typical situations are the conversation with a child trying the best to respond exactly as he or she believes the researcher expects, or the child who escapes the interview after a few moments.

Carrying out an informative interview requires more effort than simply figuring out how to ask understandable questions – although of course that is essential. It requires that the whole situation be considered in order to make it meaningful to the interviewee. Obviously, such reflections are important in any kind of interviews, yet they seem to be particularly acute when dealing with young children. All ethnographic research makes use of both informal conversations and formal interviews. When dealing with young children, it may prove useful to downplay the formality in favour of a more spontaneous dialogue with one or more children. This requires, however, careful preparation, making clear for oneself the topics to be addressed, in order to be able to ask questions at every opportunity that arises. Our experience is that insights into children's ideas and views often come more fluently while walking with a group of children or while helping someone getting dressed. Sitting with a small group of children drawing, while reflecting on a specific incident, may prove very informative, as may a guided tour by a single child who will not only point out important sites but also illustrate important points through body language. As we have both noticed, it is easier to have an in-depth conversation when not looking the child straight in the eye like in a more formally organised interview. In continuation of this, it is necessary also to pay attention to the way one's own body is part of the conversation. In the same way that downplaying the formality can be a way to create an atmosphere of trust, the generational distance can be moderated by physically positioning oneself where the children are (on the floor, on the same kind of chairs, up in a tree) in order to communicate interest and parity.

Regardless of the degree of formality, the most important thing is, however, to base the conversation on actual incidents that the child has experienced. Abstract or general questions produce vague answers (if any at all) that can be rather difficult to analyse. The specific starting point does not mean that the conversation will not provide general knowledge. In Lisbeth's (Skreland, 2015) studies of rules in kindergartens, regular talks with the children provided interesting insights into the amount of rules the children experienced, although the teachers believed there were only a few basic guidelines. In contrast to the teachers, children could, for example, easily articulate many restrictions concerning behaviour at the playground, such as 'do not jump from the playhouse-roof', which had great impact on their activities. Lisbeth's extensive knowledge of daily activities made her able to ask precise questions, thus gaining insight into more general aspects of institutional life.

7.10 Using participant-based methods

Some researchers work systematically with research methods directed at engaging children in the research process, e.g., using drawings, diaries, schedules, photographs, etc. (for a detailed discussion see Christensen & James, 2000; Punch, 2002). There are several benefits to adding such participant-based approaches to the methodological toolbox. Because the children involved produce the material themselves, they are often more engaged and better at recalling episodes in follow-up interviews. In addition to the benefits of the specific material, the process itself offers many opportunities for informal talks, elaborations and reflections on incidents in everyday life. Furthermore, it allows the child over time to build up familiarity with the researcher (Punch, 2002). (See also Chapters 6 and 9 for further consideration of using art-based methods and children's drawings in qualitative research.)

Yet, caution is required when using participant-based methods. First of all, drawings, photographs and diaries may provide inspiring insights into thoughts and perceptions, but obviously these will be strongly influenced by the medium of production. Drawings are not neutral representations of thoughts, and photographs do not objectively reproduce their motives. They are taken out of context, and selections and adjustments have been made that are no longer visible. Second, there is a risk of regarding this kind of material as significant primarily because children produce it. Unnoticed, an idea of authenticity might sneak into the methodological design, the participant-produced material implicitly coming to represent an authoritative expression of a true child perspective. In short, participatory methods can be a fine complement to other research methods. Used in combination with observations and interviews, such techniques can contribute with a different kind of insights into children's everyday lives.

7.11 Dilemmas for the adult researcher

Conducting ethnographic research always involves a number of dilemmas concerning the researcher's role in relation to the social setting. We will point out three dilemmas that we have found particularly acute in our studies of young children in early child institutions.

The first dilemma concerns the organisational features of the setting. To enter a day-care centre means to move into an already established social world with distinct roles, authority structure, rules and regulations defining what children can, must and should do. Neither the children nor the adult participants are unaffected by these organisational features, and also the researcher will have to adapt to the structural expectations. The researcher will often feel torn between an unspoken demand to enforce existing rules and the fascination, curiosity, and need to explore the children's transgressions and explorations of institutional rules and regulations; an exploration that often means crossing boundaries. Being caught between expectations of loyalty to the adults who have granted access and the possibility of collecting valuable information on children's challenges to the prevailing order, the researcher needs to find a way to balance the different interests at the same time reflecting the impact these have on the study.

The second dilemma relates to the question of adult authority. According to Punch (2002), it is a challenge for the adult researcher to enable children to express their points of view, as children are not always used to being heard. In this way, it becomes necessary to reflect on generational asymmetry. Again, however, it is important not to view the difference between children and adults as absolute. A strong focus on asymmetry entails a risk of presenting children one-sidedly as powerless, limited, constrained and marginalised in an adult-dominated world. As stated by Johansson, it is crucial to acknowledge children's ability to possess power at least in specific situations (Johansson, 2011). According to our experiences from studies of children's everyday lives in Scandinavian day-care centres, children will often address and question adult priorities and decisions – of both staff and researcher. As already mentioned, children may not always behave as respectfully as adults during an interview. Children may announce loudly that they find the topics boring or that they would rather talk about a trip to Granny's or riding a bicycle without training wheels. In our experience, the distribution of power between adults and children is dynamic; it is not necessarily in favour of adults. Research with children requires flexible strategies and different perspectives on authority. In many childcare centres, children are used to this seemingly contradictory and perhaps inconsistent adult role; sometimes friendly and empathetic, sometimes distant and controlling. It is, thus, possible to develop a research role that involves at the same time closeness and distance, openness and control (Johansson, 2011), thereby addressing the complexity of power relations and authority structures, as well as taking into account the differences between children.

A third dilemma relates to the adult position of the researcher and concerns the feeling of uselessness that can occur when other adults are busy helping children, preparing for fieldtrips, mediating conflicts or putting babies to sleep. The idea of participant observation is, obviously, to observe while participating. However, when studying children this does not mean doing the same as the professional staff. Many fieldworkers have found themselves entangled in everyday chores and activities, or giving into demands made by institutions, putting their project at risk. Clarifying mutual expectations between researcher and teachers is essential for being able to take on a different kind of adult role, where the researcher again will have to balance between closeness and distance (Repstad, 2009).

7.12 Ethical challenges in ethnographic research

There are ethical concerns in every research project, some general and some – like those addressed here – more specifically related to ethnographic research. The ethnographer enters what Seland, with reference to Goffman, has termed the 'backstage' of people's worlds and lives (Goffman, 1961; Seland, 2009). Becoming involved in other people's lives, they will gradually tell you of their thoughts, feelings, choices and priorities – often revealing their perceptions of other informants. This trust should be handled carefully. In order not to end up with conflicting loyalties it is necessary to stress that all information is treated with respect, yet also to emphasise that the role of an ethnographer differs from that of a friend or an ally. (See also Chapter 15 for a broader discussion of ethical procedures in research with children.)

Furthermore, the researcher enters the field knowing that their presence is temporary, a fact that might be particularly difficult for young children to grasp. It calls for ethical considerations on how to balance the interest in creating as much empirical material as possible in the time available, while at the same time paying attention to the relationships one has become part of. In one of her studies, Eva experienced how a 4-year-old girl became closely attached to her. The girl had difficulty being welcomed into the other children's activities, obviously ranking low in the hierarchy. The staff was too busy to take special care of this somewhat lonely child, which is why the seemingly inactive ethnographer appeared to be an obvious prospect for a great friendship. Eva would like to listen, and the child was very excited about this attention. The problem was, however, that Eva was not really interested in having this girl following her around in all situations, because it would limit her opportunity to gain access and observe. In addition to this, Eva was cautious of developing a genuine friendship, since she knew it would not continue when she left the day-care centre. Eva decided that the most considerate thing to do was to mark explicitly when they could talk and play, and when the girl had to be by herself – and, moreover, involve the staff in the girl's situation.

While this example concerns a challenge for the researcher of relationships that appear to be 'too close', there is an equally difficult issue concerning respecting children who find the researcher's observations intimidating. When it comes to young children, access to the field is almost always granted by adults – parents and teachers. But that does not mean that children cannot speak up in other ways, such as demanding that the researcher stop asking questions or leave the room.

Ethnography is a fragile enterprise that needs to build on trust and confidence. Johansson claims it is a vital balance between approaching children while at the same time respecting their communication and reactions to the researcher's presence, and that the responsibility for creating this relation always falls to the researcher (Johansson, 2011).

In any ethnographic project, the researcher must strive to make the participants aware of the fact that participating in a research project is voluntary, and that they can withdraw their consent at any phase in the project without stating the reason. Yet, as in many other aspects of life, young children's worlds and their potential rights are managed by parents and other significant adults. When ethnographic research includes young children, it has been argued that it is sufficient to inform the parents. It is definitely important to do so, but we do not find that sufficient. Rather, the researcher needs to inform all participants in a comprehensive and accurate way. The claim of informed consent includes some specific ethical considerations when informants are young children, as they are not able to sign an information sheet or, perhaps, fully aware of the implications of being participants. Informing, making the project known to the informants, and ensuring their consent, is not something that is done once and for all, but a continuous part of an ethnographic project. Being sensitive to the informants' expressions towards the researcher is an ethical stance, whether they express curiosity, invite contact or reject the presence. The researcher must keep a close eye on the uneasy body, the face turning away, the silly jokes or the glances at the door. Making sure that informants can choose their presence, whether or not they have given their consent, is also a means of empowerment.

A final ethical point is the importance of ensuring confidentiality and anonymity by using pseudonyms of personal names and locations, and omitting certain details in the descriptions (Bryman, 2008). When it comes to young children, however, the dominance of adult relations might sometimes challenge their right to anonymity. As pointed out by Kampmann (2003), researchers often find themselves negotiating and cooperating with parents and teachers about the children. It is tempting to share information with other adults who know the specific child, and it often feels quite challenging to have a conversation without letting any information slip. Most of the time, this may be insignificant and slightly trivial information, but as pointed out by Kampmann, it gives cause for ethical considerations when the child has shared information expecting confidentiality. This challenge becomes very demanding when the researcher comes across troubling and disturbing information that needs to be communicated in order to ensure the child's wellbeing. When informants choose to share critical aspects of their lives, this raises an ethical dilemma, as the researcher may feel obliged to inform authorities while at the same time respecting the child's trust. Lofland and Lofland (1995) state that sympathy and the impulse to help are commonly experienced by researchers during fieldwork and that they need to deal with this. In general, concern for the child's wellbeing must have the highest priority. In cases where one's consciousness demands the involvement of other adults (parents, teachers, authorities), it is an ethical obligation first to inform the child that such a step will be taken and ensure that the child knows what will happen.

As has been shown in this chapter, ethnographic methods involve many ethical dilemmas, because the researcher becomes so closely involved in the lives of others. Ensuring that all participants are informed and well taken care of is a difficult task. There are ethical principles to be followed (see for instance Alderson, 1995). Although we consider ethical guidelines valuable, we hesitate to grant them status as absolute. As shown in the discussion above, every project entails a number of considerations and dilemmas depending on people involved, location and purpose of the study. We will argue that ethical considerations should be a part of the beginning, execution and conclusion of the project, making them a vital part of any ethnographic exploration.

7.13 A short note on validity in ethnographic studies

An important part of any research process is to ensure that the project is valid. Bryman (2008) states that many researchers have sought to apply the concept of validity to the practice of qualitative research, while others have argued that the basis of these ideas in quantitative research renders them inapplicable or even inappropriate in qualitative research. According to Bryman (2008), it is particularly the word 'measure' that has caused the debate, as it indicates fixed standards that are not readily found in qualitative studies. Ethnographers spend extensive time in the field, striving to obtain a deep understanding of knowledge that occurs through personal encounters with informants (Creswell, 2007). In these encounters, there are no fixed guidelines or measurable criteria for knowledge production. Instead, there are continuous interpretations of how other people create meaning, communicate and act. Ethnographic analyses consist of such processes of interpretation, and therefore it is essential that they are made transparent. What happens in the encounters between informants and researcher? What is the researcher's role, and how is the data provided? Which analytical themes have been used, and for what reason? The validity of ethnographic projects depends on the degree to which the methodological choices and process of analysis are made visible.

7.14 Conclusion

In this chapter, we have in a short format presented some key issues in ethnographic studies involving children. We have pointed out the importance of being aware of the unnoticed preconceptions that may influence the way we interpret what people do and how they communicate – something that becomes particularly relevant when the object of study is children in educational institutions. We have also emphasised the need to make careful and systematic observations, not only of the children themselves but also of the social, physical and cultural surroundings they relate to. This focus on the contextual embeddedness of social life is the key characteristic of ethnography. The basic premise is that it is not possible to understand children's actions and understandings without including in the analysis the conditions to which they relate. This involves not only the immediate physical and social environment, but also the systems of knowledge, meanings, distinctions and values their communication and actions are part of.

Ethnographic research is basically an interpretive science carried out through the personal encounter between researcher and informants. This fact means that the ethnographer faces a number of dilemmas that require thorough ethical reflection and motivated choice of methods. In this way, there is a strong subjective touch to the approach, which neither can nor should be avoided. Instead, the validity and relevance of a project relies on the researcher's systematic methodological design and ability to reflect and clarify all aspects of the research process, from generating of data to analysis, in order for results to be discussed. Carefully ensuring such transparency is particularly important when the object of study is young children who have poor chances of challenging the ethnographer's interpretations.

Practical tips

1 Use as much time as possible observing in the field. You do not have to stay with the children from morning to evening, but you should have an overall idea of what their days look like.

2 Make careful registrations of categories and speech, as well as use of bodies, facial expressions and gestures. Don't just note the words being said but also how they are being said. Register who is present and where you place yourself in relation to them. Also make notes on moods and atmosphere. Such notes are very valuable in the process of interpretations and analyses.

3 Record thoroughly and systematically not only the actions and interactions of individuals, but also the social and physical environment they interact with, and the cultural categories and meanings they orient themselves in relation to.

4   Be careful to explain your own categories and preconceptions. Matters relating to children and educational institutions are particularly charged with values and opinions that might, unacknowledged, influence the researcher's focus and interpretations.

References

Albon, D., & Rosen, R. (2013). *Negotiating adult-child relationships in early childhood research*. London: Routledge.

Alderson, P. (1995). *Listening to children: Children, ethics and social research*. London: Barnardos.

Alvesson, M., & Sköldberg, K. (2008). *Tolkning och reflektion: vetenskapsfilosofi och kvalitativ metod*. Lund: Studentlitteratur AB.

Bluebond-Langner, M. (1980). *The private worlds of dying children*. Princeton, NJ: Princeton University Press.

Bourdieu, P., Chamboredon, J. C., & Passeron, J. C. (1991). *The craft of sociology. Epistemological preliminaries*. Berlin: Walter de Gruyter.

Boyden, J., & Ennew, J. (1997). *Children in focus: A manual for participatory research with children*. Stockholm: Rädda Barnet.

Bryman, A. (2008). *Social research methods*. Oxford: Oxford University Press.

Christensen, P. H., & James, A. (Eds) (2000). *Research with children. Perspectives and practices*. London: Falmer Press.

Connolly, P. (1998). *Racism, gender identities and young children. Social relations in a multi-ethnic, inner-city primary school*. London and New York: Routledge.

Corsaro, W. A. (1985). *Friendship and peer culture in the early years*. New York: Norwood.

Creswell, J. W. (2007). *Qualitative inquiry and research design: Choosing among five approaches*. Thousand Oaks, CA: Sage.

Ferguson, A. A. (2001). *Bad boys. Public schools in the making of black masculinity*. Ann Arbor, MI: The University of Michigan Press.

Fine, G. A., & Sandstrom, K. L. (1988). Knowing children. Participant observation with minors. *Qualitative Research Methods*, *15*, 7–85.

Goffman, E. (1961). *Asylums: Essays on the social situation of mental patients and other inmates*. New York: Anchor Books, Doubleday & Co.

Gulløv, E., & Højlund, S. (2003). *Feltarbejde blandt børn. Metodologi og etik i etnografisk børneforskning*. København: Gyldendal.

Hirschfeld, L. A. (2002). Why don't anthropologists like children? *American Anthropologist*, *104*, 611–27.

James, A. (1993). *Childhood identities: Social relationships and the self in children's experiences*. Edinburgh, Edinburgh University Press.

James, A., Jenks, C., & Prout, A. (1998). *Theorizing childhood*. Cambridge: Polity Press.

James, A., & Prout, A. (1990). *Constructing and reconstructing childhood. Contemporary issues in the sociological study of childhood*. London: The Falmer Press.

Johansson, E. (2011). Investigating morality in toddler's world. In E. Johansson & J. White (Eds), *Educational research with our youngest: Voices of infants and toddlers* (pp. 39–63), Dordrecth, Heidelberg and London: Springer Science.

Kampmann, J. (2003). 'Etiske overvejelser i etnografisk børneforskning'. In E. Gulløv & S. Højlund (Eds), *Feltarbejde blandt børn* (pp. 167–78). København: Gyldendal.

Lærke, A. (1998). By means of re-membering. Notes on a fieldwork with English children. *Anthropology Today*, *14*(1), 3–7.

Lancy, D. (2008). *The anthropology of childhood*. Cambridge: Cambridge University Press.

Lofland, J., & Lofland, L. H. (1995). *Analyzing social settings: A guide to qualitative observation and analysis*. Belmont, CA: Wadsworth.

Mandell, N. (1991). The least-adult role in studying children. In F. Waksler (Ed.), *Studying the social worlds of children* (pp. 38–60). London: Falmer Press.

Mayall, B. (2000). Conversations with children: Working with generational issues. In P. H. Christensen & A. James (Eds), *Research with children. Perspectives and practices* (pp. 109–24). London: Falmer Press.

Montgomery, H. (2009). *An introduction to childhood. Anthropological perspectives in children's lives*. Oxford: Wiley-Blackwell.

Punch, S. (2002). Research with children. The same or different from research with adults. *Childhood*, *9*(3), 321–41.

Repstad, P. (2009). *Mellom nærhet og distanse – enda en gang. Å forske blant sine egne: universitet og region – nærhet og uavhengighet*. Kristiansand: Høyskoleforlaget.

Schilhab, T. S. S, Juelskjær, M., & Moser, T. (2008). *Learning bodies*. Copenhagen: Danish School of Education.

Seland, M. (2009). *Det moderne barn og den fleksible barnehagen: en etnografisk studie av barnehagens hverdagsliv i lys av nyere diskurser og kommunal virkelighet*. Norges Teknisknaturvitenskapelige Universitet, Trondheim.

Skreland, L. (2015). *På mandager er det ikke lov med papirfly. En studie av regler og yrkesutøvelse*. Unpublished Thesis, University of Agder, Kristiansand.

Solberg, A. (1996). The challenge in child research: From 'being' to 'doing'. In J. Brannen & M. O'Brien, (Eds), *Children in families. Research and policy* (pp. 53–66). London: Falmer Press.

Thorne, B. (1993). *Gender Play. Girls and boys in school*. Buckinghamshire: Open University Press.

Willis, P. (1977). *Learning to labour: How working class kids get working class jobs*. Aldershot: Gower.

8

QUALITATIVE RESEARCH WITH A 'DOUBLE LIFE'

A mixed methods approach to research and advocacy with adolescents

Jayme Hannay, Robert Dudley,
Stephanie Milan, Paula Kellogg Leibovitz
and Valerie L. Rodino

8.1 Introduction

Community-based participatory research (CBPR) is increasingly used in health research to help assess the needs of communities and to empower those communities to change at the systems, environment or policy level. Conducting CBPR projects with teens presents unique opportunities and challenges because with the right choice of methodologies and effective mentoring from adults, teens can participate as full partners in the project's research and advocacy aims. Methodologies such as Photovoice can serve a dual function: as a research tool and leadership building intervention. In this chapter we discuss how a mixed methods approach using two qualitative methodologies, focus groups and Photovoice, can inform, enrich and sustain a CBPR project with adolescents. The chapter begins with an overview of CBPR. Next, we examine strengths and weaknesses of focus groups and Photovoice when used with adolescents and their families within a CBPR framework. Our final section provides a rationale for combining the two methodologies. To illustrate our points, we draw on our experiences as partners in a long-running community-based obesity prevention programme for Latina teens.

8.1.1 Why a community-based participatory research (CBPR) approach works in research with adolescents

Programmes that aim to improve health, educational and career opportunities for teens from disadvantaged or minority communities often use youth empowerment and leadership building as key strategies. The extent to which these methods are successful often depends on how well they are tailored to the specific needs and goals of community members and participating youth. However, the needs and goals of diverse stakeholders often differ and may not be clear to programme developers.

One way to identify different community needs and goals is to conduct quantitative (e.g., surveys) and/or qualitative (e.g., focus groups) research. While these strategies have many benefits, youth and family members are typically 'subjects' of the research from whom information is collected. In contrast, incorporating youth and family members into the research process in more meaningful ways can provide different types of insights for programme evaluation and development. CBPR may be especially compelling as a framework for youth empowerment programmes because youth participation in the research process can be integrated into the intervention itself by giving teens powerful roles as researchers and advocates for translating the research into policy change (Hannay, Dudley, Milan, & Leibovitz, 2013).

8.2 Hallmarks of the community-based participatory research (CBPR) approach

A frequently used definition of CBPR is that of the W.K. Kellogg Foundation's Community Health Scholars Program. CBPR is:

> A collaborative process that equitably involves all partners in the research process and recognizes the unique strengths that each brings. CBPR begins with a research topic of importance to the community with the aim of combining knowledge and action for social change to improve community health and eliminate health disparities.
>
> (Minkler & Wallerstein, 2008, p. 6)

The roots of CBPR can be traced to the work of psychologist Kurt Lewin who defined 'action research' as a means of addressing social inequalities through a collaborative process of group planning and discussion resulting in practical solutions to immediate problems (Lewin, 1946). In the 1970s, the Brazilian educator Paulo

Freire and others emphasized the participatory nature of research (Freire, 1970). Communities that were formerly the objects of research became full participants in solving problems that they had defined themselves.

Investigators who contribute to 'real-world' community-based projects, either as members of the project team or 'outside' evaluators, must keep in mind that the goal of knowledge generation is secondary to practical applications, such as improving programme quality, attracting more resources (e.g., grant funding) and above all enhancing the wellbeing of youth and families. CBPR aligns with these goals because its approaches are not research 'methods at all but *orientations to research* with a heavy accent on issues of trust, power, dialogue, community capacity building, and collaborative inquiry toward the goal of social change to improve community health outcomes and eliminate health disparities' (Minkler & Wallerstein, 2008, p.7).

Numerous researchers have defined the hallmarks of the CBPR approach. Among the most widely cited are those of Barbara Israel and her colleagues (Israel, Schulz, Parker, & Becker, 1998; Israel *et al.*, 2008). The following section will outline these principles, illustrating them with examples drawn from our experience with Healthy Tomorrows (2007–18), a CBPR project that engages predominantly Latina teens, parents and researchers in an afterschool obesity prevention programme emphasizing healthy eating, physical activity and leadership.

The first principle identified by Israel *et al.* (1998; 2008) is that CBPR is collaborative, engaging diverse partners equitably in all phases of the research process. The core of the partnership, its driving force, is the community whose shared concerns are addressed through the research and empowerment process. Partners outside that community contribute to and benefit from the process. These may include academic researchers, community-based organizations, local and state government officials, funders, businesses and others with an interest in and commitment to the community. Over the course of a long-running programme, the number of partners will naturally expand. Although the composition of each collaboration is different, programmes engaging teens should encompass the full spectrum of institutions (education, health, religious, political and economic) that impact their lives. Adults should seek out opportunities to engage teens in frequent formal and informal discussions of design, purpose and application of the research. In the Healthy Tomorrows project, teens gave valuable feedback to project partners through participation in a Project Advisory Board, and also through informal conversations that occurred naturally as trust between teens and adults increased.

Second, CBPR research needs to address the priority concerns of the community. Tangible problems, such as crime, poor education, lack of jobs and neighbourhood decay are often of more immediate concern to teens than more abstract health problems that are the focus of researchers and funders (Minkler & Hancock, 2008). However, even when the choice of topic is constrained by outside considerations, such as a funding mandate, a commitment to the CBPR process and emphasis on group dialogue can ensure that teens' voices are heard in setting the direction of the project. For example, teens recognized that obesity, the focus of the Healthy Tomorrows programme, was a problem but they perceived it as a lower priority than issues such as stress, teen pregnancy, racism and a general lack of activities for teens in New Britain. To find a common ground, it is important for researchers to engage teens in a broader dialogue about how socioeconomic factors contribute to health and disease, and how an issue of concern to them, such as stress, may be interconnected with problems like obesity.

Third, CBPR is usually a co-learning process, meaning that all participants have knowledge to share and knowledge to gain from others. When working with teens, whose voices are often ignored, adults need to reinforce the message that youth are co-researchers, with valuable knowledge about their own lives and communities that partners want and need to know. To build teens' confidence, the Healthy Tomorrows research team gave them multiple opportunities to present their findings directly to adult audiences as well as acknowledging their contributions in publications and presentations (Hannay et al., 2013).

In addition, CBPR involves systems development and local community capacity building, meaning that the outcomes of the research should have direct benefits for community members. As 'end users' of research findings, partners should be able to identify specific ways that findings will support their mission, and result in better service to community members. For example, the YWCA, a core Healthy Tomorrows partner, used information about barriers to Latinos' access to the facility to plan new programmes to attract more Latino users.

A further principle of CBPR is the need to balance research and action. Whether or not partners choose to move forward with direct action to improve their community, the project must 'incorporate a commitment to the translation and integration of research results with community change efforts' (Israel et al., 2008, p. 57). In research with teens, the emphasis on action can have many advantages, because it taps into teens' 'natural activism' and their need to see tangible results from their work, for example by rallying around a project to reopen community pools (Hannay et al., 2013). This in turn increases engagement in programmes that often struggle to attract and retain older teens.

CBPR also requires partners to make a long-term commitment to the community. Because of the time and effort required to carry out CBPR processes and to build trust among partners and community members, that commitment must extend 'beyond a single research project or funding period' (Israel et al.,

2008, p. 52) and include a willingness to sustain the programme during gaps in outside funding.

A final principle of CBPR is that participation in the research is an empowering process through which participants can increase control over their lives. For teens, the opportunity to contribute to CBPR projects as both researchers and advocates for policy changes is especially empowering because it builds concrete skills and experiences that can expand educational and career options. Teens in the Healthy Tomorrows programme used their experience speaking before a city council to enhance resumes and college or job applications. For researchers who wish to apply CBPR principles in their practice, Campus-Community Partnerships for Health offers a comprehensive curriculum and related resources (available online).

8.3 Focus groups and Photovoice: advantages and disadvantages

Within the CBPR framework, a variety of qualitative research methodologies can be utilized to meet evolving needs for programme planning, outcome evaluation or sustainability as they emerge over the life cycle of a community-based programme. In this section we discuss two qualitative methodologies, focus groups and Photovoice, the advantages and disadvantages of each, and how they contributed to the planning and implementation of the Healthy Tomorrows programme over its 10-year life cycle.

8.3.1 Focus groups

A focus group is a traditional qualitative research methodology in which participants respond to interview questions on a specific topic. There are many resources available that provide practical guidance on conducting focus groups for applied research purposes (e.g., Krueger & Casey, 2008). In general, a group of six to twelve participants is advisable in order to create an environment that encompasses a variety of viewpoints, but ensures that all participants have an opportunity to speak. Researchers generate core questions prior to the group's meeting, but typically allow for some flexibility in follow-up or 'probe' questions depending on the direction in the discussion. Sessions last from 30 minutes to 2 hours and are ideally led by two researchers (a moderator and a note taker). In contrast to individual interviews (see discussion Chapter 6), participants hear each other's responses and are able to offer further comments based on what others have to say. Data is generated in a social context and is not contingent on the group reaching a consensus (or disagreement) (Patton, 1987). To ensure that findings are not idiosyncratic, researchers will often conduct multiple sessions addressing the same questions until little new information is generated, indicating that a point of 'saturation' has been reached. In order to analyse data, focus group sessions are often audio recorded and then transcribed verbatim.

Analysis of material generated from focus groups can be done in many ways. Often times, investigators will simply read through the transcript to generate ideas or to better understand participants' views. They may also use the 'scissor and sort' technique, which involves first reading through the transcript in order to locate all the places in which material relevant to a specific question is present, and then putting these responses together for interpretation (Krueger & Casey, 2008). These approaches are usually time efficient, but interpretations may be highly subjective. Another analytic strategy is content analysis, which involves researchers making inferences from the text in ways that are meant to be valid and replicable through application of scientific principles (Krippendorf, 2004). Usually, this involves multiple analysts independently extracting themes or specific content from the transcripts and assessing whether similar material is extracted by the analytic team (i.e., the same themes or specific examples of themes are identified consistently within the text by multiple analysts). The extent to which these themes or examples are consistently identified across researchers can be computed using reliability statistics (e.g., Krippendorf's alpha) so that only reliably identified themes or topics are used for subsequent interpretation. Software programs for content analysis (e.g., nvivo or Nudist) can also be used to transcripts, although they are more often used when qualitative researchers need to analyse multiple transcripts (e.g., ethnographic interviews from a sample of thirty participants; see Chapter 7 for more detail on ethnographic studies with children). The findings (i.e., themes or ideas generated) can then be used for programme development, refinement or evaluation, and potentially disseminated for use by other practitioners, programme planners, and researchers.

Advantages of focus groups

One advantage of focus groups is that they are efficient, and therefore relatively inexpensive. Since multiple participants are interviewed together, rather than one-on-one, the sample size can be increased significantly. In addition, focus groups are effective in needs assessment. They can elicit candid, often detailed, responses in a short amount of time, making them a useful tool for needs assessment, project planning, and evaluation at different stages in the evolution of community-based programmes (Leung & Savithiri, 2009).

A further advantage of focus groups is that the group dynamics allow the most important topics to emerge. Focus groups have some 'built in' quality controls.

Participants tend to provide checks and balances on each other, weeding out false or extreme views, and helping to determine whether there is a shared view. Healthy Tomorrows' focus groups yielded detailed information about subjects that teens were expert in and felt strongly about, such as barriers to their participation in school-based physical education (PE). Participants 'piggybacked' on each other's ideas. For example, one teen's comment that she did not like participating in PE because it involved 'getting sweaty' during the school day triggered multiple related observations including concerns about messy hair, dirty uniforms, and boring and repetitive activities such as running.

Disadvantages of using focus groups

Focus groups have a number of disadvantages that need consideration by the researcher. Since many participants must respond to each question, the number of questions that can be addressed in a given focus group is limited. This will limit the scope of the topics that you can include. In addition, conversations can be 'hijacked'. Facilitators must be adept at managing group dynamics to prevent one outspoken participant from creating an atmosphere that discourages contributions from quieter group members. With teens, there is the additional problem of groups of friends ('cliques') dominating the discussion or responding with negativity to a particular participant. In adolescent groups, moderators often need to be more active in engaging quiet participants (e.g., asking individuals specifically about their thoughts), validating all responses (e.g., thanking a participant by name following a response), and using verbal and non-verbal signals to facilitate the group process (e.g., standing closer to participants who are in a side conversation).

Community members may be reluctant to disclose personal information. The professional atmosphere of focus groups, facilitated by a researcher or academic from outside the community, can also put a damper on the candid sharing of information, particularly by teens. To mitigate this problem, Healthy Tomorrows' focus groups were held at the Spanish Speaking Centre, a social service agency where participants already used other services. In some groups, agency staff served as co-facilitators with academic partners. This comfortable setting promoted more candid responses to sensitive issues.

8.3.2 Photovoice

Photovoice is a powerful CBPR methodology that qualitative researchers are increasingly using to partner with community residents. Through Photovoice, people, often those marginalized by poverty, race, language or other circumstances, use photography or video images to document their experiences, share them with others, and engage in collective action to promote change in their environment. Photovoice integrates Freire's (1970) theory, with its emphasis on knowledge generated from people's lived experiences; feminist theory, with its focus on voice; and documentary photography, often used to help bring about social change. Although each Photovoice project is unique, the process includes three core components: (1) it engages people in photographing their everyday health and work realities to document and reflect on their community's strengths and concerns; (2) participants reflect on their photographs through critical dialogue and group discussions, thereby highlighting personal and community issues of greatest concern, and (3) it reaches policymakers, health planners, community leaders and other people who can be mobilized to make change (Wang & Pies, 2008).

Photovoice is a flexible methodology that can be adapted for research with diverse communities on a wide variety of issues. Caroline Wang, a professor at the University of Michigan, School of Public Health and an early proponent of Photovoice, used it in the 1990s to help rural Chinese women document their lives using the power of photographic images (Wang & Burris, 1997). It has since been used by Wang and others to explore homelessness, mental health, HIV/AIDS, poverty and other issues of concern to marginalized communities. A number of curricula are available for researchers to adapt in integrating Photovoice into their CBPR projects (Bandurraga, Gowen, & The Finding Our Way Team, 2013; KU Work Group, 2014; Innovation Centre for Community and Youth Development, 2008; Palibroda, Krieg, Murdock, & Havelock, 2009).

Practical issues in conducting Photovoice research

Photovoice requires a commitment of time and effort that can be challenging for participants, particularly teens. Therefore, the selection of a strong facilitator/mentor with both a thorough understanding and commitment to Photovoice and an ability to empathize with and motivate teens is essential. Facilitators must ensure that teens fully understand and see the value of their multiple roles as co-researchers and advocates for change. A co-facilitator with expertise in photography or the selected research topic can enhance the effectiveness of the project. The Healthy Tomorrows project was co-facilitated by a registered dietician who reinforced the key tenets of CBPR while contributing practical knowledge about healthy eating and answering diet-related queries that arose during sessions. She provided a knowledge base that added to the teens' credibility when they proposed their ideas for change to health professionals and other community leaders.

The length of a Photovoice project and the number of participants will vary based on the research and action or policy change goals of the partners. Small groups (of ten participants or fewer) allow for maximum bonding and emergence of a collective identity, which can build momentum for the later stages of policy action. Participants can be recruited from an existing programme or group (e.g., school, clinic or community centre) or can be identified through outreach and 'word-of-mouth' in the community. Projects can be conducted in as little as 6 to 8 weeks or can extend over many months, depending on the topic, budget, timeframe, and needs and concerns of participants. Longer projects allow for the development of greater trust among participants and facilitators, but, if the goal is policy action, the timeframe may need to be more compressed to meet external requirements (e.g., presenting at a legislative session or town council meeting). Orientation should also cover the technical aspects and ethics of taking photos or videos. The facilitator should discuss and obtain informed consent from participants for the use of both their photos and images of them in future presentations and exhibits.

As in all CBPR projects, selection of a topic requires careful consideration, and resolution of any discrepancies between a researcher's interests and those of community residents. Although obesity prevention was not a priority concern of teens in the Healthy Tomorrows programme, they were able to take 'ownership' of the topic through an extended discussion with researchers. They formulated, in their own words, three framing questions that served as a guide to taking photos. The first two questions focused on barriers and facilitators of access to physical activity as well as healthy foods and directly addressed the mandated research topic. The third was an open-ended question that explored why teens are so 'stressed out', a high-priority issue. Following the planning period, participants are given cameras (options include disposable or digital cameras or cell phones) and a set period of time (ranging from as little as a week or two to over a year) in which to collect their photos or videos to document the research topic.

The heart of the Photovoice experience is reflecting – individually or in groups – on the photographic images that participants take and the powerful stories they tell. Having teens write individual reflections prior to group discussion can help them to gain confidence in the authority of their own impressions, and their unique voice. A series of questions can be useful in enabling participants to structure their ideas. The SHOWeD mnemonic (Shaffer, 1983; Wang & Pies, 2008) asks:

> What do you **S**ee here?
> What's really **H**appening here?
> How does this relate to **O**ur Lives?
> **W**hy does this problem, concern, or strength exist?
> What can we **D**o about it?

Whether reflections are written or oral, structured as in the SHOWeD mnemonic or more conversational, facilitators should guide the process to ensure that all voices are heard. In the Healthy Tomorrows project, each teen chose six photos that best answered the framing questions and wrote reflections that explained why she took the photo, what story it told, what its significance was for her family and community, and what could be done about the problem depicted. The participants next engage in a group discussion of the photos and individual reflections, and with guidance from the facilitator, identify shared themes. Through a consensus process, the group selects a subset of photos (typically six to eight) that illustrate the themes and becomes the basis for the shared narrative or story that the group will present to the community along with recommendations for policy change.

Policymakers and community leaders should be recruited and engaged in the project at an early stage. Teens benefit from making informal presentations to adults who can provide feedback and information about how 'systems work' and concrete ideas for follow-up steps that can advance their agenda. Such encounters increase teens' sense of self-esteem and their confidence in that they can see that their contribution is valued and that they can make a difference in the community (Marne, Snyder, & Gadin, 2012). Policymakers for their part are usually eager to participate as a way of gaining a better understanding of the needs of their constituents. Such engagement creates a climate that is conducive to the success of later policy initiatives. Wang recommends setting up a 'guidance committee' of community leaders for this purpose (Wang & Pies, 2008, p. 193).

Photovoice projects culminate with teens making formal and informal presentations of their photos, reflections and ideas for changes to audiences of health providers, educators, policymakers and community members. Options for these presentations abound and most community organizations are highly receptive to hosting them. They can range from exhibitions of photos in a local museum with teens acting as 'docents' who explain the meaning of their work, to poster presentations to advisory boards, to more formal presentations at city councils, statewide meetings or conferences. These positive experiences empower teens and convince them of their value as researchers and advocates. As a Healthy Tomorrows participant observed following a presentation to a health clinic's advisory board: 'It felt good talking in front of people. I let them know how things are in New Britain. They didn't know.'

Advantages of using Photovoice

A key advantage of using Photovoice is that it builds leadership and other essential skills in teens. Unlike focus groups, Photovoice not only elicits information from teens, it directly benefits them by giving them practice in leadership and advocacy as well as a wide range of other essential academic and career-related skills, including research, writing, analysis and public speaking. Photovoice also promotes important psychosocial qualities such as self-confidence, cooperation, and the ability to work as a team and bond with teens outside their own group.

A further advantage of using Photovoice is to highlight teens' assets. Many adult 'authorities' and community leaders view teens from disadvantaged communities through the lens of risk, focusing on problems of school failure, teen pregnancy, drug abuse and gang involvement (Checkoway, Allison, & Montoya, 2005). Through Photovoice, teens have multiple opportunities to interact with adults in their positive roles as researchers and advocates, offering photographic evidence of community needs and recommendations for addressing them. Policymakers, health professionals and educators recognize the need to hear the voices of their marginalized teen constituents, who are, as one city official put it: 'the future of the community'.

Additionally, Photovoice is a powerful tool for assessing community assets and deficits. By combining visual images with the written and oral reflections, Photovoice is an especially powerful tool for assessing the needs of a community and mobilizing it to action (Sanon, Evans-Agnew, & Boutain, 2008). Participants in 'Picture This', a Photovoice project to determine the needs of low-income mothers and children, initiated actions to clean up parks and keep a local recreation centre open (Wang & Pies, 2004; Wang & Pies, 2008). Healthy Tomorrows participants took over 700 photos documenting the assets and deficits of New Britain and the condition of its schools, parks and streets. Evidence of neighbourhood and city deterioration was documented by images of garbage, graffiti, vacant buildings, broken bottles and gang tags. In their written reflections, teens explored not only the personal, but also the local and even global impact of such conditions. For example, one participant stated: 'All you see around is people with cars polluting the world . . . it is also bad for themselves.'

Furthermore, Photovoice is a cost-effective, easily shared tool for building community capacity. The Photovoice methodology itself can be shared with partners and other organizations to support a collective response to common concerns. In New Britain, Photovoice was adapted for a mentoring programme to help reduce the dropout rate by easing the transition from middle to high school. Pairs of eighth and ninth grade students took photos of high school locations and settings that evoked anxiety for younger students and then discussed how to cope with the situation.

Finally, Photovoice products are permanent assets and learning tools for the researcher, teens and their community. Photos, posters or videos can be passed along from one group of community residents to another, supporting an ongoing conversation about community needs and assets and thus provide tangible evidence of progress – or lack of progress – in improving the quality of life.

Disadvantages of using Photovoice

It is important to consider the disadvantages of this method before embarking on any project using Photovoice. Policy change is a slow process. Most of the initiatives advanced by teens are not achievable within the limited timeframe of a Photovoice project. While lack of progress can be frustrating, teens are realists and appreciate the value of the empowerment process itself, independent of the outcome. Although the Healthy Tomorrows' petition to reopen city pools was not immediately successful, the two teens who presented it to the city's Common Council were proud and regarded their presentation as preparation for the future. For example, following the presentation, one girl stated that: 'We let our voices be heard.' The second told us: 'The first time is always hard but the next time will be better.'

A further consideration is that Photovoice requires a significant investment of time and resources. Patience is required to prepare teens to take the lead as researchers, defining the scope of the investigation, interpreting the data and setting priorities for translating research into action. The most effective Healthy Tomorrows projects involved 20 hours per week of engagement with teens over a 2-month period.

One other issue to consider is that abstract concepts are difficult to capture with photographs. Photovoice is more effective in documenting tangible conditions in the environment than the less tangible topics that are often of most concern to teens such as abuse and violence, bullying and stress. Capturing such concerns photographically requires an understanding of symbolic and metaphoric representation that can be difficult for teens.

8.4 A mixed methods approach: combining focus groups and Photovoice

There are many reasons why researchers might consider combining the two qualitative methodologies of focus groups and Photovoice in their CBPR projects. Three key considerations are related to the hallmarks of CBPR projects discussed in the first section. The first is the need for flexibility. Focus groups can give researchers a broad perspective on a wide range of topics, while Photovoice allows them to drill down more deeply into specific and complex issues of concern to the community (Downey, Ireson, & Scutchfield, 2009). The second consideration is the need for sustained trust building with the community. Photovoice fosters rich, ongoing conversations that give community residents confidence that researchers are concerned about the issues raised in focus groups. The third and final consideration is the need to balance research and social justice impacts. Adding Photovoice as a complement to focus groups creates the potential for increasing awareness about issues of concern, initiating actions to address them, and ultimately transforming a community by mobilizing its citizens to advocate for change.

8.4.1 Design and analysis issues

Our discussion of the benefits of a mixed method approach draws in part from a mid-course evaluation of Healthy Tomorrows conducted between July 2009 and June 2011 with funding from *Salud-America!*, a research programme of the Robert Wood Johnson Foundation (https://salud-america.org/research; Ramirez, Gallion, Despres, & Adeigbe, 2013). The goal was to gain a greater understanding of the barriers and facilitators of physical activity and healthy eating among participants and use findings to strengthen the programme at its midpoint.

The project was designed as a series of nine focus groups and five Photovoice sessions that were conducted with Latino parents and teens over a 2-year period. Photovoice, which had been used first as a leadership intervention, was later integrated into the research design to supplement and enrich the feedback from focus groups. The additional goals of Photovoice – using research to promote policy change and community improvement – directly addressed the larger project goals of empowering parents and youth as leaders. By conducting the focus groups and Photovoice sessions during the same time period, researchers, who led the focus groups, and programme staff, who facilitated the Photovoice sessions, were able to exchange information on a regular basis. An alternative design is a two-phased sequential process in which participants take part in a focus group, then conduct a Photovoice project, and after an interval are questioned again to determine if they provide more in-depth responses (Cooper & Yarbrough, 2010).

In our project, the research team assessed the value added by the mixed method approach by analysing Photovoice products: the photos, written reflections, transcripts, and notes from group dialogues with participants and policymakers, and presentations. These were compared with the thematic analyses of the focus group findings to determine whether the Photovoice data provided additional, complementary or more nuanced information.

We found a number of ways in which research can benefit from combining focus groups and Photovoice. Researchers can revisit data in an iterative process that yields a deeper understanding of teen needs. The mixed method approach allows for the 'reflexive iteration (which) is at the heart of visiting and revisiting the data and connecting them with emerging insights, progressively leading to refined focus and understandings' (Srivastava & Hopwood, 2009, p. 77). Anecdotal evidence from the Healthy Tomorrows' mid-course evaluation points to the benefits of this approach for both knowledge generation and clinical practice. During extended conversations triggered by photos (the connection between fast food restaurants, poor diet and diabetes, for example), teens disclosed detailed, personal information about important health topics that were not shared within the time-limited, more professional setting of the focus group. In the atmosphere of trust that was generated in the sessions, many teens shared the anxieties of having – and in many cases caring for – family members who had been diagnosed with diabetes. As group members talked about their own diagnosis of pre-diabetes or diabetes, their fear of the disease and their tendency to ignore rather than manage it became apparent. The registered dietician/co-facilitator was able to dispel myths surrounding diabetes by providing evidence-based information that integrated nutrition education with self-management goal setting. This gave students confidence that they could manage the disease in small increments rather feeling overwhelmed.

Second, Photovoice provided a vehicle for taking action on problems identified in focus groups. Focus groups give participants a forum for voicing concerns (e.g., frustration about the lack of 'anything to do' in New Britain) but seldom led to concrete follow-up action. Photovoice by contrast leads to the articulation of a detailed action agenda. For example, teens' photos of vacant buildings and their reflections that they should be torn down or 'fixed up and turned into more useful buildings' led to their vision of a teen centre (which became known as the House of Teens or HOT). Staff incorporated teens' photos and reflections into a proposal that secured a second Healthy Tomorrows grant from the Maternal and Child Health Bureau (2013–18). This included funding for the teen centre.

The policymaker dialogues, which are a key component of Photovoice, also allow ideas from focus groups to surface and be acted on. In focus groups teens talked extensively about barriers to engaging in physical PE classes that had contributed to a PE failure rate of 53 per cent among Latinas. When teens met with the assistant superintendent of the New Britain school district as part of their Photovoice project, their wide-ranging conversation included a discussion of these concerns. This triggered a decision by school administration to approve an out-of-school 'PE credit recovery course', which teens that had failed PE at school could take at the YWCA.

A further benefit of combining focus groups and Photovoice is that involvement in both methods can help teens to probe more deeply into the connection between conditions in the environment and their health. In focus groups teens responded vaguely to questions about how environmental conditions influenced their health and their ability to exercise or eat healthy foods. For example, one teen observed:

> I guess if you lived in a place that really wasn't safe or right off the highway, then you couldn't really go out walking or running or anything. But there are other things like the Y here or other places you can go that are not like that. And lots of different stores and restaurants. So, maybe that's true for some people but not other people. I think it would depend on where you live.

In contrast, in answer to the framing question 'what helps or prevents us from exercising in our neighbourhoods?' a Photovoice participant took a dramatic photo of a graffiti-covered dumpster (Figure 8.1) and reflected assertively: 'Our community is damaged by dirty things.' In conversation she was more emphatic: 'Dumpsters stink! I live here, and I know it's a problem!'

In group discussions, she and her peers were able to move even further, drawing connections between external conditions and interior correlates, such as stress and

FIGURE 8.1 Mount Pleasant dumpster: A stressor for teens

Photograph reproduced from Hannay *et al.* (2013) with permission from Elsevier Publishers and Monica Little

depression, and finally linking that to the motivation to exercise in their shared theme: 'In our neighbourhood, we saw eyesores, such as bad smelling dumpsters that make us unhappy. These discourage us to exercise.'

Additionally, Photovoice yields rich, nuanced and unpredictable information about teens that may provide directions for future research. In focus groups, parents and teens described New Britain parks as neglected, vandalized places where families were afraid to go. A Photovoice project designed to document this problem both confirmed and contradicted the focus group responses. Parks in predominately Latino neighbourhood were in a state of deterioration but teens' responses were complex.

The image of an abandoned pool can be seen in Figure 8.2. A teen's lengthy, poetic reflection on this photo evokes her remembrance of summers past when the pools were open and 'full of life'. She explained:

> I used to go to the pool in Washington Park and now that it's closed there's no memories left. I remember jumping off the diving board with my friend and feeling the cold refreshing water . . . but now all I see is garbage and graffiti.

FIGURE 8.2 Empty pool: Lost memories

Photograph reproduced from Hannay *et al.* (2013). Thanks to Elsevier Publishers for permission to reproduce this photograph. This photograph is used with the permission of Jayme Hannay

The nostalgia expressed by several teens combines a sense of loss with positive memories and suggests that teens, even those who lead highly mobile lives, have a strong attachment to place. These insights may contribute to an understanding of how nostalgia functions as a positive, future-oriented emotion during times of transition (Cheung *et al.*, 2013).

Our experience has been that Photovoice yields powerful stories that challenge cultural assumptions. The story that a photo taken by a teen tells is often not what the researcher, health provider or other 'authority' initially sees. By interpreting the story, the teen helps researchers and providers examine their cultural perceptions and misperceptions, which can ultimately improve the quality of research or of clinical care. For example, consider the image of a father and daughter walking down a snow-covered street (Figure 8.3) that we used in our Salud-America! research project.

When asked to interpret this photo, physicians and other health professionals saw a generally positive image of exercise and parental engagement. The parent's reflection, however, was very different: 'We walk to exercise our bodies, but I would like it better if there weren't any gangs to mess up our streets.' This called

FIGURE 8.3 Walking: Benefits and risks

Photograph reproduced from Hannay *et al.* (2013). Thanks to Elsevier Publishers for permission to reproduce this photograph. This photograph is used with the permission of Vilma Padilla

FIGURE 8.4 Empty table: Absent family

Photograph reproduced from Hannay *et al.* (2013). Thanks to Elsevier Publishers for permission to reproduce this photograph. This photograph is used with the permission of Francesca Reyes

the researchers' attention to the 'real' story, which includes the threat of crime symbolized by the gang tag on the wall.

A further example depicted a dining room table covered with a pristine white tablecloth and red flowers, as shown in Figure 8.4.

Salud-America! project staff saw this photo as a positive depiction of home and family during the holidays. However, the reflection by the teen photographer tells a different story, one of stress evoked by the empty table and the absence of family who remained in Puerto Rico: 'One of the things that stresses me during the holidays is to see my house, my table . . . and not have my loved ones there.' The photo triggered a group discussion of how Latinos may compensate for such stress by overeating. Recognizing these differences in perspective may result in more culturally competent care.

8.5 Conclusion

Research into the effectiveness of youth programmes is critical for a variety of stakeholders. For academic researchers, findings are essential to building the evidence base about which youth development programmes work best to achieve positive outcomes. Policymakers faced with tight budgets can use the findings to decide where to direct scarce resources. For programme planners and clinicians, research and evaluation may produce 'actionable' evidence that they can use to strengthen programmes and services, recruit participants, or expand the funding base. Most important, for community partners (i.e., teens and parents) community-based research may trigger collective action to improve schools and neighbour-hoods. One way to accomplish these goals is to conduct mixed methods research within a CBPR framework. Although this approach can be particularly challenging with adolescents, the benefits make the effort worthwhile, by enhancing the quality of the research, leading in some cases to policy change, and building a new generation of researchers and advocates who are key to the long-term health and vitality of communities nationwide.

Practical tips

1 Be prepared to negotiate dynamics within adolescent groups, particularly in focus groups: some participants might know each other, while others may be strangers, and you need to be aware of specific challenges with group dynamics: e.g., 'cliques', or a person loudly telling another to shut up. Research with teens might thus require a lot more moderator redirection than in groups with strangers or adults.

2 Draw on the diverse strengths of your partners to help negotiate the roles of researcher and interventionist with teens and families. In working with vulnerable adolescents, researchers often want to be as helpful as possible, correcting misinformation about health issues that surface in focus groups, for example. The focus group format did not lend itself to addressing this issue, but the mixed method approach with its collaborative team (including, in our case, a nutritionist) allowed us to take material from one setting and incorporate it into Photovoice and other subsequent intervention efforts where it could be addressed.

3 Give teens plenty of coaching and encouragement to help them fill their roles as researchers and advocates. Both the concept and acceptance of powerful roles may be foreign to teens, particularly Latinas and other adolescent girls raised in cultures where female assertiveness is not encouraged. Facilitators should anticipate teens' resistance and be willing to invest time and attention in preparing teens to advance through the stages of the empowerment process. At an early stage, requiring an informal presentation of photos and reflections, with facilitators providing detailed feedback, helps teens overcome shyness and build confidence for later more formal presentations.

References

Bandurraga, A., Gowen, L. K., & the Finding Our Way Team. (2013). *'I bloomed here': A guide for conducting Photovoice with youth receiving culturally – and community – based services.* Portland, OR: Research and Training Center for Pathways to Positive Futures, Portland State University.

Checkoway, B., Allison, T., & Montoya, C. (2005). Youth participation in public policy at the municipal level. *Children and Youth Services Review, 27,* 1149–62.

Cheung, W. Y., Wildschut, T., Sedikides, C., Hepper, E. G., Arndt, J., & Vingerhoets, A. (2013). Back to the future: The effect of nostalgia on optimism. *Personality and Social Psychology Bulletin, 39,* 1484–96.

Cooper, C., & Yarbrough, S. (2010). Tell me – show me: Using combined focus group and photovoice methods to gain understanding of health issues in rural Guatemala. *Qualitative Health Research, 20,* 644–53.

Downey, L., Ireson, C., & Scutchfield, D. (2009). The use of photovoice as a method of facilitating deliberation. *Health Promotion Practice, 10,* 419–27.

The Examining Community-Institutional Partnerships for Prevention Research Group. (2006). *Developing and sustaining community-based participatory research partnerships: A skill-building curriculum.* Retrieved from www.cbprcurriculum.info on 24 June 2015.

Freire, P. (1970). *Pedagogy of the oppressed.* New York, NY: Herder and Herder.

Hannay, J., Dudley, R., Milan, S., & Leibovitz, P. (2013). Combining photovoice and focus groups: Engaging Latina teens in community assessment. *American Journal of Preventive Medicine, 44 (3S3),* S215-S24.

Hurworth, R. (2003). Photo-interviewing for research. Social Research UPDATE. University of Surrey. Retrieved from www.sru.soc.surrey.ac.uk/SRU40.html on 10 July 2015.

Innovation Center for Community and Youth Development (September 2008). *Collective leadership works: Preparing youth and adults for community change.* Section 7: Part 2: Activity Photovoices. (pp.164–79). Retrieved from www.theinnovationcenter.org/files/file/Collective-Leadership-ALL-LINKS.pdf on 22 June 2015.

Israel, B. A., Schulz, A. J., Parker, E. A., & Becker, A. B. (1998). Review of community-based research: Assessing partnership approaches to improve public health. *Annual Review of Public Health, 19,* 173–202.

Israel, B. A., Schulz, A. J., Parker, E. A., Becker, A. J., Allen, A. J., & Guzman, R. J. (2008). Critical issues in developing and following CBPR Principles. In M. Minkler & N. Wallerstein (Eds), *Community-based participatory research for health: From process to outcome* (2nd edn, pp. 47–66). San Francisco, CA: John Wiley & Sons.

Krippendorf, K. (2004). *Content analysis: An introduction to its methodology.* Thousand Oaks, CA: Sage.

Krueger, R., & Casey, M. (2008). *Focus groups: A practical guide for qualitative research.* Thousand Oaks, CA. Sage.

KU Work Group for Community Health and Development. (2014). Chapter 3, Section 10. *Implementing Photovoice in Your Community.* Lawrence, KS: University of Kansas. Retrieved from the Community Tool Box: www.ctb.ku.edu/en/table-of-contents/assessment/assessing-community-needs-and-resources/photovoice/main on 23 June 2015.

Leung, F., & Savithiri, R. (2009). Spotlight on focus groups. *Canadian Family Physician, 55*, 218–19.

Lewin, K. (1946). Action research and minority problems. *Journal of Social Issues, 2*, 34–46.

Marne, M., Snyder, K., & Gadin, K. G. (2012). Photovoice: An opportunity and challenge for students' genuine participation. *Health Promotion International, 28*, 299–310.

Minkler, M., & Hancock, T. (2008). Community-driven asset identification and issue selection. In M. Minkler & N. Wallerstein (Eds), *Community-based participatory research for health: From process to outcome* (2nd edn, pp.153–69). San Francisco, CA: John Wiley & Sons.

Minkler, M., & Wallerstein, N. (2008). *Community-based participatory research for health: From process to outcome* (2nd edn). San Francisco, CA: John Wiley & Sons.

Palibroda, B., Krieg, B., Murdock, L., & Havelock, J. (2009). *A practical guide to Photovoice: Sharing pictures, telling stories and changing communities*. Winnipeg, Manitoba: The Prairie Women's Health Center of Excellence.

Patton, M. Q. (1987*). How to use qualitative methods in evaluation*. Newbury Park, CA: Sage.

Ramirez, A. G., Gallion, K. J., Despres, C. E., & Adeigbe, R.T. (2013). *Salud America!* A research network to build the field and evidence to prevent Latino childhood obesity. *American Journal of Preventive Medicine, 44*, S178–S85.

Sanon, M., Evans-Agnew, R., & Boutain, D. (2008). An exploration of social justice intent in photovoice research studies: From 2008 to 2013. *Nursing Inquiry, 21*, 212–26.

Shaffer, R. (1983). *Beyond the dispensary*. Nairobi, Kenya: Amref.

Srivastava, P., & Hopwood, N. (2009). A practical iterative framework for qualitative data analysis. *International Journal of Qualitative Methods, 8*, 76–84.

Wang, C., & Burris, M. (1994). Empowerment through Photovoice: Portraits of participation. *Health Education Quarterly, 21*, 171–86.

Wang, C., & Pies, C. (2004). Family, maternal, and child health through photovoice. *Maternal and Child Health Journal, 8*, 95–102.

Wang, C., & Pies, C. (2008). Using Photovoice for participatory assessment and issue selection: Lessons from a family, maternal, and child health department. In M. Minkler & N. Wallerstein (Eds), *Community-based participatory research for health: From process to outcome* (2nd edn, pp.183–97). San Francisco, CA: John Wiley & Sons.

9

NOVEL AND CREATIVE QUALITATIVE METHODOLOGIES WITH CHILDREN

Karen Winter

9.1 Introduction

The use of creative qualitative methodologies in research with children is now a taken for granted aspect of the research process backed up by a wide knowledge base that spans disciplines and that describes: the methods, their application, the theoretical standpoints underpinning their usage, ethical issues, and the benefits and limitations of employing such methodologies (see review by Winter, 2014a). In one sense it could be argued that there is little new to say. However, the literature often lacks a detailed exploration of particular methods as applied in the research process, their transformational properties and possibilities as well as some of the limitations. It is within this context that the focus of this chapter is a detailed consideration of two arts based methods (picture construction and reality boxes) that I applied in research with young children ages 4–7 years old in 'out-of-home' care to elicit their in-depth experiences, perspectives and feelings about their lives at home; their knowledge of the reasons behind the transition into 'out-of-home' care; their experiences since moving including their involvement in decision making. The chapter will consider children's engagement in the research process, strengths and weaknesses, the impact of the methodology to our understanding and future directions. The chapter will end with three practical tips for students planning to undertake research with young children using these methods.

9.2 'Novel' and 'transformational' methods

The methods used in my research have variously been referred to as 'innovative' or 'novel' and could also be perceived as 'transformational'. These terms sound impressive and yet, as Wiles, Pain and Crow (2010) as well as Wise, Bengry-Howell, Crow and Nind (2013) and others (Taylor & Coffey, 2009; Travers, 2009) remind us, there is a need to be measured and specific about the claims that are being made. And so, at the outset it is important to consider in what sense these methods could be called 'novel' and 'transformational'? Research literature uses the term 'novel' to mean pioneering a new methodological innovation or the novel application of pre-existing methods in new contexts. Wiles *et al.* (2010) helpfully identify 'innovation' or 'novel' at three levels: at inception, adaptation and/or adoption. The use of reality boxes, an idea I derived from a presentation by young people at an international conference titled Childhoods 2005 Oslo (www.child hoods2005.uio.no/), was a novel application of a pre-existing method in a new context. So too was the construction of pictures using arts based materials. My own research was the first social work of its kind to employ these methods with this particular group of young children under the age of 7 years old who lived in 'out-of-home' care and where, prior to my own work (Winter, 2011; 2012; 2014a; 2014b), it was common in social work practice to, at best, underestimate the competence of young children to express their experiences and perspectives or, at worst, to assume that they could not do this.

Informed by a child rights based approach and rooted within sociological understandings of children and childhood these aspects to my research were also novel at the time. With regards to children's rights, the *United Nations Convention on the Rights of the Child* (UNCRC) (UN, 1989), establishes children as a group requiring separate 'rights' provisions, as individuals who can exercise rights, and also creates a set of standards to which governments should comply and against which legislation, policy and practice should be evaluated. References to the UNCRC often divide it into three broad categories: rights to provision, protection, and participation. In terms of participation rights, a theme which informed my own research study, these include: the right to information (Article 13), the freedom to express views and to have his or her views taken into account in all matters affecting them (Articles 12), freedom of information (Article 13), and that in making decisions in children's 'best interests' (Article 3) due regard has to be given to their views (Article 12). Through *General Comments*, the United Nations acknowledges that very young children face particular challenges in getting their voice heard. *General Comment No. 7 Implementing Child Rights in Early Childhood* (United Nations, 2005, p. 6–7, para. 14) notes, for example, that young children are exposed to age-related discrimination and that this should be tackled within a framework of evolving capacities (*General Comment No. 7*, United Nations, 2005).

A sociological approach to children and childhood also informed my research design. This allowed for a consideration of the influence of social and cultural factors on the lives of children and young children's own social agency (James, Jenks, & Prout, 1998; Jenks, 1982). As Jenks (1982, p. 205) argued, evidence showed that 'cross-culturally children vary enormously in terms of their degree of responsibility, the expectations held of them, their level of dependency, need for care, life expectation and more generally the nature of their relationship with adults'. Again my approach was novel because at the time, views of children and childhood within the social work profession were predominantly informed by a rigid, narrow, if not inaccurate understanding of a Piagetian developmental focus on 'age and stage' with the result that the abilities of young children were sometimes underestimated (Knight & Caveney, 1998; Winter, 2006).

The term 'transformational' research, as noted by Given (2008, p. 887), is multifaceted in its meaning. It can refer to the research process (the choice, application and use of methods by researchers). It can also refer to the intended impact of the research and this might include offering new insights that seek to challenge stereotypical and discriminatory attitudes and assumptions, to educate or enlighten, and/or to transform practice in a certain area. The latter is certainly the case with my own research in which findings revealed that young children can hold deep insights. These findings firmly challenged the 'taken for granted' assumptions held by social work professionals that negated young children's competence and capacity (Winter, 2011). The remainder of the chapter considers the methods used, their application in practice as illustrated through some of my research case studies, their strengths and weaknesses, and their contribution to the field. The chapter ends with three practical tips for those considering the use of these methods.

9.3 The arts based methods

Knowles and Cole (2008) define arts based research as:

> The systematic use of the artistic process, the actual making of artistic expressions in all of the different forms of the arts, as a primary way of understanding and examining experience by both researchers and the people that they involve in their studies (p. 29).

The methods are many and include the use of puppets, Lego, toys, role-plays and modelling clay (Mand, 2012; Winter, 2014a). My own contribution involves two types of arts based method – picture construction and reality boxes. Each, using a detailed case example from my own research, is discussed in turn.

9.4 Picture construction

Picture construction has long been used as a therapeutic, diagnostic, and research tool (Backett-Milburn & McKie, 1999; Rollins, 2005; Winter, 2014a). With regards to *why* researchers might wish to use picture construction, it is argued that: 1) the method is child-friendly (appealing to the skills set of young children); 2) it includes an activity with which children might already be familiar (through their everyday play for example); 3) and that drawings represent a powerful form of communication allowing children (through colour, shapes, patterns, and lines) to articulate their experiences and perspectives in a more detailed way than reliance on verbal interactions alone (Duncan, 2013). In terms of *when* researchers use this method, drawings can be used to measure children's abilities (Horstman, Aldiss, Richardson, & Gibson, 2008) or to gain children's perspectives (Clark & Moss, 2011; Coates & Coates, 2006; Driessnack & Furukawa, 2012).

How researchers use the drawing method varies. At times there is a structured approach to the drawing within the research process, with children being invited to complete mapping exercises of their social and physical environments (Clark & Moss, 2011; Darbyshire, MacDougall, & Schiller, 2005), to draw spider diagrams (Punch, 2002), to construct time lines (Gawler, 2005), and to discuss them. Other researchers have used picture construction in a more flexible way to engage children in the exploration of sensitive issues about their illnesses, their worries, fears or perspectives but where the content of their pictures may not relate directly to what has been spoken about (Duncan, 2013). In this sense the method acts as a vehicle to a conversation or to the expression of their inner world, feelings and thoughts (Hamama & Ronen, 2009). Given that the method connects with the lived experiences of children, it is often carried out within their local social contexts – schools, homes, surgeries and hospitals for example (Duncan, 2013). Further practicalities of this approach are explored in the case studies that follow.

In relation to *what* makes this method 'novel' in the context of my own research three things are worth highlighting: 1) there was then no other research with young children in 'out-of-home' that used this approach; 2) there was no other research with this group that sought to elicit their perspectives and feelings; 3) and there was no other research with this group of children which illustrated how and in what ways young children exerted their own social agency in the interview process (Winter, 2011; 2012). Examples of social agency in the interview context include the fact that by 'talking and doing' children can diffuse some of the intensity of the interview encounter by choosing to be busy making pictures while talking, thus avoiding eye contact with the interviewer if they feel shy, upset or awkward. Children can also take 'time out' of the interview by switching the conversation from the issues to their construction (Winter, 2011; 2012). Appropriately used, the method is seen as one that will provide the best chance of supporting children to express their views especially on sensitive issues. To illustrate this the next section considers a case study from my research involving Harvey.

The case study of Harvey is part of a bigger research project, that underwent rigorous ethical approval and which explored the participation rights of young children in 'out-of-home' care, and took place between 2005 and 2008. It centred on ten case studies selected from families with whom I had previously worked in my capacity as a Guardian ad Litem (an Officer of the Court appointed to independently represent the best interests of the child) but where my professional role had ended. In total thirty-nine semi-structured interviews were undertaken with young children, their parents and their social workers. As part of this fourteen children, who were each seen once as part of the study, were interviewed: five female and nine male. For children to be involved in the study they, their carers and social workers had to give consent and the process was constructed as multilayered, 'opt-in', and ongoing rather than a 'one-off' event. The research process, ethical issues and findings are reported elsewhere (Winter, 2011; 2012; 2014).

The interviews with children took place in social service buildings that were familiar to the children, where there was a quiet room with table and chairs, and where arts based methods could be used. Interviews, which were digitally recorded, lasted between 40 and 90 minutes and were based on the practice of 'talking and doing' where children were engaged in conversations (which were digitally recorded) alongside also being engaged in creative methods. As part of this research, I purchased a large, plastic, multicoloured arts storage box – that could be carried like a big brief case, and that contained small and larger pull out drawers in which I stored felt tip pens, coloured pencils, sheets of varied stickers, pom-poms, fuzzy felt shapes, buttons, feathers, beads, ribbons, string, cotton, pipe cleaners, matchsticks, glue sticks, glitter, wool, scissors, as well as gold and silver cardboard shapes. I had a separate box that contained plastic toy figures, shoeboxes and plain facemasks that children could make into their own designs. Children could choose from a range of activities including drawing, cutting, sticking, picture construction, writing, playing with figures as well as the possibility of constructing reality boxes. Children's constructions were photographed. Some children opted just to talk rather than use any of the activities on offer.

9.4.1 Case example using picture construction – Harvey (aged 4 years)

By way of a brief background the H family had been known to social services for several years. Harvey was one of four children born to Ms Hill (Helen). The children were removed from her care under an emergency court order following cumulative concerns regarding Ms Hill's own alcohol misuse, mental health issues (suicide attempts), violent relationship with an unstable partner and concerns regarding the children's wellbeing. When Harvey was at home, he spent a lot of time being looked after by his sister Heather. Following a series of unsuccessful attempts by Ms Hill to address her alcohol misuse, the plan for Harvey became one of adoption. Harvey was staying with foster carers (Henrietta and HJ) until this happened. His older sister (Heather) and brother (Henry) were initially placed with extended family members before moving into two different residential units. It was the view of the social workers that because Harvey was young, had been in foster care for about 18 months and had limited contact with his birth family, that his memories of his birth family were hazy and that his birth family were no longer that significant to him anymore. It was also recorded on reports for formal meetings that Harvey was too young to express his views. The purpose of this research interview was to explore Harvey's views of his circumstances, his experiences and his feelings.

At the start of a research interview with young children, using this approach, there are five practical hints for researchers. First, at the outset the researcher should state the interview purpose in a clear, accessible, short and jargon free manner. Second, the researcher should introduce the digital recorder saying that this keeps everything that is said and makes sure the researcher does not forget anything important. The researcher should ask the child if they would like to see how the digital recorder works and to hear the sound of their own voice. Most children say yes. Given that this may take about 10–15 minutes the additional time should be factored into the interview. Third, the researcher should be clear about how he/she intends to talk with the child during the interview. I explained to Harvey that I had brought along an art box and that if he liked we could draw and make things together while talking with each other. I asked Harvey if that was okay. He nodded to indicate yes. Fourth, the researcher may need to support and facilitate children's engagement with the materials on offer by playing with them first and then inviting the child to do the same. Fifth, the researcher should pay attention to the child's body language. In my research interview with Harvey we had a low table at which I knelt and he stood. This positioning meant that we were at the same level in terms of eye contact. Harvey chose some coloured paper and began to look at ribbon, wool and glue. I then invited Harvey to tell me who lived in his family (I left the definition of 'family' to Harvey). Harvey immediately began to name members of his *birth family* rather than his foster family:

Interviewer:	Harvey, can you tell me who lives in your family with you?
Harvey:	Everybody.
Interviewer:	Everybody? [. . .] You tell me who's in your family.
Harvey:	Helen. [Birth mother]
Interviewer:	Helen? So there's mummy Helen? [*Pointing to a piece of paper where Harvey is beginning to assemble ribbon from the art box.*] There she is. And what does your mummy Helen look like?
Harvey:	Got black hair.

As the session moves on Harvey makes a picture of his birth mother (see Figure 9.1) while naming other *birth family members*:

Harvey:	I'm making that for Helen. [*Pointing to the picture that he is constructing.*]
Interviewer:	Are you making that for Helen?
Harvey:	Yeah.
Interviewer:	That's lovely [. . .] so in your family there's Helen? Who else is there?
Harvey:	[*Mumbles word Heather – birth sister and someone else – inaudible.*]
Interviewer:	Heather? And who's the other one?
Harvey:	Henry. [*Birth brother*]
Interviewer:	Henry! Ah! Let's see. Now where does Henry live at the moment? Where does he live? [*No answer.*]
Harvey:	Look what I done. [*Shows me some paper he is sticking together.*]
Interviewer:	Oh, good boy! That's lovely! Henry, does he live with you? [. . .]
Harvey:	No, that's my house, that's his house. [*Pointing to two ends of the table as if they are two houses.*]
Interviewer:	OK. You're going to stick that on there? [*Harvey is sticking ribbon on a piece of paper to make legs.*]
Harvey:	Because he's my brother and I'm going to make it and look what I done. [*Harvey has picked up some glitter to make a tummy.*]

Given the social worker's view that Harvey had a hazy memory of home and tenuous relationships with birth family, it was highly significant that given the time,

FIGURE 9.1 A picture of mummy by Harvey

space and tools, Harvey was very capable of identifying the significant people. His words and pictures represented an immediate challenge to the prevailing social workers' view. As we continued to focus on the construction of the picture that he was making, I asked Harvey if he remembered going from his mother's house to his foster carers' house. It was the view of the social worker that Harvey was 'too young' to remember much about it. Again Harvey's words and picture constructions revealed otherwise as noted below:

Harvey: Put glue on there.
Interviewer: Yeah, put some glue there?
Harvey: And her hair.

Interviewer:	And her hair? [*Long pause while Harvey concentrates on gathering wool, which is bound together in small packs.*] Who looked after you when you were a baby?
Harvey:	Helen. [*Birth mother*]
Interviewer:	Helen did? [*Long pause to watch Harvey as he tries to gather more wool and glue.*] At her house? And do you remember when you moved to Henrietta's house?
Harvey:	Yeah.
Interviewer:	Yeah? What was that like?
Harvey:	Open it myself? [*Another pause as I observe Harvey opening the art box.*]
Interviewer:	Who helped you move in there?
Harvey:	Helen.
Interviewer:	Helen did? And were you happy when you went to Henrietta's house or sad?
Harvey:	Sad, I didn't want to go to school there.
Interviewer:	You were sad? You didn't want to go to the school there?

Unusually, Harvey's birth mother accompanied him during his admission to the foster placement. Most children removed from their birth families are separated at the family home. There can be pain and confusion accompanying the transition process (Winter, 2011; 2014a). Although Harvey did not recount the reasons for this move, he remembered it happening and the changes it brought about. During this type of research interview the researcher should be attuned to the verbal and non-verbal cues of the child. A child may be communicating, through gesture, movement, body language, facial gesture and words that they are bored, tired, upset, disengaged, interested, engaged or ready to move on. In the case of Harvey, he finished one picture and engaged in making another when asked if he wanted to carry on. In this sense it could be said that within the structured space of the interview (set up by me, facilitated by me and using materials chosen by me) Harvey was able to articulate his own choices that were then supported by me through my words and actions.

This raises a question about who controls the content, pace and nature of the interview – the child or researcher (Winter, 2010)? There is no blueprint to follow but rather there should be a process of careful planning that takes account of the child, their age, abilities, circumstances and context, the research questions and the methods available. In Harvey's case (below) he chose to spend time constructing a picture of his sister Heather (see Figure 9.2), carefully choosing materials and colours to make different parts of her (clothes, legs and eyes). The careful attention to detail seemed at odds with the social worker's view, which was that his birth family members were no longer of significance to him.

Interviewer:	[. . .] Would you like to make a picture of anyone else?
Harvey:	[*Nods to indicate yes.*]
Interviewer:	Who would you like to make a picture of?
Harvey:	Of Heather. [*Birth sister.*]
Interviewer:	Heather?
Harvey:	Girls wear, girls wear pink.
Interviewer:	Yes, girls wear pink?
Harvey:	Here's pink.
Interviewer:	And there's pink too. So let's see, how could we make Heather?
Harvey:	I want to make her legs. [*Pointing to strips of fabric.*]
Interviewer:	Yes, those could be her legs, Heather's legs. Does Heather like wearing pink?
Harvey:	Yeah . . . Her legs are pink and pink and pink and pink.
Interviewer:	Her legs are pink and then pink and pink and pink and pink?
Harvey:	There.

Having collated the data in this way, a key question for researchers is how to interpret and analyse such data. Work by Duncan (2013) highlights that there are a range of approaches that reflect differing ontological and epistemological standpoints regarding the nature of reality, how we define knowledge, and how we come to know what we know. Two broad types are mentioned here. One is to code the imagery in the pictures – the shapes, forms, colour – in line with an individualistic developmental approach where, it is argued, differences can reflect age-related stages in the development of understanding of/and representation of reality. This reflects a positivist standpoint – that is there is an objective truth to be found and it can be labelled, quantified, and categorised. Luquet's Stage Theory (1927) is a good example here with its four stages that delineate in an 'age and stage' fashion the children's drawing development from drawing what they know, to what they actually see. Others argue that this categorisation is too rigid, linear, and does not reflect the cultural and social context in which each child's reality is constructed, understood and experienced.

Furthermore, it does not take account of what the researcher brings to the process in the making of meaning. This Interpretivist standpoint acknowledges that what is known as 'truth' is socially constructed. The analysis of data therefore, has to take account of these nuances and subtleties. Duncan's work (2013),

FIGURE 9.2 A picture of my sister by Harvey

informed by social semiotics (studying signs and meaning making within specific cultural and social contexts), presents a four-stage framework to the analysis of pictures that combines coding imagery and taking account of the nuances of cultural and social contexts. My own research, as indicated earlier, was approached from an Interpretivist standpoint.

9.4.2 Strengths and weaknesses of picture construction as one form of arts based method

Although, in the example of Harvey, the benefits of using picture construction are clear, it is important to be mindful of associated weaknesses. I have raised these as a series of questions for researchers to consider. First, how much of the choice of this method is really child led? It may be that the choice of this method stems from pre-existing stereotypes of young children, and hence reinforces the view that it is only through picture construction that they can communicate (Gallacher & Gallagher, 2008; Thomson, 2007). Second, does the choice of this method mask researcher fear and lack of confidence in more straightforward verbal communi-cation with children (Warming, 2011)? Third, could the choice of this method be disempowering to children in that they might perceive engagement in the task as some kind of test which, if they do not feel confident with arts based materials, might hinder their engagement through fear of failure?

In addressing these first three issues, the following practical suggestions are ones I have found helpful: take some time to get to know a little about the child before they are seen. Ensure that the right venue is chosen for the interview. Choices should be informed by considerations such as what is familiar to the children, and whether it is permissible and possible to comfortably engage in these methods in this location. Researchers should take along a range of materials. The choice here is researcher led – how much money there is to spend on materials, how confident is the researcher in their use, do they have the potential to act as a barrier (too difficult, too messy), how will they be stored, will children feel overburdened by choice or underwhelmed by lack of choice, what are the questions to be explored? There is no checklist as such because each child is different. Make clear at the outset the 'rules' of the interview (what it's for, how long it will last, how it can be stopped, where the toilet is, whether a snack is needed or not). Within the parameters of the interview and the materials available, the child should be permitted choice about what (if anything) they wish to engage with. The role of the researcher might include introducing new materials to children, helping them (open packets, take lids off, use scissors), engaging in the construction of the picture with the child if invited to by the child (e.g., 'Can you stick that there? Can you cut this?'), asking them what different things mean, and offering reassurance that there is no right or wrong answer; that the interview is not a test to see who can make the best picture; that no marks are awarded but that the interview is a place to talk about certain things and to make things if they like.

Another related and common concern is whether the invitation to young children to explore difficult issues through this method might actually cause more harm than good? In addressing this concern researchers need to take a balanced approach, weighing up a consideration for the child's wellbeing against the hoped-for benefits of the research (Alderson & Morrow, 2011; Winter, 2011). In the case of my own work, there is a clear need for research using this type of method and to bring the hidden and invisible perspectives of very young children in 'out-of-home' care into the public domain with the aim of challenging and galvinising changes in practice. However, there is also a clear need for proper ethical protocols (Winter, 2011; 2012). One last issue is a question as to whether researchers have the necessary skills required to use creative methods effectively? The case study of Harvey reveals that researchers require well-developed verbal and non-verbal communication skills and high levels of reflexivity (that is the ability to identify the influences they bring to bear on the research process) (Alderson & Morrow, 2011; Winter, 2011). Researchers should begin by being clear about whether they have the requisite skills before embarking on research involving this type of method.

9.5 Reality boxes

Another form of arts based method, and my own specific contribution, is the 'reality box' (Winter, 2011; 2012). As noted earlier, the concept was based on an idea that I came across at a conference on Childhoods in Oslo (www.childhoods2005. uio.no). The reality box was an empty, undecorated shoebox with a lid. On the outside of the box children were invited to construct an image that best reflected how they came across to the outside world (their public person). For children this was explained as 'what they think they look like to people around them'. On the inside they were invited to construct images of their thoughts and feelings (their private person). For children this was explained as 'what is hidden away in their heads and their hearts'. The difference between the reality boxes and picture construction (referred to above) is that the box (with an inside and an outside) can be used to provide a symbolic representation of a person (with an outer appearance and inner thoughts and feelings). This method works well when it might be difficult to draw feelings and could be used for children (and young people) of different ages and backgrounds. This chapter reports the case example of Grady (not previously published).

9.5.1 Case example using the reality box – Grady (aged 4 years)

By way of background, social services became involved with the G family when Grady was about 2 years old following concerns regarding Ms Getty's life style including late night parties, substance misuse, multiple and sudden house moves due to paramilitary threats, and large debts. After a very violent domestic incident, all of the children were removed from their family home. Grady was separated from his siblings and placed with foster carers.

The research session began with a long 'lead in' where Grady spent time looking through the art box and bags that I had taken with me. Grady took most of the materials out of their bags and containers, laid them on the coffee table (which I sat next to and he stood next to). He then asked me if it was okay to make boxes into houses to which I said 'yes'. Hence, in this research session, Grady made the reality boxes into the three houses (see Figure 9.3) each with figures living in. These represented his family home (Figures 9.4 and 9.5).

This was a departure from the work of other children in the research (Winter 2011; 2012) where they had engaged with the boxes in the way in which I had intended the boxes to be used (the outside of the box to represent how the child looks and the inside of the box to represent thoughts, experiences and feelings). In my work with Grady I respected his choice and supported it. This, in turn, did enable him to explore his feelings – as seen below:

Interviewer:	And do you know why you don't live at mummy's house anymore?
Grady:	Because my mummy, mummy don't look after, mummy don't look after us properly.
Interviewer:	Mummy don't [*using same word as Grady for symmetry in the interview process*] look after you's properly?
Grady:	Aha.
Interviewer:	What kind of things?
Grady:	Us!
Interviewer:	Mummy didn't look after you properly?
Grady:	Yeah.
Grady:	[*Silence. Grady cuts out some paper.*]
Interviewer:	Grady, you see when you say to me that mummy didn't look after you properly, what do you mean? Did she feed you?
Grady:	No.
Interviewer:	No?

FIGURE 9.3 The inside of Grady's three boxes (his three homes together)

Grady:	No.
Interviewer:	Did she put clean clothes on you?
Grady:	Yes.
Interviewer:	But she didn't feed you?
Grady:	No.
Interviewer:	Were you always hungry?
Grady:	Yeah, my stomach was rumbling.
Interviewer:	Your stomach was rumbling?

Here Grady recalls his experience of being removed:

Interviewer:	OK, oh, right, we've got to do those ones as well. OK. [*Referring pictures being completed while talking.*] And who took you from your mummy's house to Gwendolyn's [*foster carer*] house?

Grady:	A social worker.
Interviewer:	A social worker? And do you know why she took you away from your mummy's house?
Grady:	No.
Interviewer:	No? And how did you feel when she took you from your mummy's house?
Grady:	Happy.
Interviewer:	You felt happy? Did you not want to stay with your mummy?
Grady:	Yeah.

While he spoke of his happiness at being away from his family home, he was also able to identify the feeling 'not happy'. This is evidenced in the excerpt below when talking about the people he was drawing to go into one of the reality boxes – the family home (Figure 9.5).

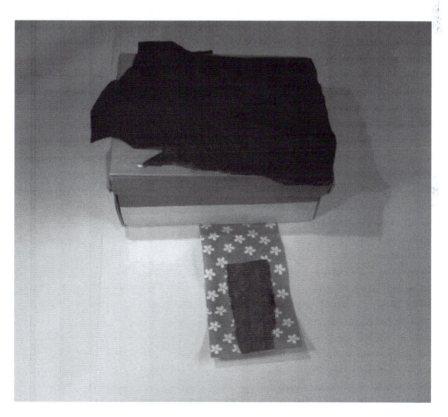

FIGURE 9.4 The outside of Grady's family home

Interviewer:	And is this house a happy house where all these people live?
Grady:	It was. [*Drawing mum and stepdad, Gerard, on paper.*]
Interviewer:	This used to be a happy house?
Grady:	Yeah. And now it isn't.
Interviewer:	And now it isn't? Why is it not happy anymore?
Grady:	Cause we don't live with mummy and Gerard.

The exploration of his feelings continued as he was constructing his boxes (Figure 9.5). He went on to identify the feeling 'sad' when, without prompt, he introduced his nanny into the conversation:

Interviewer:	Oh, there's some room there. Who else is there?
Grady:	Nanny.
Interviewer:	Nanny?
Grady:	Nanny is the same size as mummy and Gerard [*Drawing her*].
Interviewer:	Nanny is the same size as mummy and Gerard? And do you like nanny?
Grady:	Yeah.
Interviewer:	Did you used to go to nanny's house?
Grady:	Yeah.
Interviewer:	Yeah?

FIGURE 9.5 The inside of Grady's family home

Grady:	But now I don't.
Interviewer:	Now you don't? And how do you feel about that?
Grady:	Sad.

While it is clear from the discussions above that Grady had strong attachments to his birth family, he also had strong relationships with his other carers and identified the feeling 'happy' in relation to them all as indicated below:

Interviewer:	You're not sad in anybody's house?
Grady:	Just happy.
Interviewer:	You're just happy? So you're happy in mummy's house? You're happy in Giselle's house?
Grady:	[*Nodding to say yes.*] Put them together [. . .]
Interviewer:	All of them? [. . .]
Grady:	All of them.
Interviewer:	All of them? There, that's [*Moving the three boxes – see Figure 9.3.*]
Grady:	Oh, put them together!

9.5.2 Strengths and weaknesses of reality boxes as one form of arts based method

The use of reality boxes in my research with Grady generated insightful data about his changing identify and his feelings that he may not have been able to articulate in a traditional 'face-to-face' interview. The contribution of the method was that it acted as a vehicle, a support, something that Grady could turn to, appropriate and express experiences in a way that he may not have been able to by words and/or pictures alone. For researchers therefore, it is important to be aware of the fact that it is not the method alone that should be focused on but rather children's relationship with the method and the ways they choose to engage with it (Winter, 2010; 2011; 2014a).

There are limitations, noted below, followed by practical suggestions as to how to address these. First, how do researchers avoid an over-focus on the resultant artefact when the child's narrative that accompanies the work is equally important? Ideally, the narrative should run alongside a record of the work as it is evolving *in situ* (which could be achieved by filming for example). However, similarly to other reported findings from the use of arts based methods, this raises the issue of confidentiality (Winter, 2011; 2014). A practical suggestion for researchers is to make sure that the narrative is digitally recorded and to seek agreement, as part of the ethical protocol, that photographs will be taken *in situ* of the emerging arts based constructions and a note made of the time the photographs were taken so they can be matched up against the verbal narrative for the purposes of analysis and reporting the findings.

Second, how do researchers report findings from arts based methods that respect the views of those that have been expressed but that do not lead to over-generalisations? It is important to report that findings might not be generalisable or quantifiable, and to engage with questions about rigour and robustness. To illustrate this further, in my own research, it is impossible to make the claim that all young children in 'out-of-home' care feel like this, think like this and can express themselves like this. The very nature of the research, with its emphasis on the social agency of children and their rights, aimed to involve children as far as possible as subjects rather than objects of the research. This relied on establishing meaningful relationships with children and sensitively respecting their individuality, their choices and freedoms, being flexible and offering opportunities for negotiation, and collaboration in the research process (Alderson & Morrow, 2011; Christensen, 2004; Dockett & Perry, 2007). This by its very essence means that the research was not concerned with quantifying issues, generalising them to the population as a whole, or producing a design that could be replicated and produce the same results over and over again, but it was concerned to engage with and to reveal personal experiences, views and feelings of this group of young children which people have overlooked and/or underestimated.

The few case studies that I used in my own research serve the function of introducing at least the possibility that some young children in 'out-of-home' care have the potential to engage in meaningful discussions around difficult issues with the right levels of support, space and skill. In engaging further with issues of rigour and robustness in qualitative research, writers such as Spyrou (2011), and Thyer (2012), note that rigour and robustness is related to reflexivity – the researcher needs to be clear what they bring to the research process, what biases, assumptions, motivations and attitudes they hold, as well as how and in what ways these influence the whole research design from start to finish. As Thyer (2012) indicates, there is a need to be explicit about sample size, research design, collation and analysis of findings, discussion of alternative explanations and interpretations and explicit reference to underpinning epistemological and ontological leanings.

9.6 Concluding thoughts and three practical tips

With all these caveats in place, and by way of drawing the key points together, this chapter has illustrated the use of picture construction and reality boxes as novel and transformational. While accepting that there is no blueprint, I end this chapter by outlining three practical tips for researchers who are thinking of employing these methods.

Practical tips

1   When do these methods work and when do they not work? These methods are most likely to work well if the researcher is familiar and confident with them, if the child is positively inclined towards and familiar with them (seeing them as 'fun' rather than as a test or challenge), and if there is enough support and time for a child to engage with them fully.

2   What instructions and how much choice do you give the child? The level, nature and type of instructions given by the researcher varies depending on: whether the researcher wishes the child to draw or make something specific (in which case a direct instruction is given) or whether the method is used as a vehicle to engage a child in a wider discussion (in which less instruction might be given). Sometimes children may lack confidence and may need researcher permission to begin to play with what is available. This might involve a direct invitation (please feel free to take what you like) or it might involve an indirect invitation (the researcher exploring the materials themselves and indicating to the child that they can do the same). Once started the researcher can withdraw to more of the non-participant observation role again). The choice offered to children will vary and depend on carefully 'weighing up' the characteristics of the child (age, abilities, interests, circumstances, cultural, religious, family and social background), the context of the research interview, the research questions and the materials actually available.

3   How do you analyse these methods? As highlighted in the chapter the analysis of these methods is dependent on ontological, epistemological and theoretical frameworks. It is important to be consistent, and to make sure it is consistent with the aims, objectives of the research project and with the questions it is seeking to answer.

References

Alderson, P., & Morrow, V. (2011). *The ethics of research with children and young people: A practical handbook*. London: Sage.

Backett-Milburn, K., & McKie, L. (1999). A critical appraisal of the draw and write technique. *Health Education Research*, *14*, 387–98.

Childhoods 2005 Oslo. Children and Youth in Emerging and Transforming Societies. International Conference 29 June–3 July. Retrieved from www.childhoods2005.uio.no/ on 5 February 2015.

Christensen, P. (2004). Children's participation in ethnographic research: Issues of power and representation. *Children and Society, 18*(2), 165–76.

Clark, A., & Moss, P. (2011). *Listening to young children: The mosaic approach* (2nd edn). London: National Children's Bureau.

Coates, E., & Coates, A. (2006). Young children talking and drawing. *International Journal Early Years Education, 14*(3), 221–42.

Darbyshire, P., MacDougall, C., & Schiller, W. (2005). Multiple methods in qualitative research with children: More insight or just more? *Qualitative Research, 5*(4), 417–36.

Dockett, S., & Perry, B. (2007). Trusting children's accounts in research. *Journal of Early Childhood Research, 5*(1), 47–63.

Driessnack, M., & Furukawa, R. (2012). Arts-based data collection techniques used in child research. *Journal of Special Pediatric Nursing, 17*(1), 3–9.

Duncan, P. A. (2013). Drawing as a method for accessing young children's perspectives in research. School of Education, University of Stirling: Unpublished Thesis.

Gallacher L. A., & Gallagher M. (2008). Methodological immaturity in childhood research? Thinking through 'participatory methods'. *Childhood, 15*, 499–516.

Gawler, M. (2005). *Useful tools for engaging young people in participatory evaluation.* Geneva: UNICEF.

Given, L. (Ed.) (2008). *The SAGE encyclopedia of qualitative research methods.* Thousand Oaks, CA: Sage.

Hamama, L., & Ronen, T. (2009). Children's drawings as a self-portrait measurement. *Child and Family Social Work, 14*, 90–102.

Horstman, M., Aldiss, S., Richardson, A., & Gibson F. (2008). Methodological issues when using the draw and write technique with children aged 6 to 12 years. *Qualitative Health Research, 18*(7), 1001–11.

James, A., Jenks, C., & Prout, A. (1998). *Theorizing childhood.* London: Polity Press.

Jenks, C. (Ed.). (1982). *The sociology of childhood: Essential readings.* London: Batsford Academic and Educational.

Knight, T., & Caveney, S. (1998). Assessment and action records: Will they promote good parenting? *British Journal of Social Work, 28*(1), 29–43.

Knowles, J. G., & Cole, A. L. (2008). *Handbook of the arts in qualitative research. Perspectives, methodologies, examples, and issues.* Thousand Oaks, CA: Sage.

Luquet, G. H. (1927). *Le Dessin Enfantin* (Children's drawings), translation and commentary by A. Costall (2001). London and New York: Free Association Books.

Lundy, L. (2007). 'Voice' is not enough: Conceptualising Article 12 of the United Nations Convention on the Rights of the Child. *British Educational Research Journal, 33*(6), 927–42.

Mand, K. (2012). Giving children a 'voice': Arts-based participatory research activities and representation. *International Journal of Social Research Methodology, 15*(2), 149–60.

Punch, S. (2002). Research with children: The same or different from research with adults?' *Childhood, 9*(3), 321–41.

Rollins, J. A. (2005). Tell me about it: Drawing as a communication tool for children with cancer. *Journal of Pediatric Oncology Nursing, 22*(4), 203–21.

Spyrou, S. (2011). The limits of children's voices: From authenticity to critical, reflexive representation. *Childhood, 18*(2), 151–65.

Taylor, C., & Coffey, A. (2009). Editorial. Special issue: Qualitative research and methodological innovation. *Qualitative Research*, *9*(5), 523–6.

Thomson, F. (2007). Are methodologies for children keeping them in their place? *Children's Geographies*, *5*(3), 207–18.

Thyer, B. A. (2012). The scientific value of qualitative research for social work. *Qualitative Social Work*, *11*(2), 115–29.

Travers, M. (2009). New methods, old problems: A sceptical view of innovation in qualitative research. *Qualitative Research*, *9*(2), 161–79.

United Nations. (1989). *Convention on the Rights of the Child*. Geneva: United Nations.

United Nations. (2005). *General Comment No. 7. 2005. Implementing Child Rights in Early Childhood*. Geneva: United Nations.

Warming, H. (2011). Getting under their skins? Accessing young children's perspectives through ethnographic research. *Childhood*, *18*(1), 39–53.

Wiles, R., Pain, H., & Crow, G. (2010). *Innovation in qualitative research methods: A narrative review*. ESRC National Centre for Research Methods: University of Southampton: Southampton.

Winter, K. (2006). Widening our knowledge concerning young looked after children: The case for using sociological models of childhood. *Child and Family Social Work*, *11*(1), 55–64.

Winter, K. (2011). *Building relationships and communicating with young children: A practical guide for social workers*. London: Routledge.

Winter, K. (2012). Ascertaining the perspectives of young children in care: Case studies using reality boxes. *Children and Society*, *26*(5), 368–80.

Winter, K. (2014a). Innovative qualitative research methods with children aged 4–7 years. In O. Saracho & B. Spodek (Eds), *Handbook of research methods in early childhood education*. Vol I. Research Methodologies. (pp. 271–93). Charlotte, NC: Information Age Publishing.

Winter, K. (2014b). Understanding and supporting young children's transitions into state care: Schlossberg's transition framework and child-centred practice. *British Journal of Social Work*, *44*(2), 401–17.

Wise, R., Bengry-Howell, A., Crow, G., & Nind, M. (2013). But is it innovation? The development of novel methodological approaches in qualitative research. *Methodological Innovations Online*, *8*(1), 18–33.

PART 3

Mixed methods designs in research with children

10

USING MIXED METHODS IN DEVELOPMENTAL PSYCHOLOGY

From scale errors to death

*Karl S. Rosengren, Isabel T. Gutiérrez
and Matthew J. Jiang*

10.1 Introduction

Many investigators use a small set of research methods in their research, with some sticking to a single approach for most, if not their entire, career. While this tactic can be highly effective in certain research areas, we would suggest that many research questions cannot be sufficiently addressed by using a single method or approach. In this chapter we use our own research on children's scale errors (DeLoache, Uttal, & Rosengren, 2004; Rosengren, Gutiérrez, Anderson, & Schein, 2009a), behaviours where children attempt to perform an action on an object that is too small to accommodate the action, and children's understanding of death (Gutiérrez, 2009; Rosengren, Miller, Gutiérrez, Chow, Schein, & Anderson, 2014) to highlight the use of multiple methods in research. We examine reasons for embarking on a mixed method approach in research, consider some difficulties with taking a mixed method approach, and use examples of our own research. The end of the chapter discusses some of the challenges we have encountered while trying to weave together a research programme using multiple methods and provides some practical tips for researchers.

10.2 Reasons why a researcher might want to use mixed methods in their research

There are many reasons for researchers to employ multiple methods in their research. One reason for using a mixed method approach in research is that different research techniques can help you gain better insights into a problem. A second reason is that complex research questions, especially ones that are interdisciplinary in nature, may need to be tackled from multiple angles. A third reason for using mixed methods is that this approach can provide converging evidence for some phenomena. The use of multiple methods may help the researcher establish that the research can be generalized across tasks and situations to a larger extent than a single method. Researchers may also choose to employ multiple methods given that there is no perfect research method; by using multiple methods in research, different methodologies can overcome limitations of a single research design or method.

By overcoming the weaknesses of different methodologies and obtaining converging evidence through multiple methods, researchers ultimately gain a clearer and deeper understanding of complex issues. Research involving children often limits the kinds of designs and methods that are available – and thus, achieving deep understanding in certain areas may be particularly difficult. Next, we discuss types of scenarios in which applying multiple research methods can be leveraged.

10.3 What types of research might benefit from a mixed method approach?

We suggest that a mixed method approach to research may be beneficial in addressing particular types of phenomena. Specifically, we suggest that this approach may be most beneficial for: 1) studying important but infrequent behaviours, 2) addressing broad research questions, 3) studying complex issues, and 4) studying topics that society or the participants may view as sensitive in nature (see also Chapters 11, 12, 13 and 14 for further consideration of mixed method approaches). We use examples from our research on scale errors to highlight how using mixed methods can be informative in investigations of infrequent behaviours and use our research on children's understanding of death to address the value of mixed methods in studying broad, complex and sensitive questions.

10.3.1 Studying infrequent behaviours

We suggest that studying important behaviours that are relatively infrequent can benefit from using mixed methods. Using mixed methods can aid researchers in understanding the contexts and conditions that are more likely to elicit the infrequent behaviours. One relatively infrequent behaviour we have examined using mixed methods is the production of scale errors in young children. Scale errors occur when a child attempts to perform an action on an object that is too small to afford the action to be completed successfully. An example of a scale error is when a young child attempts to sit in a doll-sized chair. These behaviours are of interest to developmental psychologists because these behaviours suggest that a) children may not realize what their bodies afford for action, b) different brain pathways related to object identification and the control of action may not be integrated in young children, and c) children have difficultly inhibiting an action that is not appropriate for a small replica of a larger object. We had observed this behaviour in our own children and in laboratory tasks involving scale models, but it was not at all clear how common this behaviour was, or whether it could be elicited in children under more controlled conditions.

We began our formal study of these behaviours with a laboratory study, but then went on to conduct a prospective parent diary study, a retrospective Internet study and a series of preschool studies. We chose to use these other methods due to concern that conducting tasks in the laboratory would prime children to do something they wouldn't normally do. We describe each of these approaches briefly.

Laboratory study

For our initial attempt to investigate scale errors we designed a study (DeLoache et al., 2004) to determine whether these behaviours could be elicited in controlled laboratory conditions. In this study, children were brought in to a laboratory containing three large toys, a chair, a slide and a car. These toys were sized so that children could effectively sit on the chair, slide down the slide and climb into the car. Children were then taken to another room and the toys were replaced with tiny replica versions of the toys (a 5 cm tall chair, a 10 cm high slide, and a 10 cm high car). Children were then returned to the laboratory room and their behaviour with the replica objects was observed. Roughly half (46 per cent) of the children in this study performed at least one scale error behaviour. These behaviours included attempting to sit on, slide down and climb in to the tiny replica objects. This laboratory study confirmed that these behaviours could be elicited in a controlled laboratory task, but they did not tell us much more.

Parent diary study

The prospective parent diary provided information regarding the extent to which parents observe scale errors in their own children in their homes. In this study, we asked parents to maintain an on-going record of any scale errors performed by their children (Rosengren et al., 2009a). We first brought parents in to our laboratory for a 30-minute training session to learn about the behaviours. Parents were then sent home with a binder to record if their child performed any scale errors and (if they did) to provide details about the behaviour and situation where it occurred. We contacted parents on a regular basis to help maintain participation and address any questions. At the end of the 6 months parents returned the diaries. Twenty-nine of the thirty (97 per cent) mothers reported that their children had performed at least one scale error. The scale errors described were similar to those we had recorded in the laboratory. This study provides an important result, suggesting that these behaviours appear to be performed by most, if not all, children in the familiar home environment. This study provides more detail than the single episode of behaviours obtained in the original laboratory study. A limitation of this approach is that it required a relatively long time to collect data on a relatively small number of children.

Internet study

An Internet study (Ware, Uttal, & DeLoache, 2010) was also conducted to examine the frequency of scale errors in the home. In this study, parents were recruited to complete an online, retrospective study. At the beginning of the survey scale errors were described and parents were asked if they had ever seen a scale error, and if so, to describe the behaviour. One advantage of using the Internet to examine scale errors is that it is much more efficient in terms of time and resources than doing a 6-month diary study. In this study, data were collected from 221 parents over the course of only a few weeks.

Forty parents in the Internet study reported at least one scale error (18 per cent). The discrepancy in the frequencies between the diary study and the Internet one is likely to be due to the use of prospective (diary study) versus retrospective (Internet survey) approaches. In addition, as these behaviours are relatively infrequent, parents primed to look for them may provide more accurate information about their frequency than parents who were not primed to be on the lookout for scale errors. One limitation of both the diary study and the Internet study is that scale errors can only occur if small replica versions of larger objects (e.g., chairs, slides) are present in the environment, and we did not know to what extent this was actually the case.

Preschool studies

We conducted two studies to examine whether we could elicit scale errors in laboratory preschool classrooms (Rosengren, Carmichael, Schein, Anderson, &

Gutiérrez, 2009b; Rosengren, Schein, & Gutiérrez, 2010). In order to overcome the potential limitation of our other studies that children might not be exposed to objects likely to elicit scale errors, we seeded a number of preschool classrooms with small replica objects. The laboratory preschool setting enabled us to observe the children's behaviour from an observation booth equipped with a one-way mirror. We placed the replica objects in infants' (4 to 16 months), toddlers' (17 to 28 months), and 2-year-olds' (29 to 40 months) classrooms only when researchers were present so that we could observe all interactions with the objects. In the first study, we observed for a total of 280 minutes in each of the classrooms over a period of 12 weeks (Rosengren *et al.*, 2009b). We observed 53 per cent of the children performing at least one scale error. This result is similar to the frequency of behaviours found in the original laboratory study. Most of the scale errors occurred in the 2-year-olds' preschool classrooms so we conducted a second study to more closely focus on this age (Rosengren *et al.*, 2010). In the second study, we conducted three 20-minute observations for 10 weeks for a total of 600 minutes of observation. We found that 88 per cent of the children performed scale errors, with one child performing sixteen scale errors over an 8-week observation period.

Overall results of scale error studies

Taken together these results suggest that scale errors can be elicited in highly controlled laboratory tasks, structured observations in the preschool and in children's homes. The use of multiple methods across a variety of studies enabled us to conclude that most, if not all, children will perform a scale error at some point provided they are exposed to small replica objects. The research also suggests, based on results from very different methods, that there exist relatively large individual differences in the production of these behaviours. Finally, converging results obtained from our research group and other laboratories (Brownell, Zerwas, & Ramani, 2007) provide important replications and extensions of the initial laboratory task that could not be obtained using a single approach. In these studies the use of multiple methods helped us gain insights into this relatively uncommon behaviour that could not have been obtained using a single type of method.

10.3.2 Addressing broad, complex and sensitive research questions

Investigating a behaviour that occurs relatively infrequently, as we described in the exploration of scale errors, is one situation where using multiple methods in a series of studies can be very advantageous. Additional situations that can benefit from using multiple methods in a series of studies, or mixing the methods used in a single study, include research investigating broad research questions, complex issues or sensitive research topics.

Broad questions

Researchers are often interested in broad, overarching questions that can be difficult to examine using a single method. One obvious solution is to narrow the research question so that it can be addressed with a single approach. This is the typical approach used by many researchers, and some broad research questions can be addressed with a series of studies, all employing the same methods. However, breaking a broad question down into parts that can be easily studied in a set of discrete studies, each with a narrow focus, can sometimes make it challenging to connect all the studies back together to inform the original broad question. Further, as is the case with our investigations of scale errors, use of a single method in a series of studies may not help us find clear answers to a broad research question. Our research on how children understand death in different cultural contexts is one example of a broad research question that we argue benefited greatly from using a variety of methods. We describe this research in a later section (see section 10.4).

Complex issues

Studying complex issues may benefit from using mixed methods. One reason for this is that complex issues often require collaboration between researchers with different types of knowledge, skills and expertise. Research in the social sciences is becoming more interdisciplinary, likely due in part to the growing awareness that many important research questions are complex and require researchers with a range of different skills and expertise in research methods.

A clear example of using a variety of methods to examine a complex issue is research conducted by Karmiloff-Smith and her colleagues (Karmiloff-Smith, Casey, Massand, Tomalski, & Thomas, 2014). These investigators were interested in studying how genes and environment dynamically influence gene expression and developmental trajectories at the neural, cognitive and behavioural levels. Over a series of studies they employed five different approaches that included assessment of infant and child behaviour, neuroimaging techniques including EEG/ERP electrophysiology, structural/functional MRI, non-human animal models and neurocomputational modelling. Each of these methods provided partial information in a much more complex story of how genes and the environment interact over development. They suggest that this type of multi-method approach enables the collection of a far richer data set, and ultimately a richer theoretical analysis of the data that have been collected.

Sensitive topics

We suggest that the use of mixed methods may be useful for conducting research on sensitive topics, such as children's understanding of reproduction, children's religious beliefs or children's understanding of death. These are all important issues to study, but parents and their children may find them difficult, or uncomfortable to discuss, especially if these topics are the sole focus of an interview. Conducting research on these topics can also be ethically challenging, due to the need to be respectful of different beliefs, concern for potential emotional distress, and the need to have sensitive, highly trained researchers conducting the research. (See also Chapter 15 for further discussion of ethical issues.) Creatively designing and conducting research to minimize ethical challenges often involves the use of a variety of different methods.

10.4 Research on children's understanding of death in context

We completed a set of studies that employed mixed methods to investigate children's understanding of death (Gutiérrez, 2009; Rosengren *et al.*, 2014). Prior to our set of interconnected studies, most investigations of children's understanding of death employed a single methodological approach through the lens of one of two very different perspectives. On the one hand, researchers from a clinical perspective primarily used open-ended interviews to examine children's emotional and affective responses to death (e.g., Corr & Corr, 1996; Grollman, 1995; Shapiro, 1994; Webb, 2010). On the other hand, researchers from a cognitive developmental perspective primarily used highly structured interviews to examine how children think about death as a biological concept (e.g., Carey, 1985; Nguyen & Gelman, 2002; Poling & Evans, 2004). We felt that this previous research was limited by the use of single approaches, and we were concerned about the lack of connection between these two research literatures. We also felt that both approaches, which were based heavily on Piaget's (1929) work, underestimated children's emotional and cognitive capacity to cope with death.

Our research programme grew out of a desire to bring these two different perspectives together and to address some of the limitations of previous research on this topic. One of the most notable limitations of past research was the failure to examine children's understanding of death in context. Children do not experience and learn about death completely on their own, but do so in the context of their family and larger cultural context. From our perspective, children are likely to come to understand death in collaborations with their parents, family, and the culture at large (e.g., Callanan & Valle, 2008; Cole, 1996; Miller, 1994; Rogoff, 1998; Shweder *et al.*, 2006). For this reason we expected that children's understanding of death might vary by culture, based on the cultural construals of death that are common in their community.

A second goal of our research was to provide a more inclusive perspective of the complex nature of children's understanding of death. In our research programme, we investigated both affective and cognitive dimensions of death in the same children, while also exploring the religious and spiritual dimensions of children's understandings. Researchers have explored children's afterlife beliefs (Bering & Bjorklund, 2004; Bering, Hernández Blasi, & Bjorklund, 2005) using similar techniques to those used by most cognitive developmentalists (i.e., highly structured interviews), but generally have not done so in conjunction with an examination of the larger religious and cultural context in which children experience death.

We believe that the choice of method (or methods!) should be driven to a large extent by your research question. Our research programme (Gutiérrez, 2009; Rosengren *et al.*, 2014) was designed around three main questions: 1) How do children reason about both the cognitive and emotional aspects of death, 2) How do children come to acquire an understanding of death in their families and cultures, 3) How do children negotiate the complex, multifaceted nature of death?

Each of these main questions had a number of more specific questions associated with them, and we used a variety of different methods to examine these research questions. Figure 10.1 provides a brief overview of our research programme, presenting the research questions, methods and analytical approaches. More detailed information about the research programme can be found in Rosengren *et al.* (2014). In this next section, we explore how we used a variety of methods to address the main questions and related sub-questions.

10.4.1 How do children reason about both the cognitive and emotional aspects of death?

To examine how children reason about cognitive and emotional aspects of death, we conducted individual interviews with children while their parents completed questionnaires. To make the task highly relevant to children, we developed a procedure that involved showing children a photograph of a child (matched to the interviewee in age, ethnicity and sex) and telling them that this was a girl/boy

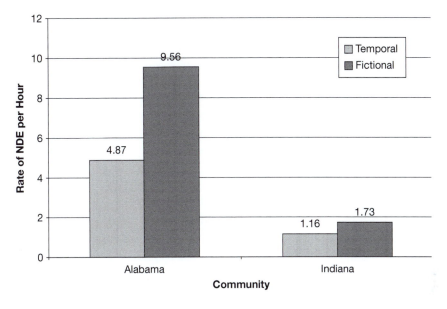

FIGURE 10.1 Research questions, methodology and analysis approach used in research investigating children's understanding of death in context

named 'Terry' who was just like them. We then showed the child photographs of Terry's aunt/uncle, Terry's pet dog and a plant owned by Terry (the order was counterbalanced across children). We told the child that one of these items (i.e., the aunt/uncle, pet dog or plant) had died and then asked questions about biological and psychological properties of the 'dead' relative/dog/plant. We also asked a number of open-ended questions about what the child thought Terry should feel about her/his 'dead' relative/pet dog/plant and what Terry's parents should tell Terry about the 'dead' relative/pet dog/plant. After asking questions about one item, we went on to the next item, repeating both the structured and open-ended questions. This main 'death' interview was embedded in a larger interview about life processes so that the questions about death came in the middle. We did this out of ethical concerns that the children might find an interview that focused solely on death disturbing, though only one of our children found the questions about death stressful (we stopped the interview early for this child).

As described above, both the child interviews and the parent questionnaires contained a combination of highly structured questions (e.g., Do all *people/animals/plants* have to die?) This required a yes/no response, as well as some open-ended questions (e.g., What are some things that cause *people/animals/plants* to die?). The highly structured child interview was based on past research in cognitive development (Nguyen & Gelman, 2002; Speece & Brent, 1992), but was extended to include both open-ended questions and questions about the emotional aspects of death (e.g., How do you think Terry feels about the death of her/his relative/dog/plant?). We also extended previous work by attempting to make the interview highly relevant to children and not to try to avoid aspects that might trigger strong emotions (i.e., we did not restrict our questions to only asking about plants or objects that are unlikely to elicit strong emotional attachments in children).

We also used parental questionnaires to examine how children reason about the cognitive and emotional aspects of death. As with the child interviews, we used both highly structured questions (e.g., Has your child ever questioned you about death and dying?) and open-ended probes (e.g., Please describe any questions your child has asked you about death and how you responded) on the questionnaires. The data from the child interviews and parental questionnaires provided a wealth of quantitative (e.g., number of children responding that all animals die) and qualitative information (e.g., parents' thoughts and beliefs about their child's ability to cope cognitively and emotionally with death).

There were two related questions that we wanted to investigate as part of the overall question about children's cognitive and emotional understanding of death. These were: 1) how children's reasoning was influenced by the age of the child, and 2) how do children, who had experienced a significant death, cope cognitively and emotionally? To address the first of these follow-up questions, we interviewed children between the ages of 3 and 6 years and examined whether responses varied by age. A full description of the study and results is beyond the scope of this chapter but may be found in Rosengren *et al.* (2014).

To address the second follow-up question (how did children who had experienced a significant death, cope cognitively and emotionally?) we used a multiple step procedure. First, we identified children who had experienced a significant death from information provided in the parent questionnaires. From these data we invited ten parents of children who had experienced a significant death to participate in individual interviews. For these parents we used an open-ended interview that was based on their original questionnaire responses. We chose to interview parents, rather than the children, due to ethical concerns regarding potential emotional distress, and because we did not have a trained clinician as part of our research team.

To further address how children who have experienced death handle it emotionally and cognitively, we interviewed four clinicians who primarily worked with grieving children. Again due to ethical considerations and concerns about whether parents of grieving children would feel comfortable with us asking their children questions, we contacted clinicians who worked with grieving children, rather than attempting to interview children ourselves. Finally, we also were able to interview the director of a local preschool that had been the focal point of a horrible tragedy that also served as the inspiration for this entire research programme.

The tragedy involved a young boy who attended a local preschool and his family. Following participation in a school trip with the boy's older brother, the mother of the young boy murdered the older brother and attempted to kill the young boy, stabbing him over 50 times. The boy survived, but this event rocked the preschool he attended as well as the surrounding community. Soon after this tragic event, the preschool hosted a number of meetings that included parents, teachers and local clinicians. We interviewed the director of the preschool to gain insights about how the children (and their parents) coped both cognitively and emotionally with this event and its aftermath. The data from interviews with the parents, clinicians and preschool director were transcribed and qualitatively coded for unified themes. One of the key findings from this aspect of the study was that parents, clinicians and a preschool director who had interacted with children who had experienced a significant death, all thought that young children under the age of 5 years could handle death both emotionally and cognitively.

10.4.2 How do children come to acquire an understanding of death?

To address our second main question, we used a variety of different methods and subject populations. The main data that we used to address this question were our parent questionnaires. For example, we asked parents whether their children asked questions about death and how the parents responded. We also asked parents how comfortable they felt talking about death, whether they attempted to shield their children from experiences of death in real life or in different forms of media (e.g., books, videos). If they did shield their children, we asked them why they did so. Thus, we drew on both highly structured and open-ended questions to examine the extent to which parents communicated information about death to their children in both direct (e.g., responses to specific questions) and indirect (e.g., attempting to avoid discussions and exposure to death related events) methods.

A key issue that we were interested in investigating was whether parents thought that their young preschool children were able to cope cognitively and emotionally with death. In a sense, we were interested in determining whether there was a cultural narrative about death that seemed to capture the environment in which the children were growing up. To explore this issue more thoroughly, we conducted research with three different main samples of children and their parents. Our principal sample was families of European descent living in a midsize midwestern community. We augmented this sample with a smaller sample of Mexican descent children and their parents living in and around this community in the United States. We chose the second sample for two reasons. The first is that we expected this group to approach death in a very different manner from that of most families of European descent in the United States. Parents in the United States attempt to shield their children from death (Ariès, 1974) while in Mexico death is embraced on a daily basis (Paz, 1961) and even considered to be the national symbol (Brandes, 2003; Lomnitz, 2005). The second reason we chose to study Mexican descent children and parents is that we wanted to use these interviews and questionnaires as pilot work for a more extensive study we planned to launch in Mexico (see Gutiérrez, 2009). Thus, our third main sample was collected in and around the city of Puebla, Mexico. These questionnaires and interviews involved a mixture of structured and open-ended questions and the data were analysed both quantitatively (e.g., the number and types of death questions) and qualitatively (e.g., common themes emerging from the interviews and question-naires). For the qualitative analysis we read over transcripts of the interviews to identify different themes and cultural narratives. A fuller description of these analyses can be found in Rosengren *et al.* (2014).

We also used focus groups as a second approach to exploring the cultural narratives related to death. We conducted two focus groups, one with teachers from a university laboratory preschool and one with teachers from a multicultural preschool primarily serving Mexican descent families. Both of these preschools were in the local community. The focus groups were transcribed and then examined using a qualitative approach to identify common themes and narratives that the teachers had encountered with respect to children's cognitive and affective responses to death.

We used a third approach to explore the cultural narratives related to death. In this approach we analysed three different types of books. The first set of books included Caldecott Medal award-winning books and a list of favourite books obtained from the parent survey. The second set of books were ones specially designed to be read to or given to young children who have recently experienced the death of a loved one. We analysed the books both quantitatively (e.g., the number of times death or a sub-concept of death were mentioned) and qualitatively (e.g., common themes such as a biological or religious perspective on death). We also examined a set of commonly used advice books for parents for information regarding children's ability to cope with death both cognitively and emotionally, and for specific advice for parents. We used a qualitative approach with these books in which we looked for common themes (e.g., be honest with children, don't avoid talking about death with your child).

A final way that we attempted to understand prevailing cultural narratives was through the use of participant observers. All of the researchers lived in the community where the tragic event described earlier occurred, and one of the researchers had a daughter who attended the same preschool as the young boy. She was a close friend of the boy who had been stabbed. This researcher also attended all of the meetings at the school involving parents, teachers and clinicians. During these meetings the researcher participated as a concerned parent, but also observed common themes that emerged from the parents' discussions and the clinicians' comments.

In addition to the researcher who was a participant/observer in the preschool, a second member of the team travelled to Mexico twice to live for an extended period of time (at least 4 months) as well as returned on multiple occasions to participate and observe in the annual celebration for Day of the Dead (*día de los muertos*). While living within the community, this researcher collected detailed ethnographic information about the community and rituals related to death. These data were analysed qualitatively for common themes that captured the cultural narratives surrounding death.

10.4.3 How do children negotiate the complex, multifaceted nature of death?

Our final main research question focused on how children negotiate the complex, multifaceted nature of death. Death is complex. Death can be viewed as a biological process, involving the cessation of all biological processes. Death can be viewed from a psychological perspective, where death results in the end of psychological processes such as thinking and feeling. Death can also be viewed from a religious or spiritual perspective. We were interested in whether we could find any evidence that children either kept these different models of death (i.e., biological, psychological, religious) separate or attempted to combine them in different ways. In particular, we were interested in whether children attempted to fit the information that they had acquired about death into a unified cognitive model or some sort of co-existence model (see Evans, Legare, & Rosengren, 2011; Legare, Evans, Rosengren, & Harris, 2012).

To address this question we read through all the interviews and surveys looking for responses that suggested that the individuals viewed death from mostly a biological, religious or combined perspective. Participants were categorized as having a unified biological model if their responses were dominated by ones that treated death as the cessation of biological and psychological processes. Participants were categorized as holding a religious model if frequent references to God or spiritual aspects were mentioned. Participants were categorized as having a co-existence model if they appeared to blend aspects of the biological and religious model. For example, in one instance a parent told her daughter that their nanny had died in a car crash (providing a real world cause for the cessation of biological processes) but then explained that 'God had decided that she should be with him'.

10.4.4 Results from our studies of children's understanding of death in context

The use of multiple methods enabled us to extend our work on children's understanding of death beyond past research. By combining highly structured interviews with open-ended questions, focus groups, clinician interviews, participant-observations, and analysis of books in the United States and Mexico, we were able to obtain a rich understanding of children's cognitive and affective responses to death (see Gutiérrez, 2009; Rosengren *et al.*, 2014 for more details about this research). Our results suggest that parents and preschool teachers in the United States generally believe that it is important to shield young children from death as the children are viewed as unable to cope emotionally or cognitively with death. This view contrasts sharply with that of clinicians who have worked with bereaved children in the US, and parents in Mexico. Both of these groups suggested that children should not be shielded from death, with Mexican parents viewing death as 'a part of life'.

By employing a mix of different methods and analytic approaches ranging from interviews to focus groups, and combining both qualitative and quantitative analyses of the data, we were able to obtain a richer and more nuanced understanding of how children handle death both cognitively and emotionally. Further, we were able to gain insights into different narratives held by parents and teachers and how these narratives varied by culture. We suggest that overall, using a mixed method approach can provide a great way to examine broad, complex questions on sensitive topics.

10.5 Challenges to conducting mixed method research

Conducting research using mixed methods is not without some major challenges. Using different methods and the appropriate analytic techniques associated with these requires a greater range of knowledge and experience than simply using one method in your research programme. For this reason, a mixed method research programme can benefit from collaborations among researchers who bring different skills and expertise. This type of collaboration may be a necessity for addressing certain broad and complex interdisciplinary problems (see also Chapters 13 and 14 for further discussion of some of the challenges of using mixed methods in research with children).

A second issue related to the use of different types of methods is that researchers trained from different perspectives may hold very different, and even incompatible, assumptions about what is the appropriate way to conduct research and analyse data. This is generally more of a problem when researchers from qualitative and quantitative traditions take extreme positions, than when researchers take a more moderate view regarding the goals and assumptions of both of these approaches. But in collaborations among researchers that cross the qualitative/quantitative divide, it may take some time and effort for researchers to understand and appreciate the alternative approach. This issue of effective communication among researchers can be one of the greatest challenges in mixed methods collaborations and apply to interdisciplinary research more generally.

An additional challenge to conducting mixed method research programmes concerns resources. Most laboratories are set-up to perform one type of research and it may be difficult to configure them in ways that enable flexibility of methods. Likewise conducting both laboratory and non-laboratory research as part of a research programme requires more time, personnel and other resources than doing one type of research in either a laboratory or non-laboratory setting.

A further challenge of mixed method approaches is the problem of putting the separate parts of the research package together in a coherent whole. When results from different methods converge, this is really not an issue. However, when the results from different methods fail to converge, it may be difficult to explain the reasons for the lack of congruence. Resolving these inconsistencies may require a further study designed to explicitly address the lack of convergence. A related issue is how to evaluate the results obtained from very different methods. While it is often relatively easy to compare measurements obtained in different quantitative approaches (as we did with the scale error studies), it is much more difficult to directly compare data collected and interpreted using a combination of qualitative and quantitative methods. In this case, it is important to consider how the entire research programme helps to build a narrative that addresses the main research question.

A final, practical challenge when using mixed methods is the issue of finding a suitable outlet to publish your research findings. While this is not really an issue with research that is either strictly quantitative or strictly qualitative, when these two approaches are combined it may be more difficult to find a journal (and reviewers) that is (are) welcoming of this approach.

Even with these challenges to conducting mixed methods research, we suggest that it is a fruitful and rewarding approach to doing research. We have certainly found, in our own research, that we can understand behaviours that occur relatively infrequently, and ask broad, complex questions on sensitive topics more deeply by employing a variety of different methods for collecting, interpreting, and analysing our data.

Practical tips

1   Let the research question guide your design: Plan your research around a specific research question. In developing your research consider how your own theoretical assumptions influence and potentially bias your questions and choice of design.
2   Consider when and why a mixed methods approach is appropriate: Before designing a mixed methods approach to address your research question, be sure that this approach provides more advantages than disadvantages. Do the challenges and disadvantages outweigh the benefits?
3   Consider the type of data you are collecting and how it will be analysed before collecting it: Be cognizant of the kind of data that you want to collect and how you will interpret or analyse it before you start data collection. In conducting a mixed method research, consider if and how the data will be interpreted and integrated across the different methods.

References

Ariès, P. (1974). *Western attitudes towards death: From the Middle Ages to the present*. Baltimore, MD: The Johns Hopkins University Press.

Bering, J. M., & Bjorklund, D. F. (2004). The natural emergence of reasoning about the afterlife as a developmental regularity. *Developmental Psychology, 40*, 217–33.

Bering, J. M., Hernández Blasi, C., & Bjorklund, D. F. (2005). The development of 'afterlife' beliefs in religiously and secularly schooled children. *British Journal of Developmental Psychology, 23*, 587–607.

Brandes, S. (2003). Is there a Mexican view of death? *Ethos, 31*(1), 127–44.

Brownell, C. A., Zerwas, S., & Ramani, G. B. (2007). 'So big': The development of body self-awareness in toddlers. *Child Development, 78*, 1426–40.

Callanan, M., & Valle, A. (2008). Co-constructing conceptual domains through family conversations and activities. *Psychology of Learning and Motivation, 49*, 147–65.

Carey, S. (1985). *Conceptual change in childhood*. Cambridge, MA: MIT Press.

Cole, M. (1996). *Cultural psychology: A once and future discipline*. Cambridge, MA: Harvard University Press.

Corr, C. A., & Corr, D. M. (Eds) (1996). *Handbook of childhood death and bereavement.* New York: Springer.

DeLoache, J. S., Uttal, D. H., & Rosengren, K. S. (2004). Scale errors offer evidence for a perception-action dissociation early in life. *Science, 304,* 1027–9.

Evans, E. M., Legare, C. H., & Rosengren, K. (2011). Engaging multiple epistemologies: Implications for science education. In M. Ferrari & R. Taylor (Eds), *Epistemology and science education: Understanding the evolution vs. intelligent design controversy* (pp. 111–39). New York: Routledge.

Grollman, E. A. (Ed.). (1995). *Bereaved children and teens: A support guide for parents and professionals.* Boston, MA: Beacon Press.

Gutiérrez, I.T. (2009). *Understanding death in cultural context: A study of Mexican children and their families* (Unpublished doctoral dissertation). University of Illinois, Champaign.

Karmiloff-Smith, A., Casey, B. J., Massand, E., Tomalski, P., & Thomas, M. S. C. (2014). Environmental and genetic influences on neurocognitive development: The importance of multiple methodologies and time-dependent interventions. *Clinical Psychological Science, 2(5),* 628–37.

Legare, C. H., Evans, E. M., Rosengren, K. S., & Harris, P. L. (2012). The coexistence of natural and supernatural explanations across cultures and development. *Child Development, 83(3),* 779–93.

Lomnitz, C. (2005). *Death and the idea of Mexico.* New York, NY: Zone Books.

Miller, P. J. (1994). Narrative practices: Their role in socialisation and self-construction. In U. Neisser & R. Fivush (Eds), *The remembering self: Construction and accuracy in the self-narrative* (pp. 158–79). New York: Cambridge University Press.

Nguyen, S., & Gelman, S. A. (2002). Four and 6-year-olds' biological concept of death: The case of plants. *British Journal of Developmental Psychology, 20,* 495–513.

Paz, O. (1961). *The labyrinth of solitude: Life and thought in Mexico.* New York: Grove Press.

Piaget, J. (1929). *The child's conception of the world.* London: Routledge and Kegan Paul.

Poling, D. A., & Evans, E. M. (2004). Are dinosaurs the rule or the exception? Developing concepts of death and extinction. *Cognitive Development, 19,* 363–83.

Rogoff, B. (1998). Cognition as a collaborative process. In W. Damon (Series Ed.), D. Kuhn & R. S. Siegler (Volume Eds), *Handbook of child psychology: Vol. 2. Cognition, perception, and language* (5th edn, pp. 679–744). New York: John Wiley & Sons.

Rosengren, K. S., Carmichael, C., Schein, S. S., Anderson, K., & Gutiérrez, I. T. (2009b). A method for eliciting scale errors in preschool classrooms. *Infant Behavior & Development, 32,* 286–90.

Rosengren, K. S., Gutiérrez, I. T., Anderson, K., & Schein, S. S. (2009a). Parental reports of children's scale errors in everyday life. *Child Development, 80,* 1586–91.

Rosengren, K. S., Miller, P. J., Gutiérrez, I. T., Chow, P. I., Schein, S. S., & Anderson, K. N. (2014). Children's understanding of death: Toward a contextualized and integrated account. *Monographs of the Society for Research in Child Development, 79,* 1–142.

Rosengren, K. S., Schein, S. S., & Gutiérrez, I. T. (2010). Individual differences in children's production of scale errors. *Infant Behavior and Development, 33,* 309–13.

Shapiro, E. R. (1994). *Grief as a family process: A developmental approach to clinical practice.* New York: Guilford Press.

Shweder, R. A., Goodnow, J. J., Hatano, G., Levine, R. A., Markus, H. R., & Miller, P. J. (2006). The cultural psychology of development: One mind, many mentalities. In W. Damon (Series Ed.) & R. M. Lerner (Vol. Ed.), *Handbook of Child Psychology: Vol. 1. Theoretical models of human development* (6th edn, pp. 716–92). New York: John Wiley & Sons.

Speece, M. W., & Brent, S. B. (1992). The acquisition of a mature understanding of three components of the concept of death. *Death Studies, 16,* 211–29.

Ware, L., Uttal, D. H., & DeLoache, J. S. (2010). Everyday scale errors. *Developmental Science, 13,* 28–36.

Webb, N. B. (Ed.). (2010). *Helping bereaved children: A handbook for practitioners* (3rd edn). New York: Guilford Press.

11

COUNTING IN CONTEXT

Studying children's everyday talk by combining numbers and words

Douglas E. Sperry and Linda L. Sperry

11.1 Introduction

Words are pervasive in every child's life. Parents use them to play with, teach and protect their children. The importance of the acquisition of language extends far beyond that of other accomplishments in the lifespan of a child, for the achievement of language brings along with it the ability to be a fully functioning member of one's culture. Language provides the means through which culture is transmitted from one generation to the next as the actions and meanings of community members are reproduced in the language they use in their daily interactions with each other (Bourdieu, 1977). In this chapter, we examine one approach to the study of how these meanings are conveyed from caregiver to child through language, an approach grounded in ethnographic methods but reliant on detailed quantitative analyses, in addition to the qualitative analyses typically employed in ethnographic studies (see Chapter 7 for a detailed discussion of using ethnographic studies with children).

We borrow the first portion of the title for this paper from Dell Hymes' introductory notes to Sankoff (1980). In earlier work, Hymes (1974) had suggested that all children must learn to use language in everyday life, thereby achieving expertise he termed 'communicative competence'. This expertise exists in counterpoint to 'linguistic competence' as described by Chomsky (1965), and is realized in everyday conversation as stylistic choices that vary depending on the speaker's attitudinal stance to the speaking situation and cultural belief systems underlying the communicative exchange itself. The concept of communicative competence underscored Hymes' belief that stylistic choices are used by speakers to tailor their language to the needs of current situations and conversation partners, indexing the speaker's own position and beliefs about the listener with regard to such variables as class, ethnicity, age and gender. Although to some extent the notion of communicative competence emerged from evidence that considerable heterogeneity of language use exists within individual speakers and communities, Sankoff's work helped to demonstrate that this heterogeneity was not random: that communicative competence involves regular, systematic choices on the part of the speaker. In other words, a given speaker's verbal performance across time and place is subject to the same laws of probability characteristic of other behavioural phenomena.

In this chapter, we extend this notion of 'counting in context' to the language used by children and their caregivers in their everyday lives. We suggest that the notion of 'counting in context' consists of multiple layers. If everyday behaviours are meaningful in the lives of children and their caregivers, they must certainly recur with enough regularity and coherence that children recognize, appreciate and eventually learn their significance. However, 'counting in context' implies another meaning for us. Behaviours must 'count' in the everyday lives of families. Words and other linguistic phenomena do not exist in isolation. Rather they occur in the context of everyday interactions delimited by conversational goals, participant roles and social structures. These everyday interactions are located within cultural beliefs and values that provide both product and process for the interactions themselves (see also Chapters 5 and 10 for further consideration of studying language in everyday interactions).

In the search for behaviours that 'count', ethnographic researchers have long endeavoured to situate their observations within multiple layers of meaning ascribed to those behaviours by the participants themselves. This 'thick description' (Geertz, 1973) necessarily involves complex descriptions of the behaviours, their contexts and interpretations of the behaviours by community members as well as the researcher. Unfortunately this approach to the study of behaviour as situated within a web of cultural significance has often placed ethnographic description at odds with other scientific approaches that seek to establish significance of behaviour through the analysis of its frequency of occurrence (cf. Brown & Gaskins, 2014). Simply put, the identification and analysis of behaviours that 'count' often renders difficult the process of counting how often those behaviours occur. This tension between analysis by words and analysis by numbers extends to the study of children and their language development, and reflects a larger set of conflicts in the social sciences that has persisted for some time between advocates of quantitative, positivistic methodologies and qualitative, interpretative methodologies. Our goal in this chapter is to present one solution to the resolution of this tension by the careful delineation of language phenomena that both acknowledges how those phenomena occur naturally within the contexts of children's everyday lives, and in turn allows us to identify how often those phenomena actually occur.

In the larger field of developmental psychology, many attempts in recent years have been made to adopt a more pragmatic approach to research with children, one that incorporates both quantitative and qualitative methodologies simultaneously in any one of a number of different approaches specifically tailored to the studies themselves (e.g., Rosengren *et al.*, 2014). (See also Chapter 10 by Rosengren, Gutiérrez, & Jiang for further consideration of how to combine qualitative and quantitative methodologies in research with children).

We use a slightly different approach, grounded in the paradigm of language socialisation (D. Sperry, L. Sperry, & Miller, 2015). Unlike studies conducted with mixed methods approaches, we do not mix quantitative and qualitative data collection techniques simultaneously. Rather, we analyse corpora of everyday talk, collected according to ethnographic principles, using both numbers and narratives. We both count and describe language artefacts that have emerged from the context of the entire data as significant markers of the aspects of development that interest us. For example, in this chapter we describe our work with children's earliest attempts to engage in narrative-like conversation, identified through examination of talk surrounding their statements describing an action or occurrence that is not happening at the time of the conversation. Using this method, we aim to tease apart not only the earliest cognitive understandings of narrative that our young participants possess, but also the implications these narratives have for emerging meaning-making as children learn about their culture.

11.2 Language socialisation as theory and method

Language socialisation is the study of socialisation through language and socialisation to use language (see D. Sperry *et al.*, 2015, for a complete review). We view socialisation as any process through which cultural experts help children to learn the values, beliefs and practices of the prevailing contexts in which they live. Socialisation is not something that is given wholesale to the child, however. In our view, the child is a meaning-making agent within these everyday contexts rather than an empty vessel waiting to be filled with the messages of socialisation (Miller, Fung, Lin, Chen, & Boldt, 2012). Children are presumed to be partners, if immature, in the on-going negotiations of their households. By contrast, they are not presumed to accede passively to the socialisation goals of others through the simple reproduction of those goals in their subsequent actions (Corsaro, 2005).

We consider language to be one of the most essential tools through which caregivers transmit and children learn to make meaning in their lives. Language socialisation, as a method, studies language use and development within context. Language socialisation takes as its point of analytical departure the assumption that language phenomena and socialisation goals are imbricated within the everyday lives of children and their caregivers (Ochs & Schieffelin, 1984). To examine this interconnectedness, the paradigm of language socialisation created by Ochs and Schieffelin combined elements of anthropology, linguistics and developmental psychology into a unique approach to understanding human growth within a cultural context. Based upon these intellectual commitments, language socialisation relies upon the microanalysis of longitudinal observations collected ethnographically. By definition, language socialisation employs a comparative approach to the study of development since it views as its subject the investigation of developmental principles as they are realized both within and across cultural groups.

Language socialisation views language as a constituent force in the establishment and maintenance of the everyday practices that define who we are as individuals and how we fit into the world around us (Miller and Goodnow, 1995; cf. Bourdieu, 1977). To that end, language socialisation studies have often focused on routine talk during caregiving practices, such as stories of personal experience, shaming routines and classroom discourse (D. Sperry et al., 2015). The analysis of routine talk depends on detailed investigation of all aspects of the communicative situation, including, but not limited to, the goals and intentions of the participants, the physical and historical setting of the interaction, and the cultural beliefs attending the type of interaction that are held by the participants themselves. Through its focus on routine talk, language socialisation seeks to establish construct validity by its insistence on the importance of establishing recurrence of any given practice (Kulick & Schieffelin, 2004; D. Sperry et al., 2015).

11.2.1 A new approach

Despite the insistence placed by language socialisation theory on the demonstration of the routine nature of any phenomenon both within the context at hand and across developmental time, work within this tradition has sometimes favoured the study of the comparative nature of specific practices across different cultural groups over establishing how frequently the practices actually occur within any given group (Brown & Gaskins, 2014). In other words, some studies have preserved the focus of language socialisation on 'thick description', or the microanalysis of naturally occurring interactions between caregivers and children, but have sought to establish the importance of these interactions through the careful delineation of how, when and where the interactions fit into the daily routines of families without reference to how often the interactions themselves occur.

One possible tactic suggested by Brown and Gaskins (2014) to augment the careful analysis of the nature of a given interaction with additional analyses of its frequency of occurrence is to undertake analyses of data that combine detailed examination of one or more specific examples of the type of behaviour under study, with a broad sampling of the distribution of the behaviour itself. Following the work of Peggy Miller, this approach is the one we have adopted in our work (cf. Miller *et al.*, 2012). Miller's work breaches the divide between qualitative and quantitative analyses by situating the phenomena she studies within everyday practices identified through meticulous ethnographic investigation. However, her work insists on the establishment of recurrence through the documentation of the frequency of these phenomena. Miller's work embraces language socialisation as theory and method, but also represents natural outgrowth of the early work in developmental psycholinguistics that relied on frequency counts to establish baseline measures of early grammars and vocabulary production.

In early studies of language acquisition (including Miller's own 1982 monograph), the number of participants studied was frequently small, too small for quantitative analyses based on probability distributions. This methodological choice was paralleled in language socialisation, but we suggest that this fact might represent an unfortunate by-product of ethnographic inquiry that may not be necessary. Of course, the intensive nature of ethnographic data collection and the sheer amount of data it generates often preclude amassing a sufficient number of participants to employ probability analyses. However, in our observational work on child development, we have endeavoured to involve enough participants (twelve in our Alabama corpus and fifteen in our Indiana corpus) to make probability analyses tenable. We view our use of probability analyses to be descriptive in nature, a vehicle for illustrating comparative differences across groups. We do not consider our use of probability analyses to justify generalized statements about populations beyond those we have studied; in that manner, we veer from the common use of statistical procedures to make inferences about populations at large. Nevertheless, we consider robust statistical procedures to be an important tool in our analytic arsenal, one that can help to establish the significance of a particular behaviour to the individuals within a particular group.

To illustrate this approach, we turn to a discussion of our research on the development of narrative in the conversation of young children. Oral narrative provides an excellent example of the approach of language socialisation to the study of verbal practices in the lives of young children, because it is a universal practice across cultures that allows children to participate in meaning-making practices along with their caregivers as they are socialised into the beliefs and values of their communities (Miller *et al.*, 2012). In addition, oral narrative serves in many cultures as an important stepping-stone into school and literacy as children are asked to participate in practices such as sharing time (Michaels, 1991). Children in the United States continue to rely upon oral narrative skills as they learn literacy as late as the fourth grade (Hester, 1996).

The fact that narrative serves as a repository for cultural meaning is aptly demonstrated in many studies that report the different storytelling styles children take with them from their homes to the classrooms, many of which place them at odds with the mainstream styles of their teachers (Corsaro, Molinari, & Rosier, 2002; Genishi & Dyson, 2009; Michaels, 1991). The roots of these differences lie in the fertile ground of home interaction (see also Chapter 5 for further consideration of children's conversations in the home). The talk displaced from the here and now in which children and their families engage predicts later academic achievement (Curenton & Justice, 2004; Rowe, 2012). Furthermore, conversational storytelling has been shown to be a particularly important discourse phenomenon within lower-income homes (Burger & Miller, 1999; Miller, Cho, & Bracey, 2005; Miller & L. Sperry, 1988; L. Sperry & D. Sperry, 1996), and it has the potential to serve as an important antidote to the misrecognition of young children's verbal abilities in prevailing notions of linguistic deprivation in recent literature (Miller & D. Sperry, 2012).

In sum, our investigations of early narrative-like conversation have been in service of the elucidation of these cross-cultural differences in narrative content, storytelling style and socialisation goals of caregivers. The ultimate purpose of this work has been to provide information that might serve to inform curriculum and later school-based practices aimed towards the education of children from different backgrounds. What follows is a brief example of the type of work we have conducted, with an eye towards focusing on the methodology principles underlying this research.

11.3 The emergence of narrative competence in 2 and 3 year olds: an illustration

Miller, Hengst and Wang (2003) described four essential characteristics of ethnographic inquiry. First, ethnographic observations should be sustained and engaged within the community under study. Second, all ethnographic inquiry assumes an implicitly multicultural perspective. Third, data collection occurs in simultaneously microscopic and holistic manners as the researcher records both detailed interactions for subsequent analysis and broad moment-by-moment interpretations. Finally, the approach to a given study must be flexible enough to allow emerging understandings to redefine on-going processes of data collection and analysis. We present here a brief synopsis of how we have instantiated these goals in our work with two low-income, rural communities within the United States.

11.3.1 Choice of community and participants

In terms of choice of community and participants, our research embraces selection effects due to our goal of investigating cross-cultural differences (cf. Yoshikawa, Weisner, Kalil, & Way, 2008). Although our first study reported here employed a sample of convenience (African Americans in rural Alabama where we lived at the time due to our employment), the second study (European Americans in rural Indiana) was selected to match the Alabama community in terms of geographic dispersion (rural), social class (impoverished to working class) and age of child participant at the onset of data collection (approximately 24 months). Through this deliberate selection, we hoped to observe the course of child language acquisition and adult socialisation of development cross-culturally between two groups living in similar geographic and social circumstances. Of course, choice of community and participants will vary depending on the research goals and questions of the investigator, given the goal that ethnographic inquiry be cross-cultural in its perspective. In our case, our choices of communities were made based on the desire to investigate traditionally understudied American communities comparatively with the theoretical goal of elucidating reasons why impoverished children in general, and impoverished children of colour in particular, tend to fare poorly in the American school system.

11.3.2 Methods of interaction and data collection

Our research relies principally on analyses of the everyday verbal interactions of children and their families recorded in systematic, videotaped observations. However, in keeping with the goals of ethnographic inquiry, our work is grounded in extensive, deliberate contact with the community under study before this systematic recording of individual participants begins. We place great value on the familiarity accorded by persistent, routine contact with the community and its members before the onset of formal data collection. This familiarity with the local scene is essential for it both accords us initial understandings of the everyday lives of the participants and permits a period of time for the participants to become as comfortable as possible with the presence of us as both researchers and outsiders. All people may feel vulnerable to a certain extent when they open their homes and lives to outsiders; this vulnerability is only exacerbated by any differences in cultural or socioeconomic background that may exist between researcher and participant.

There are no easy answers, however, with regard to questions that arise concerning the relationship between researcher and participant. In the Alabama case, the researcher was a European American woman entering the homes of African American families. In the Indiana case, the European American research assistant who collected the data was herself a member of the European American community under study. On the one hand, dissimilarity between the researcher and participant contributes to the sense of vulnerability that some participants may feel in the research context. On the other hand, similarity between the researcher and participants limits analytic integrity due to the difficulties associated with viewing one's own culture as usual. To the greatest extent possible, we endeavour to address the first problem through the assiduous establishment of familiarity with the local scene described in the preceding paragraph, and the second problem through meticulous attention to data coding to which we turn later in this chapter.

Extensive field notes are maintained throughout the initial stages of community familiarisation. In the Alabama case, fieldwork prior to the onset of systematic recording involved observations in area day centres, private tutoring, piano lessons and child development classes offered through the local community education programme. The importance of thorough, organized field notes cannot be overemphasized. Field notes provide more than a record of observations about the community under study and its comings and goings. Field notes provide a means of on-going and retrospective analysis of the researcher's positioning with respect to the study, the community and the participants.

Throughout the systematic data collection process, extreme value is placed on achieving ecological validity by making every effort to construct the data collection situation in a manner designed to make all participants, adult and child alike, as comfortable as possible. As researchers, we attempt to 'fit' into the homes of our participants in the manner of a friendly visitor. The very young children who are the central actors in the scene often come to see the researcher as more than a visitor, perhaps even as a teacher or friend. Our adult participants have often referred to us as their child's 'teacher', and have occasionally demonstrated their comfort with our presence around their children by leaving the research scene momentarily while they perform another small household task such as seeing after another child, preparing a snack in the kitchen or retrieving water from an outside well.

Extreme care must be taken to safeguard the best interests of the participants at all points in the data collection process (see also Chapter 15 for a discussion of ethical issues when working with children). Necessarily, procedures will need to be created and modified according to the situation of the data collection. In our work, recording times were always set up in advance at the convenience of the caregiver. The length of observation times varied depending on the age of the child; children under the age of 2 years were recorded for 1 hour while children over the age of 2 years were recorded for 2 or more hours. Observations were terminated in the event that the child fell asleep or the caregiver decided that they could not continue for any reason. In terms of the recording situation, participants were assured that the video camera would always be focused on the child under study. The video camera was always set up in plain view in an area of the home determined by the caregivers. In the event that the very young children left the room, no attempt was made to follow them to other portions of the house. Rather, the researcher relied upon the caregiver to fetch the child back to the recording area. Finally, the rights of participants were respected in terms of providing incentives that on the one hand acknowledged the time they spent accommodating the research process, but on the other hand were not so great as to be coercive. In our case, a small cash payment was given to participants at the time of each observation, and a videotape compilation of all observations (for the caregiver) and a toy (for the child participant) were given to participants at the final observation time.

11.3.3 Data analysis

We rely on meticulous, verbatim transcription of the videotaped observations made during longitudinal observations as our primary data. We privilege words in transcription, remaining fully aware that the theoretical orientation of a researcher is determined in no small part by what she chooses to transcribe (Ochs, 1979). We also record contextual information, gaze and intonation patterns in our transcripts, although not in a manner consistent with the more exhaustively detailed transcripts commonly used in conversation analysis (Schegloff, 2007). In so doing, we make an intellectual commitment to the belief that the information we seek to discover exists across broader conversational interactions, more consistent with larger units of discourse.

We believe the language data we study should 'have the first say' in any analytical approach undertaken for their reduction and interpretation because these words represent symbolically the beliefs, values and everyday actions of the people we seek to understand. We do not consider our work to be atheoretical, however, a criticism often assailed against qualitative work. Rather, we pursue greater understanding of phenomena that we believe to exist in some form across cultures (an etic perspective) through the exploration of specific variations and contrasts of that phenomena occurring within and across cultures (an emic perspective; cf. Pike,

1966). To accomplish this goal, we attempt to specify the most essential aspects of the phenomenon we wish to study, thereby creating a frame of reference, or 'etic grid' for identifying examples of the phenomenon in the data. The establishment of an etic grid prior to the onset of data analysis may help the researcher to remain alert to and potentially discover missing pieces of data in theory (Goodnow, 2002) while simultaneously remaining true to established theoretical knowledge concerning the phenomenon under study.

11.3.4 Determining the etic grid

We turn to an example of the construction of an etic grid for analysis of the emergence of narrative competence in 2 and 3 year olds. Many theoretical orientations to understanding mature storytelling exist in both the linguistic (e.g., Labov & Waletzky, 1967) and the psychological (e.g., Stein & Glenn, 1979) literatures. Based on these theoretical orientations, we devised an etic grid for incipient storytelling in young children, defining what we called narrative-like, displaced-event episodes (NDE). This definition relied on two components. First, a child had to tell at least one event displaced from the here and now. For example, a child had to refer to an action that occurred in a different temporal frame (e.g., 'I gonna ride [the school bus] in morning time' – Kendrick, 28 months) or in a fictional frame (e.g., 'Scoredini [an imaginary character] not gonna get my feet' – Keisha, 24 months). Second, a child had to say one other statement topically related to the displaced event in a contiguous conversation turn. For example, in his next utterance, Kendrick repeated his brother's declaration of the bus driver's name, 'Ms. Cole'. Keisha reinforced her first utterance with the assertion, 'Ain't,' in reference to the threat of Scoredini getting her feet. (All personal names used in transcripts are pseudonyms.)

We reported on the emergence of narrative skills in the everyday talk of eight African American toddlers (Sperry & Sperry, 1996). Observation of these toddlers was begun when they turned 24 months of age with the assumption that these young language learners had not begun to employ narrative features in their talk at that very early age. We were wrong. From the earliest recordings, all of the toddlers performed one or more conversational exchanges that met our definition for a NDE. Earlier work had focused exclusively on stories of past personal experience (cf. Miller & L. Sperry, 1988). Yet, it became evident early on that these toddlers were engaging in talk about fictional or fantastic events with almost the same frequency, as they were engaging in talk about past events.

It cannot be overstated that we did not enter the data collection or analysis process with any notion that these results would emerge. In fact, as referenced in the previous paragraph, our beliefs prior to the outset of data collection were more consistent with the idea that these very young children would be telling little if any narrative. We deliberately set our sights low as we defined our etic grid with the goal of identifying the very earliest attempts of these young participants to tell stories. Ironically, our low expectations proved beneficial in the long run, for it is unlikely that we would have observed the vast array of genre types existing in the speech of these young children (and socialised by their caregivers) had we entered the data collection process looking only for stories of personal experience.

Recently, we have looked at the data from Indiana to consider what differences might exist cross-culturally in the emergence of narrative competence. These data have been coded in the same manner as were the data from Alabama. The Alabama data set consists of twenty-four half-hour samples. The ages of the children in these samples range from 24 to 42 months, with a mean age of 30.2 months. The Indiana data set consists of 135 half-hour samples. The ages of the children in these samples range from 18 to 42 months, with a mean age of 30.8 months.

What emerged from the comparison was an entirely different picture of narrative development, as shown in Figure 11.1. Compared with the children in Alabama, the children in Indiana told many fewer NDEs. Overall, the Alabama children told 13.58 NDEs per hour, while the Indiana children told only 2.89 NDEs per hour ($F = 21.78$, $p < .001$). Children in both communities told more fictionally displaced stories than temporally displaced stories. However, children in Alabama were more likely to tell stories about events that would not or could not ever happen (fantasy events) whereas children in Indiana were more likely to tell stories about events that not only could happen but whose retelling was supported by objects in the environment (pretend events). Nevertheless, there was a significant Community X Displacement Type interaction ($F = 7.47$, $p = .012$) that necessitated reconsideration of the above results. Not only did the Alabama children tell more NDEs overall than did the Indiana children, but the amount of difference between the groups in terms of the rate of fictionally displaced stories far exceeded the amount of difference between the groups in terms of the rate of temporally displaced stories.

We suspect that these differences are the result of extensive socialisation patterns concerning the value of displaced talk in general, and fantasy talk in particular, across these two culturally defined groups, a suspicion that must await additional analysis. Nevertheless, in the Alabama case, mothers, especially of the boys, strongly encouraged fantasy talk as measured by the number of elicitations they produced (L. Sperry, 1991). An examination of one example from each community is instructive in understanding the relative persistence of Alabama mothers in their encouraging of displaced-event talk as compared with Indiana mothers.

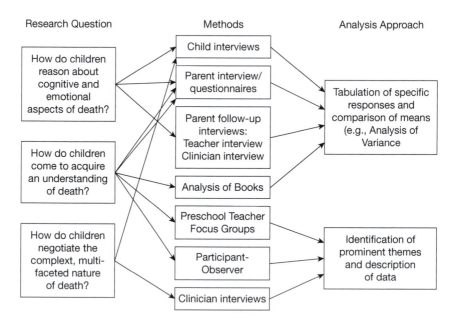

Research Question   Methods   Analysis Approach

FIGURE 11.1 Mean rates of fictionally and temporally narrative-like displaced-event episodes in two low-income communities

Stillman, 28 months (Alabama)

Mother:	Where your truck at?
Stillman:	'at. In a 'at. (gazes at furnace door, then at Mother)
Mother:	In a what? (leaning towards Stillman)
Stillman:	In 'at! (loudly, pointing over Mother's shoulder)
Mother:	In the closet.
Stillman:	Eh. ('yes')
Mother:	Oh, the rat in the closet.
Stillman:	Eh.
Mother:	You scared to get the truck? (nods, eyes widen)
Stillman:	Ma, Ma, Ma it scare me rat. (gazes floor to right)
Mother:	Oh, Lonnie gonna get the rat for you?
Stillman:	Eh.
Mother:	Oh. Okay.
Stillman:	Ma, Ma, Ma, Ma, Ma rat go?
Mother:	The rat'll bite your nose off. (gazes at Stillman)
Stillman:	Mm. (shakes head 'no' briefly)
	Where my rat at?

Mother:	In the closet where your truck at.
Stillman:	Unh. (negatively)
Mother:	Yes, it is. (nods)
Stillman:	Mmm my, my rat in the buh.
Mother:	In the bushes?
Stillman:	Eh.
Mother:	There's no rat in the bushes.
Stillman:	A man get 'at in buh.

In this episode, 28-month-old Stillman is unwilling to retrieve his truck from the closet. Stillman's initial response to his mother's request seems ambiguous at first, given his articulation and stuttering problems. Regardless of whether or not he said 'rat' or 'that', the important point here is that his mother soon interpreted his statement as referring to a rat in the closet, an interpretation somewhat inconsistent with Stillman's acceptance of her reply: 'In the closet', after he pointed to the door and loudly exclaimed: 'in 'at!'. Stillman accepted her initiation of talk about the rat equally as quickly, convincing the listener that he was referring to it all along. This type of conversation seems well rehearsed within the conversations of Stillman and his mother, each interlocutor spinning the tale in different directions until soon the rat is in the bushes outside, perhaps along with an unidentified stranger. Both interlocutors contributed new information to this episode, generating a complex story line. These conversations seldom generated any real fear in Stillman; rather they seem more like a delicious verbal diversion within this dyad's warm relationship.

We now compare this example from the Alabama corpus with an example from the Indiana corpus of a conversational exchange between Shane and his mother. This exchange was not considered to be a NDE in our analysis since Shane never engaged in talk displaced from the here and now. Nevertheless, it provides an interesting contrast to the example from Alabama since Shane's mother does make a limited attempt to fantasize the current happenings, an attempt that goes nowhere.

Shane, 24 months (Indiana)

Mother:	There goes the choo-choo train, Shane. (hearing the train outside) It's out there.
Shane:	(stands up against the back of the couch, and looks out of the window; he turns to face his mother and laughs, then looks back out the window)

	Oh I see.
	C' c' c' coming! (gets down off the couch)
	C' coming.
	The choo coming. (runs into the kitchen)
Mother:	Is it gonna get you?
Shane :	Coming.
	C' coming.
	(runs through the kitchen and past the table to a back sliding door; he stands there looking outside)
Mother:	It's goin' now. It's all gone.
Shane :	Uh.
	I'm sad.
	Gone.
	Train gone.
	Train gone.

In both of the above examples, Stillman's and Shane's mother each began their respective exchanges with a conversation nomination situated in the here and now: i.e., Stillman's mother asking him to get his truck and Shane's mother calling his attention to the train. Although in Stillman's case it is unclear whether or not he began the fantasy, in both conversations the boys' mothers soon turned the topic into a potentially scary story based on their child's reactions: i.e., Stillman's loud proclamation and point to the closet, and Shane's running into the kitchen, presumably to catch a glimpse of the train as it passes behind the house. The similarities between these episodes end here, however, because Shane failed to take up his mother's fantasy nomination in the way Stillman did. Rather, he continued remarking on the train's coming, and then concluded the conversation by his expression of sorrow that the train has gone.

Our preliminary analysis of these data is insufficient to determine the impact of socialisation patterns on these children's varied performances. In both of these examples, the mothers did nominate a fantasy topic. We suspect that additional analyses will confirm that these nominations occurred much less frequently overall in the Indiana corpus than they did in the Alabama corpus. In fact, the relative paucity of narrative in the Indiana corpus suggests that any nomination of displaced talk by caregivers is rare in this community. Future work will examine utterance-level elicitations of narrative-like talk by caregivers as well as the relative original contributions of both child and caregiver participants within NDEs in terms of the introduction of new information in order to shed light on the semantic/syntactic support children receive within episodes from their interlocutors. In this manner, we reiteratively interrogate our findings to seek new understandings of both the phenomenon under study and its aetiology in the conversations of children and their families.

11.4 Discussion

In sum, our research is conceptualized as language socialisation and grounded in ethnography. It employs what Erickson has termed *multiple methods* (Moss *et al.*, 2009), a methodology we believe to be consistent with the original intent of language socialisation as a paradigm designed to uncover developmental pathways through the establishment of their recurrence within communicative practices. In our research, the use of the term multiple methods is to be understood as distinct from the more common use of the term mixed methods. The term *mixed methods* has come to imply a dialectical give-and-take between quantitative and qualitative approaches existing within the same study. In that sense, although our approach relies on both quantitative and qualitative data, it is not consistent with mixed methods. We make no attempt to modify the original qualitative work based on subsequent quantitative analyses or reiterative qualitative investigation. Our research may be considered corpora studies given the fact that our analyses are limited to the data at hand. Nevertheless, our work is not simply a corpora study of any random set of data. Analyses of data are grounded in the theoretical motivation of the original studies to capture language in use and to elucidate how that language illuminates the belief and value systems held by the participants. Furthermore, as new findings are uncovered in one investigation, new lines of inquiry emerge as we seek to understand the context in which the original findings are situated. For this purpose, we are able to interrogate the data reiteratively, constantly situating new ideas within old. In this manner, our approach represents what Johnson and Onwuegbuzie (2004) called a pragmatic solution to any disagreements or tensions between explicitly quantitative or qualitative ideologies.

Many calls for methodological pragmatism have emerged in recent years as one solution for the so-called quantitative versus qualitative wars (Biesta & Burbules, 2003; Howe, 1988; Johnson & Onwuegbuzie, 2004; Onwuegbuzie & Teddlie, 2003; Yoshikawa *et al.*, 2008). Greene (2007) described the pragmatic approach as consistent with a call for an alternative paradigm, one where neither traditional paradigm (quantitative or qualitative) is considered adequate for the discovery of behavioural truths. Of course, our work is initially grounded in methods more consistent with qualitative inquiry, and we might therefore consider our work more in keeping with Greene's dialectic stance to mixed methods where paradigmatic assumptions (specifically for us, the importance of context) guide methodological choices. However, we view our approach to 'counting in context' as a choice grounded in pragmatism.

The pragmatic approach represents perhaps the best justification for 'counting in context' as it argues for using all of the tools available in each approach to find the procedures best suited for answering the research questions at hand (cf. Johnson & Onwuegbuzie, 2004). Specifically, we reject the notion of what some have called the 'incompatibility thesis' (Howe, 1988), namely that qualitative and quantitative paradigms exist in philosophical opposition one to the other, and that the methods they enjoin cannot be combined. Johnson and Onwuegbuzie (2004) discussed the undeniable commonalities across these two paradigms: their use of empirical observations, their insistence on rigorous methods to avoid threats to validity and their practice of reliance upon warranted assertions to make epistemological claims about human behaviour. This lack of entailment from epistemology to methodology suggests that there is no reason for the practitioner of either qualitative or quantitative methods to avoid the collection or analysis of data within the complementary paradigm (Onwuegbuzie & Teddlie, 2003). As Yoshikawa and his colleagues noted (2008), the world is not inherently quantitative or qualitative. Regardless of how we analyse human behaviour, we are imposing on that behaviour a scheme of analysis that, whether it is based on numbers or words, is simply an analytic tool for helping us to understand and categorize that behaviour. To that end, the pragmatic approach is well suited for the discovery of behavioural truths, but it is perhaps best suited for the representation of them in public discourse since it offers the scientist the flexibility necessary to discuss the wide range of human behaviour, some of which is better suited to analysis by numbers and some of which is better suited to analysis by words.

In our study of narrative, we have sought to discover the earliest attempts by very young children to tell stories through the use of an etic grid based on linguistic and psychological theory. Of course it is not always necessary or desirable to rely upon the determination of an etic grid for analysis of data. Our observational work has also relied upon the principles of grounded theory in order to let understandings emerge from the data themselves (Glaser & Strauss, 1967). Charmaz (2011) discussed using data to allow relevant categories of analysis to emerge before consulting the relevant literature for comparative analysis. The length of time we have worked with these data has afforded us an intimacy with them consistent with what Charmaz might suggest allows for an immediate recognition of both differences between the two communities and 'sharp' distinctions between the data themselves and relevant theory concerning interaction styles between caregiver and child. Regardless of whether data are approached through theoretical approaches based on a predetermined scheme such as an etic grid or through grounded theory where the analysis emerges from the data themselves, we consider the final result to be most compelling when the data demonstrate that any noticed pattern is both recurrent and thoroughly enmeshed in the everyday practices of children and their families.

Practical tips

1   Remember that the world cannot be defined by words or numbers alone. Describing a phenomenon does not guarantee that it occurs often enough to be meaningful; counting a phenomenon does not guarantee that it is understood. Keep your investigative imagination open by being willing to think outside of methodological boxes. Be familiar with the principles of both qualitative and quantitative methodologies in order to use all techniques judiciously, with respect to their essential epistemologies.

2   Define your phenomenon broadly but precisely, relying on basic first principles within the area in which you are working to establish an etic grid for data analysis. In this manner, you can then analyse the phenomenon broadly across socially and culturally defined groups to capture the range of possibility inherent to the phenomenon under study.

3   Acknowledge your position as researcher and your significance on the scene. Spend the time necessary in advance of systematic data collection to learn local ways and to allow participants to grow familiar with you. In this manner, you reduce the vulnerability participants may feel as they enter the research situation and ultimately give them voice.

References

Biesta, G. J. J., & Burbules, N. C. (2003). *Pragmatism and educational research.* Lanham, MD: Rowman & Littlefield.

Bourdieu, P. (1977). *Outline of a theory of practice.* New York, NY: Cambridge University Press.

Brown, P., & Gaskins, S. (2014). Language acquisition and language socialisation. In N. J. Enfield, P. Kockelman & J. Sidnell (Eds), *Cambridge handbook of linguistic anthropology* (pp. 187–226). Cambridge, England: Cambridge University Press.

Burger, L. K., & Miller, P. J. (1999). Early talk about the past revisited: A comparison of working-class and middle-class families. *Journal of Child Language, 26,* 1–30.

Charmaz, K. (2011). Grounded theory methods in social justice research. In N. K. Denzin & Y. S. Lincoln (Eds), *The Sage handbook of qualitative research* (4th edn, pp. 359–80). Thousand Oaks, CA: Sage.

Chomsky, N. (1965). *Aspects of the theory of syntax.* Cambridge, MA: MIT Press.

Corsaro, W. A. (2005). *The sociology of childhood* (2nd edn). Thousand Oaks, CA: Sage.

Corsaro, W. A., Molinari, L., & Rosier, K. B. (2002). Zena and Carlotta: Transition narratives and early education in the United States and Italy. *Human Development, 45*, 323–48.

Curenton, S. M., & Justice, L. M. (2004). African American and Caucasian preschoolers' use of decontextualized language: Literate language features in oral narratives. *Language, Speech, and Hearing Services in Schools, 35*, 240–53.

Geertz, C. (1973). *The interpretation of cultures.* New York, NY: Basic Books.

Genishi, C., & Dyson, A. H. (2009). *Children, language, and literacy: Diverse learners in diverse times.* New York, NY: Teachers College Press.

Glaser, B. G., & Strauss. A. L. (1967). *The discovery of grounded theory.* Chicago, IL: Aldine.

Goodnow, J. J. (2002). Adding culture to studies of development: Toward changes in procedure and theory. *Human Development, 45*, 237–45.

Greene, J. C. (2007). *Mixed methods in social inquiry.* San Francisco, CA: Jossey-Bass.

Hester, E. J. (1996). Narratives of young African American children. In A. G. Kamhi, K. E. Pollock & J. L. Harris (Eds), *Communication development and disorders in African American children: Research, assessment, and intervention* (pp. 227–45). Baltimore, MD: Brookes.

Howe, K. R. (1988). Against the quantitative-qualitative incompatibility thesis (or dogmas die hard). *Educational Researcher, 17*(8), 10–16.

Hymes, D. (1974). *Foundations in sociolinguistics: An ethnographic approach.* Philadelphia, PA: University of Pennsylvania Press.

Johnson, R. B., & Onwuegbuzie, A. J. (2004). Mixed methods research: A research paradigm whose time has come. *Educational Researcher, 33*(7), 14–26.

Kulick, D., & Schieffelin, B. B. (2004). Language socialisation. In A. Duranti (Ed.), *A companion to linguistic anthropology* (pp. 349–68). Malden, MA: Blackwell.

Labov, W., & Waletzky, J. (1967). Narrative analysis: Oral versions of personal experience. In J. Helm (Ed.), *Essays in the verbal and visual arts* (pp. 12–44). Seattle, WA: American Ethnological Society.

Michaels, S. (1991). The dismantling of narrative. In A. McCabe & C. Peterson (Eds), *Developing narrative structure* (pp. 303–51). Hillsdale, NJ: Lawrence Erlbaum.

Miller, P. J. (1982). *Amy, Wendy, and Beth: Learning language in South Baltimore.* Austin, TX: University of Texas Press.

Miller, P. J., Cho, G. E., & Bracey, J. R. (2005). Working-class children's experience through the prism of personal storytelling. *Human Development, 43*, 115–35.

Miller, P. J., Fung, H., Lin, S., Chen, E. C-H., & Boldt, B. R. (2012). How socialisation happens on the ground: Narrative practices as alternate socialising pathways in Taiwanese and European-American families. *Monographs of the Society for Research in Child Development, 77*(1), 1–140.

Miller, P. J., & Goodnow, J. J. (1995). Cultural practices: Toward an integration of culture and development. In J. J. Goodnow, P. J. Miller & F. Kessel (Eds), *Cultural practices as contexts for development: New Directions for Child Development* (Vol. 67, pp. 5–16). San Francisco, CA: Jossey-Bass.

Miller, P. J., Hengst, J. A., & Wang, S-H. (2003). Ethnographic methods: Applications from developmental cultural psychology. In P. M. Camic, J. E. Rhodes, & L. Yardley (Eds), *Qualitative research in psychology: Expanding perspectives in methodology and design* (pp. 219–42). Washington, DC: American Psychological Association.

Miller, P. J., & Sperry, D. E. (2012). Déjà vu: The continuing misrecognition of low-income children's verbal abilities. In S. T. Fiske & H. R. Markus (Eds), *Facing social class: How societal rank influences interaction* (pp. 109–30). New York, NY: Russell Sage Foundation.

Miller, P. J., & Sperry, L. L. (1988). Early talk about the past: The origins of conversational stories of personal experience. *Journal of Child Language, 15,* 293–315.

Moss, P. A., Phillips, D. C., Erickson, F. D., Floden, R. E., Lather, P. A., & Schneider, B. L. (2009). Learning from our differences: A dialogue across perspectives on quality in education research. *Educational Researcher, 38*(7), 501–17.

Ochs, E. (1979). Transcription as theory. In E. Ochs & B. B. Schieffelin (Ed.), *Developmental pragmatics* (pp. 43–72). New York, NY: Academic Press.

Ochs, E., & Schieffelin, B. B. (1984). Language acquisition and socialisation: Three developmental stories and their implications. In R. A. Shweder & R. A. LeVine (Eds), *Culture theory: Essays on mind, self, and emotion* (pp. 276–320). Cambridge, England: Cambridge University Press.

Onwuegbuzie, A. J., & Teddlie, C. (2003). A framework for analyzing data in mixed methods research. In A. Tashakkori & C. Teddlie (Eds), *Handbook of mixed methods in social and behavioral research* (pp. 351–83). Thousand Oaks, CA: Sage.

Pike, K. L. (1966). Etic and emic standpoints for the description of behavior. In A. G. Smith (Ed.), *Communication and culture: Readings in the codes of human interaction* (pp. 152–63). New York, NY: Holt, Rinehart, & Winston.

Rosengren, K. S., Miller, P. J., Gutierrez, I. T., Chow, P. I., Schein, S. S., Anderson, K. N., & Callanan, M.A. (2014). Children's understanding of death: Toward a contextualized and integrated account. *Monographs of the Society for Research in Child Development, 79*(1), 43–61.

Rowe, M. L. (2012). A longitudinal investigation of the role of quantity and quality of child-directed speech in vocabulary development. *Child Development, 83,* 1762–74.

Sankoff, G. (1980). *The social life of language.* Philadelphia, PA: University of Pennsylvania Press.

Schegloff, E. A. (2007). *Sequence organization in interaction: Vol. 1. A primer in conversation analysis.* Cambridge, England: Cambridge University Press.

Sperry, D. E., Sperry, L. L., & Miller, P. J. (2015). Language socialisation. In K. Tracy, C. Ilie, & T. J. Sandel (Eds), *International encyclopedia of language and social interaction.* Malden, MA: Wiley-Blackwell.

Sperry, L. L. (1991). *The emergence and development of narrative competence in African-American toddlers from a rural Alabama community* (Unpublished doctoral dissertation). The University of Chicago.

Sperry, L. L., & Sperry, D. E. (1996). Early development of narrative skills. *Cognitive Development, 11,* 443–65.

Stein, N. L., & Glenn, C. G. (1979). An analysis of story comprehension in elementary school children. In R. O. Freedle (Ed.), *Advances in discourse processes. Vol. 2: New Directions in Discourse Processing* (pp. 53–120). Norwood, NJ: Ablex.

Yoshikawa, H., Weisner, T. S., Kalil, A., & Way, N. (2008). Mixing qualitative and quantitative research in developmental science: Uses and methodological choices. *Developmental Psychology, 44,* 344–54.

12

THE USE OF Q SORT METHODOLOGY IN RESEARCH WITH TEENAGERS

Larry Owens

12.1 Introduction

Brown and Good (2010) defined Q methodology as 'a combination of conceptual framework, techniques of data collection, and method of analysis that collectively provides the basis for the scientific study of subjectivity' (p. 1149). It involves the collection of data in the form of Q sorts, and the inter-correlation and factor analysis of those sorts. The aim of this research methodology is to reveal and understand the key viewpoints on a particular topic that exist among a group of participants (Watts & Stenner, 2012). Q methodology has been used successfully in a wide range of research disciplines including psychology, education, nursing, health sciences, political science, sociology, environmental science and philosophy. Paradoxically, although it was developed within behaviourism, it has been used by postmodernists, social constructionists, feminists, discourse and narrative analysts, cognitive scientists, psychoanalysts, geographers, as well as both quantitative and qualitative researchers (Brown, 2004). Like any research paradigm, Q methodology has its critics (e.g., Kampen & Tamás, 2014) but these criticisms have generally been rebutted (e.g., Brown, Danielson, & van Exel, 2015). This chapter contains the following sections: the origins of Q methodology, theoretical foundations, how to conduct a Q study, Q methodology research with children and teenagers, advantages and limitations of Q methodology, and the author's own Q studies on popularity among teenage girls.

12.1.1 Origins of Q methodology

Q methodology was invented by British physicist/psychologist William Stephenson and first introduced by him in a letter to the journal *Nature* (Stephenson, 1935). Stephenson had been a student of Charles Spearman, the originator of factor analysis, and later an associate of Cyril Burt. Spearman and Burt made major contributions to the individual differences tradition in psychology through their use of R methodology factor analysis which involved correlating items or traits or tests (called variables) and determining the latent variables across a large population of people being measured on these items. Stephenson (1953) argued that R factor analysis, by measuring the associations and differences between individuals at the population level, could not reflect the different characteristics of specific individuals. Stephenson broke from his mentors in his use of Q methodology which involved inverting the R correlation matrix and using people as variables and the items or tests or traits as the sample or population (Watts & Stenner, 2012). From early in the twentieth century, behaviourism, with its emphasis on objective behaviour and rejection of mentalism, consciousness and subjectivity, had become the predominant paradigm in psychology. Stephenson challenged the behaviourist view with his belief that subjectivity was real and could be measured in a scientifically rigorous way.

12.2 Theoretical underpinnings

12.2.1 Behaviourism

John B. Watson (1913) famously proclaimed: 'psychology, as the behaviourist views it, is a purely objective experimental branch of natural science' (1913, p. 158). The behaviourist paradigm dominated psychology until the late 1950s. With its focus on observable behaviour, it rejected consideration of the inner world of thoughts, feelings or emotions. B. F. Skinner is best known for his work on operant conditioning whereby he developed principles of behaviour based upon the foundation that behaviour is controlled by its environment. Skinner (1938; 1953) defined operant behaviour as actions undertaken voluntarily by people and animals that result in some sort of consequence, the nature of which serves to either increase or decrease the behaviour. Although Stephenson (1935; 1953) began his work and retained his belief in behaviourism, he broke from many behaviourists in his belief that subjectivity is in fact behavioural.

12.2.2 Subjectivity

'Within the context of Q methodology, "subjectivity" is regarded as a person's communication of a point of view on any matter of personal or social importance' (McKeown & Thomas, 2013, p. ix). With the rejection by many behaviourists of anything unobservable including subjectivity, it is perhaps counter-intuitive that Stephenson (1935; 1953) used the term 'operant subjectivity'. By doing so, he was making the point that subjectivity does not belong to subconscious or inner mental processes, but that it is a behaviour or activity. Stephenson (1953) saw the act of conducting a Q sort as the operant or behavioural expression of subjectivity or an individual's point of view. In essence, Stephenson (1953) rejected behaviourism's rejection of subjectivity! He argued that Q methodology enabled subjectivity to be studied reliably, utilizing all the procedures of the scientific method. In other words, Q methodology could provide a first person or subjective science as rigorous as the third-person behaviourist science that was holding sway in psychology at least through the first half of the twentieth century (Watts & Stenner, 2012). Indeed, Stephenson (1953) like William James before him, rejected the subjectivity/objectivity dualism to which many behaviourists adhered. To Stephenson (1953) a subjective viewpoint relating to, for example, one's opinion about this current chapter is something real or substantive or factual. Your opinion of my writing is real at this point in time and such a self-referential point of view can be investigated scientifically (Watts & Stenner, 2012).

12.2.3 Self-reference

Absent from R methodology but central to Q is self-reference. Q methodology is concerned with an individual's subjective perspective including feelings, thoughts, preferences and opinions relating to facts or issues. According to Q methodology, subjective points of view are communicable and advanced from a self-referential position. In fact, McKeown and Thomas (2013, p. 3) argued that: 'subjectivity is always self-referent'. The subjective communication is able to be analysed objectively providing that the self-referent nature of these communications is preserved and not compromised by use of an external frame of reference brought by researchers (as happens in R methodology) (McKeown & Thomas, 2013). In Q methodology, individuals respond to a set of statements by providing their own opinions, views and so on, and these self-referential positions can be subjected to scientific scrutiny via Q sorting, Q factor analysis, and interpretation (Brown & Good, 2010; Watts & Stenner, 2012).

12.2.4 Concourse

Concourse refers to 'the universe of subjective communicability surrounding any topic' (Brown & Good, 2010, p. 1149). The sources of the concourse are diverse and include ordinary conversations, back-fence gossip, internet blogs, social network sites, chat room discussions, literature reviews, surveys, letters to newspaper editors, television talk shows, and may include any widespread sources of discourse about the topic or issue (Brown & Good, 2010; McKeown & Thomas, 2013). Concourses are not restricted to words, but could include collections of paintings, art, photographs, and music (Watts & Stenner, 2012). A concourse is 'the overall population of statements from which a final Q set is sampled . . . it is to Q set what population is to person sample (or P set)' (Watts & Stenner, 2012, p. 34).

12.2.5 Quantum theory

Physicist Richard Feynman (1965) said, 'I think I can safely say that nobody understands quantum mechanics' (p. 129). Given this complexity, I do not intend to provide much detail here. Suffice to say that quantum mechanics is concerned with physical phenomena at the atomic and subatomic levels. The ideas within quantum physics do not fit easily with classical Newtonian cause and effect scientific principles. In the quantum sphere, there is no objective real world – instead reality can only be defined in relation to the context of its action or measurement. Stephenson (1988) believed that Q methodology is connected through its mathematics to quantum theory. Just as in quantum physics there must be quantum stuff (e.g., an atom), altered through an experimental manipulation and a measured result, in Q methodology the quantum stuff is the set of self-referential viewpoints (the Q set), which is altered in systematic ways via different conditions of instruction for Q sorting, and the result measured through factor analysis and interpretation of the final Q sort (Brown & Good, 2010; Watts & Stenner, 2012).

12.2.6 Abduction

Abduction is central to the reasoning of Q methodology. To assist in our understanding we need to define two other concepts – deduction and induction. Deduction is top down logic, which begins with a theory and hypothesis, and through data gathering an attempt is made to confirm the hypothesis. Induction is bottom up logic whereby there is no original hypothesis, but data are gathered and observed, and descriptions and generalizations are then made. Like induction, abduction is bottom up and involves studying collected data and devising a theory to explain the observations. Abduction differs from induction in its generation of explanations or hypotheses rather than only descriptions of data. In Q methodology, factor analysis is used to generate theories, explanations or hypotheses about the observed Q sorts. In Q methodology, it is recommended that the factor rotations are done manually or judgementally in order to retain the opportunity for abductive logic. Automated rotation (e.g., varimax) can be undertaken but the logic employed is statistical rather than abductive (Watts & Stenner, 2012).

12.2.7 Constructivism and social constructionism

Constructivism is well recognized from the work of Jean Piaget (1950) as being concerned with the creation or construction of meaning by individuals. Objects in the world are interpreted by us as individuals, i.e., their meanings are not stable or objective but constructed by us. Q methodology has often been used for constructivist purposes particularly in relation to single-participant designs and the emphasis on self-reference. Constructionism, in contrast, is concerned with social or shared understandings of the world (Elder-Vass, 2013; Hacking, 2000). Beginning with the work of Rex and Wendy Stainton Rogers (R. Stainton Rogers, 1997; W. Stainton Rogers, 1997) on discourse analysis, Q methodology is now often used with multiple participants in a constructionist sense to identify the social or dominant viewpoints or shared understandings of particular phenomena.

12.3 How to conduct a Q study (in brief)

I suggest both Watts and Stenner (2012) and McKeown and Thomas (2013) as excellent manuals that provide comprehensive detail about how to do a Q study. There is also the Q methodology website (International Society for the Scientific Study of Subjectivity, 2011), which provides resources, references, tutorials, references to online sorting packages, and a listserve for sharing information and addressing Q research problems. I now provide a very brief outline of the steps involved.

12.3.1 The concourse

In order to do Q methodology research, we must first have an area of subjectivity to investigate, i.e., there must be a stimulus, issue or topic about which people have varying opinions.

Having established the aims of the study, the next step is to establish the concourse. As explained above, this can be done via a range of measures, including literature reviews and interviews with people who are likely to have an opinion on the topic. This will result in a number of statements (often more than 100 from a variety of sources) in the form of opinions about the topic or issue.

12.3.2 The Q sample

For the purpose of Q sorting, a subset of statements, called a Q sample, needs to be drawn from the larger concourse. This is the set of statements that will be presented to research participants in the form of a Q sort. This set of statements must be small enough to be manageable for the participant group (e.g., perhaps thirty to sixty) but representative of the larger concourse from which the Q set is drawn. A suggested way of achieving representativeness of the Q sample is to use Fisher's (1960) balanced-block experimental design principles (for details of this see: Brown, 1980; McKeown & Thomas, 2013). Reduction of items to make a Q set will usually involve careful examination of each item in the concourse and combining together similar ones, in addition to pilot testing to ensure that items are clear and unambiguous.

12.3.3 The P sample

The P or participant sample is not randomly drawn, as in R methodology, but selected on theoretical grounds, i.e., relevance to the aims of your study. In Q methodology, our concern is not with generalizing to the larger population but to do with revealing meanings of a limited number of participants. What we generally want to sample are people who do have a point of view on the topic of interest. This is usually done with a P sample size of forty to sixty (Stainton Rogers, 1995).

12.3.4 Q sorting

Usually the Q set of items are presented to the participants in the form of small cards with a condition of instruction to arrange them from, for example, 'most agree' to 'most disagree' or 'most like' to 'most unlike'. Typically the sorting is completed on a grid, which takes the shape of an inverted normal curve (for an example see Figure 12.1). To assist the participants, a good strategy is to ask them first to sort the Q items into three piles, e.g., agree, disagree and a neutral group. Then the participants are required to take the single card with which they most strongly agree and place it on the extreme right hand side of the grid. They then place cards in the grid spaces moving from the right side of the grid (the strongly agree side) working across to the left side of the grid (the strongly disagree side).

A record is taken of each participant's completed sort, and usually a post-sort interview is conducted (and recorded) during which the researcher discusses the participant's choices in order to clarify and elicit greater understanding. Although personal one-to-one administration of Q sorts is recommended, there are at least three online sorting packages – Flash Q, WebQSort and QAssessor (the third one can also assist with data analysis). The web addresses for these on-line tools can be found on the Q methodology website (International Society for the Scientific Study of Subjectivity, 2011).

12.3.5 Q factor analysis and interpretation

There are two dedicated software packages available to analyse Q data – PQMethod (Schmolck & Atkinson, 2013) (available for free) and PCQ (Stricklin & Almeida, 2004). First, the Q sorts are correlated, followed by factor analysis of the correlation matrix and factor rotation. The factor rotation can be done manually (preferred in order to be consistent with the philosophy underlying Q) or automatically (usually varimax). Ultimately, the factors are made up of groups of people who share similar views on the topic of interest. The final step is to interpret the factors by examining carefully the make-up of each factor and using the post-sort interview data to assist with interpretation. During the post-sort interview participants are asked to explain their reasons for placing cards in particular grid locations, especially at the extreme strongly agree and strongly disagree ends of the distribution.

12.4 The usefulness of Q methodology in studies of children and teenagers

12.4.1 Range of studies

Q methodology has been used in a diverse range of studies of children and teenagers including: identifying priorities that adolescents place on adolescent tasks (Nitzberg, 1980); using a social constructionist perspective to explore the influence that children have on their parents (De Mol & Buysse, 2008); a mixed methods study to examine Italian and Japanese language policy implementation in Melbourne schools (Lo Bianco & Aliani, 2013); identifying the views of 14–17 year olds on alcohol marketing (Scott, Baker, Shucksmith, & Kaner, 2014); a discourse analysis investigating attitudes of Dutch youth about their health lifestyle (van Exel, de Graaf, & Brouwer, 2006); identifying preferences for health care and self-management of Dutch adolescents who have chronic health conditions (Jedeloo, van Staa, Latourb, & van Exel, 2010); a study of the concept of family held by Norwegian adolescents (Ellingsen, Shemmings, & Størksen, 2011); and a study of the feelings and experiences of day-care children whose parents are divorced (Størksen, Thorsen, Øverland, & Brown, 2012).

12.4.2 Particular advantages of Q methodology in research with children and teenagers

A major challenge for researchers is to find methods that will enable teenagers and children, especially younger ones, to be able to provide the information that scholars seek (see also discussions about children's verbal competencies in Chapters 5 and 6). For instance, traditional verbal responses in interviews in phenomenology studies would be difficult to obtain from young children. Phenomenology is concerned with eliciting individuals' understandings of personal experiences with phenomena in the world around them. These personal experiences are often explored, with individuals who have experienced the phenomena, via multiple interviews. The researcher analyses the data carefully and systematically to eventually arrive at the essence of the phenomena as experienced by the individuals (Moustakas, 1994; van Manen, 1990). Taylor, Delprato and Knapp (1994) described the difficulties that young children have in participating in phenomenological studies because of their limited language and speech skills. However, Taylor *et al.* (1994) showed that 3- and 4-year-old children could convey the phenomenal information required via a Q sort process involving the use of pictorial rather than verbal stimuli.

Ellingsen, Thorsen and Størksen (2014) argued for the importance of including the views and ideas of children in research, but the difficulties of having children express themselves in research tasks, especially in relation to sensitive issues (such as parental divorce) (see also Chapters 6 and 9 concerning researching sensitive issues with children). Most parents could relate to the situation where they ask their child: 'How was school today?' and the response is 'Okay'. It does require more specific concrete questions to get the detail that parents are seeking, but then there is the danger of asking children leading questions. Ellingsen *et al.* (2014) documented some of the limitations of traditional research methodologies when the participant group is children. For instance, qualitative in-depth interviews require good verbal skills (see Chapter 6), surveys require reasonable reading skills, and quantitative studies often require large samples and the need for parental consent can make it difficult to obtain the requisite sample size. Q sort methodology can overcome these difficulties. Ellingsen *et al.* (2014) recounted a study of the feelings and experiences of 5-year-old children of divorced parents. It would be very difficult for children to express their perceptions and feelings on such a sensitive issue in typical research interviews. Instead, the researchers used Q sorting with visual images illustrating various emotions and experiences relating to divorce. Despite their young age and the sensitivity of the topic, the children were able to express their feelings and perceptions via the Q sorting process. Ellingsen *et al.* (2014) reported a second study, this one focusing on the meaning of family to Norwegian adolescents living in foster homes. Again this was a very sensitive issue and many adolescents would find it difficult to express their feelings in traditional interviews, but the Q sort process did enable the teens to engage in the research process in a participatory and effective way. Together the two studies show that Q methodology is child friendly, participatory, non-threatening and non-intrusive, enabling children and teens to express their views on very sensitive issues.

12.5 Critiques of Q methodology

Generally Q methodology is claimed to have a number of strengths, including being able to study subjectivity in a scientific way, being appealing to both quantitative and qualitative researchers, and requiring small non-random samples. However, Q methodology is not mainstream, and definitely not well understood by R methodologists, and there have been numerous critiques of Q methodology. I refer the reader to a recent article by Kampen and Tamás (2014) and a response by Brown, Danielson and van Exel (2015). I now provide a summary of the major criticisms of Q methodology made by Kampen and Tamás (2014) and the responses to each of these by Brown *et al.* (2015).

Kampen and Tamás argued: (i) Q methodology is ineffective in measuring internal subjective states and the closest science has come to this is through Magnetic Resonance Imagery (MRI) technology; (ii) Q methodology does not provide a systematic approach to the construction of a concourse or test its completeness and therefore, it is not valid to claim that the Q sample is representative of the concourse; (iii) the recommendation that the P sample can be small and in fact smaller than the Q sample is mathematically and logically flawed; (iv) there is no proven connection between subjectivity as measured in Q card sorting and people's views in their daily lives; (v) there are threats to internal validity in the Q process particularly relating to lack of control of researcher bias. In response, Brown *et al.* contended: (i) Kampen and Tamás have adopted a nineteenth century internal mentalistic conception of subjectivity, whereas Q methodology is concerned with the operant or behavioural expression of subjectivity (e.g., points of view) that can be measured and analysed via Q sorting and factor analysis; (ii) there are many sources of guidance about how to assemble a concourse and derive a Q sample from it (e.g., Brown, 1980; McKeown & Thomas, 2013; Watts & Stenner, 2012); (iii) while the ratio of number of participants to number of items is important in R methodology, it is of little significance in Q methodology; (iv) specificity is important, i.e., the context in which people respond to research questions will and ought to make a difference, and there is no argument to be had about that; (v) the potential for bias by unscrupulous researchers is real in any form of scientific enquiry, but the specific accusations relating to Q research are based on assertion and innuendo.

Readers will need to make up their own minds in relation to this debate, but a good starting point would be to carefully read the articles and the sources referred to in each. Of course, in determining whether to use any research methodology, the researcher needs to consider the aims or research questions, and the strengths and limitations of each research design. For instance, if generalization to a larger population is desired then a Likert scale survey instrument may be appropriate, but if the desire is to find out about the points of view that exist within a participant group then Q methodology has the advantages previously described.

12.6 Q studies of popularity among teenage girls

Traditional sociometric research conceptualized popularity as being well-liked, pro-social, and non-aggressive (e.g., Asher & Coie, 1990; Rubin, Bukowski, & Parker, 1998). Concurrent sociological research (e.g., Adler & Adler, 1998; Eder, 1985; Merten, 1997), however, saw popularity as being publically visible, prestigious and not necessarily well-liked. Later social psychologists (Cillessen & Rose, 2005; de Bruyn & Cillessen, 2006; Parkhurst & Hopmeyer, 1998), using peer nomination, found a form of popularity concerned with social power, influence and visibility (similar to the sociological findings). These peer-nominated popular children and teens could be aggressive and were not necessarily well-liked or pro-social. Our own previous work (Duncan, 1999, 2004; Owens, Shute, & Slee, 2000a, 2000b, 2001) suggested that popular teenage girls can play a powerful role in determining social relationships within schools through the use of socially harmful aggressive behaviours. Based on this background, we decided to explore popularity from the point of view of girls themselves and, given our concern with subjectivity, Q methodology seemed an ideal way to proceed. Three studies are briefly described below.

12.6.1 Study 1. Adelaide, South Australia: 'Druggies and Barbie dolls' (Owens & Duncan, 2009)

To collect data we used Q methodology and follow-up semi-structured interviews with forty 15-year-old girls (the P sample) from two schools (one middle class and the other from a low-income area) in metropolitan Adelaide, the capital city of South Australia. A sixty-five-item concourse was developed from the literature on girls' peer relationships and via a series of discussions with teachers and teenage girls in earlier studies (Duncan, 1999; 2004). The Q sample consisted of thirty-five representative items derived from the concourse. The students were required to arrange the statements from items most associated with popularity to those most associated with unpopularity (see Figure 12.1 for the layout of the Q grid). An audiotaped post-sort discussion was held at the end of the Q sort activity, during which the girls explained their Q choices. Although it is not necessarily a standard procedure in Q studies, we later returned to the girls' schools and shared with them our preliminary analysis of the data. The purpose of this feedback session was to check with the girls to see whether our understanding of the Q sort results and interviews matched their views (Guba & Lincoln, 1981; Owens et al., 2000a; Sandelowski, 1986).

The Q sorts were correlated and factor analysed (including varimax rotation), using PQMethod version 2.11 (Schmolck & Atkinson, 2002), revealing two perspectives on popularity – the predominant one being labelled by the girls in the credibility checking session as 'girly girly' or 'Barbie doll' popularity and the second one (adhered to by a small group of girls in the low-income school) as 'mean' or 'scary' or 'druggy' popularity. Based on Z scores 1.0, girls who subscribed to factor 1 saw popular girls (in rank order) as being very well-liked by boys, having a lot of friends, being very fashionable, being really pretty and well-liked by other students. In contrast, based on Z scores -1, unpopular girls (in rank order from most unpopular) were seen as very quiet, having special needs, may be lesbians, well-behaved, overweight, well-liked by teachers, drug taking and having one very close friend. Based on Z scores 1, for the girls who subscribed to factor 2, popularity was associated, in rank order, with taking drugs, smoking, drinking alcohol and being very well-liked by boys. Based on Z scores -1, girls who subscribed to factor 2 saw unpopular girls (in rank order from most unpopular) as

	Most Unpopular			Neutral			Most Popular		
Score	-4	-3	-2	-1	0	1	2	3	4
No. of Statements	1	3	4	6	7	6	4	3	1

FIGURE 12.1 Layout of the Q sort grid in the Adelaide and Wolverhampton studies

very good at school work, well-liked by teachers, very well behaved at school, kind to other students, very quiet, virgins and having special needs. The interviews assisted in our interpretation of the factors.

In summary, Q methodology revealed that the girls generally saw popular peers as being physically attractive, liked by boys and having a rebellious anti-authority attitude with some risk-taking behaviours, even more so in the low-income school. Being well-liked was part of the picture of popularity, but many other features around appearance, attractiveness to boys, public visibility and a 'cool' non-conformism were at play. We argued that the girls from the low-income school, who subscribed to a more hard-edged anti-social view of popularity, did not see their schooling as providing them with benefits so they adopted anti-authority models and nothing-to-lose attitudes to their risk-taking behaviours as a way of enhancing their reputations among peers (Becker & Luthar, 2007; Kreager, 2007).

12.6.2 Study 2. Wolverhampton, UK: 'Boys like them' (Duncan & Owens, 2011)

In this study, twenty-eight 15-year-old girls from two Wolverhampton schools (one middle- and one working-class) sorted the same statements under the same conditions as in Study 1 above. In the Wolverhampton study, there appeared to be no difference between the perspectives of girls in the two schools with one factor being evident, onto which all the girls loaded. Popularity was associated (in order) with: being really pretty, very fashionable, well-liked by boys, very loud, having many friends, having a certain type of make-up or hairstyle, being quite thin, and going out with older boys. Unpopularity was associated (in order) with: may be lesbian, very quiet, well-behaved in school, liked by teachers, overweight, misses a lot of school, and being religious. We interpreted these results (confirmed in the interviews and in the credibility feedback session) as popularity being based on heterosexual attractiveness and mild school rebelliousness. So there was a degree of similarity between the views of the girls in Wolverhampton and those in Adelaide, particularly those Adelaide girls who subscribed to factor 1, but there was only one dominant perspective, regardless of social class background, according to the Wolverhampton girls.

12.6.3 Study 3: Shanghai, China: 'They are friendly and helpful' (Owens, Feng, & Xi, 2014)

Because of the cultural differences, in this study we started again in generating a concourse of items and deriving a Q set for sorting. In this study fifty-five 16- to

19-year-old senior high school girls from two Shanghai schools (assumed to be different in social class background) sorted forty items relating to popularity. Analysis produced one dominant factor, explaining 75 per cent of the variance. All participants from both schools loaded significantly and positively onto it. Items most closely associated with popularity (in rank order) were: is even-tempered, is sincere to others, is forgiving, is outgoing and energetic, is kind to others, helps other students and has a good sense of humour. Items most closely associated with being unpopular in rank order were: is double-dealing, sows discord among others, talks about people behind their backs, looks down on others, often shows-off, laughs at other students, considers herself always right, behaves pretentiously, seldom thinks about others and excludes others from the group. Once again, follow-up individual interviews and consultation with the participants assisted us in our interpretation of the results. Our summary of this factor is that popular girls are seen as friendly and pro-social but unpopular girls are seen to be self-centred and relationally aggressive. The Shanghai girls saw popular peers as friendly and cooperative and not at all rebellious, aggressive or anti-social.

Because participant samples are small and not drawn randomly in Q studies, we need to be careful about making generalizations to the wider population from results. However, we can say that our participants from Wolverhampton and Adelaide did see popularity in a different way from the girls in Shanghai. Our explanations for these variations are necessarily tentative but it could be that cultural differences are at play. We speculate that the Chinese girls, with a collectivist Confucianist background, are influenced in school, home and society by concepts relating to social harmony and the common good. Relational aggressiveness and rebelliousness will lead to disharmony, so this is not valued or appreciated by the teenage girls (Fujihara, Kohyama, Andreu, & Ramirez, 1999; Li, Wang, Wang, & Shi, 2010; Li, Xie, & Shi, 2012). Instead forgiveness, sincerity and helping others are admired. In contrast, in Western societies, where the emphasis is on individualism, the girls might consider what is of most benefit to themselves and the concept of benefit to the whole group is not at the forefront of their minds. To the Western girls, rebellious and anti-authority attitudes serve as a declaration of autonomy and are admired by peers (Corsara & Eder, 1990; Glendinning & Inglis, 1999; Mayeux, Sandstrom, & Cillessen, 2008; Moffitt, 2003; Owens & Duncan, 2009). However, in China, the emphasis is on harmonious interpersonal relationships and not rule-breaking and risky behaviours. In addition, whereas in the West, popular girls were seen as attractive, fashionable and liked by boys, in China there is a strong moral education at home and in school, which emphasizes internal qualities rather than external physical beauty (Chen, Li, Li, Li, & Liu, 2000; Li et al., 2012). In an overall sense, the views of our Western participants align with a peer or publically perceived view of popularity, but the girls from Shanghai more closely aligned with the sociometric view of popularity, i.e., as being well-liked.

In coming to these conclusions, we are well aware of the criticisms made of cultural differences explanations and particularly the way in which the distinction between individualism and collectivism has been criticised for not adequately considering the heterogeneity that exists within and across cultural groups (Fiske, 2002; Miller, 2002). Q methodology has provided us with some interesting results relating to the perspectives on popularity of samples of girls in Adelaide, Wolverhampton and Shanghai. Our work points the way for further research, particularly in Mainland China where very few studies have been conducted relating to popularity.

12.7 Conclusion

Q methodology has been described as 'the best developed paradigm for the investigation of human subjectivity' (Dryzek & Holmes, 2002, p. 20). It had its origins in the work of Stephenson in the 1930s. Although it is not a mainstream approach in the social sciences, it has a strong theoretical basis and systematic rigorous techniques for collecting and analysing data and it has been used in a wide range of disciplines and topics relating to human subjectivity. It has been criticised, but the criticisms have been well addressed. The author has used Q in several studies relating to popularity among teenage girls and further work, particularly in Mainland China, is warranted.

Although it uses quantitative methods of analysis, Q methodology appeals also to qualitative researchers and it shares many of the goals and procedures of qualitative research. As Brown (2008) explained: 'Central to this enterprise are the meanings and understandings that individuals bring to their endeavours, and it this preservation of the person's perspective . . . that has rendered Q methodology attractive to investigators who are partial to qualitative methods' (p. 699). McKeown and Thomas (2013) argued that Q methodology breaks down the barriers between quantitative and qualitative researchers (see also Chapters 10, 11, 13 and 14 for further consideration of breaking the barriers between qualitative and quantitative research). For example, qualitative research traditions such as phenomenology are concerned with the lived experiences of individuals and articulating the essence of these experiences across groups of people. In a similar way, the goals of the statistical analyses inherent in Q methodology are to preserve the subjectivities of individuals and to reveal how these subjectivities are shared across groups of people. As McKeown and Thomas wrote (2013, p. 1): 'Q methodology brings qualitative research into the quantitative realm'.

Practical tips

1   If it is your first Q study, use the excellent guidance provided in Watts and Stenner (2012) and in McKeown and Thomas (2013). In addition, join the Q Listserve (International Society for the Scientific Study of Subjectivity, 2011). It is the official email information and discussion list for the International Society for the Scientific Study of Subjectivity (ISSSS). Members of the listserve are very active and a source of excellent advice relating to Q studies.

2   It is crucial to spend considerable time developing the concourse for your study. If the concourse is not exhaustive, then the Q sample will not be truly representative of the population of ideas and views relating to the issue. In developing the concourse, do a thorough review of the literature relating to your topic. In addition, conduct individual and group interviews with children and/or teenagers in the age groups that you will use for your participant sample.

3   Before working with your participants, ensure that you pilot test your Q sorting procedures. During the pilot testing, solicit advice and opinions from your pilot group to ensure wording is understandable and lacking in ambiguity and that all procedures are clear. During the Q sorting, provide guidance to your participants, especially during the early stages of Q sorting, until you are confident that the participants understand the requirements. After you have completed a preliminary analysis of your data, it is a good idea (if it is possible) to return to your participants to share with them your findings and seek their reaction and further comment.

References

Adler, P. A., & Adler, P. (1998). *Peer power: Preadolescent culture and identity.* New Brunswick, NJ: Rutgers University Press.

Asher, S. R., & Coie, J. D. (1990). *Peer rejection in childhood.* New York: Cambridge University Press.

Becker, B. E., & Luthar, S. S. (2007). Peer-perceived admiration and social preference: Contextual correlates of positive peer regard among suburban and urban adolescents. *Journal of Research on Adolescence, 17,* 117–44.

Brown, S. R. (1980). *Political subjectivity.* New Haven: Yale University Press.

Brown, S. R. (2004). Q methodology. In M. S. Lewis-Beck, A. Bryman & T. Futing Liao (Eds), *The SAGE encyclopedia of social science research methods* (Vol. 3, pp. 887–8). Thousand Oaks, CA: Sage.

Brown, S. R. (2008). Q methodology. In L. M. Given (Ed.), *The SAGE encyclopedia of qualitative research methods* (pp. 699–702). Thousand Oaks, CA: Sage.

Brown, S. R., Danielson, S., & van Exel, J. (2015). Overly ambitious critics & the Medici effect: A reply to Kampen and Tamás. *Quality & Quantity, 49,* 523–37.

Brown, S. R., & Good, J. M. M. (2010). Q methodology. In N. J. Salkind (Ed.), *Encyclopedia of research design* (Vol. 3, pp. 1149–55). Thousand Oaks, CA: Sage.

Chen, X., Li, D., Li, Z., Li, B., & Liu, M. (2000). Sociable and prosocial dimensions of social competence in Chinese children: Common and unique contributions to social, academic, and psychological adjustment. *Developmental Psychology*, *36*, 302–14.

Cillessen, A. H. N., & Rose, A. J. (2005). Understanding popularity in the peer system. *Current Directions in Psychological Science*, *14*, 102–5.

Corsara, W. A., & Eder, D. (1990). Children's peer cultures. *Annual Review of Sociology*, *16*, 197–220.

de Bruyn, E. H., & Cillessen, A. H. N. (2006). Heterogeneity of girls' consensual popularity: Academic and interpersonal behavioral profiles. *Journal of Youth and Adolescence*, *35*, 435–45.

De Mol, J., & Buysse, A. (2008). Understandings of children's influence in parent child relationships: A Q-methodological study. *Journal of Social and Personal Relationships*, *25*, 359–79.

Dryzek, J. S., & Holmes, L. T. (2002). *Post-communist democratization: Political discourses across thirteen countries*. Cambridge, UK: Cambridge University Press.

Duncan, N. (1999). *Sexual bullying: Gender conflict and pupil culture in secondary schools*. London: Routledge.

Duncan, N. (2004). It's important to be nice, but it's nicer to be important: Girls, popularity and sexual competition. *Sex Education*, *4*, 137–52.

Duncan, N., & Owens, L. (2011). Bullying, social power and heteronormativity: Girls' constructions of popularity. *Children and Society. The International Journal of Childhood and Children's Services*, *25*, 306–16.

Eder, D. (1985). The cycle of popularity: Interpersonal relations among female adolescents. *Sociology of Education*, *58*, 154–65.

Elder-Vass, D. (2013). *The reality of social construction*. Cambridge, UK: Cambridge University Press.

Ellingsen, I. T., Shemmings, D., & Størksen, I. (2011). The concept of 'family' among Norwegian adolescents in long-term foster care. *Child and Adolescence Social Work Journal*, *28*, 301–18.

Ellingsen, I. T., Thorsen, A. A., & Størksen, I. (2014). Revealing children's experiences and emotions through Q methodology. *Child Development Research*, *2014*, 1–9.

Feynman, R. P. (1965). *The character of physical law*. Cambridge, MA: MIT Press.

Fisher, R. A. (1960). *The design of experiments* (7th edn). Edinburgh: Oliver & Boyd.

Fiske, A. P. (2002). Using individualism and collectivism to compare cultures – a critique of the validity and measurment of the constructs: Comment on Oyersman *et al*. *Psychological Bulletin*, *128*, 78–88.

Fujihara, T., Kohyama, T., Andreu, J., & Ramirez, M. J. (1999). Justification of interpersonal aggression in Japanese, American and Spanish students. *Aggressive Behavior*, *25*, 185–95.

Glendinning, A., & Inglis, D. (1999). Smoking behaviour in youth: The problem of low self-esteem? *Journal of Adolescence*, *22*, 673–82.

Guba, E. G., & Lincoln, Y. S. (1981). *Effective evaluation*. San Francisco, CA: Jossey-Bass.

Hacking, I. (2000). *The social construction of what?* Oxford, UK: Oxford University Press.

International Society for the Scientific Study of Subjectivity. (2011). *Q methodology. A method for modern research.* Retrieved from www.qmethod.org/about on 24 June 2015.

Jedeloo, S., van Staa, A., Latourb, J. M., & van Exel, N. J. A. (2010). Preferences for health care and self-management among Dutch adolescents with chronic conditions: A Q-methodological investigation. *International Journal of Nursing Studies, 47*, 593–603.

Kampen, J. K., & Tamás, P. (2014). Overly ambitious: Contributions and current status of Q methodology. *Quality & Quantity, 48*, 3109–26.

Kreager, D. A. (2007). When it's good to be 'bad': Violence and adolescent peer acceptance. *Criminology, 45*, 893–923.

Li, Y., Wang, M., Wang, C., & Shi, J. (2010). Individualism, collectivism, and Chinese adolescents' aggression: Intracultural variations. *Aggressive Behavior, 36*, 187–94.

Li, Y., Xie, H., & Shi, J. (2012). Chinese and American children's perception of popularity determinants: Cultural differences and behavioral correlates. *International Journal of Behavioral Development, 36*, 1–10.

Lo Bianco, J., & Aliani, R. (2013). *Language planning and student experiences: Intention, rhetoric and implementation.* Bristol, UK: Multilingual Matters.

Mayeux, L., Sandstrom, M. J., & Cillessen, A. H. N. (2008). Is being popular a risky proposition? *Journal of Research on Adolescence, 18*, 49–74.

McKeown, B., & Thomas, D. B. (2013). *Q methodology* (2nd edn). Los Angeles, CA: Sage.

Merten, D. E. (1997). The meaning of meanness: Popularity, competition, and conflict among junior high school girls. *Sociology of Education, 70*, 175–91.

Miller, J. G. (2002). Bringing culture to basic psychological theory – beyond individualism and collectivism: Comment on Oyserman *et al. Psychological Bulletin, 128*, 97–109.

Moffitt, T. E. (2003). Life-course-persistent and adolescence-limited antisocial behavior: A 10-year research review and a research agenda. In B. B. Lahey, T. E. Moffitt & A. Caspi (Eds), *Causes of conduct disorder and juvenile delinquency* (pp. 49–75). New York: Guilford.

Moustakas, C. (1994). *Phenomenological research methods.* Thousand Oaks, CA: Sage.

Nitzberg, M. (1980). Development of modified q-sort instrument to measure priorities adolescent places on developmental tasks. *Adolescence, 15*, 501–8.

Owens, L., & Duncan, N. (2009). 'Druggies' and 'Barbie dolls': Popularity among teenage girls in two South Australian schools. *Journal of Human Subjectivity, 7*, 39–63.

Owens, L., Feng, H., & Xi, J. (2014). Popularity among teenage girls in Adelaide and Shanghai: A pilot Q-method study. *Open Journal of Social Sciences, 2*, 80–5.

Owens, L., Shute, R., & Slee, P. (2000a). 'Guess what I just heard!' Indirect aggression among teenage girls in Australia. *Aggressive Behavior, 26*, 67–83.

Owens, L., Shute, R., & Slee, P. (2000b). 'I'm in and you're out . . .' Explanations for teenage girls' indirect aggression. *Psychology, Evolution & Gender, 2*, 19–46.

Owens, L., Shute, R., & Slee, P. (2001). Victimization among teenage girls. What can be done about indirect harassment? In J. Juvonen & S. Graham (Eds), *School-based peer harassment: The plight of the vulnerable and victimized* (pp. 215–41). New York: Guilford.

Parkhurst, J. T., & Hopmeyer, A. (1998). Sociometric popularity and peer-perceived popularity: Two distinct dimensions of peer status. *Journal of Early Adolescence, 18*, 125–44.

Piaget, J. (1950). *The psychology of intelligence.* New York: Routledge.

Rubin, K. H., Bukowski, W. M., & Parker, J. G. (1998). Peer interactions, relationships, and groups. In N. Eisenberg (Ed.), *Handbook of child psychology: Social, emotional, and personality development* (5th edn, Vol. 3, pp. 619–700). New York: Wiley.

Sandelowski, M. (1986). The problem of rigor in qualitative research. *Advances in Nursing Science, 8*, 27–37.

Schmolck, P., & Atkinson, J. (2002). *PQMethod* (2.11). Computer program, available at www.qmethod.org on 10 January 2009 (note: latest version is PQMethod 2.35, 2014).

Schmolck, P., & Atkinson, J. (2013). *PQMethod* (2.33). Retrieved from www.qmethod.org on 10 February 2015 (note: latest version is PQMethod 2.35, 2014).

Scott, S., Baker, R., Shucksmith, J., & Kaner, E. (2014). Autonomy, special offers and routines: A Q methodological study of industry-driven marketing influences on young people's drinking behaviour. *Addiction, 109*, 1833–44.

Skinner, B. F. (1938). *The behavior of organisms.* New York: Appleton-Century-Crofts.

Skinner, B. F. (1953). *Science and human behavior.* New York: Macmillan.

Stainton Rogers, R. (1995). Q methodology. In J. A. Smith, R. Harre & L. Van Langenhove (Eds), *Rethinking Methods in Psychology* (pp. 178–92). London: Sage.

Stainton Rogers, R. (1997). Q methodology and 'going critical': Some reflections on the British dialect. *Operant Subjectivity, 21*, 19–26.

Stainton Rogers, W. (1997). Q methodology, textuality, and tectonics. *Operant Subjectivity, 21*, 1–18.

Stephenson, W. (1935). Technique of factor analysis. *Nature, 136*, 297.

Stephenson, W. (1953). *The study of behavior: Q-technique and its methodology.* Chicago, IL: University of Chicago Press.

Stephenson, W. (1988). The quantumization of psychological events. Operant Subjectivity: *The International Journal of Q Methodology, 12*, 1–23.

Størksen, I., Thorsen, A. A., Øverland, K., & Brown, S. R. (2012). Experiences of daycare children of divorce. *Early Child Development and Care, 182*, 807–25.

Stricklin, M., & Almeida, J. (2004). *PCQ: Analysis Software for Q-technique* (revised academic edition). Retrieved from www.pcqsoft.com on 10 February 2015.

Taylor, P., Delprato, D. J., & Knapp, J. R. (1994). Q-methodology in the study of child phenomenology. *The Psychological Record, 44*, 171–83.

van Exel, N. J. A., de Graaf, G., & Brouwer, W. B. F. (2006). 'Everyone dies, so you might as well have fun!' Attitudes of Dutch youths about their health lifestyle. *Social Science & Medicine, 63*, 2628–39.

van Manen, M. (1990). *Researching lived experience.* New York: State University of New York Press.

Watson, J. B. (1913). Psychology as the behaviorist views it. *Psychological Review, 20*, 158–77.

Watts, S., & Stenner, P. (2012). *Doing Q methodological research: Theory, method and interpretation.* Thousand Oaks, CA: Sage.

13

METHODOLOGIES FOR PAEDIATRIC SLEEP RESEARCH IN TYPICAL AND ATYPICAL POPULATIONS

Frances Le Cornu Knight and Dagmara Dimitriou

13.1 Introduction: sleep research with children

In a world of increasing environmental distractors, the appeal of getting a good night's sleep is diminishing for many children and adolescents. And yet, more and more research is surfacing showing sleep to be fundamental for healthy development. First, sleep promotes the production of growth hormones, which facilitate healthy brain and bodily development. Second, sleep supports processes of memory consolidation that lead to stable long-term memories, and facilitate learning. Finally, sleep helps to support healthy brain development, by promoting neural plasticity and ridding the brain of the neurochemical toxins that build up during the day (Xie *et al.*, 2013). Similarly, we now know that insufficient sleep duration and poor sleep quality have negative effects on academic performance and daytime behaviour. Children with poor sleep perform worse on schoolwork, find it harder to concentrate and display more disruptive behaviours (Sadeh, Gruber, & Raviv, 2002).

Given that physical growth, knowledge acquisition and brain development are all at the centre of healthy childhood development, understanding sleep through comprehensive research is vital. There are a variety of research tools that allow us to examine sleep in children, ranging from simply asking about sleep behaviours to measuring the neural or biological activity underlying sleep. Each method comes with its distinct set of benefits and costs, which will be considered further as we work through a range of instruments available. The paediatric sleep researcher should bear in mind that owing to the distinct benefits and costs associated with each technique, using a combined approach is usually advocated.

13.2 Overview of sleep research tools

Sleep poses a difficult problem for the researcher: How can we ask a person to help us understand an activity for which they themselves are not conscious? When talking to a participant about their sleep, you are asking them to give their perspective on an activity about which they are only vaguely aware. Researching sleep in children further compounds this issue, as a child's own insight into their sleep may be incomplete or not easy to glean. In many cases, this means asking the participant's primary caregiver (using questionnaires or interviews) or relying on objective physiological and biological measures, which monitor sleep patterns through brain activity (polysomnography), movement (actigraphy) or hormone secretion.

This section will first take you through the variety of participant response measures of sleep, and then go on to describe physiological and biological measures. We will compare and contrast the types of information that each tool can be used to obtain, while also considering their relative strengths and weaknesses. This information is crucial in selecting the appropriate tool to allow the researcher to capture the most relevant information for the specific purposes of their research. We will pay particular attention to the balancing act between objective reliability and relative disruption to habitual sleep patterns.

13.2.1 Participant response measures: questionnaires, sleep diaries and interviews

Participant response measures are assessment tools that question the participant or primary caregiver about their sleep. Currently, the most popular measures are sleep diaries/logs, questionnaires and interviews. They allow for the capture of abundant descriptive data, which can either be quantitative or qualitative in nature. The researcher is able to extract information that is directly relevant to their research question by adapting existing assessment tools, or developing their own. Such tools represent a relatively inexpensive and non-invasive means of collecting sleep data, making them accessible to researchers without major funding. The aim of each participant response tool is to obtain useful insight into the participant's nighttime behaviour. However, each will vary slightly in terms of the type of information it is able to capture. It is important to understand the distinctions in order to select the most appropriate instrument for your study's needs.

One key distinction is whether you are interested in habitual sleep patterns (how an individual typically sleeps), or immediate sleep patterns over a set period of time (how they sleep over the course of time). Because of the immediate nature of sleep diaries or logs, these will chiefly monitor the latter. *Sleep diaries or logs* include a selection of questions about sleep behaviours to be answered on a daily basis over a set period of time. For example, they can provide insight into bed and rise times, the number of nighttime awakenings, the types of nighttime disturbances (such as nightmares or toilet trips) and concurrent daytime mood fluctuations. They are commonly used when trying to associate sleep with a measurable daytime activity over the same period of time. For example, one could look at the direct relationship between exercise and sleep, by measuring or manipulating daily exercise and recording concurrent sleep behaviours using a sleep diary. They have the advantage of being easily adapted so that the child themselves can complete them (under adult supervision to avoid errors).

Questionnaires have the benefit of being able to capture either immediate or habitual sleep data. Generally speaking, questionnaires collect more information at one time than sleep diaries. For this reason they commonly require the parent's contribution. Long questionnaires are deemed too demanding for young children, and older children and adolescents with intellectual impairments.

Finally, *interviews* can be used to gain deeper insight into a child's sleep behaviours and perceptions. Like questionnaires, interviews can be used to collect immediate or habitual sleep data. On the whole, interviews obtain rich qualitative data from questions that can be modified to fit the study objectives exactly. They have the additional benefit that the researcher can flexibly discuss new constructs as they arise through conversation. Interviews can be performed with the child, the primary caregiver or both. However, this is a skill that should not to be taken for granted. The ability to listen and guide participants into discussing topics of interest without interrupting the natural flow is not easy. Before undertaking interview research, the researcher should ideally been trained in interview skills with children (see Chapter 6 for a detailed discussion of interviews with children).

Another key distinction is whether you wish to produce a quantitative, a qualitative or a mixed methods report. All three of the instruments above can collect either quantitative or qualitative data. The key to knowing which you wish to produce, is whether you wish to describe sleep patterns in a few individual cases in depth, or whether you wish to investigate sleep in a larger sample (using statistical analyses) with the aim of generalising to a wider population. The researcher can ascertain whether an existing participant response tool is qualitative or quantitative by looking at the questions that are asked. Although there are exceptions to any rule, typically closed questions produce quantitative data; data that will be coded into numbers and statistically analysed. *Closed questions* can take the form of dichotomy or binary items (e.g., Did you go to bed at a normal hour? yes/no), multiple category items (e.g., Circle the mood that best describes how you have felt today; happy/grumpy/sleepy/alert) or continuum or scale items (e.g., How did you sleep? very well/well/average/not well/not well at all). Alternatively, *open questions* produce qualitative data, comprising unrestricted descriptions of sleep-related behaviours, attitudes and beliefs. The data derived from open questions are less constrained, and therefore reflect the respondent's personal opinions more closely. For example, if I asked you to tell me what mood describes best how you have felt today, you may pick one of the four items suggested above in the multiple category items. However, you may have felt differently from the moods described in the list, or indeed felt a broad description of moods throughout the day. The open-ended interview format is aimed at eliciting a freer response. To this end as stated above, it necessitates adequate training in order to usefully engage with the interviewee and be responsive to emerging themes of interest.

Finally, the type of information acquired depends on the respondent. In paediatric sleep research, most of the information is gathered from the child's primary caregiver. One can reasonably assume that the parent of a young child will be able to provide more detailed information, to a greater degree of accuracy and with fewer misunderstandings, than the child themself. That said, it is still extremely important that questions are succinct and unambiguous in order to reduce misunderstanding or misinterpretation. As a rule of thumb, questionnaires should take less than 20 minutes to complete (Spruyt & Gozal, 2011), so as to avoid response fatigue or carelessness. The researcher may be interested in the views and perceptions of the child about their own sleep, in which case it is of utmost importance to select a participant response tool that is age-appropriate. The instrument must match the level of understanding of the respondent and be in an easily accessible, age-appropriate language. The process of designing and validating interviews or questionnaires is a lengthy one. Spruyt and Gozal (2011) give a good explanation of the processes and problems associated with doing so. It is advisable for the novice, or even intermediate researcher, to select an established and well-validated research tool. While participant response tools represent a cheap and easy way to collect sleep data about child participants, they have one key drawback, the issue of subjectivity (see Box 13.1).

The issue of subjectivity is compounded further in sleep research, in that the responses gained are in fact the participant's experience of the waking periods surrounding sleep. The participant cannot give you an accurate reflection of the

BOX 13.1 PARTICIPANT RESPONSE MEASURES: THE ISSUE OF SUBJECTIVITY

Participant response tools can be a source of rich information from a range of perspectives. They can provide accounts of an individual's sleep habits, as well as a measure of a participant's perception of their sleep habits (itself an interesting topic). However, they have one inherent flaw: subjectivity. In paediatric sleep research, this issue is further compounded as relying on parent-reports displaces this subjectivity one step further from the participants themselves. Below are a number of potential sources of subjective bias:

The questions: Error can be introduced through individual interpretations of questions. Take the question; 'What time does your child get up?' One person might interpret this as the time at which their child becomes active, whereas another might interpret it as meaning the time at which they physically get up out of bed. What if a child were to read in bed? The first person might respond with the time that their child wakes and begins reading, the second with the time their child finishes reading and leaves their bed. Making sure that questions are clear and unambiguous is of the utmost importance.

Respondent bias: Participants may exaggerate the truth in order to live up to their expectations of the research. For example, the respondent may neglect to mention negative aspects of the bedtime routine (such as allowing sugary drinks before bed) so as to avoid embarrassment or criticism.

Lack of knowledge: Bias in parent-responses may be a result of ignorance. For example, a parent's ability to accurately report how many times their child wakes in the night is dependent on the parent's awareness of the occurrence. If the child sleeps in their own room there are a multitude of questions for which lack of knowledge may be an issue. In these instances, parents may be reliant on communication with their child, which in itself represents a source of bias.

The child: When relating activities that are generally discouraged, the child might be tempted to misrepresent the truth when in conversation with their parents. For example, if the child is not allowed to play on their laptop in bed, the child may tell their parent that they read instead.

sleep period itself, because by definition they are not conscious for it. For example, if I were to ask you how you slept last night, you might tell me you slept well, based on the fact that you did not have any trouble getting off to sleep and that you woke feeling refreshed. You might tell me you slept poorly, because you found it hard to get to sleep and awoke throughout the night. However, your perception of how the participants have slept may be inaccurate in terms of the processes that underlie sleep. During typical sleep, individuals cycle through sleep stages throughout the night. Each sleep stage is associated with a different kind of sleep (with a distinct pattern of brain waves) that is important for different sleep-dependent processes. From a participant response measure, a participant might relay that they had a good night's sleep, however this might not be reflected in the quality of sleep in terms of these underlying processes. For these reasons (considering Box 13.1), it is advisable for the paediatric sleep researcher not to rely on participant response methods alone; they are best accompanied by a more objective measure of sleep.

13.2.2 Physiological measures

Polysomnography

Polysomnography (PSG) is the method of measuring sleep by recording the neural activity that occurs during it. It has long since been considered to be the gold standard in sleep research, because it is considered an accurate and truly objective observation of the processes underlying sleep. It provides the researcher with a wealth of information about when and how a participant has slept, as well as revealing the sleep stages that they went through and how long they spent in each. PSG has helped identify five physiologically distinct sleep stages, which humans typically cycle through throughout the night. Sleep stages one to four are classified as non-rapid eye movement (NREM) sleep and each increases in depth. NREM stages three and four represent slow wave sleep (SWS), and are sometimes considered together as one stage. The fifth sleep stage is identified by rapid eye movements (REM), in which most of the rest of the muscles in the body are paralysed. PSG has advanced sleep research as a whole, in highlighting the importance of each individual sleep stage to specific cognitive processes. For example, from polysomnographic studies we now know that sleep-dependent learning in children is associated with increased SWS (see Hoedlmoser et al., 2014)

PSG records physiological activity from a small number of electrodes placed on the participant's scalp, face, neck and chest. These electrodes record activity across four domains; brain activity (electroencephalography; EEG), eye movements (electro-occulography; EOG), muscle activity (electro-myography; EMG) and heart rhythms (electro-cardiography; ECG). This data is then sent to a central box, via a system of wires, from which it can be downloaded and analysed offline. The EEG electrodes record the underlying electrical impulses produced by neurons. Because the brain produces different patterns of activity during different sleep stages, the recordings can be scored and categorised accordingly. With this information, we are then able to detect whether a child's sleep activity is typical or atypical. One of the key advantages of PSG, over and above any other sleep measure, is that we are also able to measure whether daytime activities or cognitive events influence sleep, increasing or decreasing certain sleep stages.

The key drawback to PSG is its potential to disturb sleep. The equipment itself is cumbersome; sensors are applied around the participant's head and chest. Unsurprisingly, this can feel awkward to the participant, and even threatening to a child participant. Furthermore, owing to the technical equipment, testing typically takes place in a laboratory. This takes the child out of their natural environment. All of which is likely to upset natural sleep. Newer mobile PSG technologies, allow for the data to be collected in the participant's own home, which better accommodates their normal nightly routine. Nonetheless, it is assumed that the unnatural equipment will introduce some disruption. To attenuate this issue, many studies perform one night of adaption, in order to get the participant used to sleeping with the apparatus on, and then data is collected on the second night.

Actigraphy

Actigraphy is the method of measuring sleep/wake cycles through movement. It works on the assumption that participants will be physically active while they are awake and inactive during sleep. While traditionally PSG has been considered the gold standard of sleep research, actigraphy has become increasingly popular in academic research. This is because it has a number of key benefits over and above PSG, and yet retains a high level of reliability with it. Some researchers suggest that the agreement between PSG and actigraphy measures in children is around 85–88 per cent (Hyde et al., 2007).

Movement is measured using an accelerometer set into a small device (which typically takes the form of a wrist watch, see Figure 13.1) that the participant wears for a set period of time. The accelerometer measures and stores units of movement sampled several times a second, which can then be downloaded and analysed offline. The output of the actigraph analysis produces a range of sleep variables in terms of individual and averaged nightly activity. Nightly measures include; sleep onset, sleep efficiency, sleep bouts, time in bed, and time asleep, nighttime awakening,

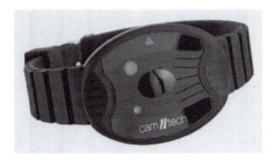

FIGURE 13.1 An example of a typical actigraphy device

time awake during bedtime, among others. Averaged measures include: the most active and least active hours (providing both time of onset and average movement), relative amplitude between the most and least active hours, and the inter- and intra-daily stability of movement patterns. All of these measures give us an idea of the entire sleep/wake cycle of each child participant.

As you can see, there is a wide variety of information available to the researcher from actigraphy data. The data available reveals information both about sleep duration and sleep quality. The richness of the data covering actual sleep quality is greater than that which could be collected using participant response instruments, and is not liable to subjectivity. There are also a number of key benefits that make it more appealing to use than PSG: namely, that it is relatively inexpensive, non-invasive, and involves little or no disruption to the participant's habitual sleep routine. The participant is able to move freely during the day and night, which in itself renders actigraphy data more generalisable to typical daily life. Importantly, actigraphy apparatus is less invasive than PSG, making it a more attractive option for use with children, especially those with developmental disorders. Like all methods, it does have associated costs. The method does not measure sleep per se, rather it infers sleep indirectly by measuring movement. The way the watch is attached can also introduce some inter-individual variability. A watch might be more tightly fitted on one individual than another, which will affect the recording but may not be taken into consideration in data analysis.

13.2.3 Biological measures

An alternative method of studying sleep patterns is by means of examining the biological mechanisms that regulate the sleep/wake cycle. The human sleep/wake cycle is controlled by a central internal timekeeper in the brain, called the suprachiasmatic nuclei. This regulates the expression of a group of genes known as CLOCK genes, which in turn prompt the release of the sleep/wake hormones melatonin and cortisol. By monitoring daily fluctuations in cortisol, melatonin and CLOCK gene expression, we can understand the typical (and atypical) biological patterns that promote efficient sleep. It is important to bear in mind that such measures do not examine sleep per se, but the circadian rhythm that supports sleep. The chief benefit of using biological measures with children is that they are obtained simply by means of buccal (mouth) samples or saliva swabs. This makes them relatively non-invasive and extremely child-friendly.

These biological systems have a consistent and measurably daily pattern that is largely comparable across healthy individuals. The hormones fluctuate in a diurnal pattern, meaning they typically show one peak and one trough in roughly 24 hours. Hence they are known as circadian rhythms, from the Latin *circa* – (meaning roughly) – and *diem* (meaning a day). The hormones cortisol and melatonin work in tandem. Cortisol aids awakening with cortisol levels peaking in the morning and diminishing throughout the day (Buckley & Schatzberg, 2005). Melatonin has the opposite pattern. Its role is to aid sleep. Melatonin is low in the morning and peaks in the evening just before rest (Waldhauzer, Kovacs, & Reiter, 1998). Circadian Locomotor Output Cycles Kaput (CLOCK) genes are more complex. Their patterns of expression vary according to the specific gene. Understanding the rhythmicity of these endocrine and molecular measures, has allowed researchers to investigate their role in sleep and neurodevelopmental disorders (for an explanation of how CLOCK genes apply to childhood disorders see Dueck, Thome, & Haessler, 2012).

An important practical issue to consider here is that the time and number of samples the researcher obtains can have a meaningful effect on the results. Some studies focus on one or two key time-points. For example, cortisol peaks roughly 30 minutes after waking (known as the cortisol awakening response; CAR). Consequently, many studies have compared this one time-point between experimental groups (e.g., Zinke, Fries, Kiegel, Kirschbaum, & Dettenborn, 2010). Other studies focus on the entire circadian cycle, sampling a number of time-points throughout the day (e.g., Baird, Coogan, Siddiqui, Donev, & Thome, 2012). These two methods are commonly compared between studies, but often produce discrepant results. This is because they each afford the researcher slightly different insight. For example, one time-point measures have led to confusion about whether Attention Deficit Hyperactivity Disorder (ADHD) involves higher or lower cortisol levels than normal (e.g., Ma, Chen, Chen, Liu, & Wang, 2011; and Wang *et al.*, 2011). However, recent circadian rhythm studies (sampling fluctuations in cortisol over 24 hours) show that the full diurnal pattern is unstable (e.g., Imeraj *et al.*, 2012). This explains the discrepancy in hyper- or hypo-arousal in the ADHD group; rather than being consistently high or low at a given point during the day, cortisol fluctuates in a less consistent manner throughout the day.

Biological measures allow the researcher to weigh up the relative appeal of avoiding disruption to habitual sleep patterns and increasing objective reliability. If maintaining habitual sleep patterns is more important to the study's objectives, endocrine and molecular measures can be taken throughout the day and on either side of sleep only. In this case, typical sleep patterns are not disturbed. However, this method will not provide an objective measure of sleep itself, but only of the waking hours either side of it. If the researcher is interested in how these biological mechanisms fluctuate during sleep, they must take a number of readings throughout the night, waking the participant intermittently. In this case, the researcher increases the objective reliability as a measure of sleep, but with the associated cost of disturbing the participant's sleep cycle. On the whole in sleep research with children, researchers favour the former approach.

13.2.4 Summary of sleep research tools: a combined approach

There are a number of well-established tools available to the paediatric sleep researcher, each with its own unique set of benefits and costs (see Figure 13.2). Participant response measures provide information about approximate sleep duration and typical daily sleep patterns by collecting subjective data about sleep behaviours. Actigraphy offers a means of objective information about sleep quantity and quality by monitoring nocturnal movement in order to indirectly infer sleep patterns. PSG extends further providing direct objective information about sleep quantity, sleep quality and sleep stages, by monitoring the neural activity associated with sleep. Biological measures provide an observation of the underlying circadian rhythms that prompt the sleep/wake cycle. In order to select the most appropriate tool for your particular study, you must have a clear understanding of the kind of data that will best help answer your research questions. Perhaps the most important consideration is the balance between maintaining habitual sleep behaviours during the course of participation and gaining a truly objective insight into sleep patterns.

While each has its individual use in paediatric sleep research, without doubt the most reliable approach to collecting sleep data is to combine one or more sources of information. In this sense, the data derived from one can be used to support that derived from another. For example, actigraphic analyses require bed and rise times to be inputted, in order to establish individual levels of day and night time activity. Hence, it is necessary to compliment actigraphy data with a simple sleep

OBJECTIVE RELIABILITY			
MAINTENANCE OF HABITUAL SLEEP			
Polysomnography	**Biological**	**Actigraphy**	**Participant Response**
Benefits: Rich objective profile of sleep	Benefits: Objective profile of biological mechanisims underlying sleep/wake cycle	Benefits: Non-invasive and child-friendly objective physiological measure. Minimal disruption to sleep	Benefits: No disruption to sleep. Broad range of descriptive data
Costs: Disruptive to sleep, invasive and expensive	Costs: Disruptive to sleep, invasive and expensive	Costs: Sleep patterns are inferred indirectly through movement. Wrist watches may vary in tightness from one individual to another	Costs: Prone to subjective bias

FIGURE 13.2 Displays the main benefits and costs of four paediatric sleep research tools. The box focuses on the balance between obtaining objective reliability and maintaining habitual sleep patterns. The light and dark grey bars at the top of the figure portray this relationship. The strength of the colour in each bar represents the relative strength of each testing constraint, such that as one becomes stronger the other weakens

diary or log. Likewise, participants undergoing PSG will usually only do so for one or two nights, and so using a parent report measure of habitual sleep behaviours is a good way of augmenting one-off PSG data. Baird and colleagues (2012) provide an excellent example of using multiple methods to produce a comprehensive study of sleep.

13.3 Atypical populations

Sleep is a particularly interesting subject in children with neurodevelopmental disorders. Sleep is important for neural plasticity (the way in which the brain functionally develops according to new knowledge and experience). Sleep allows for the strengthening of existing neural connections and the formation of new ones. As such, disturbed sleep interrupts this important process and may therefore have long-lasting functional consequences on the brain and general daily performance. Given that sleep problems are prevalent in a number of neurodevelopmental disorders, and that severity of sleep disturbances can contribute to the manifestation of such disorders, research has turned to the investigation of sleep in trying to understand and explain some of these issues. In this section, we will briefly look at some of the differences in sleep that have been reported across three neurodevelopmental disorders, with a focus on the research methods that have allowed such insights. We will also contemplate some practical considerations for using sleep measures with atypical populations.

13.3.1 Autism Spectrum Disorder (ASD)

Autism Spectrum Disorder (ASD) is a well-known neurodevelopmental disorder affecting three core components: social interactions, communication and stereo-typed repetitive behaviours (Le Couteur et al., 1989). In the UK in 2010, prevalence rates were estimated at roughly 1/1000 for girls and 4/1000 for boys (Taylor, Jick, & MacLaughlin, 2013). Disorders of sleep co-occur in 50–85 per cent of children with ASD (Richdale, 1999; Xue, Brimacombe, Chaaban, Zimmerman-Bier, & Wagner, 2008). One reason for the sizeable range in reported co-occurrence could be due to the methods used to obtain the estimates. Parental reports consistently describe atypical sleep onset delay (an increased amount of time between going to bed and falling asleep), nighttime awakenings and parasomnias (atypical movements or behaviours during sleep, e.g., sleep walking). However, while some parents might be very aware of their child's sleep difficulties, others may not. Indeed, some specialists suggest that children with ASD, who suffer from sleep disturbances, rarely complain about their issues to their parents. A recent polysomnographic study (Limoges, Bolduc, Berthiaume, Mottron, & Godbout, 2013) has confirmed differences in sleep onset (delayed), sleep efficiency (reduced), and percentage of time spent awake following sleep onset (increased). The authors further reported increased percentage of sleep stage one (NREM) and decreased SWS. Interestingly, the same study found no difference in total sleep time. These results show that there may be underlying differences in sleep that would not have been identified if PSG had not been performed. In a population that is not prone to complain about their difficulties, sleep disturbances may prevail without parents being aware of them.

13.3.2 Williams Syndrome (WS)

Williams Syndrome (WS) is a neurodevelopmental disorder caused by deletion of some twenty-eight genes on the long arm of chromosome 7q11.23, with around a 1/20,000 prevalence rate (Schubert, 2009; Tassabehji, 2003). It is characterised by overly social behaviour and good expressive language, despite having an IQ range between fifty and seventy. Again, sleep disturbances are often reported. Parents report problems settling, night awakenings, bedtime resistance, and daytime sleepiness (Annaz, Hill, Ashworth, Holley, & Karmiloff-Smith, 2011). A recent actigraphy study (Ashworth, Hill, Karmiloff-Smith, & Dimitriou, 2013) confirmed the presence of longer sleep onset latencies in children with WS compared with controls. However, despite parental reports, the authors found no difference in sleep duration or the number of night awakenings. There are two practical considerations with regards to these discrepant findings. First, children with WS have difficulty self-soothing (getting themselves back to sleep of their own accord), and are therefore more likely to alert their parents. This means that parents of children with WS may be more aware of nighttime awakenings than those of TD controls. Parent report measures are likely to reflect this. Second, it may be that parents of children with WS are more sensitive to their child's daily behaviours, being more responsive to minor difficulties than parents of TD children may be. In this sense, if the child wakes during the night, the parent might be more likely to a) be aware of it, and b) view it as an issue.

Polysomnographic studies have shown reduced REM, reduced NREM sleep stages one and two, and increased SWS in children with WS. This pattern is almost the exact reverse to that of ASD. This highlights a key practical issue with both participant response measures and actigraphy; on the surface, sleep disturbances may present in a similar way, yet the underlying mechanisms may be completely different. So while parent reports and actigraphy are useful in identifying and highlighting problematic sleep patterns, only PSG is able to allow us insight into the mechanisms underlying such differences (Mason *et al.*, 2011).

13.3.3 Attention Deficit Hyperactivity Disorder (ADHD)

ADHD is characterised by the core behavioural symptoms of inattention, hyperactivity, and impulsivity. In the UK, ADHD prevalence rates vary between 1.7–3.8 per cent in school-aged boys, with the prevalence in girls being much lower (around 0.8 per cent; Russell, Rodgers, Ukoumunne, & Ford, 2014). Sleep disturbances are commonly reported in ADHD. Indeed, many researchers have reported that sleep problems correlate strongly with the behavioural manifestation of ADHD (Choi, Yoon, Kim, Chung, & Yoo, 2010; Gruber *et al.*, 2011). However, despite numerous parental reports of sleep disturbances in ADHD, actigraphy and PSG studies have produced inconsistent findings. While the findings of some actigraphy studies are consistent with parent reports (Moreau, Rouleau, & Morin, 2014), others are not (Hvolby, Jorgensen, & Bilenberg, 2008). PSG data too have been inconsistent. Prehn-Kristensen and colleagues report three studies, in which one shows increased REM sleep (confirmed by Kirov *et al.*, 2004) and shorter SWS latency in ADHD children (Prehn-Kristensen *et al.*, 2011a), and two others that find no differences between ADHD participants and controls (Prehn-Kristensen *et al.*, 2011b; 2013). Owing to discrepancies in PSG data, researchers have begun investigating neural activity during sleep using more sensitive, high-density EEG arrays. Such studies have found immature SWS distribution through the cortex (Ringli *et al.*, 2013) and differences in arousal activity (Miano *et al.*, 2006). In a study of the biological mechanisms underlying sleep, Baird *et al.* (2012) report that the typical circadian expression of CLOCK genes is lost in the ADHD sample. These studies highlight the seemingly inconsistent results that different methodologies in sleep research can produce. Relying on one measure may bias the results towards the information that measure is able trace. However, this may not be the full story. So while some actigraphy and PSG studies might not pick up on difference in sleep between ADHD and control, more sensitive methods might.

13.4 Selecting a tool: questions to ask yourself

As we have seen, there are a variety of sleep research tools available for use with children. The paediatric sleep researcher must be aware of their relative strengths and weaknesses, and consider them with respect to their own specific research questions. First, consider your research objectives: Are you interested in habitual sleep patterns, or immediate sleep over the course of participation? Do you want to produce a qualitative or quantitative report? Are you interested in the subjective experience of sleep, or the objective observation of it? Are you interested in sleep patterns, sleep stages, or circadian rhythms? Second, you must consider your sample and their capacities: How old is your sample? Do they have any specific difficulties that might influence your choice of tool? If you are interested in the subjective experience of sleep, do they have the capacity to give you adequate information on their sleep habits themselves, or will you rely on parent report? Are you confident and trained in performing interviews with children? If you are interested in an objective observation of sleep, will the child be comfortable with the equipment? How might the equipment affect their typical sleep patterns? Does this represent a meaningful problem for your report? Finally, each researcher has a different set of resources available to them. It is important to consider your means: How long will testing take per participant? Do you have access to the preferred assessments or equipment? Do you have the time and the funding to perform a study with physiological or biological measures? Will a participant response measure allow you to capture sufficient information to answer your research question?

If you consider all of these questions with respect to the information covered in this chapter, you should be in a good position to select a tool to fit your research objectives. Remember, that the answers to these questions need not be either/or. Indeed, a mixed methods approach will allow you to obtain a more holistic perspective of sleep (see section 13.2.4). If you have selected a parent-response measure, would a simple participant response measure with the child help corroborate the caregiver's perceptions? If you have decided to investigate immediate sleep over the course of participation, a participant response measure of habitual sleep will enable you to see if this sleep is typical. If you have selected a physiological or biological measure, a sleep diary will help validate the sleep/wake information a physiological measure returns. Ultimately, before embarking on sleep research with children, it is important to think fully about the information you wish to examine, and the most reliable ways of obtaining it with your given sample.

13.5 Summary

Sleep research in children is both interesting and important. The way sleep develops across childhood, how sleep influences daytime learning and behaviour, and the effects of disturbed sleep are all worthy topics of research. There are a variety of tools available to the paediatric sleep researcher, each of them providing slightly different information, and each with its unique set of strengths and weaknesses. Participant response measures provide an abundance of data with minimal disruption to sleep. However, they are victim to subjective bias. On the whole, physiological methods represent reliable, objective measures of sleep. They vary in the objective information they provide, and their relative disruption to sleep. PSG allows an in depth objective observation of sleep in terms of quality, quantity, and sleep stages. However, it is expensive and fairly invasive for use with children. Actigraphy is non-invasive and much less expensive, but the information it provides is indirect (measuring movement rather than sleep itself) and comparatively less detailed. Biological measures represent a method of obtaining objective information about circadian rhythms, and are easy to use with children. However, such methods do not measure sleep patterns per se. Instead, they provide insight into the mechanisms underlying the daily sleep/wake cycle. The choice of sleep tool(s) selected will ultimately affect the capacity the paediatric sleep researcher has to answer their research question. For this reason, these methodological considerations must be well researched before testing begins.

Practical tips

1   Know your sample, and their capabilities: This will inform your selection of tool and study design.
2   Select you tool on the basis of your research question and the data you wish to capture.
3   Use a combined approach to data collection: This will allow a more rounded perspective of sleep.

References

Annaz, D., Hill, C. M., Ashworth, A., Holley, S., & Karmiloff-Smith, A. (2011). Characterisation of sleep problems in children with Williams syndrome. *Research in Developmental Disabilities, 32*, 164–69.

Ashworth, A., Hill, C. M., Karmiloff-Smith, A., & Dimitriou, D. (2013). Cross syndrome comparison of sleep problems in children with Down Syndrome and Williams Syndrome. *Research in Developmental Disabilities, 34*, 1572–80.

Baird, A. L., Coogan, A. N., Siddiqui, A., Donev, R. M., & Thome, J. (2012). Adult attention-deficit hyperactivity disorder is associated with alterations in circadian rhythms at the behavioural, endocrine and molecular levels. *Molecular Psychiatry, 17*, 988–95.

Buckley, T. M., & Schatzberg, A. F. (2005). On the interactions of the hypothalamic-pituitary adrenal (HPA) axis and sleep: Normal HPA axis activity and circadian rhythm, exemplary sleep disorders. *Journal of Clinical Endocrinology & Metabolism, 90*, 3106–14.

Choi, J., Yoon, I. Y., Kim, H. W., Chung, S., & Yoo, H. J. (2010). Differences between objective and subjective sleep measures in children with attention deficit hyperactivity disorder. *Journal of Clinical Sleep Medicine, 6*, 589–95.

Dueck, A., Thome, J., & Haessler, F. (2012). The role of sleep problems and circadian clock genes in childhood psychiatric disorders. *Journal of Neural Transmission, 119*, 1097–104.

Gruber, R., Wiebe, S., Montecalvo, L., Brunetti, B., Amsel, R., & Carrier, J. (2011). Impact of sleep restriction on neurobehavioral functioning of children with attention deficit hyperactivity disorder. *Sleep, 34*, 315–23.

Hoedlmoser, K., Heib, D. P., Roell, J., Peigneux, P., Sadeh, A., Gruber, G., & Schabus, M. (2014). Slow sleep spindle activity, declarative memory and general cognitive abilities in children. *Sleep, 37*(9), 1501–12.

Hvolby, A., Jorgensen, J., & Bilenberg, N. (2008). Actigraphic and parental reports of sleep difficulties in children with attention-deficit/hyperactivity disorder. *Archives of Pediatrics and Adolescent Medicine, 162*, 323–29.

Hyde, M., O'Driscoll, D. M., Binette, S., Galang, C., Tan, S. K., Verginis, N., . . . & Horne, R. S. (2007). Validation of actigraphy for determining sleep and wake in children with sleep disordered breathing. *Journal of Sleep Research, 16*(2), 213–16.

Imeraj, L., Antrop, I., Roeyers, H., Swanson, J., Deschepper, E., Bal, S., & Deboutte, D. (2012). Time-of-day effects in arousal: Disrupted diurnal cortisol profiles in children with ADHD. *Journal of Child Psychology and Psychiatry, 53*, 782–89.

Kirov, R., Kinkelbur, J., Heipke, S., Kostanecka-Endress, T., Westhoff, M., Cohrs, S., . . . & Rothenberger, A. (2004). Is there a specific polysomnographic sleep pattern in children with attention deficit/hyperactivity disorder? *Journal of Sleep Research, 13*, 87–93.

Le Couteur, A., Rutter, M., Lord, C., Rios, P., Robertson, S., Holdgrafer, M., & McLennan, J. (1989). Autism diagnostic interview: A standardized investigator-based instrument. *Journal of Autism & Developmental Disorders, 19*, 363–87.

Limoges, E., Bolduc, C., Berthiaume, C., Mottron, L., & Godbout, R. (2013). Relationship between poor sleep and daytime cognitive performance in young adults with autism. *Research in Developmental Disabilities, 34*, 1322–35.

Ma, L., Chen, Y. H., Chen, H., Liu, Y. Y., & Wang, Y. X. (2011). The function of hypothalamus–pituitary–adrenal axis in children with ADHD. *Brain Research, 1368*, 159–62.

Mason, T. B., Arens, R., Sharman, J., Bintliff-Janisak, B., Schultz, B., Walters, A. S., . . . & Pack, A. I. (2011). Sleep in children with Williams Syndrome. *Sleep Medicine, 12*, 892–7.

Miano, S., Donfrancesco, R., Bruni, O., Ferri, R., Galiffa, S., Pagani, J., . . . & Pia Villa, M. (2006). NREM sleep instability is reduced in children with attention-deficit/hyperactivity disorder. *Sleep, 29*, 797–803.

Moreau, V., Rouleau, N., & Morin, C. M. (2014). Sleep of children with attention deficit hyperactivity disorder: Actigraphic and parental reports. *Behavioral Sleep Medicine, 12*, 69–83.

National Institute for Health and Clinical Excellence (2008). *Attention deficit hyperactivity disorder: Diagnosis and management of ADHD in children, young people and adults.* CG72. London: National Institute for Health and Clinical Excellence.

Prehn-Kristensen, A., Göder, R., Fischer, J., Wilhelm, I., Seeck-Hirschner, M., Aldenhoff, J., & Baving, L. (2011a). Reduced sleep-associated consolidation of declarative memory in attention-deficit/hyperactivity disorder. *Sleep Medicine, 12*(7), 672–9.

Prehn-Kristensen, A., Krauel, K., Hinrichs, H., Fischer, J., Malecki, U., Schuetze, H., . . . & Baving, L. (2011b). Methylphenidate does not improve interference control during a working memory task in young patients with attention-deficit hyperactivity disorder. *Brain Research, 1388*, 56–68.

Prehn-Kristensen, A., Munz, M., Molzow, I., Wilhelm, I., Wiesner, C. D., & Baving, L. (2013). Sleep promotes consolidation of emotional memory in healthy children but not in children with attention-deficit hyperactivity disorder. *PloS One, 8*(5), e65098.

Richdale, A. L. (1999). Sleep problems in autism: Prevalence, cause, and intervention. *Developmental Medicine & Child Neurology, 41*, 60–6.

Ringli, M., Souissi, S., Kurth, S., Brandeis, D., Jenni, O. G., & Huber, R. (2013). Topography of sleep slow wave activity in children with attention-deficit/hyperactivity disorder. *Cortex, 49*, 340–7.

Russell, G., Rodgers, L. R., Ukoumunne, O. C., & Ford, T. (2014). Prevalence of parent-reported ASD and ADHD in the UK: Findings from the Millennium Cohort Study. *Journal of Autism and Developmental Disorders, 44*, 31–40.

Sadeh, A., Gruber, R., & Raviv, A. (2002). Sleep, neurobehavioral functioning, and behavior problems in school-age children. *Child Development, 73*, 405–17.

Schubert, C. (2009). The genomic basis of the Williams–Beuren syndrome. *Cellular and Molecular Life Science, 66*, 1178–97.

Spruyt, K., & Gozal, D. (2011). Development of paediatric sleep questionnaires as diagnostic or epidemiological tools: A brief review of dos and don'ts. *Sleep Medicine Reviews, 15*, 7–17.

Tassabehji, M. (2003). Williams–Beuren syndrome: A challenge for genotype–phenotype correlations. *Human Molecular Genetics, 15*, 229–37.

Taylor, B., Jick, H., & MacLaughlin, D. (2013). Prevalence and incidence rates of autism in the UK: Time trend from 2004–2010 in children aged 8 years. *British Medical Journal open, 3*(10), e003219.

Waldhauzer, F., Kovacs, J., & Reiter, E. (1998). Age-related changes in melatonin levels in humans and its potential consequences for sleep disorders. *Experimental Gerontology, 33*, 759–72.

Wang, L. J., Huang, Y. S., Hsiao, C. C., Chiang, Y. L., Wu, C. C., Shang, Z. Y., & Chen, C. K. (2011). Salivary dehydroepiandrosterone, but not cortisol, is associated with attention deficit hyper- activity disorder. *The World Journal of Biological Psychiatry, 12*, 99–109.

Xie, L., Kang, H., Xu, Q., Chen, M. J., Liao, Y., Thiyagarajan, M., . . . & Nedergaard, M. (2013). Sleep drives metabolite clearance from the adult brain. *Science, 342*(6156), 373–7.

Xue, M., Brimacombe, M., Chaaban, J., Zimmerman-Bier, B., & Wagner, G. C. (2008). Autism spectrum disorders: Concurrent clinical disorders. *Journal of Child Neurology, 23*, 6–13.

Zinke, K., Fries, E., Kliegel, M., Kirschbaum, C., & Dettenborn, L. (2010). Children with high-functioning autism show a normal cortisol awakening response (CAR). *Psychoneuroendocrinology, 35*, 1578–82.

14

DIGITAL AND NEW TECHNOLOGIES

Research tools and questions

David Messer and Natalia Kucirkova

14.1 Introduction

Changes in technology, even small changes, have always been with us and in the lives of children. It also seems that these changes are accelerating in pace and involving younger and younger children. For example, there are widely circulated examples of infants swiping and tapping on iPads, while the availability of the Internet and the accessibility of digital information are significantly changing the working and non-working lives of all who use these systems. In this chapter, we first consider the use of iPads/tablets and other computer devices as ways to gather information about children and young people (e.g., as recording devices of their behaviours). This is similar to chapters in this book that are concerned with specific research techniques, such as eye-tracking, where the technique provides a way of understanding psychological processes. Second, we consider more general issues about research methods and design in relation to major research questions about the use of technology. In this case technology is not simply a research tool, but a subject of enquiry. We use the term *research tools* when discussing the ways new technologies can be used to collect information and the term *methods* to refer to general paradigms that are used in investigations, such as experimental, participatory and so on.

Our subject matter concerns new technologies and digital technologies and we use these terms to refer to various kinds of hardware such as iPads, tablets, smartphones as well as desktop computers (PCs) and entertainment devices such as PlayStations. We use the term technological tools when considering inter-connected networks or specific approaches, such as for example learning analytics and the Internet. Examples are often drawn from our own work (simply because we know it best), and often concern issues related to the use of technology for educational purposes or in educational settings. We conclude by outlining new issues and new directions for research in this area.

14.2 Using technological tools to gather data and information

In this section we outline the way that commonly available forms of digital technology can aid the collection of information from children and young people. We consider: simulations and games, eye-tracking, iPads, learning analytics and the Internet.

Before considering these tools it is useful to make some general points. Most children and young people are fascinated by technology and do not have the inhibition or concerns of some adults who may worry they will 'break' the device or fail to master a task. As a result, children are often eager to participate in investigations that make use of technology, especially new and unfamiliar tech-nology and may even feel disappointed if they do not take part. Although using technology has many advantages, one has to be careful about the time and financial costs in setting up a computer-based activity and the ease of collecting information about the activity. Furthermore, one needs to consider whether access to the Internet is necessary for the research; many schools block this access because of concerns about children's access to unsuitable sites. It also is useful to bear in mind the possibility of theft or damage; often the researchers have to be prepared to bear these costs. However, in our experience such events are very rare, though with portable equipment such as iPads/tablets the purchase of protective covers can be helpful. Thus, there are a number of general issues that need to be worked out at an early stage of research planning.

14.2.1 Virtual worlds: games and simulations

Many investigations make use of the attractive and engaging properties of technology to collect information about cognitive processes. For example, standardised tests are now often presented on computer, which may be more motivating and provides gains in relation to the time taken to score the tests (for a more detailed discussion see Chapter 4). Games, puzzles and problems presented on digital devices often make the tasks more interesting and engaging.

In some cases, commercial games are used for research purposes. For example, virtual car racing games have been used to investigate risk-taking in adolescents (Gardner & Sternberg, 2005). In this investigation, recordings of brain waves were obtained to locate regions of the brain that were associated with risk-taking (Chein, Albert, O'Brien, Uckert, & Steinberg, 2011). Although it cannot be assumed that the risk-taking seen in a virtual game exactly corresponds to the behaviour seen when driving, the simulation provided insights into risk-taking in competitive situations.

In other research projects, simulations are used as a less difficult and less dangerous way of obtaining information about behaviour. A good example is the use of virtual, interactive, simulations of walking around city streets to investigate the navigation abilities of children (Courbois, Blades, Sockeel, & Farran, 2013). This is less dangerous than carrying out research in 'real' streets, and provides standardised experience for all children without the need to construct a physical environment. Furthermore, keyboard responses can be automatically recorded to aid data collection. A 3D simulation of a Geology field trip based in the Lake District has been developed by Minocha (2015), using Unity 3D software. The interactions and the learning activities within the 3D environment are designed both to mirror the experience of a real field trip and to enhance it with additional functionality. This is very useful for students with limited mobility who cannot take part in real field trips and also for teachers who can complete risk assessment and take part in professional development training anytime and anywhere in the world.

These examples show how technology can engage children and also provide a way to look at responses in a safe environment that sometimes can be less costly to construct than similar activities in the physical world. There is evidence that virtual worlds provide a very good indication of children's responses to real world activities; an issue that always needs to be considered (Sheehy, Ferguson, & Clough, 2010). Thus, new technologies have opened up new possibilities for research into a range of behaviours and thought processes.

14.2.2 Eye-tracking

Eye-tracking makes it possible for tablets or computers to know where users are looking (see Chapter 2 for a detailed discussion). This is relevant to the development of websites and digital material (e.g., games), but also for measuring children's engagement. For example, Southgate, Senju, and Csibra (2007) have used recordings of eye gaze to look at anticipatory in infancy and in this way provide a detailed record of events. Eye-tracking is a direct and powerful tool for revealing what information the brain is processing. For children with special needs, the technology can be used to generate a click or other command and supplement traditional communication mechanisms. As such, children with profound communication difficulties can control resources around them with gaze without the need for use of hands or speech.

14.2.3 iPads

In this section we outline the way that iPads (and comparable tablets) can be used in research. This section is more detailed than the others because of comparatively less research with these new tools. iPads/tablets can be used as effective research tools for three main reasons: 1) the devices contain several data collection tools embedded in one: camera, digital notepad, audio-recorder; 2) they are portable and lightweight, facilitating fieldwork; and 3) they are easy to access and intuitive to use. In addition, there are many applications (software programs) facilitating data collection. For instance, researchers can use annotating apps, apps supporting representation of ideas (various mind-maps apps), or apps facilitating editing videos and audio files. iPads are intuitively designed and therefore easier to use than some of the older technologies for both the participant and the researcher. Moreover, unlike many other data collection tools (e.g., eye-trackers), iPads are commonplace in many classrooms and homes. As such, they are non-intrusive data collection tools. This makes iPads particularly suitable for studies that require children's focused attention and close manipulation of the device.

Our investigations of iPads have focused on Our Story (OS hereafter; free from iTunes; see www.open.ac.uk/creet/main/projects/our-story) in educational settings. We have been involved in the design and development of this iPad/tablet app. The app enables the creation of narratives around digital photographs, and text and/or audio recording can be added to each photograph. The screen shots below (see Figure 14.1) illustrate some of the app's characteristics. The user interface shows that pictures can be dragged from the camera role at the top onto the storyline at the bottom. Text and/or sound can be added to the pictures in the storyline and it can be played, printed or sent to others. We describe two of our projects to illustrate how the OS app – and comparable tablet apps – can be used in research.

Using Our Story (OS) to promote and collect information about narrative abilities

We have used the OS app both as an intervention and a way of collecting information about children's progress. In one instance, we worked with an Early Years

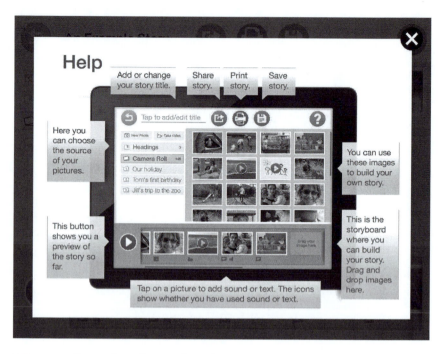

FIGURE 14.1 Screen shot of a page from Our Story

teacher who contacted us with the explicit intention of using the OS app to support the narrative development of children who were 3–5 years old in her preschool. In the course of 6 months, the teacher used the app to motivate children in narrative and literacy activities, especially those children who lacked such engagement at home or could not fully participate in classroom group activities because of their limited oral language skills. The teacher used the app to display, in an attractive digital format, some of the children's favourite books. She, together with class-room assistants, encouraged children to narrate their own stories by taking their own photos and recording sounds to accompany them. A formal evaluation of the approach, comparing pre- and post-test activities, found that as a result of the intervention, children produced more utterances in their digital stories and their narratives were also richer in detail than at the start of the study (Kucirkova, Messer, & Sheehy, forthcoming). In this way technology was used as a way to provide early literacy-related experiences, and their digital (and other) narrative abilities, before and after this experience, were compared. The ease of use of the app enabled the research to be set up reasonably quickly, and the interest of the teacher in technology enabled a co-operative research project to take place.

Using Our Story for participatory research

The use of the app can provide an impetus for more collaborative and participatory data collection. Punch (2002) explains that participatory research with children is different from research with adults given children's marginalised position in adult society. iPads and other similar novel technologies provide children with the opportunity to place themselves in a reverse role and showcase their expertise at managing new devices, which is often better than adults' (Hutchison, Beschorner, & Schmidt-Crawford, 2012). In addition, several researchers have engaged in research where children's voices are not only respected but also actively sought and where new technologies set the stage for learner-centred participatory research (Conole, Scanlon, Littleton, Kerawalla, & Mulholland, 2010). We found that participatory research with iPads meets several ethical criteria and best practice guidelines, including allowing children to collect, view and interpret the data together with the researchers (Alderson, 2000).

In one project undertaken with colleagues at The Open University, we encouraged twelve preschoolers from six different early year settings to use OS when retelling their experiences of specific story acting/storytelling activity delivered by a private theatre company. Pictures to scaffold children's retellings were taken by the researcher, while the children were involved in the storytelling/ story acting or by the children themselves. When asked how they liked the activity, the children recorded their answers using the microphone feature of the app or produced short captions to accompany the digital pictures. Without the need for prompting, the children helped us interpret the data in that they played the recorded sounds back to us and talked us through their storylines (Kucirkova, 2013). Such a participatory research approach was invaluable in ascertaining children's own perspectives on the activity and provided a window into children's personal story worlds. The data generated through children's retellings could be used as further evidence of the value of the technique for the theatre company, but was of great interest also to researchers, the teachers and us. For example, the teachers were keen on using children's digital narratives as part of tracking their early literacy-related development. We, as researchers, were intrigued by children's portrayal of self in these narratives and have further analysed the data for the evidence of children's novel self-representations in new media (Kucirkova, 2013). From this perspective, new technologies can provide easy-to-use methods for children to present their own viewpoints which are based around photographs and speech, rather than being constrained by written text and paper-based materials.

14.2.4 Learning analytics

Automatic recording of participants' responses is often possible with technological devices. This has provided an impetus to learning analytics with student responses collected to identify learning needs and provide tailored or customised support. In this case, the technologies used can range from smartphones to PCs. This has attracted the interest of researchers and educators in higher education, but is also relevant to educational organisations where there are large cohorts such as in secondary schools. However, as Clow (2013) describes, learning analytics 'is a "jackdaw" field of enquiry, picking up "shiny" 7 techniques, tools and methodologies, including web analytics (the analysis of logs of activity on the web), social network analysis, predictive modelling, natural language processing, and more' (p. 6). There have been concerns that this form of data collection has aspects of 'big brother' institutional scrutiny, although it also should be said that the purpose of such analytics is to be supportive.

The idea of using data collected via technology to support learning through individualised tutorials has had a relatively long history (Mandle & Lesgold, 1988). Still, this approach has not become widespread partly because of the cost of research and development to produce the software and also because agreed theories about learning processes are rare. The presence of many apps that are sold to parents on the basis of their learning and educational potential has transformed this situation. Although it should be admitted that few of the apps are grounded in psychological and educational principles, there is now a possibility for both teachers and parents to select apps that fit with the learning style they believe suitable for children (Chau, 2014).

In many ways the success of learning analytics has yet to be established as a research and education tool, we suspect the major factor governing success is the ease and ability to identify critical markers of a students' progress and the effectiveness of interventions that can be given when this is identified. Thus, the availability of information may be less important than the use made of the information that is collected. In our experience the sheer volume of the data that is collected and the difficulties of understanding the context of the responses can make it difficult to know what are the key events (e.g., an error in a calculation can be due to a range of factors). Thus, research using these data is likely to be helped by clear testable hypotheses that are based around theory or previous findings (Hirsh-Pasek et al., 2015).

14.2.5 Using the Internet as a research tool

The Internet also offers possibilities for both quantitative and qualitative research and for the use of existing research tools in new ways. Questionnaire surveys can be based on the Internet and specialist providers (e.g., Opinium; Surveymonkey) are available to host these questionnaires and make the data analysis relatively simple. In addition, the Internet can be used to collect data from large populations of respondents when this is associated with sites that attract many users. For example, in our own work information has been collected about a range of topics as a result of the Open University's association with the BBC's *Child of Our Time* series. These have resulted in obtaining over 100,000 responses in some instances. In one study, we have investigated the relations between questionnaire answers about food preferences, television watching and worries about appearance/weight in relation to enjoyment of exercise in young people (Wright, Messer, Oates, & Myers, forthcoming). This involved participants answering a relatively large number of questions on the Internet, so it was possible for them to return to their answers if they took a break. The very large number of responses would not have been possible without both using the draw of a television programme and automatically recorded responses. One additional feature that might have helped maintain interest was that participants could see their own response in relation to those of other participants; when the questionnaire had been completed the participants could opt to review their own responses and a summary of the responses from all the previous respondents. However, a large sample collected in this way has its own problems. For example, the population is going to be self-selected and care needs to be taken to exclude responses that are fraudulent from anonymous data collection. Issues of ethics need to be considered in what are for most investigators unusual circumstances (see also Chapter 15). In addition, with such large samples many statistical tests will reveal significant effects so more attention needs to be paid to effect size rather than significance, i.e., to the size of the effect rather than confidence in whether there is an effect). Furthermore, it should be remembered that online questionnaires are not always successful, especially when it is difficult to publicise their existence, and for some participants the ease and immediacy of paper-based questionnaires is more likely to result in a response.

Chat rooms, Facebook and other social media provide a basis for qualitative research into a whole range of topics about social processes. These Social Network Sites (SNS) now form an important aspect of the social worlds of many children and young people, with many hours/week being devoted to these sites. As Underwood and Farrington-Flint (2015) point out behaviour is different on SNS and face-to-face interactions; and the popularity of these sites indicates that they are addressing important psychological needs. Research about these processes often involves participant observations and ethnographic approaches. This type of research can provide valuable information about activities and processes that often are neglected, and provide insights into new and emerging ways that we communicate and present ourselves. However, not only can there be technical difficulties (Orthmann, 2000), there are important and difficult ethical issues about the disclosure of the researcher's identity and their participation in discussions (Convery & Cox, 2011; Hudson & Bruckman, 2004).

14.2.6 Summary

In general terms, the technological tools that we have discussed provide many advantages for research into cognitive processes, they can provide interesting tasks and with many of them, data can be collected automatically. Technological tools also can provide many advantages when trying to understand the opinions of participants: web-based questionnaires can result in a high number of respondents and the multimedia of iPads/tablets can provide a way to understand children's and young people's perspectives. Social processes can be recorded using digital technology and the technology itself provides new forms of social interaction.

14.3 Research questions, research methods and new technologies

Research that considers children's use of technology, by its very nature, is likely to focus on the technology rather than the psychological processes associated with its use. In this section we consider three major questions that often are asked about new technologies and the research methods that can be used to answer these questions: 1) How are new technologies used? 2) Are new technologies harmful? 3) Can new technologies enhance learning and education?

14.3.1 How are new technologies used?

With new technologies, researchers often ask questions around the frequency and length of use as well as the competence levels of the users. In relation to schools, there also are questions about the introduction of new technology and identification of the barriers to introduction (see Flewitt, Messer, & Kucirkova, 2014; Flewitt, Kucirkova, & Messer, 2014).

Observations into the use of new technologies can be carried out in schools and homes. However, observational studies are usually costly in terms of researcher time, so that qualitative methods often are favoured to provide in-depth information about a small number of participants. An example is the observations we carried out with two mother–child pairs into their use of the OS app (Kucirkova, Sheehy, & Messer, 2014). Although the study was small in scale, it offered examples of the type of positive and rewarding social interaction that can occur between preschool children and their mothers and raised interesting issues about the application of Vygotskian theory to new technology.

More generally interviews and questionnaires are used to collect information from larger samples. A particular issue that has generated recent interest is the claims of Prensky and others that today's generation of children, because they are growing up in a digital world, can be regarded as 'digital natives' and expert in these matters. However, these notions of expertise have been challenged. For example, Helsper and Eynon (2009) collected information from face-to-face interviews with over 2000 respondents who were age 14 years or above. They concluded that there were not 'unbridgeable differences' between young and older respondents, and on this basis provided an evidence-based challenge to the idea of 'digital natives'. This suggests that it should not be assumed that all children will be familiar with new technology, an important point when considering how they take part in the research.

When BBC computers were introduced into primary schools in the 1980s, one of us was involved in a survey of computer use in primary schools and this was followed up 2 years later with a comparable survey. The second survey showed that drill and practice activities (i.e., activities where similar tasks/questions are re-presented until success is achieved) continued to be the main use of the computers, although there were suggestions that the use of more innovative software might be increasing and this was related to training possibilities (Jackson, Fletcher, & Messer, 1988). Although there appear to have been changes since then in the use of PCs with a greater emphasis on collaborative activities (Condie, Munro, Seagraves, & Kenesson, 2006), there are indications that drill and practice activities are often used with iPads and tablets perhaps because of the changing nature of the interface (e.g., size and touch) as well as the availability of relevant software (Flewitt, Messer, & Kucirkova, 2014).

In general terms, qualitative research can deliver findings which are relevant to understanding the interests and the perspectives of the participants, as well as understanding how participants construct and interpret their activities. For example, a qualitative description concerning the use of the Internet can provide more insights and detailed information than would be possible from a questionnaire survey. However, there are issues about whether the insights from these more detailed observations can be generalised more widely. In this case, a questionnaire-based survey might be more appropriate, even though as is generally accepted less detailed information can be obtained and the questions are more likely to be misinterpreted. Furthermore, we believe that both techniques provide useful information about the use of new technology and are complementary rather than in opposition to each other.

14.3.2 Do new technologies have harmful effects on children and young people?

The introduction of new technologies is often accompanied by concerns about the effects on children. However, experimental investigations of this issue are unlikely to be possible because of ethical concerns: random assignment to a potentially harmful experience is not acceptable. As a result, many investigations of this topic involve quasi-experimental research where one compares children who have a target experience with those who do not have or have less of a target experience. These methods have been used to investigate the effects of gaming violence or Internet pornography (see Boyle & Hibberd, 2005). The matching of groups on relevant characteristics or the statistical adjustment of the influence of other variables (e.g., regression analysis) can help to control for the effects of confounds. Even so, these types of investigations cannot provide definitive answers because it is always possible to argue that certain children may like violent computer games and be more disposed to fights, rather than one leading to the other. In the case of concerns about computer (Underwood & Farrington-Flint, 2015) and Internet addiction (Cash, Rae, Steel, & Winkler, 2012), this is again something that is difficult to address in both quantitative and qualitative research.

Undoubtedly, there have been changes in the amount of time children spend on computer-related activities. Yet, it is very difficult to make accurate comparisons with activities in previous generations or, for example, in the proportion of children who appear to isolate themselves from others (e.g., the 'book worms' of previous generations). Thus, although the question of the effects of new technology on children are extremely important, obtaining objective answers is extremely difficult, and any conclusion is likely to come out of a body of research findings rather than a single definitive study.

14.3.3 Can technology enhance learning and education?

We devote more space to this question, partly because different perspectives about the methods that should be used when answering questions about causality, particularly between psychologists and educationalists, exist. Many psychologists argue that experimental investigations, especially those that involve a randomised control design are the *gold standard* to determine causality. In contrast, many educationalists criticise this method and argue that it is difficult to carry out true randomisation without large and costly investigations involving large numbers of schools and classrooms. In addition, experimental conditions involving new technology are likely to be more motivating for teachers and children especially compared with a control condition of *learning as* usual, so the effect of new technology is confounded with the attitudes of teachers/children. Furthermore, questions are raised about whether findings can be generalised to other schools and children. In the next sections, we provide examples of methods used to investigate the effects of new technology on children's skills, and discuss some of their strengths and limitations.

Experimental investigations

An example from our own work provides an illustration of the reasons for carrying out experimental investigations, an evaluation of computer-based support for literacy abilities. There is good evidence from well-controlled investigations that a range of non-computer interventions, particularly those that concern phonological abilities, can be effective with children who have literacy difficulties (Hulme & Snowling, 2009). However, at least with English-speaking children who are 'struggling readers', there is very little positive evidence about computer-based interventions of positive effects and few randomised controlled trails. Cheung and Slavin (2013) in a review of this topic only identified twenty studies, and of these only thirteen involved a randomised control investigation. Our investigation concerned the effectiveness of the Easyread tutorial system for children with literacy difficulties using a randomised controlled trial (Messer & Nash, in preparation). In this investigation, seventy-eight children aged about 8 years were identified by their schools as needing support for reading were randomly assigned to an intervention condition and a waiting list control condition. Both groups continued to receive the support normally given by their school. The intervention group had short 10–15-minute sessions over 13 months. All children were given a pre-test that involved standardised assessments of reading and reading-related abilities, and they also received a post-test of the same assessments when this phase of the study ended.

The findings indicated that the intervention group made significant gains in reading (decoding) and phonological awareness as predicted from the nature of the intervention and they had reached a level of ability that would be expected for their age. Importantly, a waiting list control group was used, who did not show similar gains; these children received the intervention after the randomised controlled trial. This opportunity was important for ethical reasons and also helped with recruitment, as parents often are reluctant for their children to take part in a study that is of no potential benefit. Furthermore, our experience indicated that special care needs to be taken when explaining the randomisation to parents and it is likely that there will be a higher drop-out rate from a waiting list control group.

The Easyread tutorial system contains a number of techniques designed to help the development of reading. This illustrates a dilemma, one can either put together what one believes is an effective collection of techniques, in which case the intervention is more likely to be effective, but one will not know which particular technique is effective. Alternatively, one can evaluate each technique on its own which allows for better understanding, but the research is likely to be more lengthy and costly. Another general issue is the experience of the control group and it is worth giving this some careful thought, as it will influence the conclusions that can be drawn. A waiting list control group means the intervention is compared with what usually happens, and so whether it is more effective than the usual support. However, if there are resources it can be useful for the waiting list group to have an unrelated intervention (e.g., arithmetic) or some other experience to control for the possible effect of the motivating properties of receiving special attention.

Action research and formative experiments

Another way to investigate and develop techniques to assist educational processes concerns action research. Action research has several definitions and meanings, we subscribe to the definition provided by Reason and Bradbury and the view that action research brings together several approaches that are participative, grounded in experience, and action-oriented (Reason & Bradbury, 2001). Reflection is a fundamental element of the approach, as it serves as a connecting point between action and research (Coughlan & Coghlan, 2002). In the research concerning the effectiveness of the OS app, we were keen on producing practical knowledge that would be of direct use and benefit to specific research organisations, community groups and charities. Action research was very suitable for this objective given that it is oriented towards improvement and given that it invites research participants into the research process. Action researchers are not interested in developing robust theories that would deal with infinite possible scenarios, but rather in theories that work in specific contexts and circumstances. In developing such theories (Reinking, 2001), action researchers need to engage in reflection during several stages of the research process. Reflection is a useful tool for the researchers to learn about participants' views but also, in collaboration with the research participants, to 'contemplate what can be learned from the experiences' (Lau, 1997, p. 52). Action research can employ a diverse range of study designs and methodologies (Cargo & Mercer, 2008). In the next section, we describe the methodological approach adopted in our work.

An example concerns an exploratory investigation when we were interested in finding out about whether the OS app contributed to educational experiences in a holistic way. As a result different tools were used and a qualitative approach was adopted (Kucirkova, Messer, Critten, & Harwood, 2014). This study involved OS being used in two schools by children with complex needs. In one school the whole of a small class of nine children used OS to construct a narrative about their visit to a spinney that related to the theme of the 'Great Outdoors' with sessions of about 30–45 minutes occurring every week for 7 weeks. In the second school one pupil used OS to relate an event where there was a successful achievement; these sessions occurred for about 45 minutes over 6 weeks. The main research tools that were used involved documenting what was done in the sessions, looking at whether the teaching aims for each child had been achieved and for the teachers to reflect on the process. In general terms, the aims were achieved, the app provided a focus for motivation and engagement, and the children expressed pleasure and pride in their achievements.

Formative experiments

Formative experiments are an effective methodology for research, which aims to ascertain how instruction-related design might support specific outcomes as well as the conceptual development of the actual intervention (Lim, 2001). By definition, formative experiment implies a collaborative teacher–researcher investigation. In contrast to large-scale controlled experiments or in-depth case studies, formative experiments are concerned with scalable improvements and, unlike traditional inter-vention research which often relies on 'fix it approaches', formative experiments are located in the perspective of multiple realities (Labbo & Reinking, 1999).

David Reinking (2001), the 'father' of design and formative experiments, wrote that:

> Formative experiments seek deep pedagogical understanding informed by iterative, data-driven modifications of a promising intervention aimed at achieving a valued pedagogical goal in authentic instructional contexts. The aim is to generate recommendations, not prescriptions, and pedagogical principles (humble theories) useful to practitioners, thus closing the gap between research and practice. This approach challenges the reductionism of conventional experiments and the observational passivity of naturalistic approaches (p. 190).

As the quote suggests, formative experiments are very effective if researchers wish to, for example, develop a framework for school professional learning communities to reflect upon, reimagine and redesign their communication with families about literacy and communication with families. Cooperation and collaboration with practitioners and ongoing mini-cycles of reflections are fundamental principles of such an approach. Also, when designing instruction for children, this usually takes the shape of working closely with the classroom teacher. Researchers who embed process-focused reflections into the design itself often do so with the aim of enabling the teachers to be both learner and designer and feel agency and ownership of the process.

In the example of qualitative research there were informal assessments of progress by experienced practitioners. Both the formative experiment and action research methodologies can be useful techniques for showing how children with complex needs engage in a storytelling activity, mediated by a technological tool (the app) and by effectively embedding this approach in existing practice, the teaching aims were achieved as a result of this engagement. The findings are useful to practitioners and more generally in understanding the way that these types of app can be employed in a school setting. The research provided an exemplar of what could be done with a specific technological tool and the teaching aims that were achieved, with the aims of this research being very different from those traditionally identified by psychologists, particularly those using experimental designs. Thus, practical research about technology involves a consideration of what questions need to be answered and about the appropriate methods to answer these questions.

Summary

We hope these examples illustrate the way that different research tools and different research methods/approaches can be used to answer questions about new technologies. Psychologists and other researchers need to consider a range of methods and often there are both positives and negatives about any method that is chosen with each method providing different insights into the process. Research into the way that new technologies are used is relatively straightforward with decisions having to be made about the depth of questioning and the size/breadth of the sample. In the case of the questions about the negative effects of new technology, these are difficult to definitely answer because ethical considerations mean that experimental investigations are not possible. In contrast, experimental investigations are possible into the positive effects of new technology, although there is debate about the usefulness of these and other methods. In relation to such debates we believe that quasi-experiments can often provide important insights into what effects might be occurring (and importantly what effects might not be occurring) and if sufficiently important experimental investigations can follow up the findings from quasi-experiments.

14.4 Future directions

In terms of the tools that are used to study children's use of technology there undoubtedly will be developments. It is foreseeable that in the near future, the embedded camera in iPads and the possibility to track students' eyes and finger movements with the embedded camera will become a favourite data collection tool in psychology research. Furthermore, more research funders may be prepared to support the development of state of the art research tools and assessments that can be used by individual researchers to collect data while at the same time contributing to large data bases of performance, a situation where everyone appears to gain (see www.nihtoolbox.org/). In addition, it seems likely that there will be greater integration between different methods of data collection, using the ever present camera on computers and tablets, integrating behavioural data and that about brain activity or eye movements is likely to become much more prevalent as the ease of use and cost of such are reduced. Where there is likely to be a large change in the research agenda is when voice recognition becomes reliable and common-place, this will both transform children's (and researchers') use of technology and transform our ability to collect information about speech.

Another future direction that is likely to involve children, young people and adults is a more participatory research environment. Using the power of the Internet it seems likely that research may be directed not just by an isolate group of researchers in their ivory tower, but may become something that is supported, advised and participated in by a web-based community. We already have discussed the issue of children's voices and their ability to research issues that concern them, and the future is likely to involve more examples of participatory research. Thus, not only the research tools but also the research methods seem likely to change in the future.

We suspect that in the near future there will be increasing interest in the coding and programming abilities of children. In England, a new part of the national curriculum specifies that all children aged 5 years and up will have to learn to code. This policy change follows an emphasis in the United States on teaching children not just to use but also to create technologies. It is likely that Australia and other countries will soon follow the lead. This change is being accompanied by a surge of resources aimed at helping children code and engage in computational thinking, for example non-digital board games such as Robot Turtles or Google's visual, character-free programming language. Recently, Nesta, a UK innovation charity, analysed the attitudes of young people, parents, carers and teachers towards digital making activities and showed that a great proportion of them are already making apps, games and even robots (www.nesta.org.uk/project/digital-makers), thus rebutting the concern that children only passively absorb information on the screens.

The report also showed how digital meaning making can be a social activity, with several projects (e.g., Code Club, Young Rewired State centres) encouraging children to get together when creating their digital projects (Quinlan, 2015).

In thinking about future directions we, as researchers who are carrying out research in schools and children's homes, believe it is important to outline a topic which often is ignored, that is the way that research can contribute to promoting innovation and good practice in children's learning with technology. The recent impact of technology on our working and social lives has been profound. This contrasts with an education system in the UK that is concerned with the three Rs (reading, writing and arithmetic) and an assessment system that focuses on the knowledge of factual information, rather than on ways to equip the new generation of children to function effectively in the new digital age.

If one accepts these arguments then effective research which has impact should not simply be concerned with *augmentation* of the existing educational system by improving learning in the existing curriculum, but should also make arguments about *innovations* in both the learning experiences and learning objectives to take account of new social and employment opportunities. Clearly this is not an easy task. For one thing, psychologists (and other social scientists) usually lack the research tools to answer big questions, for example, a set of tools to assess the degree to which pupils are equipped to become effective citizens (Twining, 2012).

In the past, changes have often occurred because of innovative theories or case studies rather than the accumulation of research evidence. For example, Piagetian theory had a profound influence on UK primary education in the 1960s and resulted in an emphasis on discovery learning rather than formal teaching. A more recent question is whether the availability of information on the Internet will make classrooms and possibly teachers obsolete. One investigation that has been widely cited in this debate is Mitra's 'hole in the wall' study where children could access a computer and taught themselves advanced computer-based and other skills with no support. Furthermore, in developing countries in particular, there are many projects that advocate or investigate the effects of teacher-less educational environments. The common rationale for why technology can replace teachers is that technology can provide one-to-one personalised teaching and necessary support in classrooms with few teachers and many children. There is also an implicit belief that children are capable of learning for themselves with very little adult support. Although the vision of a teacher-less school is often criticised (see useful blog by Harrison, 2014), the challenge facing researchers concerned with technology is what research methods can be used if they wish to support or transform existing systems. Furthermore, the presence of the National Curriculum in the UK and the concerns of many schools about their league positions in terms of conventional learning outcomes mean that there is a great reluctance to make changes that have associated risks.

14.5 Summary

Research related to technology cannot be neatly pigeon holed as based around a particular research tool or to one methodology. We have described technological tools that can be used for collecting information and data, with an emphasis on the novel uses of iPads and tablets, and have given examples of a range of methodologies that can be applied to three significant issues related to children's use of new technologies. In this way we hope to alert you to the diversity of tools and methods and, at the same time, link choices about these to a careful reflection by investigators about the question that the research is designed to address. We also hope to have alerted you to broader issues particularly when research about technology concerns educational processes.

Practical tips

1   Using new technologies as research tools might be time-consuming given that many need to be proof-tested. Do allow extra time for this in your research plan.
2   Try to think of technologies not only as providing you with a wealth of data but also the added value of their use in a given context.
3   Children sometimes know better than adults how new technologies work and involving them in the research process can bring interesting insights.
4   There are different types of question that can be asked about digital technologies; think about the methods you need to use to answer your research question(s).

References

Alderson, P. (2000). Children as researchers. In P. Christensen & A. James (Eds), *Research with Children* (pp. 241–57). London: Falmer Press.

Boyle, R., & Hibberd, M. (2005). Review of research on the impact of violent computer games on young people. Stirling Media Research Institute. Retrieved from www.video games.procon.org/sourcefiles/Reviewofresearch.pdf on 30 June 2015.

Cash, H., Rae, C. D., Steel, A. H., & Winkler, A. (2012). Internet addiction: A brief summary of research and practice. *Current Psychiatry Reviews, 8*(4), 292–8.

Cargo, M., & Mercer, S. L. (2008). The value and challenges of participatory research: Strengthening its practice. *Annual Review of Public Health, 29,* 325–50.

Chau, C. L. (2014). *Positive technological development for young children in the context of children's mobile apps*. (Doctoral dissertation, Tufts University.)

Chein, J., Albert, D., O'Brien, L., Uckert, K., & Steinberg, L. (2011). Peers increase adolescent risk taking by enhancing activity in the brain's reward circuitry. *Developmental Science, 14*, 1–10.

Cheung, A., & Slavin, R. E. (2013). Effects of educational technology applications on reading outcomes for struggling readers: A best-evidence synthesis. *Reading Research Quarterly, 48*(3), 277–99.

Clow, D. (2013). An overview of learning analytics. *Teaching in Higher Education, 18*(6), 683–95.

Condie, R., Munro, B., Seagraves, L., & Kenesson, S. (2006). *The impact of ICT in schools – a landscape review*. Coventry: Becta.

Conole, G., Scanlon, E., Littleton, K., Kerawalla, L., & Mulholland, P. (2010). Personal inquiry: Innovations in participatory design and models for inquiry learning. *Educational Multimedia International, 47*(4), 277–92.

Convery, I., & Cox, D. (2011). A review of research ethics in internet-based research. *Practitioner Research in Higher Education, 6*(1), 50–7.

Coughlan, P., & Coghlan, D. (2002). Action research for operations management. *International Journal of Operations and Production Management, 22*(2), 220–40.

Courbois, Y., Blades, M., Sockeel, P., & Farran, E. (2013). Do individuals with intellectual disability select appropriate objects as landmarks when learning a route? *Journal of Intellectual Disability Research, 57*, 80–9.

Flewitt, R. S., Kucirkova, N., & Messer, D. (2014). Touching the virtual, touching the real: iPads and enabling literacy for students with learning disabilities. *The Australian Journal of Language and Literacy Special Issue, 37*(2), 107–16.

Flewitt, R. S., Messer, D., & Kucirkova, N. (2014). New directions for early literacy in a digital age: The iPad. *Journal of Early Childhood Literacy*, published online before print 20 May 2014.

Gardner, M., & Sternberg, L. (2005). Peer influence on risk taking, risk preference, and risky decision making in adolescence and adulthood: An experimental study. *Developmental Psychology, 41*(4), 625–35.

Harrison, J. (2014, September 24). Not the SOLE way to go: The fundamental flaws of Sugata Mitra's framework. Retrieved from www.mikejharrison.com/2014/09/not-the-sole-way-to-go-the-fundamental-flaws-of-sugata-mitras-framework on 30 June 2015.

Helsper, E., & Eynon, R. (2009). Digital natives: Where is the evidence? *British Educational Research Journal, 36*(3), 503–20.

Hirsh-Pasek, K., Zosh, J. M., Golinkoff, R. M., Gray, J. H., Robb, M. B., & Kaufman, J. (2015). Putting education in 'educational' apps lessons from the science of learning. *Psychological Science in the Public Interest, 16*(1), 3–34.

Hudson, J. M., & Bruckman, A. (2004). 'Go away': Participant objections to being studied and the ethics of chatroom research. *The Information Society, 20*, 127–39.

Hulme, C., & Snowling, M. (2009). *Developmental disorders of language, Learning and cognition*. Chichester: Wiley-Blackwell.

Hutchison, A., Beschorner, B., & Schmidt-Crawford, D. (2012). Exploring the use of the iPad for literacy learning. *The Reading Teacher, 66*(1), 15–23.

Jackson, A., Fletcher, B., & Messer, D. J. (1988). Effects of experience on microcomputer use in primary schools: Results of a second survey. *Journal of Computer Assisted Learning, 4,* 214–26.

Kucirkova, N. (2013). iPads in early education. *Early years educator, 14*(9), 24–6.

Kucirkova, N., Messer, D., Critten, V., & Harwood, J. (2014). Story-making on the iPad when children have complex needs: Two case studies. *Communication Disorders Quarterly, 36*(1), 44–54

Kucirkova, N., Messer, D., & Sheehy, K. (forthcoming). Implementing 'The Our Story app' to increase children's narrative skills: Lessons learnt from one English preschool classroom. In E. Veneziano & A. Nicolopoulou (Eds), *Narrative literacy and other skills: Studies in interventions.* Amsterdam: John Benjamins.

Kucirkova, N., Sheehy, K., & Messer, D. (2014). A Vygotskian perspective on parent-child talk during iPad story-sharing. *Journal of Research in Reading,* published online before print 3 June 2014.

Labbo, L. D., & Reinking, D. (1999). Negotiating the multiple realities of technology in literacy research and instruction. *Reading Research Quarterly, 34*(4), 478–92.

Lau, F. (1997). A review on the use of action research in information systems studies. In: A. Lee, J. Liebenau, & J. I. DeGross (Eds), *Information systems and qualitative research* (pp. 31–68). Chapman & Hall: London.

Lim, C. P. (2001). The dialogic dimensions of using a hypermedia learning package. *Computers & Education, 36*(2), 133–50.

Mandle, H., & Lesgold, A. (1988). *Learning issues for intelligent tutoring systems.* New York, NY: Springer-Verlag.

Messer, D., & Nash, G. (in preparation). The effectiveness of a computer-based intervention for children identified as needing support for their literacy abilities.

Minocha, S. (2015). Retrieved from www.open.ac.uk/researchprojects/open-science/3d-virtual-geology-field-trip on 30 June 2015.

Orthmann, C. (2000). Analyzing the communication in chat rooms: Problems of data collection. *Forum Qualitative Sozialforschung/Forum: Qualitative Social Research, 1*(3). Retrieved from www.qualitative-research.net/index.php/fqs/article/view/1053 on 9 February 2015.

Punch, S. (2002). Research with children: The same or different from research with adults? *Childhood, 9*(3), 321–41.

Reason, P., & Bradbury, H. (2001). *Handbook of action research.* London: Sage.

Quinlan, O. (2015). *Young digital makers.* Nesta: London. Retrieved from www.nesta.org.uk/sites/default/files/young-digital-makers-march-2015.pdf on 9 February 2016.

Reinking, D. (2001). Multimedia and engaged reading in a digital world. In L.Verhoeven & K. Snow (Eds), *Literacy and motivation: Reading engagement in individuals and groups* (pp. 195–221). New Jersey: Taylor & Francis.

Sheehy K., Ferguson R., Clough G. (2010). *Virtual Worlds: Controversies at the frontier of education.* New York: Nova Science.

Southgate, V., Senju, A., & Csibra, G. (2007). Action anticipation through attribution of false belief by 2-year-olds. *Psychological Science*, *18*(7), 587–92.

Tanenhaus, M. K., Spivey-Knowlton, M. J., Eberhard, K. M., & Sedivy, J. C. (1995). Integration of visual and linguistic information. *Science*, *268*, 1633–4.

Twining, P. (2012). Preparing digital citizens. *SecEd*. Retrieved from www.sec-ed.co.uk/blog/preparing-digital-citizens on 30 June 2015.

Underwood, J. D., & Farrington-Flint, L. (2015). *Learning and the e-generation*. Chichester: Wiley-Blackwell.

Wright, M., Messer, D., Oates, J., & Myers, L. (forthcoming). What predicts young people's enjoyment of exercise? An Exploratory UK Study of 8 to 16 year olds.

15

ETHICAL PRACTICE IN RESEARCH ABOUT CHILDREN

Lindsay O'Dell and Charlotte Brownlow

15.1 Introduction: ethical practice and procedural ethics

In this chapter we outline ethical issues that arise from research about children. We take the view that ethics involves a 'set of moral principles and rules of conduct' (Morrow & Richards, 1996, pp. 90–1), in which researchers draw on moral judgements to ensure their work respects others and treats people fairly. We explore the challenges involved in producing ethically robust research about, with and for children through considering key issues in the ethical production of research with children outlined in international ethical guidelines, in particular interrogating key issues of informed consent and protection from harm. However, we also critically examine these concepts as they link to ideas about children and the social construction of childhood. It is clear that researchers' theoretical standpoint in psychology as well as their understanding of the abilities of children and the construction of childhood impacts on their choice of research design, their approach to researching children, and therefore to the ethical choices and the decisions they make. Finally, we consider current and future directions in the approach to research *with* rather than *on* children and the establishment of children as co-researchers and co-producers of research knowledge.

15.2 What do we mean by 'children'?

The concept of 'children' and 'childhood' is one that has been considered for many years within disciplines including sociology and psychology. What we understand by the concept 'child' and the child's various capabilities influences the way that we engage with children in a range of situations, including research. Understandings of the skills and capabilities of children has undergone significant shifts in developmental psychology, as well as many other areas of psychology, over the past twenty years, which has led to a view of children as more capable individuals who have agency.

As well as changes in understanding the skills and abilities of children, there is also uncertainty about whom we are referring to when we talk about 'children'. A 'child' is defined by the UN Convention on the Rights of the Child (1989) as anyone who is under the age of 18 years. However, McLaughlin (2015a) argues that this seemingly clear definition is not without its problems. Greig, Taylor and Mackay (2013) posit that despite such definitions, there is no universally accepted definition of childhood, and understandings vary quite considerably depending on culture and context. McLaughlin (2015a) notes that such differences may be in terms of the adoption of social roles, such as the age that someone can legally marry, or the right to exercise democratic rights and engage with the governmental systems in the country they live in. McLaughlin (2015a) also notes the mixed messages sent out to children concerning their role and position within a society. He reflects that in the UK children may, for example, get married with parental consent at 16 years and have a child, but they cannot exercise their right to vote or buy alcohol until they are 18 years, yet are expected to pay full fare on public transport at 14. The issues of age being a complex and sometimes contested marker of maturity and adulthood are further complicated for individuals with neurodevelopmental disorders, who may remain a 'vulnerable population' despite achieving the chronological milestone of adulthood.

The use of chronological age as a way of demarking who is a 'child' is therefore complex and invoked inconsistently within legislation and social policy at national and international level. Such complexities resonate strongly in research practices where, for example, drawing on chronological age as a mechanism for deciding who can provide informed consent to take part in research projects may be problematic. For many researchers a child's age is not the most important aspect in determining whether they should participate in research, but rather issues of competency are also important to consider.

> Perhaps searching for a minimum threshold age for children's consent is asking the wrong question ... the child's competency to consent to research participation should not be regarded as an inflexible limitation deriving from the child's age, but rather as an interaction of the child, the context, and the nature of the (decision-making) task.
>
> Thompson (as cited in Morrow & Richards, 1996, p. 60)

However, there are some projects where an age based decision needs to be made. For example, where the activity being researched has an age based legal sanction, such as alcohol use or sexual activity. This has been an issue for us as researchers who use social media to research Autism Spectrum Disorders (ASD) identities and communities. Social networking sites such as Facebook have an age restriction; children under 13 years old are not permitted to have a Facebook account (Facebook, 2015). While there is anecdotal evidence that younger children do use the media, it is difficult for us as researchers to design a study based on this assumption.

15.3 Legislative and professional frameworks for research ethics

There are several key frameworks that are drawn upon internationally to inform ethical research, as well as specific frameworks developed within countries, and within particular research disciplines. The United Nations Convention of the Rights of the Child was the first international treaty to safeguard the rights of the child and has been approved by all United Nation member states, except for the USA and Somalia (McLaughlin, 2015a). In addition to having a protective role for children, the convention also focuses on children's agency and their ability to participate in decisions about their lives and communities. For example, Article 12 states that: 'Every child has the right to say what they think in all matters affecting them, and to have their views taken seriously' Article 12, UN (as cited in McLaughlin, 2015a, p. 6).

In addition to internationally shared principles, there are also national ethical statements in many countries, as well as guidelines produced by professions such as the British Psychological Society (BPS). There is also guidance on specific ethical practices from government and non-government organisations (NGOs). For example, in the UK Research Councils, such as the Economic and Social Research Council, and charities such as Barnardo's and the National Children's Bureau, all have expectations and guidelines on research with children. In this chapter we focus on our own national contexts, i.e., the BPS in the UK, and the National Statement on Ethical Conduct in Human Research in Australia, developed jointly by the Australian Government, the National Research Councils and the Australian Vice-Chancellors Committee (The Australian Government, 2007/2014).

The BPS's Code of Human Research Ethics outlines a set of common ethical principles for all research with human participants: respect for the autonomy and dignity of persons, scientific value, social responsibility, and maximising benefit and minimising harm. Research with children is expected to conform to all elements of these general expectations, although additional information about research with children is given in a section on research with 'vulnerable groups', which in the BPS's code includes children, persons lacking capacity, and individuals in dependent or unequal relationships. The assumption is that children are able to participate in research and should be 'given ample opportunity to understand the nature, purpose, and anticipated outcomes of any research participation' (BPS, 2010, p. 31).

In Australia, the National Statement on Ethical Conduct guides and governs human research. It presents ethical considerations that apply to all research, but also identifies specific categories of research participants who have more complex requirements in terms of research ethics. Children and young people form one of these specific categories in addition to: pregnant women, the human foetus, people in dependent or unequal relationships, people highly dependent on medical care who may be unable to give consent, people with cognitive impairments, an intellectual disability, or a mental illness, people who may be involved in illegal activities, Aboriginal and Torres Strait Islander peoples, and people in other countries (The Australian Government, 2007/2014).

In the following sections we examine two key issues for research ethics with children, which are broadly conceptualised in most ethics procedures: issues involved in gaining informed consent and the protection of children from harm. However, we, along with many other social scientists, argue that a thorough engagement with ethics is sustained through the research process rather than by an exercise of box ticking at the beginning of a study. Many elements of a procedural view of research ethics are common to research with both adults and children. However, we share the view of many researchers, such as Thomas and O'Kane (1998) as well as Morrow and Richards (1996) that key ethical issues may be conceptualised and addressed by researchers working with children quite differently from research with adults. Specifically, researching with children presents some key challenges in establishing, for example, benchmarks for obtaining informed consent and complexities in the management of power differentials within the research relationship. Hence, the next two sections of the chapter discuss informed consent and protection from harm. In the final sections of the chapter we draw on our theoretical approach to research with different childhoods to argue that a truly ethically engaged research project involves a consideration of ethics and of the role and capabilities of children throughout the process.

15.4 The provision of informed consent

According to the BPS (2010) and the Australian National Statement on Ethical Conduct (Australian Government, 2007/2014), researchers must consider and respect the capacity of children in terms of being able to provide consent to take part in research. In considering capacity, the National Statement on Ethical Conduct in Australia identifies four distinct levels of maturity that reflect children's ability to engage in decision making for research purposes. These include young children who do not have the capacity to discuss research and young children who may understand some relevant information but whose consent is not required. A third group are young people of developing maturity who may understand relevant information but who are considered vulnerable due to lack of maturity. Consent would be required from this third group, but the giving of consent from this population would not be sufficient to authorise the research. The final group comprise young people who are mature enough to both understand the research and its requirements, and to provide consent. This final group are not considered vulnerable and additional consent from a parent or guardian would therefore not be warranted (Australian Government 2007/2014).

While these groupings seem relatively clear, difficulties exist in terms of attaching ages to each level, as the capacities described above may differ greatly between children. In addition, it is not possible to assume that any individual child of a specific age would be at the same level of ability for every research project, with different requirements in relation to a child's understanding and development being posed by different research projects (Australian Government, 2007/2014). Given such complexities, the Australian National Statement on Ethical Conduct encourages researchers to engage with all children about the research outcomes and expectations at a level that is suitable to them, rather than making assumptions regarding capacities of individuals.

In the UK, researchers may additionally draw on a notion of competence derived from a legal case, the Gillick ruling 3 A11 ER 423 Gillick (as cited in Boddy, 2014). This ruling was made following the unsuccessful challenge by a mother against doctors prescribing her daughter contraception without the mother's knowledge, and definitely against her wishes. The court ruling was that the daughter was competent to make decisions about her own medical treatment. The legal view of 'Gillick competence' states that a child can consent to participation when they have 'sufficient understanding and intelligence to enable him or her to understand fully what is proposed' Gillick (as cited in Morrow & Richards, 1996, p. 94).

Age and perceived competence are key to deciding whether the 'Gillick competence' can be applied. In Australia, there is a specific requirement for parental consent when working with young children. However, Dockett (2008) proposes that even though the legal position may require the provision of consent from adults when researching with young children, researchers should not dismiss the opportunities to seek the child's informed consent to participate. Dockett (2008) notes that this sometimes takes the form of assent rather than consent, and researchers need to be creative in developing mechanisms for children to provide this that reflect their ability – for example through the use of smiley faces in a chart (a series of cartoon style faces with a range of emotions from a smiling face, a neutral face, and a frowning or unhappy face) when working with children with limited reading or writing capacities as a way of indicating what their own feelings concerning taking part in the research might be (see also Chapters 4 and 6 for further discussion of consent in relation to specific research methods with children).

Halse and Honey (2005) note that for research with young people, the age at which individuals can provide their own consent alone is fiercely debated. Indeed, from a purely legal position it has been noted (as discussed above) that in the UK, parental consent may not be required, as is the case for older children where Gillick competence can be applied. However, it is often required by gatekeepers of the sites in which research takes place, such as head teachers in schools or health care practitioners (Boddy, 2014). Such permissions from the relevant gatekeepers may be a long process, often requiring the research to be approved by internal research ethics committees as well as external approvals from schools or health authority ethics committees. These considerations need to be carefully built in to the research planning and timelines. While such external gatekeepers may be required to provide access to participants, participants themselves still need to provide individual consent to participate. Halse and Honey (2005) argue that young people have the ability to make decisions at a comparable level to that of adults, but may not have the required emotional maturity and life experience with which to inform that decision. However, they caution against the notion that seeking and gaining consent from parents or guardians will be the solution to such challenges. The sole seeking of parental consent serves to strengthen the power differentials between children and parents, and reinforces the assumption that 'parents know best'.

There are also instances where the perspective of the child may be different from, and in contrast to, those of the parent (see for example Hepburn, 2005, whose research examined children's calls to Childline, a child protection helpline in the UK). Such tensions in perspectives raise interesting questions with regard to the provision of consent to participate in a particular research project and how consent can have an impact on other people.

Similarly, this was an issue for some of the young people in previous research undertaken by one of the authors of this chapter (O'Dell, Abreu, Cline, & Crafter, 2006) where young people aged 15–19 years were interviewed about their activities as young carers and/or language brokers (this is where children/young people translate for a family member who is unable to speak the official language of the country the family lives in). It was evident from this research that the young people interviewed had complex views of their families and the activities they undertook, which at times were different from those of their parents and other family members. The decision to provide consent to participate in the research was therefore potentially a tension due to the varying perspectives of the individuals and the roles that they took up. In order to navigate this potential tension, the research by O'Dell et al. (2006) utilised research vignettes as a way of enabling young people to discuss the issues inherent in the activities they were undertaking, but without specifically describing the things they themselves actually undertook and enabling them to discuss complex and sensitive issues within families.

There are a variety of ways in which researchers manage the process of gaining and maintaining consent from children to participate in research. Researchers often use a 'parallel process' of asking child and parent to consent to the research (see for example Morrow & Richards, 1996). Many use a process of 'on-going consensual decision making' (Halse & Honey, 2005) where the seeking of consent is revisited at several points throughout the research process, with an aim to empowering the young research participants to make active decisions about their role within the research process. Some researchers, including Thomas and O'Kane (1998), use a process of active consent from children and passive agreement of caretakers. In Thomas and O'Kane's (1998) research the children provided active consent in conjunction with discussing the research project with their parents or carers, who ultimately provided passive consent for the children to take part. Through such a process, Thomas and O'Kane (1998) argue that the children themselves expressed their own views as to whether they wished to take part in the research through actively discussing their preparedness with their parents or caregivers. As a result of these discussions, parents would return a parental consent form, indicating that the children had not only considered their role as participant, but also actively pursued this through discussions with parents. This is very much in line with the BPS guidelines, which suggest that the 'principle of monitoring assent' of the child is important (BPS, 2010, p. 32).

However, Morrow and Richards (1996) advocate the use of informed dissent, which allows children the right to refuse to participate in any given research project. Thomas and O'Kane (1998) advocate principles for research with children, which include the possibility of a child withdrawing at any point in the process and children being given as much choice as possible over how they take part. It is evident that regardless of the approach taken to gaining consent, the researcher is required to provide all the information the participant needs in order to understand the requirement of the research and its implications.

15.5 Protecting child research participants from harm

Protection from harm forms one of the cornerstones of all ethics codes. However, there are particular aspects of our understandings and experiences of 'childhood' that makes it more complex when researching with children. Sociologists of childhood such as McLaughlin (2015a) argue that children in Western societies have traditionally been seen as either in need of protection due to their perceived vulnerabilities or as a threat to a particular society. McLaughlin (2015a) argues that such views of children serve to diminish their views compared with those of adults and compromises their agency. In more recent times, the view of children as vulnerable to harm generally has predominated and this concern is carried over into research practices.

McLaughlin (2015b) argues that the vulnerability of children is due to a range of issues including physical development, a lack of knowledge and life experience when compared with adults, and also a dependence on adults such as parents, teachers and other professionals. In addition, Lansdowne (2010) argues that the structural position of children within a particular society, as dependent on adults and with very few rights, may also mean that they are more vulnerable to harm.

Within a research project, harm may arise as a direct result of the research, such as physical harm from particular experimental conditions (although this is unlikely in contemporary research with children). Psychological harm may also arise from an unintended consequence of the research, such as a child feeling embarrassed by their performance on experimental tests, or feeling increased visibility because they have been chosen to take part in the research (see also a discussion of issues relating to performance in Chapters 6 and 9). Similarly social harm could arise by relationships being focused on, such as in the sociometric nomination of children's friendship circles, and the potential realisation by individual children that they were not nominated as anyone's friend. However, researchers take care to design nomination research in ways that do not cause difficulty (see for example Litwack, Aikins, & Cillessen, 2012). Research design that carefully considers potential harm will be able to mitigate any such harm if it arises in the course of the research project. Attention to the various types of harm therefore need to be considered in all types of research, as even research techniques which may be considered by the researchers as low risk, such as simple questionnaires or non-experimental research approaches, may have unintended harmful effects on child participants.

A further consideration in relation to harm is that engagement with the researcher may lead to a child disclosing to a researcher that they have been harmed by others, or are at risk of being harmed. A key issue for researchers is with respect to the limitations of confidentiality within the research process and the question of whether they have the duty to pass on information that a child may provide to them as part of the research process. Many researchers feel a tension and conflict between the child's right to confidentiality and their obligations where a disclosure has been made. It is important for researchers who work with children to have considered their legal and moral position on disclosure and formulating a process for managing it *before* beginning research with children.

There are differing legal requirements to report disclosures of abuse dependent on the country the research takes place in and the context in which it is undertaken (for example within a school, hospital etc.). An interesting example of an approach to maintaining confidentiality and possibility of managing disclosure was reported in the UK by researchers Thomas and O'Kane (1998) who took a clear and transparent position on issues of confidentiality from the outset of their research. Their approach was that any information the children revealed to them as part of the research process would only be revealed to a third party with the child's permission. They argue that this explicit approach is at odds with the more common assumptions within research that confidentiality can never be guaranteed to child participants due to potential issues of discovering harm. Thomas and O'Kane proposed, in their research, that any disclosure of harm to a third party would be done through supporting the child in telling someone else, and any actions would be done with the child's consent. However, they argue that if the research project as a whole is approached with an assumption of competence and agency on the part of the child participants, adopting different procedures for any potential disclosures would be at odds with such a competence framework.

15.6 A sustained approach to ethics through research design

While procedural ethics are a necessary element of producing good research about children, researchers need a full consideration of the ethical practice in research from initial ideas through to publication and dissemination (Boddy, 2014). Therefore, research that is effectively designed in its methods and methodology will enable researchers to develop ethically sensitive and rigorous work (Thomas & O'Kane, 1998).

The implementations of research ethics in both quantitative and qualitative approaches are governed by the various codes of research ethics previously discussed. How these are applied, however, might have quite different implications depending on the research methodologies adopted by the researchers. Some quantitative research may be considered low risk, and hence, for example, in Australia individual schools can have the ability to seek 'standing parental consent', where prior consent is provided for low-risk projects in advance for a range of projects for a child's participation in research. The projects have to be considered to be for the benefit of children broadly and are typically anonymous or coded questionnaires that are not of a sensitive nature (Australian Government, 2007/2014). These are of course examples of what can be considered low-risk quantitative research projects, and quantitative projects can take many different forms. Specific techniques such as those drawing on brain imaging or experimental designs requiring an element of deception raise much greater ethical concerns and considerations (see also Chapters 1, 3 and 14 for a discussion).

Qualitative research may pose different ethical challenges for researchers, as participants may be more easily identifiable, especially if the population under study forms part of a community minority. This is further complicated if the information that is being gathered from such individuals is of a sensitive nature. The BPS' set of ethical principles to guide research does not offer comment at the level of particular research design or methodology, but is clear that all steps should be taken to ensure the integrity and anonymity of research participants. The Australian National Statement on Ethical Conduct (Australian Government, 2007/2014) suggests that researchers need to take particular care in protecting the identity of participants, unless the participants have chosen to be identified. This is particularly important in the final write up and dissemination of research findings. The Australian National Statement on Ethical Conduct also acknowledges the personal nature of relationships that are sometimes formed as part of a qualitative research project and the need for careful management of these and a planned withdrawal from such relationships on completion of the project. (See Chapter 7 for further consideration of this issue in ethnographic research.) As such for qualitative research projects, The Australian National Statement on Ethical Conduct suggests that informed consent must take into account a range of factors including the sensitivity of the research, the culture within which the research will take place and the gatekeeper approvals required, and the potential vulnerability of participants.

In order to seek children's engagement, researchers need to be flexible and responsive to needs within their research designs. Vignettes, for example, are an interesting way of managing ethical issues in research with children. They are usually a short story or scenario presented in written format. Using such approaches allows children to engage to the extent that they wish in that they can talk about themselves or about the character of the story. There is therefore no requirement for children to divulge personal information if they choose not to do so, and discussions can remain at the hypothetical level of the fictional character.

An example of a study using vignettes can be found in an interview based study that examined children who work, particularly focussing on young carers and language brokers (O'Dell, Crafter, Abreu, & Cline, 2012). These roles are assumed to be unusual in childhood and often stigmatised. Therefore, asking young people about their experiences of being a young carer is potentially challenging. Vignettes were used because they allowed the participants to discuss purely the fictional character of each vignette. The study used four vignettes, each giving a short written description of a 14-year-old's life: Eduardo a language broker, Samuel who did not work, Mira who was a babysitter and cleaner, and Mary who helps to care for her dad. Mary's vignette can be seen below:

> Mary is 14 years old and lives with her dad and her brother who is 15 years old. Mary's dad is disabled and needs help during the day with activities such as getting out of bed, getting dressed and making lunch. Mary loves her dad and is happy to be there for him. However, she also misses school some days if her dad has a bad day and needs extra help. Sometimes Mary wishes that she could see her friends after school like her brother does.

The young people who participated in the study were asked to read the vignettes and were then asked a series of questions such as 'what advice would you give Mary if she was your friend?', 'what do you think Mary's teacher would say about what Mary is doing for her family?' The project used the vignettes in interviews and generated purely qualitative data, but other researchers have used vignette methodology in a mixed method or as a quantitative design.

In a different approach to research, online methodologies work well for young people and adults with ASD (see for example Brownlow & O'Dell, 2006, and Enochsson, 2011, for a broader consideration of online versus face-to-face interviews with children). These may take various forms and can be modified in order to meet the needs of the participants. For example, the use of asynchronous interviewing online could enable participants to consider their responses and not to feel under pressure to keep up a reciprocal dialogue that accords with the expectations of non-ASD researchers. This would facilitate the management of questions and pace of the interview by the participants themselves, as it is quite typical in asynchronous research for answers to be given at a delayed time, sometimes days after the question has been posted. Such a research approach therefore enables participants to reflect and engage in discussions at their own pace, potentially enabling richer, more insightful data to be collected. However, one of the drawbacks from this kind of approach is the real-time discussions and co-constructions by participants and researchers online at the same time that can be achieved through the use of synchronous interviewing. Similarly, drawing on new technologies such as Photovoice provides agency for the participants to capture the issues that are important to them as individuals, rather than those directed to them by the researchers. (See Chapter 8 for a discussion of Photovoice methodology.)

15.7 Children as co-researchers

There is a growing research field that draws children into the research process as co-researchers and research *with* them rather than *on* them. This is an approach favoured by researchers such as Thomas and O'Kane (1998) who have developed a range of techniques to enable children to participate on their own terms and affording them an active role in the research process through the shaping of the research agenda and the methodologies employed (see also Chapters 8 and 14). The Children's Research Centre at the Open University in the UK has been at the forefront of developing this approach. The Children's Research Centre works with children to develop research that is of importance to children themselves. Recent projects have examined children's views on university, issues involving reading and literacy, and online safety (www.open.ac.uk/researchprojects/childrens-research-centre/research-children-young-people. See also Kellett, 2011).

In terms of identifying what the benefits might be in including children in such a co-researcher role, in a review of previous research using children as co-researchers McLaughlin (2015c) identified a number of benefits. The key factors he identified were that child co-researchers could: offer an alternative perspective to the views of adults, speak a common language with other children, and draw on this to recruit their peers as participants in ways that are inaccessible for adult researchers, allow other children to increase their self-esteem and self-confidence as participants.

Such potential benefits would seem to be good reasons for drawing on children as active co-researchers within projects. However, McLaughlin (2015c) does stress the need to consider the skills that individual children are bringing to the research project and the potential need for training in particular aspects in order for the child co-researchers to act ethically and responsibly. McLaughlin (2015c) also notes that there are some disadvantages associated with such an approach. For example, training requirements for child co-researchers in particular research methods may mean that the research will take longer, and also just because children are positioned as co-researchers, there is no guarantee that this will result in enhanced research outcomes (McLaughlin, 2015c). Further, while the involvement of children as co-researchers is potentially an important way of engaging them to drive the research agenda and respects the agency of child participants, there are still key power differentials in operation between the child and adult researchers (McLaughlin, 2015c). Morrow and Richards (1996) note that such power differentials are evident throughout the research process, but are particularly evident at the stage of data analysis. Including children as co-researchers therefore needs to be a whole programme research approach with inputs from the children at each step in the research process. If this is not the case, then there is a risk that their involvement becomes 'tokenistic', with the 'real' work of analysis and interpretation completed by the adult researchers. (See also Chapter 8 for a discussion of children as co-researchers.)

15.8 Future directions

Researchers such as Thomas and O'Kane (1998) have argued that participatory research techniques involving children as co-researchers can be an important way of meeting some of the ethical challenges of research with children and we would agree with this assertion. We would also argue that children need to be able to decide what information to provide and whether to become involved with particular research projects. Drawing on some of our previous work, we would argue that some research methodologies such as those using vignettes allows researchers to explore issues that may be sensitive for child participants and affords children the decision as to whether to disclose personal information. Similarly, using online methods of interacting with children, especially those who may for a variety of reasons find face-to-face interactions challenging, also enables children to determine the extent and the pace of their engagement with the researcher.

As researchers interested in 'different childhoods', our theoretical position links to the ethical engagement we have with our research. We begin from a position of valuing diversity and difference in the children who we work with and we seek to employ methods of data collection that will acknowledge and capture diverse experiences rather than make assumptions about children's lives. There are significant differences in the experiences of being a child, and a number of issues need to be considered such as gender, ethnicity, disability, and disposition and character traits such as shyness, confidence and sociability (Morrow & Richards, 1996). We, and many others, draw on an abilities framework, which assumes that children are capable and able and that the focus should be on what they are able to do rather than what they are lacking.

We would also argue that researchers need to capitalise on the expert knowledge that some children may have with respect to new technologies and the engagement with these. Drawing on research techniques that enable the expertise of children to be captured will allow for rich insights for researchers if they start from the perspective of viewing their child participants and potentially co-researchers as competent and capable individuals.

Practical tips

1   Good research design is essential in producing ethically robust research. It is important that you consider issues of ethics from the design stage of your study by engaging with the needs of your participants and how best to manage a balance between data collection and the safeguarding your participants. One strategy is to revisit issues of consent throughout the research process in order to ensure that continued consent is understood and agreed to.

2   Children are active agents and should be considered as such within all aspects of the research process. Researchers should always engage children in the provision of their own consent in order to take part in research even if additional consent is also sought from parents and/or caregivers.

3   Children are not a homogenous group and factors such as gender, age, ability and the child's interest in the topic are involved in decisions such as the provision of consent. Researchers should therefore be respectful to the individual needs and positions of individual children, and adopt clear ethical protocols in their research practices in order to safeguard the rights of individual child participants.

References

Australian Government, developed jointly with the National Health and Medical Research Council, Australian Research Council and Australian Vice-Chancellors' Committee. (March 2007, updated March 2014). National statement on ethical conduct in human research. Retrieved from www.nhmrc.gov.au/_files_nhmrc/publications/attachments/e72.pdf on 16 February 2016.

Boddy, J. (2014). Research across cultures, within countries: Hidden ethics tensions in research with children and families? *Progress in Development Studies, 14,* 91–103.

British Psychological Society (2010). *Code of human research ethics.* British Psychological Society.

Brownlow, C., & O'Dell, L. (2006). Constructing an autistic identity: AS voices online, *Mental Retardation, 44,* 315–21.

Dockett, S. (2008). Engaging young children in research. In Australian Research Alliance for Children and Youth & The New South Wales Commission for Children and Young People. *Involving children and young people in research: A compendium of papers and reflections from a think tank co-hosted by the Australian Research Alliance for Children and Youth and the NSW Commission for Children and Young People* (pp. 52–61). Retrieved from www.aracy.org.au/publications-resources/command/download_file/id/108/filename/Involving_children_and_young_people_in_research.pdf on 16 February 2015.

Enochsson, A-B. (2011). Who benefits from synchronous online communication? A comparison of face-to-face and synchronous online interviews with children, *Social and Behavioral Sciences, 28,* 15–22.

Facebook (2015). Help Center, www.facebook.com/help/210644045634222 on 18 February 2015.

Greig, A., Taylor, J., & Mackay, T. (2013). *Doing research with children (3rd edn)*. London: Sage.

Halse, C., & Honey, A. (2005). Unravelling ethics: Illuminating the moral dilemmas of research ethics. *Signs, 30*, 2141–62.

Hepburn, A. (2005). 'You're not taking me seriously': Ethics and asymmetry in calls to a child protection helpline. *Journal of Constructivist Psychology, 18*, 253–74.

Kellett, M. (2011). Empowering children and young people as researchers: Overcoming barriers and building capacity. *Child Indicators Research Journal, 4(2)*, 205–19.

Lansdowne, G. (2010). The realisation of children's participation rights: Critical reflections. In B. Percy-Smith, & N. Thomas, (Eds), *A handbook of children and young people's participation: Perspectives from theory to practice* (pp. 9–24). Oxford: Routledge.

Litwack, S. D., Aikins, J. W., & Cillessen, A. H. N. (2012). The distinct roles of sociometric and perceived popularity in friendship: Implications for adolescent depressive affect and self-esteem. *The Journal of Early Adolescence, 32(2)*, 226–51

McLaughlin, H. (2015a). *Involving children and young people in policy, practice and research*. London: National Children's Bureau.

McLaughlin, H. (2015b). Involving children and young people in policy, practice and research. An introduction. In H. McLaughlin (Ed.), *Involving children and young people in policy, practice and research* (pp. 5–12). London: National Children's Bureau.

McLaughlin, H. (2015c). Ethical issues in the involvement of children and young people in research. In H. McLaughlin (Ed.), *Involving children and young people in policy, practice and research* (pp. 13–25). London: National Children's Bureau.

Morrow, V., & Richards, M. (1996). The ethics of social research with children: An overview. *Children & Society, 10*, 90–105.

O'Dell, L., Abreu, G., Cline, T., & Crafter, S. (2006). *Young people's representations of conflicting roles in child development*. Final Project Report to the Economic and Social Research Council.

O'Dell, L., Crafter, S., Abreu, G., & Cline, T. (2012). The problem of interpretation in vignette methodology in research with young people. *Qualitative Research, 12*, 702–14.

Thomas, N., & O'Kane, C. (1998). The ethics of participatory research with children, *Children & Society, 12*, 336–48.

United Nations (1989). *Convention on the rights of the child*. New York: United Nations.

INDEX